Creative
Solution Finding

Creative Solution Finding

The Triumph of Full-Spectrum Creativity over Conventional Thinking

Gerald Nadler
Shozo Hibino
with
John Farrell

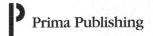

Prima Publishing

Copyediting by Ruth Letner
Production by Andi Reese Brady
Composition by Archetype Book Composition
Cover design by Lindy Dunlavey, The Dunlavey Studio, Inc.
Cover photograph by The Stock Market © 1993 Ron Lowery

Library of Congress Cataloging-in-Publication Data

Nadler, Gerald.
    Creative Solution Finding / Gerald Nadler, Shozo Hibino.
      p.   cm.
    Includes index.
    ISBN 1-55958-567-6
    1. Problem solving. I. Hibino, Shōzō, 1940– . II. Title.
BF449.N33   1994
153.4´3—dc20
                            94-19879
                            CIP

95 96 97 RRD 10 9 8 7 6 5 4 3 2 1
Printed in the United States of America

Contents

Contents

Acknowledgments

The angst of authors is high when preparing this section. Writing a book depends on the work of many, and omissions are an anxiety to be avoided. We hope we have done well.

Our motivation in writing this book arose from two sources. People in the many organizations with which we had major opportunities to use the Breakthrough Thinking or Full-Spectrum Approach ideas for finding solutions often asked why the new paradigm of thinking worked and where it came from. Our continuing interaction with research and extensive literature on thinking are the second source.

Thinking about thinking is a critical frontier for researchers in the fields of neuroscience and cognitive science through artificial intelligence to psychology and sociology. They seek to understand the basic mechanisms. The main research on which we rely is applied and conceptual, and we thank the many authors from diverse fields whose findings are described and referenced.

The following organizations from various categories of size, sector, for and not-for-profit ownership, product and service, organizing principle, and geographical location are examples of where Breakthrough Thinking is being used and where some of the questions that motivated this book arose: AIG Insurance, The Center for Breakthrough Thinking Inc., EMS Consultants, Gifu Prefecture (Japan), Hewlett-Packard, IBM Europe, Indian River Elementary School (Orlando), Kellerco Transportation Planners, KPMG Peat Marwick, Matsushita, Mitsubishi, NEC, Nestle' USA, NeuroConcepts Inc., Open University of Israel, Ralston Consulting Group, San Diego Gas and Electric, SANNO Institute of Management, Sisters of Mercy Hospitals, Toshiba, Toyota, U.S. Dept of Agriculture, University of Wisconsin Extension, Wichita State University, and so on. Many professional organizations, such as the Institute of Industrial Engineers, Japan Management Association, Japan Planology Society, Korean Management Association, Project Management Institute, Institute for Healthcare Improvement, and American

Society of Association Executives, sponsor Breakthrough Thinking seminars and workshops where participants stimulate many issues we address.

We do appreciate the encouragement and thoughtfulness of those who wrote endorsements for the book, most of which are included elsewhere. An especially crucial contribution to Chapters 2, 4, 6, and 9 was made by research assistant Tom Pieronek. Also particularly valuable were the many helpful comments given to us by the many readers of parts of the early manuscripts, especially Robert Kohler, executive vice-president of TRW Avionics and Surveillance Group.

We hope everyone in all of the above groups, including those involved with the production of the book itself—from agent to distributor—will understand and be pleased with our interpretation of this complex subject. We thank in advance those readers who share other views with us. We will respond to and/or incorporate these comments in the next edition.

This book is dedicated to those who stimulated us—people all over the world who know that finding solutions is a continuing process of change and who seek to use the most effective paradigm of thinking for the journey.

Preface

The basic premise of this book is simple—and quite complex.

Simple because it says that we must change the way we think when we seek to create and restructure solutions of any type if we are to obtain the most effective results that everyone seeks.

Quite complex because it deals with each human mind—an entity whose working is hardly understood at all and yet is the most powerful "computer" in the world with its paradigms of culture, its habits, and its reasoning patterns.

Our aim is to have you, the reader, grasp the significance of this simple premise—and then change your "computer" to approach all problems and opportunities with the new paradigm of Full-Spectrum Thinking.

This book focuses primarily on explaining the significance of the premise, with a brief review of Full-Spectrum Thinking. Other books provide how-to-do-it details: *Breakthrough Thinking: The Seven Principles of Creative Problem Solving*, 2nd Edition, written by the two of us and published by Prima Publishing in 1994, is for the general public and *Breakthrough Thinking in Total Quality Management*, written by Glen Hoffherr, Jack Moran, and Gerald Nadler and published by Prentice-Hall in 1994 is for the professional planner, designer, architect, engineer, project manager, and facilitator. These books and additional detailed resources—Participant Handbook, User Guide, Successively Detailed Roadmap for Breakthrough Thinking, etc.—are available from The Center for Breakthrough Thinking Inc., International Headquarters, P.O. Box 18A12, Los Angeles, CA 90018.

The significance of the basic premise and the brief review of Full-Spectrum Thinking are presented in an introduction and four parts of three chapters each. About two-thirds of the book is devoted to Parts I and II, the exploration of the basic premise.

The Introduction provides some insights into the world of problems, the types of errors current thinking can produce, the

principles or assumptions effective people follow in finding solutions, and illustrations of how Full-Spectrum Thinking—based
on the principles and process of reasoning used intuitively by
naturally effective people—produces outstanding results.

Part I raises the curtain on difficulties that each individual
and society in general encounter when solving problems. Chapter 1 reviews a wide range of settings—organizational, personal, governmental, international—to note that we are not
now faring well in finding good solutions. Chapter 2 explores
the characteristics of a paradigm of any sort—the systems or solutions we currently follow, such as organizational structure,
family behavior, and educational methods—and, of course, a
paradigm of thinking. In Chapter 3 we propose a link between
the relative collapse of solution finding and the current paradigm of thinking about how to create and restructure solutions.
Here, we show that A Paradigm Shift in Thinking is clearly
needed.

Part II provides background about thinking, primarily regarding human efforts to create or restructure solutions. Chapter 4 traces the history of thinking for creating and
restructuring solutions from the early Greeks to the present,
showing how the Conventional Thinking of the research approach became the current paradigm. Chapter 5 notes that
thinking is always related to some content or subject and that
human purposeful activities form the basis of thinking about
substantive solution finding. Chapter 6 summarizes a vast literature of research into thinking, to identify findings and clues that
can lead to a new paradigm of thinking for creating and restructuring solutions.

Part III sets forth the principles and process of a different
approach, along with specific supporting research. Chapter 7
explains the basic principles that replace our current mental
model. Chapter 8 sketches a general flow of reasoning for solution-finding, a process that follows from the new assumptions.
Chapter 9 introduces other research and applications to supplement that of Chapter 6, so as to establish direct and indirect
credibility for the new paradigm of thinking.

Part IV suggests how each person can modify so ingrained an instinct as the paradigm of thinking for creating and restructuring solutions. Chapter 10 discusses many different settings where the Full-Spectrum Thinking of Breakthrough Thinking might be introduced, but concludes that each individual, *you*, can and must use these new ideas right away, on every problem or situation needing a decision. Chapter 11 emphasizes that the Conventional Thinking of the Research Approach is not to be discarded but rather will be used as needed within the new Full-Spectrum Thinking. Chapter 12 states the case for consciously seeking changes that improve even the new Full Spectrum Thinking assumptions and process, thus bringing to the new paradigm of thinking itself the same concept of continuous improvement so prevalent with regard to operating and organizational paradigms.

Enjoy your journey.

Changing the world begins with changing your own thinking.

Introduction
Problems/Solutions

Thinking It Over

Think about it: It is time to change the way you think when you plan, design, solve problems, or seek to create or restructure any solution, system, structure, or artifact.

Think about it.

We have no shortage of problems or situations that require new or revised answers. On all sides, problems surround us. And those problems seem increasingly intractable. We grow impatient with the lack of solutions. We are exasperated, apprehensive, desperate. On every level, problems threaten to overwhelm us. Worse, these problems often seem insoluble.

They are not. What *is* intractable, exasperating, inefficient, self-defeating, ultimately self-destructive, is an *ineffective way of thinking*—an ineffective way of approaching a problem to find the solutions so desperately needed for the problems of your family, your neighborhood, your community, city, state, nation. With an effective approach to a problem—any problem—you can successfully tackle and contribute to finding effective solutions.

How? Think about it.

First of all, face the facts: problems exist. We will always have them, even after some have been "solved."

Second, recognize that problems are really opportunities. They almost always represent human desires to improve, to be better.

Third, understand and accept the fact that the real obstacle to overcome is not the problem itself, but rather the *approach to its solution.*

To solve the problems that so trouble, frighten, and threaten us, we must think anew. As Albert Einstein is supposed to have said, "The unleashed power of the atom has changed everything, save our modes of thinking. And we thus drift toward unparalleled catastrophe. We shall require an entirely new way of thinking, if we are to survive."

Today, half a century beyond the most spectacular (and most destructive) application of Einstein's theories, most people have yet to recognize that his momentous discoveries demand radical change in thinking processes.

Whether we like it or not, we have to make fundamental changes in our personal lives, our societies, our work-related organizations. At the most visceral level of awareness, in our very bones, indeed somewhere deep within our genetic material, we know this all too well. We sense that, within our lifetime, humanity will once again confront that point in its evolution when either human consciousness will expand sufficiently to embrace a new approach to thinking, or we will perish.

Think about it. We will change, or we will fail.

The choice is in your minds.

In your hands, at this moment, is an approach to the new kind of thinking that humanity must adopt. The book that you are now reading will guide you to finding solutions for your own and our common future.

What We Need Now

Above all, this new kind of thinking, synthesized from studies of how effective people create and restructure solutions, requires a fundamental shift in the paradigm—the mental assumptions underlying the thinking process we mistakenly apply to almost all problems today. That prevailing conventional approach is the same thinking process that has been applied to most human problems for the past 400 years. That largely outmoded process to plan, design, improve, and solve problems, known as the Research Approach, is of course, the same thinking process that created our apparently insoluble problems in the first place.

It arose in response to overcoming a similarly pervasive paradigm, that of thinking based upon inflexible theological dogma. This theocratic approach to problem-solving tended to ignore natural phenomena in favor of focusing on a faith-based view of the spiritual and supernatural, matters that by definition can neither be proven to exist nor to not exist.

Protean thinkers of the European Enlightenment such as René Descartes, Francis Bacon, and Isaac Newton, who built upon the work of Nicolaus Copernicus and Galileo Galilei, who in turn built upon the observations of Leonardo da Vinci, the mathematical theories of Paolo Toscanelli, and the intellectual product of similar "Renaissance men," developed generalizations and theories about the world that would amplify and refine the prevailing theocratic thought. Ultimately, the Research Approach they developed brought in its wake a tidal wave of change. It led to the Scientific Revolution and (in tangible application of its discoveries) the Industrial Revolution. For good and ill, it created our modern society, the way of life we know today.

For certain problems, this old approach has led to some excellent solutions. For certain problems, it still can. The terrible irony is that this 400-year-old thinking process has been so successful, for so long, in the limited and specialized realm of science, that it has come to be applied to *all* our problems— most of which it cannot solve and was never intended to solve. Most of which, inevitably, it makes worse and worse.

Because the Research Approach has such a pervasive influence upon contemporary problem solving, we are all familiar with it. Its extensive application has both greatly enhanced and greatly imperiled human existence. This dichotomy of impact is in part the result of fundamental misconceptions on the part of people since the time of Descartes, Bacon, Newton, and other seminal thinkers. As valuable as their principles of the Research Approach proved to be for developing generalizations, the error of those who followed was in equating human being and machine. Unlike machines, human beings are demonstrably more than the sum of their parts.

Since the seventeenth century, we human beings have generally believed the Research Approach to be the only way to think rationally, the only way to solve problems, even those that do not lie in the realm of science and discovery. But the theocratic method it replaced had existed for more than 1,000 years before giving way. And the Greco-Roman value system had prevailed for some 1,500 years and more before giving way to Christian theocracy. Elsewhere in the world, other attitudes, perspectives, and paradigms—other sets of mental assumptions—have taken root, blossomed, flourished, and faded, as their utility to humankind was manifest and ultimately superseded.

In life, change is the only constant. Consequently, no paradigm of human thought is destined to prevail forever. Today, the time has again arrived for we human beings to change our way of thinking, our way of approaching solution-finding in planning, design, improvement, and problem solving, and of creating or restructuring systems, artifacts, or solutions.

Almost all commentators on the political, economic, and social scene describe the urgent need for widespread, dramatic changes in or reinventions of the structures (such as hierarchical companies), systems (health care), and solutions (educational services) of modern society—that is, in the current solution paradigms that now govern our lives. Manufacturing must be revolutionized; customer service dramatically improved; the product design time cycle compressed; education overhauled; healthcare systems transformed. The list of needed paradigm changes seems to increase daily.

Yet these calls for dramatic shifts in our paradigms of living, in our basic assumptions about and methods of doing things, fail to probe the most important paradigm of all: the set of assumptions that explains *how* we come to confront so many difficulties in achieving the changes or reinventions that we all agree are necessary. These fundamental assumptions that we most need to change relate to *how we think* when we plan, design, improve, and solve problems. These are the sixteenth-century assumptions with which we approach each problem, each opportunity. Familiar and comfortable, these assumptions remain largely hidden from our conscious recognition.

A related presumption is that the Research Approach is the only way for human beings to reason, to solve problems. This has caused inflexible allegiance to the present methods and structures of solution finding. However, the pervasive influence of the Research Approach, coupled with the presumption that equates its thinking paradigm (and that paradigm alone) to reason—thus, to the solution of any and all human problems—in fact blocks the road to an array of potentially successful solutions.

As the Canadian writer John Ralston Saul has noted in his book *Voltaire's Bastards: The Dictatorship of Reason in the West,* "Reason [read Research Approach] is a narrow system, swollen into an ideology. With time and power, it has become a dogma, devoid of direction and disguised as disinterested inquiry. Like most religions, reason presents itself as the solution to the problems it has created."[1]

Thus, if the paradigms of organization structure, operating systems or procedures, and ways of doing things are to change or be reinvented, the most fundamental assumptions about the way we develop and implement the paradigm changes so desperately needed must first be challenged. If we are to find new and better solutions to our problems, we must first approach those problems in a new and better way.

Why Read This Book?

The modes of reasoning and the general flow of approach to solution-finding significantly affect the quality and quantity of results obtained, of decisions made, solutions found. This book explains the Conventional Thinking for creating and restructuring solutions which arose from the Research Approach. It is also about the last 30 years of investigation into thinking itself and alternative approaches to problem solving. Ultimately, it offers evidence supporting an alternative approach—Full-Spectrum Thinking—that leads to significantly better solutions— products, systems, structures, policies—to most problems we face.

Predictably, if paradoxically, many great scientists recognize the limitations of strict adherence to the application of the Research Approach in their own pursuit of knowledge. Cyberneticist W. Ross Ashby, for example, noted nearly forty years ago that science explored simple phenomena to which the Research Approach lent itself, thus overlooking complex world realities. Santa Fe Institute fellow John Casti explicitly writes about "the limits of reductionism as a universal problem-solving approach."[2]

Our purpose in this book is to demonstrate why and how we must now question and change our long-standing basic assumptions about thinking and problem-solving. We will report on the collapse of solution paradigms that has occurred in all segments of modern society. We will then probe new territory to identify the fundamental paradigm shift in thinking that we must first adopt in order to find and implement paradigm shifts in systems and solutions that everyone in society agrees are essential, but comparatively few know how to bring about.

We relate how a different set of assumptions would greatly improve not only human planning, designing, improving, and solution finding, but also all common, day-to-day activities of persons and organizations.

We will summarize the principles of this new paradigm— Full-Spectrum Thinking—and the general flow of reasoning of its new set of assumptions. And we will demonstrate that each person needs to be a Multi-Thinker and must learn to use the most effective set of assumptions for each purposeful human activity.

You will probe the steps of Conventional Thinking, their strengths and limitations. More important, you will learn the seven principles and the process of the new Full-Spectrum Thinking. You will learn how these principles have been applied to produce significantly better solutions to almost all problems in almost all fields of human endeavor. You will learn exactly how, for most problems, Full-Spectrum Thinking develops longer-lasting solutions, in less time, for less cost, than does Conventional Thinking. You will learn how the search for changes is built into *Full-Spectrum Thinking*.

This new approach to finding solutions has a proven record of success. There is nothing ephemeral about the ideas; the approach is no "pie-in-the-sky." To the contrary, it is deeply rooted in tangible reality, in results.

Full-Spectrum Thinking seeks and finds better solutions to real problems in personal lives, societal groups, and workplace organizations, in education, health care, government, industry, in the realms of private and public life, profit-making and not-for-profit enterprises. It increases quality, improves performance, increases innovation, reduces costs, decreases time and money spent, increases happiness. By definition, Full-Spectrum Thinking means results.

However, in order to achieve those positive results, you must first accept the need for a change in your thinking. If you make that one change successfully, the way you approach a problem will change as well. If you learn and practice the seven new principles and their resulting process, you will automatically find better solutions to your problems. Why? In part, because you will avoid the eight fundamental errors of the conventional approach to creating and restructuring solutions.

Eight Errors of Conventional Thinking in Finding Solutions

By using this new Full-Spectrum Thinking, you will significantly reduce the likelihood of:

1. applying *ineffective mental assumptions* to the problem;
2. taking an *ineffective approach* to the problem;
3. involving *ineffective* or *"standard" people;*
4. focusing on only the *visible* or *wrong problem;*

5. addressing the problem with the *inappropriate timing;*

6. exerting *ineffective control* over the search for a solution;

7. *unfortunately accepting* a predictable or incomplete "solution"; or

8. *inappropriately rejecting* a broader and effective solution.

These eight errors in solution finding—which can be systematically avoided by applying the seven new principles—stem directly from the excessive application of the conventional Research Approach mode of thinking to human problems it was not designed—and remains woefully inadequate—to solve.

In the course of reading this book, you will learn to recognize the fundamental differences between Conventional Thinking and Full-Spectrum Thinking, as well as the various types of problems to which each method of problem solving may be most effectively applied. For the moment, it is enough to know and to contrast the fundamental assumptions and principles of these two very different approaches to problem solving.

There are three fundamental assumptions of Conventional Thinking used to create or restructure solutions:

1. Every problem can be divided into its elements;

2. These elements can be replaced by other (better) elements;

3. If we solve the problem of a given malfunctioning element, and replace it, we can thus solve the problem of the whole.

In turn, these three assumptions lead to four steps by which Conventional Thinking proceeds to its conclusions:

1. identify the problem

2. gather and analyze data

3. decide what is "wrong" (formulate a hypothesis through logical argumentation)

4. replace the "wrong" element(s) (conduct experiments to verify hypothesis)

The Seven Principles of Full-Spectrum Thinking

In the new Full-Spectrum Thinking, there are seven fundamental assumptions or principles:

1. **Uniqueness:** Every problem is unique. Whatever the apparent similarities, each situation requires an initial approach that dwells on its contextual needs. Don't copy a solution from elsewhere. Only if the context of purposes shows it is useful should some available solution be considered.

2. **Purposes:** Always and continually ask the purpose of solving the problem, then ask the purpose of that purpose. Expand as far as possible the purposes of the purposes. Focusing on purposes lets the uniqueness of the situation become clear and helps strip away nonessential aspects to avoid working on just the visible problem.

3. **Solution-after-next:** Find solutions today that achieve the focus purpose, based on what might be the solution of the future. Innovation can be stimulated and solutions made more effective by working backward from an ideal target solution. Having a target solution in the future gives direction to near-term solutions and infuses them with larger purposes.

4. **Systems:** In addressing your target solution, employ a format that includes all elements and interrelationships that it will entail. Every solution or system is part of a larger system, and solving one problem inevitably leads to another. Understanding the elements and dimensions that comprise a solution lets you determine in advance the complexities you must incorporate and the actions you must take in the implementation of the solution.

5. **Limited Information Collection:** Before taking the time and wasting the effort to collect and analyze extensive data, determine what purposes would be achieved by gathering that data. Study the solution, not the problem. Excessive data-gathering may create an expert in the prob-

lem area, but knowing too much about a problem initially will often prevent the discovery of some excellent alternative solutions.

6. **People Design:** Throughout the process of finding a solution, give everyone who will be affected by that solution the opportunity to take part in its development. People are willing to explore purposes and solutions-after-next, rather than to gather data about what is wrong with the current system. Those who carry out and use the solution should be intimately and continuously involved in its development. Also, the proposed solution should include only the critical details, in order to allow flexibility for those who must apply the solution.

7. **Betterment Timeline:** Even as you design today's solution, schedule the future changes necessary to its continuing success. The only way to preserve the vitality of a solution is to build in and then monitor a program of continual change. A sequence of purpose-directed solutions and knowledge of the solution-after-next are bridges to a better future.

The Purposes Humans Seek to Achieve

With the exceptions of survival and achieving personal satisfaction, all other human activity can be categorized according to one of five fundamental purposes. These broad areas of purposeful human activity in which problems arise are:

a) operation and supervision—controlling and maintaining the existence of successful systems

b) planning and design—creating new systems or restructuring ones that no longer serve our purposes

c) research—seeking generalizations to satisfy curiosity concerning natural phenomena

d) learning—gaining knowledge and skills by transmission from one mind to another and/or by experience and repetition

e) evaluation—measuring success in achieving our purposes

The Research Approach excels at developing knowledge (purposeful human activity [c])—finding facts and organizing generalizations concerning natural phenomena. It is also useful in controlling and maintaining successful systems (a). However, in order to find innovative and useful solutions to most other human problems, Full-Spectrum Thinking must be applied. Many concepts and illustrations will also show how Full-Spectrum Thinking can be helpful in developing the plan to put into place to then pursue (a) and (c).

Both Conventional Thinking and Full-Spectrum Thinking are needed to produce the Multi-Thinking Mode essential to the solution of our problems. But these two different modes of reasoning, two different methods of approaching a problem, two different ways of thinking, have profoundly different, almost opposite, impacts on the process of problem-solving, thus, on the solutions found.

While the Research Approach of Conventional Thinking is excellent for finding facts, for arriving at generally correct observations of natural phenomena, and while this knowledge may be readily applicable to creating and using machines conceived and wrought by human intelligence and skill, it fails when applied to the other human purposeful activities. Indeed, applying Conventional Thinking to create and restructure solutions creates six obstacles to finding the best solution to the great majority of human problems.

Obstacles to finding solutions when using Conventional Thinking:

- It calls for subdivision of a problem into small parts, minimizing the possibility of finding a broadly inclusive solution;
- Its excessive analysis risks solution-finding paralysis;
- It leads to the loss of synergy, as a result of the division of a problem into discrete elements;
- It leads to the loss of interdependence, as a result of dividing the problem into discrete elements;
- It creates a culture of confrontation, as a result of the loss of mutual understanding between elements;
- It exacerbates imagined fears and risks.

Less familiar are the contrasting benefits of the new and different solution-finding method.

Benefits of using Full-Spectrum Thinking:

- It emphasizes synthesis, not analysis;
- It focuses on solutions in the future, not on problems in the past;
- It takes the attitude of belief, not doubt;
- It asks initially: Are we doing the needed thing? rather than asking: Are we doing things efficiently?
- It generates a larger solution-space;
- It provides full-spectrum creativity;
- It emphasizes implementation;
- It offers all participants a rich, multi-faceted role in developing and implementing solutions;
- It provides for continual change and improvement;
- It deals with positive methods of getting people involved.

The Fusion of East and West

One great strength of a new approach is that, in contrast to the western perspective of Conventional Thinking, Full-Spectrum Thinking fuses western and oriental perspectives on solution-finding. In one aspect of its philosophy, this approach tends toward an oriental point of view: things are in a constant state of flux, of being and becoming. The solutions to today's problems beget new problems. This inexorable evolution can be harnessed by human purpose-based thinking and constructive action, so that the progression from one solution to the next leads ultimately to the realization of our ideals. Full-Spectrum Thinking is further based on the oriental theory of holism and mutual dependence, the symbol for which is the never-ending, never-beginning mandala.

At the same time, Full-Spectrum Thinking is filled with western optimism about intentionally designing and creating a future. Each of us can make a difference, and our impact can be enhanced by applying a new kind of common sense to the solution of our problems. Starting with the seven principles of Full-Spectrum Thinking, we can gain the ability and confidence to work more constructively and more purposefully. Where the oriental concept of wholeness and unity is symbolized by the mandala, by the perspective of just being and praying, an equivalent western perspective is reflected in the concept of systems-thought. Everything is a system, both part of and reflection of a larger whole.

Thus, fusing oriental and occidental strengths provides the possibility of "full-spectrum creativity." While profoundly practical in both concept and application, it maintains that human beings are not machines, though indeed the best and most powerful computer in the world exists between our ears.

Extending the analogy, Full-Spectrum Thinking provides an agile and flexible new "software for the mind." It offers a new paradigm, a new set of mental assumptions and premises about solution finding. With Full-Spectrum Thinking, we can develop visions of where we want to be to achieve necessary purposes. And it allows us to develop systems to get where we want to go, without the burden of ponderous data collection.

Full-Spectrum Thinking—which we have elsewhere called Breakthrough Thinking—extends the process of creativity to determine the right purposes to be accomplished, to generate a large number of imaginative and original solution options, and to develop the systems to implement successful solutions. This "full-spectrum creativity" provides structure for the imaginative mind and freedom for the structured mind. The new "software for the mind" provided by Full-Spectrum Thinking involves new principles and a new process to plan, design, reengineer, improve, and find solutions to problems.

Full-Spectrum Thinking:

- removes obstacles to simple solutions in both personal and organizational affairs;
- encourages a fresh look at options in both personal and organizational affairs;
- requires minimal data collection, thus reducing analysis paralysis;

- produces implementable answers that give much greater benefits in, among other measures, quality, economic return, risk reduction, and timeliness;
- requires much less time and cost in developing these benefits;
- promotes innovative thinking to seek major changes in and develop new products, systems, and services;
- develops successful and long-lasting systems;
- causes implementation of recommendations;
- builds natural project and work teams.

The Clutter of Problem Solving

As a result, Full-Spectrum Thinking bursts the barrier of clutter—the sometimes useful but more often distracting "noise" of endless data and information produced by the Research Approach—so that we can develop and implement successful solutions to our problems, so that we can plan effectively, so that we can adapt ourselves and our actions most successfully to the often chaotic and always changing world in which we live.

In problem-solving and decision-making, clutter often affects not only the process, but also the product: the decision or solution itself. This accumulated baggage creates obstacles that often preclude us from getting where we want and need to go.

Clutter implies litter, disorder, and obstacles—all the stuff that gets in our way when we want to go from one place to another. Sometimes we create it; other times it is created for us. Sometimes we see it; sometimes we don't. Too often we see it, but don't recognize it. Whatever the case, we store it. More and more, clutter exists, piles up. More and more, it creates obstacles to the solution of our problems.

Clutter can suffocate a good idea. It chokes off our thinking, our total creativity. It can disguise reality and force us to take unnecessary detours. It can make an excellent solution impossible to achieve.

Clutter often exists in the form of a long-held system of belief. Whether derived from parents, schools, workplaces, religions, or nonprofit organizations, belief systems become clutter when they take precedence over an open process of decision-making/solution-finding.

One way that belief systems become clutter is when they become so solidified and presumably immutable that they are unquestioningly accepted as "the way we do things." Too often, belief systems become the "how" that controls the process of decision-making/solution-finding. And this in turn affects the end result: the decision, the solution. Entrenched existing practices can be detrimental to the quality of the result achieved. The "way we've always done it" is one of the most restricting pieces of clutter in the human closet.

In organizations, the culture and established policies and procedures can either hinder or facilitate achieving the results desired. Some policies and procedures are necessary for the orderly pursuit of business. Others may place unnecessary restrictions on getting things done. They clutter the process by forcing us into structures that might not be applicable to our goals. Policies and procedures are usually committee-grown. Consequently, they usually attempt to cover all possible eventualities. Thus, they leave no room for the creation of systems different from the norm.

Finally, negative prevailing attitudes can add immeasurably to clutter. "It can't be done" and "We've tried that already" are key ingredients in this recipe for dangerous and self-defeating clutter. Often, such negative attitudes clutter the attempt to clarify and solve a particular problem.

The Profusion of Problems

Problems are everywhere: The protracted ethnic, racial, religious, and economic conflicts in Northern Ireland, the Middle East, Kurdistan, and Africa. Fervent nationalism and attendant racial and religious conflicts in the Balkans, the countries of Eastern Europe, and the former Soviet Union. The recurring droughts and famines of Ethiopia, the Sudan, Somalia, and other nations of the Horn of Africa. Staggering levels of population expansion, low productivity, and national debt in most of Latin America. The depletion of mineral wealth and a glut of tourism in Australia, while its cultural values are in danger of being usurped by the pervasive influence of American entertainment norms and other imported standards.

The problems that exist in the United States and Japan are even better known. In the U.S., crippling levels of debt undermine both private and public life. The country as a whole wrestles with social problems caused by uneven productivity improvement, a loss of competitive advantage, and a consequent trade deficit of staggering proportions. After decades of political, economic, and industrial hegemony, Americans can no longer deny that, even as costs increased, their health care and educational systems faltered and must be considered inadequate, if not failures. Simply stated, what Americans set up as a structure of government, laws, organizational culture, and "ways of doing things" worked well but now does not work so well. Changes and reinventions are needed.

Japan also needs to change, just as much as does the USA. Medical costs are skyrocketing in Japan, and education is facing increasing problems. There are frightening imbalances in Japan's economy, most prominently in real estate. So inflated has the price of Japanese land become that 145,807 square miles of Japan is said to be equal in price to twice the whole 3.6-million-square-mile land area of the USA. Furthermore, due to almost continuous traffic jams, the average speed of a car in Tokyo is only 15 kilometers (9 miles) per hour. Significantly, this problem is in large measure the result of a so-called advance in Japanese manufacturing ("just-in-time" inventory control), which has had the unforeseen effect of placing many more trucks and cars on the roads than before, making a great number of deliveries, rather than only one or fewer per day.

There is no doubt that we all have problems, problems which are rapidly becoming messes. And the messes threaten to become disasters. But Full-Spectrum Thinking can and does provide an effective way to find solutions.

Success with Full-Spectrum Thinking

The principles of Full-Spectrum Thinking have repeatedly proven successful when applied to problems of business, government, and nonprofit organizations in widely diverse countries and cultures, whether in Europe, Asia, Africa, the Americas, or Oceania. Moreover, these same principles can be and have been applied with equal success to personal problems and common activities in the day-to-day lives of countless individuals throughout the world.

It has been estimated that most human beings make as many as 50,000 decisions in the course of an average day. On a personal level, then, the use of Full-Spectrum Thinking can extend from the most profound and difficult of human problems to the most tedious and mundane. From psychotherapy to career planning, from relationships to study habits, from laying out the items in a chest of drawers to deciding where to go on a vacation, from choosing the best tennis racket or set of golf clubs to choosing the best child care provider or family pet, from selecting a new wardrobe to cleaning the house and doing the laundry. In fact, Full-Spectrum Thinking principles have widely and repeatedly proven to be the best approach to solve problems on almost all levels of purposeful activity by human beings.

INDIVIDUAL SUCCESSES

We have received countless testimonials from readers of our earlier book, *Breakthrough Thinking: Why We Must Change the Way We Solve Problems, and the Seven Principles to Achieve This*. The range and depth of their experiences with this new Full-Spectrum Thinking—Breakthrough Thinking—is evidence of the power of its seven principles when applied to individual human lives.

A psychiatrist working with Native Americans in rural Alaska, who experience many social, economic, and health problems, writes that many of the problems he treats in Alaska are similar to "technology transfer" problems in economically developing countries of the so-called Third World. He laments the fact that health programs that work elsewhere are too often assumed to work in the unique setting of the Far North frontier. "Transient professionals" there too often display insensitivity to local purposes and systems, he notes. And he expresses the belief that Breakthrough Thinking will teach new health professionals, as well as local villagers, a successful process by which they can address and solve their problems.

An industrial engineer: "I am confident that Breakthrough Thinking will be of great assistance, both to professional practitioners of planning and design and to others who are exposed to the principles. I foresee your book breaking down many of the barriers to understanding that have existed in the past."

A computer scientist: "Our management of the problem-solving process traditionally depends on simplistic, deterministic models and macho attitudes. Instead, Breakthrough Thinking should be an integral part of our several corporate cultures. You pull together streams of commonsense ideas into a coherent and workable whole. I am excited by your book."

An executive: "I intend to bring Breakthrough Thinking to the attention of key managers, as your seven principles to successful problem solving are fundamental and should be reviewed periodically by all of us."

A teacher: "I found your principles and planning process to be successful not only with my seventh- and eighth-graders, but also with all levels of high school students. I am firmly convinced that it offers a method for college-bound students to learn to take control of their studying and achievement."

A school administrator: "I enjoyed *Breakthrough Thinking* very much and have found its concepts very valuable. I used them in planning a major change in the way our school district tests students. The systems matrix principle proved an extremely helpful tool as the system that we planned was quite complex."

A business person: "Thank you for writing *Breakthrough Thinking*. Reading it is a mind-clearing and focusing experience."

An engineering manager: "I find your book to be profoundly important to much of what I am trying to do. Your thoughts are fantastic, and they have made a great impact in the way I now approach all problems. The principles of Break-through Thinking are the most potent, critical thinking weapons in my professional and personal arsenals."

A hospital manager: "Breakthrough Thinking has trans-formed my outlook, my job, and my life. It unlocked my cre-ativity, which is a truly irresistible force. It has woven a network of credibility around me. As one result, the executive director of the hospital calls on me—and Breakthrough Think-ing—when everything else has failed."

ORGANIZATIONAL SUCCESSES

Applying the seven principles of Full-Spectrum Thinking, the manager of management development at a U.S.-based, multi-national conglomerate facilitated the work of a group that de-veloped a regional cost allocation system that was agreed upon by two previously feuding factions within the parent company. The system they agreed to proved better than either alternative developed independently by the feuding factions, and it was enthusiastically endorsed and implemented by both of these previously rival groups. Because it focuses on larger (thus shared) purposes and includes in the design of a solution those people who will implement it, an additional benefit of Full-Spectrum Thinking is its utility as a powerful team-building agent.

The vice-president of marketing at another American company used Full-Spectrum Thinking with a multi-functional team that designed a new product development system for a major subsidiary. The intention of the management had been to fix the old system. Using Breakthrough Thinking, the team quickly saw that the original purpose of the old system was outdated. It identified a more appropriate purpose and a com-pletely new product development system, one which not only eliminated the flaws of the old system, but also enabled the company to do things the old system had not even anticipated.

A business systems facilitator at a giant insurance compa-ny led a regional senior management team that developed a new system for enabling diverse profit centers to effectively cross-market for the first time. An additional benefit was that profit center managers were aligned behind a common purpose (cross-marketing), also for the first time. The region's cross-marketing efforts to date have substantially exceeded the regional vice-president's expectations.

A Japanese electronics conglomerate tried unsuccessfully for many months to convince its workaholic employees to put in fewer hours. From management's perspective, the company needed to convince its employees to work only 1,800 hours per year, not the 2,020 hours they had long been accustomed to working. Nonetheless, manifesting the characteristic Japanese devotion to diligent labor on behalf of a lifelong employer, the employees continued to put in hours in excess of company needs and management desires.

The best efforts of an increasingly frustrated management failed to convince the company's employees to abandon their traditional work habits. Finally, applying the principles of Full-Spectrum Thinking to this impasse, management and workers came to agree that some 40 percent of traditional tasks did not actually contribute to the achievement of the company's larger purposes. Thus, the employees' devotion to their company's best interests was enlisted to produce the necessary reduction in hours worked per year, simply by eliminating much of the work that all parties now agreed was unnecessary.

A major Japanese auto manufacturer had always been highly regarded for its efficiency. Thus, its top management was alarmed to notice that the cost-effectiveness of their research and development program was declining precipitously. Whereas, in the 1970s, three out of every 1,000 new products developed proved successful, by the late 1980s, only three in every 10,000 new products developed by the company were profitably utilized. As R&D costs increased and the market for innovative automobile products grew ever more crowded, the need for reduced product development time and increased utility was recognized as essential.

Applying the principles of Full-Spectrum Thinking, the company was able to eliminate many market research costs, to plan and design advanced solutions to its product development problem, and to greatly reduce its inventory of ultimately use-less new products. Rather than try to push a great quantity of new products toward an uncertain market (as do many of its American competitors), this Japanese auto manufacturer chose instead to let the market pull a limited quantity of high-quality, quickly developed new products toward success.

Using this new approach of purpose-driven, future-orient-ed "plan and development," not problem-driven, past-grounded "research and development," the company now finds that 30 out of every 100 new products it develops are successful in the marketplace. Full-Spectrum Thinking has resulted in a remark-able 1,000 percent increase in the company's product develop-ment efficiency.

Applying the principles of Full-Spectrum Thinking, a Japanese manufacturer of numerical control machines was able to increase productivity by 174 percent, to decrease set-up time by 383 percent, to increase production activity by 169 percent, and to improve office activity by 150 percent. A Japanese food products company was able to greatly speed product development time for a new rice-chip snack from a projected eighteen months to three—an improvement of 600 percent—then continually improve the popular new product to increase its market share. A venerable Japanese resort hotel and spa reversed its slide toward bankruptcy and is now ap-proaching a level of profitability never before achieved.

During the 1970s, a huge, federal/state, multi-agency, in-dustrial and environmental task force failed in its attempts to control the proliferation of gypsy moths in the United States, a situation that threatened to become a major environmental cri-sis. Bureaucratic infighting and massive data collection had cre-ated a deadlock among the task force experts. They made no progress until an outside consultant—applying Breakthrough Thinking—showed them that the immediate, essential prob-lem had more to do with organizing the task force itself than with controlling the moths. With the acuity of hindsight, this realization seems almost self-evident. At the time, however, the conventional approach to problem-solving resulted in a literally life-threatening paralysis.

In Gifu prefecture, a central area of Japan, the governor was eager to meet the needs of local citizens. To that end, his administration adopted Full-Spectrum Thinking as the official method of approaching problems and encouraging citizen participation in the development of public policy. Specifically, he involved all citizens who wished to participate in a movement known as Gifu Democracy or "Dream Development." Under this program, citizens submitted their ideas of which problems they thought government should address along with their ideal solutions to those problems.

In 1992, the prefecture government received some 60,000 such ideas (or "dreams") from citizens. These ideas were then sorted and categorized according to problem area. They now provide the basis for policy priorities and budget allocations throughout the prefecture, and the resulting government projects are credited to the initiative and vision of the individual citizens who suggested them. Thanks to Full-Spectrum Thinking, public policy and the perceived needs of the electorate are more closely allied than ever before, producing both responsive government and successful politics. In the words of Governor Kajiwara: "In Gifu, we learn from the future, not the past."

In the United States, a multi-city hospital corporation encountered difficulties in allocating limited financial resources to improve two separate sites, four miles apart in the same city. At a cost of some $250,000, a team composed of people from both sites hired an architectural firm to tell them how best to solve their problem. After many months of data collection and analysis, the consultants dutifully produced a three-inch thick study providing a variety of alternative solutions to the problem. However, the team still was unable to resolve the issue. There was significant bickering about which site deserved the most money.

Nearly two years later, little had been accomplished beyond critical maintenance. Finally, hospital management and the team turned to another consultant, one who used Breakthrough Thinking. Using those principles, the team—representing both separate hospital sites—accepted in *only one and a half days* the alternative solution idea it had discussed and rejected at the beginning of the deliberations: close one site! Not only did the people directly affected by the momentous decision agree to close one of the two campuses (actually, convert it to a retirement home), they even agreed which campus should be converted.

In Japan, the Junior Chamber of Commerce now utilizes Breakthrough Thinking and promotes its use by member companies. Under the leadership of Mr. Haruo Usami, president of Usami Construction Corporation, the JJCC has particularly championed the use of Full-Spectrum Thinking in solving problems of urban planning and design.

The JJCC is composed of 753 Local Organization Members, called LOMs. In 1991, the JJCC proposed a nationwide movement called "1 LOM 1 STORY" for addressing problems of town development. The goal of the movement is for each LOM to create a situation-specific town vision based on the unique culture and history of each town, then to promote town development based on this local, unique, situation-specific vision.

"In the old days," says Usami, "the JJCC utilized the conventional Research Approach to town development. We would prepare to examine a general problem, conduct surveys, analyze what was wrong, develop general solutions for what was wrong, try to replace the part that was wrong, evaluate our action, then start all over again to analyze what was wrong."

Usami reports that the principles of Breakthrough Thinking have been well received and have strongly affected JJCC members. "They understand that the old 'what's wrong here' approach is very negative. Focusing on the problem, not the solution, makes the heart dark. This new approach encourages people to be active and hopeful for the future. Now our members are using Breakthrough Thinking in their own companies' daily activities."

Professor Kouji Morooka, a leading member of the Japanese Medical Association, performs work design in the field of medical care systems throughout Japan, especially information systems in hospitals.

Morooka, a member of numerous Japanese professional scientific committees, attributes much of the prosperity and productivity of Japanese industry, especially in the area of sophisticated systems, to successful application of the principles of Breakthrough Thinking and its Full-Spectrum Creativity. In his own design of sophisticated systems, Morooka says he always tries to grasp the function, the purpose of the system; and he finds Breakthrough Thinking to be unique and very effective.

For example, in 1989, Morooka designed and established the first-of-its-kind, completely automated dispensing pharmacy in Japan, for a hospital with 1300 beds, 500 medical doctors, and 55 pharmacists. "We tried to grasp the function, the purposes, of the pharmacy," he explains, "and finally we recommended a quite new, completely automated system, three of which now operate in Japan. This system, based on Breakthrough Thinking, is now being applied to other industries throughout Japan. I find it particularly applicable to 'tertiary' industries such as hospitals, hotels, and educational institutions, the emerging successors to our 'secondary' industries such as automobile and electronics manufacturing."

Some years ago, relates Dr. Fujio Umibe, consultant and systems engineer at Japan's Toshiba Corporation, the company faced a problem with component fan blades being damaged during transport in the manufacture of its electric fans. A great deal of time and money was being lost as a result of the broken blades, and no one seemed able to devise a satisfactory solution by applying Conventional Thinking. Finally, what had been perceived as a problem of packaging technique—which was researched and analyzed so that a defective method of packaging might be detected and replaced—was instead approached by questioning the purpose of transporting the fan blades from one plant to another.

The result of applying Breakthrough Thinking was to develop an interim solution that lowered cost for packaging material, increased the quantity of blades per box from 14 to 24, and thus decreased the costs of transportation by almost 50 percent. The ultimate solution recommended had nothing to do with packaging techniques; instead, the company was advised to make the fan blades at the same plant where the completed fans were finally assembled.

The "Naturals"

Our research indicates that only about eight percent of people intuitively use the new paradigm of thinking. These people are invariably highly effective in their endeavors. Often, they are the sort of natural leaders who rise to the top of governments, corporations, and nonprofit organizations.

Among American corporations whose internal cultures and decision-making practices reflect an intuitive appreciation of Full-Spectrum Thinking principles are such highly successful companies as 3M and Procter & Gamble. It seems no accident that a floundering General Motors Corporation recently selected John Smale, retired CEO of Procter & Gamble and new chairman of the GM board, to lead the board-directed effort to turn around the ailing automotive giant. P&G's emphasis on individually designed "efficiencies of cooperation" with the retailers of its products intuitively reflects such Full-Spectrum Thinking principles as the uniqueness of every problem and the need to engage those who will be impacted by its implementation in designing a solution.

The current management of Electronic Data Systems also seems to intuit many Full-Spectrum Thinking principles, though not necessarily the process by which to apply them systematically. The company claims to help its clients achieve their business *purposes* by focusing on the *unique* needs of each client, providing *only useful information,* and *integrating systems* of information and communication with the *people* who operate and rely on them, so as to help client companies *improve over time* in a constantly changing environment. Missing from this EDS-intuited list is the *solution-after-next* principle by which those who use Full-Spectrum Thinking leapfrog ahead of competitors to anticipate future problems and solutions.

Another intuitive (if somewhat extreme) example of Full-Spectrum Thinking use is the case of Craig Benson, chairman of Cabletron Systems, a cable-television company in Rochester, New Hampshire. Mr. Benson writes in the *New York Times* that his policy is to not spend any money that does not relate directly to the purposes of the business: providing advanced cable and other electronic networking capabilities. "Overhead is like cancer," he notes. "Once it gets started, it's hard to cut out."[3]

As a result, Cabletron provides no office larger than 15 × 15 feet, including Benson's. The chairman's desk, he notes, has a broken leg. Company conferences are held around a stand-up table. If executives want to spend more than $70 per night for a hotel room, they must pay the difference out of their own pockets. No racquetball courts or marble hallways at Cabletron, insists Chairman Benson. Why? They contribute nothing to the purpose of growing the business.

Three Types of Breakthroughs

As you come to be familiar with and learn to practice its concepts, Full-Spectrum Thinking may provide you with a thrilling moment of epiphany. "Eureka! I have found it," shouted the ancient Greek physicist Archimedes, as he bolted from his bath to run naked through the streets of Siracuse, joyfully proclaiming his discovery.

That is one type of breakthrough; the *"Ah-hah!"* But this sudden, startling revelation or creative idea is only one of three ways by which you may increase your own effectiveness and help to change the world by applying Full-Spectrum Thinking.

Another sort of breakthrough is accomplished when you achieve *significantly better results* toward the goals you seek. If you can produce twice the economic returns from the same amount of time and effort spent before, that's a breakthrough. Another way of looking at it is to get the same results while expending half the time and energy spent before.

The third type of possible breakthrough is to achieve *implementation* of a good solution previously ignored or rejected as too difficult, even impossible. This happened in the case where one hospital site was converted to another use. No solution, however theoretically excellent, is worth much until you bring it into effect. Also part of the third type of breakthrough is *not using a bad idea.* Designing a factory to double its capacity could be accomplished very effectively, but it was a bad idea when Breakthrough Thinking showed that developing management control systems was the needed purpose.

All manner of excellent solutions to organizational, public, and private problems will be within your reach as you learn to practice and apply the seven principles of Full-Spectrum Thinking in your own life. But first, you must overcome the unintended tyranny of Conventional Thinking.

A Shift to the Purpose-Based Full-Spectrum Thinking

Where Conventional Thinking insists that we first study the problem, Full-Spectrum Thinking first studies the purposes we hope to achieve in solving the problem. From the start, Full-Spectrum Thinking focuses on movement toward solutions and changes. Thus, it creates a positive orientation. It uses the full range of intelligences of the people involved. Applying the seven principles of Full-Spectrum Thinking, we approach problems believing that we can indeed find at least one successful solution, if not several. Without doubt.

Our purpose now is to arouse in you the awareness that your previous assumptions about solution-finding have been only that: assumptions. And that you have now held those assumptions far too long. So have we all. It is now long past time for those failed assumptions to change.

Yes, we ask a lot of you. Not only do we ask you to change, to re-think your entire world; we further ask you to re-think your world *in an entirely new way.*

Think about it.

We want you to re-think your way of thinking. We hope to change your automatic response when you (and your groups) try to find solutions from "everybody knows you have to start by gathering all the information about what exists and finding out what is wrong" to "everybody knows you have to start by finding the biggest purpose to achieve and solutions-after-next for accomplishing it."

Like all journeys of conscious discovery, the one we ask you to embark upon is fraught with uncertainty, apparent danger. The only greater danger is to remain on the certain, ineffective, problem-replete shore. There, we can only continue to apply the same pattern of thinking that created overwhelming problems in the first place.

On that familiar shore, we are doomed to increasing failure. For no course to the future can be charted with reference to the past. We can only find our way to the solution of our problems by confronting them from that precarious, uncertain, ideal future in which, paradoxically, we will find tremendous strength. In that future, Full-Spectrum Thinking is both our shield and weapon, both our destination and our map.

We begin our journey of discovery by exploring many of the "insoluble" problems that—with the purpose-based Full-Spectrum Thinking—we can solve.

NOTES

1. John Ralston Saul, *Voltaire's Bastards: The Dictatorship of Reason in the West* (New York: The Free Press/Macmillan, 1992).

2. John L. Casti, *Complexification: Explaining a Paradoxical World Through the Science of Surprise* (New York: Harper/Collins, 1994).

3. Craig Benson, "Setting a Tone With Battered Desks," *The New York Times,* (September 29, 1991).

Part I

The Current Assumptions About Thinking

Chapter 1

The Age of the Solution-Finding Collapse

The Wholesale Failure of "Solutions"

In assessing the fundamental problems of the Soviet Union in the mid- to late-1980s, Mikhail Gorbachev described as well the fundamental problems of U.S. society in the early 1990s. The U.S.S.R. suffered, said its former leader, from bureaucratic paralysis, economic stagnation, and moral decay.[1] Precisely the same diagnosis was made for the U.S.A. by all three major candidates—albeit from different perspectives and with different emphases—during the U.S. presidential election campaign of 1992.

The problems faced by most societies as we approach the end of the twentieth century extend throughout all aspects of individual, organizational, and societal life. An age of anxiety is peaking. In Japan, there are growing problems of financial stagnation and political corruption; in Latin America, problems of political and drug-related violence; in Europe, problems of systematic political collapse, civil wars, and violent nationalism. In China, political stability is purchased only at the price of intellectual repression. In most of the economically developing world, problems of overpopulation, famine, disease, and sectarian violence increasingly appear to be endemic. We have been unable to find solutions to these problems not because they are inherently insoluble, but rather because we approach their solution with the wrong problem-solving paradigm, the wrong way of thinking. Our conventional approach either exacerbates the problem or leaves the situation no better than before.

In the United States, people struggle to overcome a pervasive sense of despair and disgust with the political failure to solve society's problems—the notorious "gridlock" of competing interests and power centers that has seemed to paralyze American public life for the last two decades. Former *Washington Post* editor and columnist Haynes Johnson suggests that, if the United States is to overcome its legion of problems, the country must "leap an abyss into an uncharted future" so as to re-create itself.[2] And all the while, fundamental problems go unsolved.

Racial and ethnic strife increase, even as American society becomes ever more ostensibly inclusive and multi-cultural. The long-term economic malaise now extends longer than at any time since the Great Depression of the 1930s. It is widely suspected that this economic decline may presage a permanent diminishment in the economic stature of the United States.

In part as a result of economic decline, crime in America continues to increase, exacerbated by widespread drug and alcohol abuse, often addiction. The U.S. crime rate has increased fivefold since 1960. Hundreds of thousands of Americans—many of them mentally ill—are homeless, left to fend for themselves on the streets, where they are both prey to and perpetrators of violent crimes.

Especially in urban areas, housing is generally inadequate, unaffordable, or nonexistent. In many places, lack of funds, as well as lack of teacher and student motivation, has caused massive failures in public education. Meanwhile, the physical infrastructure continues to deteriorate. Roads, bridges, railways, sewers, water supply systems, even electronic communications are increasingly at risk.

The American system of health care has become the most expensive yet arguably least effective in the industrialized world. Thirty-five million citizens lack even basic health insurance, thus they are treated only when their illness reaches a point of crisis, consequently the highest levels of cost. In impoverished inner cities and outlying rural communities, less and less medical care of any kind is available. While this health-care crisis grows ever more acute, we witness self-interested conflict among those who provide, those who finance, those who consume, and those who regulate medical services. As yet, no real mechanism for resolving these disputes exists.

Half of all American marriages end in divorce. Spouses are alienated from one another, children alienated from parents. Broken families both reflect and cause the increasing alienation of the sexes. The number of people seeking psychotherapy has increased dramatically, reflecting both bad conditions (more people with problems) and good (more people willing to address their concerns).

The failure of succeeding governments—local, state, and national—to make decisions of almost any sort, let alone meet basic human needs for health, public safety, education, employment, and housing has led to widespread public alienation. Citizens feel isolated from one another and abandoned by government. One result—which makes things worse—is voter apathy. In the U.S. presidential elections of 1988 barely half of the potential electorate bothered to vote. In 1992, increased voter turnout (due primarily to the three-candidate field) was hailed by commentators, though fully 45 percent of adult citizens (almost 100 million people) still chose not to participate in the electoral process.

Repeatedly, an evident lack of honesty and morality among elected officials is cited as the root cause of voter apathy and despair concerning public life. And ethical abuses are certainly not confined to government; they pervade business and nonprofit enterprises as well. In 1992, the CEO of United Way, the largest charitable institution in the United States, was forced to resign his post in the wake of revelations that he had abused the responsibilities of his office. This and similar cases in the nonprofit world pale by comparison to financial scandals such as the collapse of junk bond empires, the pillage of savings & loan institutions, and the failure of banks—all of which were aided and abetted by self-serving politicians and manifestly misguided policies of government deregulation.

Much like their government, many individual citizens continue to indulge a long-standing habit of high consumption and low savings, maintaining bloated lifestyles only on the basis of credit and the sale of fundamental assets. Others find themselves sinking ever deeper into poverty. A 1991 federal government report notes that one in four children in America exists at or below the official poverty level. In the midst of this unprecedented economic decline, U.S. financial markets are increasingly unable to effectively manage the global flow in transactions and stocks and commodities, while at the same time serving as the primary source of capital financing.

A worldwide population explosion is mirrored in increased rates of immigration to the United States and burgeoning birthrates among impoverished Americans, particularly the growing "underclass." Diseases such as cholera and tuberculosis, previously thought to be eliminated, are recurring worldwide, including in the United States. And the scourge of AIDS continues to take its unrelenting global toll, despite all efforts to halt the advance of the deadly HIV virus.

At the same time, environmental degradation and irreversible damage continues to occur. We use too much oil. We deplete the rain forests. Both problems lead to the "greenhouse effect," which results in too little oxygen, too much ozone, acid rain, foul air and water. On the ground, we face enormous problems in the disposal of nuclear and chemical wastes.

Headlines relate by-now-familiar problems: Defense Bribery Rampant; Greenhouse Effects Loom; Racism Rears Ugly Head; Troubled Seas: Global Red Tides; Whatever Happened to Ethics?; A Growing Gap between Rich and Poor; Something's Rotten in Government; Commonplace Violence is Legacy of Drug Culture; Acid Rain Imperils Sea Life; Ethical Lapses Mark Reagan Administration.

New School for Social Research economist David Gordon attributes the nearly 20-year stagnation of the U.S. economy to the top-down structure of economic power and behavior in the United States—the huge corporate bureaucracies, the maltreatment of workers, the low-wage/low-productivity dead end in which the U.S. economy has stalled, and the reliance on investment decisions by shortsighted corporate decision makers whose focus is the quarterly bottom-line, rather than the ten-year plan. These problems, Gordon notes, have been compounded, not reduced by trickle-down economic policies during the 1980s and early 1990s.[3]

What no one can deny is that a seemingly endless array of apparently insoluble problems surround us. And although almost everyone is by now well aware of these increasingly desperate dilemmas, even when we muster the courage and the will to address our problems, we invariably seem to lack the means to solve them. President Clinton's pollster, Stanley B. Greenberg, calls the 1990s the Entropy Decade, where everything tends toward disorganization and uncertainty abounds.

Adding to our frustration is the fact that, over and over, technical analysts and auditors have reported internally on deteriorating conditions, but policy officials failed to take action at a time when the needed corrections would have been easier and cheaper to make than they are now or will be in the future.

Robert Bellah (*Habits of the Heart*), Amitai Etizioni (*The Rebuilding of America Before the Twenty-First Century*), and other "communitarians" decry the vast material wealth of America, with reference to a gaping spiritual emptiness. They find Americans cynical, overworked, and profoundly isolated psychologically and emotionally.

Writing in the *Los Angeles Times Magazine*, Jonathan Rauch has noted that the best way to address issues of "moral infrastructure" and their relation to current problems is to focus on what almost all of us can agree are five indispensable, future-building—thus, problem-solving—values: lawfulness and honesty; education; thrift (saving and investing); diligence (the willingness to work hard and to do one's best); and strong family (particularly one that is dependable for its children).

"Taken together," says Rauch, "these could be aptly called a constructive ethic. A society or person with a strong constructive ethic—postwar Japan, for instance—is likely to enjoy improved fortunes over time and will have a distinct advantage over its less constructive competitors."[4]

Some values are "basic" and remain with us at all times. Rauch's values are of this sort. These basic values are good *motivators* for successful solution finding. Thus, many basic values lead to measures of success. But values only provide impetus. They are stimulators, not results.

Too often, people mistakenly turn these motivators of success into the means of achieving it. "Law and order," some claim, would solve all our problems. Taxpayer vouchers for private education would solve all our problems. Cutting the deficit would solve all our problems. Or increased productivity. Greater diligence is the "solution." Or the recently ubiquitous catch-phrase "family values."

The related measures of success in achieving our purposes are not the actual success itself. They are merely measures. Measures of the achievement of our purposes. Neither do they describe those purposes—the actual ends that we pursue. Instead, they measure our success in achieving one or more of the fundamental purposes of human activity: to develop generalizations about a natural phenomenon; to create and restructure systems; to learn; to operate, supervise, and control existing systems; to evaluate their performance.

Success in achieving our purposes may be measured with reference to such fundamental values as the five that form Rauch's "constructive ethic." And the more that we examine and expand our purposes, the more we will find that the five values Rauch enumerates will accurately measure our success.

Yet even though positive values are essential to success and we are increasingly exhorted to manifest such values in our lives, taken alone, such well intentioned exhortations seldom if ever result in positive change. The measures of success, our goals, must often change. But what will actually make the difference between success and failure is not a change in measures but rather a change in individual behavior.

Although certain systems and organizational structures are more conducive to successful solution finding than are others, simply to blame "the system" is to beg the fundamental question: Who put together those structures? Who designed them and sustained them and controlled them? Individual human beings did. Individual human beings must now change them.

To illustrate, we examine some mistakes reflected in businesses as the people in them attempt to implement change. Remember that organizations cannot make mistakes; only people—working in and with organizations—are responsible for its success or failure.

Management professor Lawrence Greiner has noted six fatal mistakes of *organizational* change, all of which stem from resistance to change that is rooted in Conventional Thinking for problem solving.

> *Mistake Number One:* Preoccupation with external events
>
> Given the short tenure of most new CEOs, there is no "honeymoon." They are under intense pressure from boards and the stock market to perform almost immediately (improve measures of profits, market share, ROA, etc.) or else grab a parachute. . . . But herein lies the trap: these new CEOs and their advisors are so concerned with looking outside their companies to satisfy immediately the sought-for measures of these external constituencies that they have forgotten or oversimplified the internal dynamics, strengths, and weaknesses of their organizations.
>
> *Mistake Number Two:* The quest for macro-level changes
>
> In the eyes of many of these CEOs and their consultants, everything must change at once about their companies—their strategies, structures, systems, technologies, and cultures. . . . The "what" and "content" of change take precedence over the "how" and "steps" of change.
>
> *Mistake Number Three:* Change by formal/rational redesign
>
> These new CEOs and their consultants are not blind bureaucrats—they have already learned in MBA programs about the value of modern contingency theory with its technological and market determinants. However, the great weakness in this thinking is the assumption that mid-

dle managers will automatically change in response to new structural cues and requirements placed on them. Much of this redesign work is directed toward decentralization and greater control over one's own destiny—thus a further assumption being that middle managers will "welcome" newfound freedom.

Mistake Number Four: Change by charismatic leadership

Reliance on individual charismatic leadership is often an oversimplified use of influence. Most middle managers do not work day-to-day for charismatic bosses. They may get an emotional high one day a year from seeing the CEO face-to-face, and then it's back to work in the trenches under leaders who are not so charismatic and who themselves may be experiencing their own internal turmoil.

Mistake Number Five: Change by "Do as I say"

To be sure, the new strategies of companies may be clearer, the performance goals specified, the job responsibilities enunciated, the new training programs on "how to do it" put in place, and the compensation tied more directly to performance. But the underlying hypocrisy lies in the behavior of senior managers who fail to behave in consonance with their verbal pronouncements. . . . Hence no role model is provided.

Mistake Number Six: Placing the burden on lower levels

Most companies today are decentralized—and for good reason, as they attempt to deal with diverse and rapidly changing markets. Unfortunately, this structure also makes it tempting for top management to lay the entire change agenda (including the consequences of "performance based" compensation plans) squarely on the shoulders of middle managers, who are supposed to make massive changes in quick order, from reducing costs to inventing new products. And then top management sits back to monitor and judge the results. This is a cruel perversion of decentralization.[5]

A Worldwide Collapse of "Solutions"

In the United States especially, we are bombarded by exhortations to challenge all assumptions about systems in place, to re-engineer the way we do business, to change our paradigms—organizational structures, customer relations, quality management, accounting practices, manufacturing strategy, product design, strategic planning, human resource development, marketing, crisis management, the healthcare system, education at all levels, infrastructure, banking, government policy making, and so on. And on and on and on.

No doubt as a result of the precipitous decline in its post-World War II economic hegemony, recent problems in the United States are perhaps easier to notice than are problems elsewhere. Almost everything written these days about American competitiveness, quality, and productivity urges that organizational systems, structures, culture, purposes/services, and customer focus must change. Moreover, in almost all cases, the models proposed to guide U.S. organizations in such changes are based upon Japanese or German so-called successes. Yet the United States is by no means alone in needing to change its problem-solving behavior.

By 1992—after decades of successful "total quality management" and "just-in-time" production models—thoughtful Japanese could no longer deny that their "bubble economy" had finally burst. Six of the country's top electronics companies posted a drastic drop in profits. According to writer and consultant Michael Schrage, Japan's global giants are "wounded and confused . . . wondering how best to reorganize themselves to cope with a low-growth economy."[6]

Schrage notes that Matsushita, the consumer electronics powerhouse, is struggling to redefine itself in a world where traditional economies of scale and scope no longer produce strong growth. Indeed, Matsushita—which about three years previously had boldly shelled out $7 billion to buy the American entertainment conglomerate MCA—found itself humbly admitting that its new financial mission was "profit with no growth."

Ikujro Nonaka, management professor at Tokyo's Hitotsu-bashi University, says that Japanese industrial giants such as Matsushita, Toyota, and Hitachi are casting about for the best way to change. "They're now desperate," says Nonaka. "Being a mass-oriented company doesn't work anymore. Just-in-time doesn't work anymore. We have to create a new management model, but we don't know what that model is."[7]

Yoshi Noguchi, a director of a Los Angeles-based executive search firm, wrote recently in the *New York Times* that the Japanese management system "works well for the benefit of the company, but often does so at the expense of employees and their families. It makes employees focus on achieving corporate objectives and works best for the majority of Japanese who, because of cultural tradition, prefer the comfort of tightly controlled systems that minimize diversity and risk."

However, notes Noguchi, "Japanese executives are beginning to believe the system stifles freedom of choice and is a psychological imprisonment against creativity and independence—the very ingredients that must be unleashed to maintain Japan's competitive position." According to Noguchi, among the increasingly serious problems in Japan is the fact that its work force is quietly undergoing a rapid transformation, as a growing number of executives are breaking with long-standing traditions of lock-step devotion to corporate goals and priorities.

Apparently, Japan's very success in foreign markets has led many of its best executives to discover the "exhilaration of non-conformity and a better quality of life." As a result, an increasing number of Japanese executives are willing to leave longtime Japanese employers. They are drawn to foreign companies that offer more flexibility, higher incomes, and opportunity for advancement. "In the end," suggests Noguchi," Japan may find its global economic preeminence threatened from within."[8]

Certainly, the Japanese people have reason to be proud of the achievements of their industrial/governmental/social system. Today, Japan leads the world in per capita income. Yet early successes in computer chips and consumer elec-

tronics led to advanced Japanese government-sponsored projects that bit off more than they could chew. Many technological mega-projects funded by the Japanese government Ministry
of International Trade and Industry (MITI) have turned into
spectacular flops. In particular, the vaunted Fifth Generation
Computer project has now shed many of its early goals and
lowered its expectations. And the commitment to the development of analog high-definition television is now abandoned.

"For perhaps the first time since it resurrected itself from
the ruins of World War II," writes Karl Schoenberger in the *Los
Angeles Times,* "Japan appears to be without a plan. The country's one-dimensional foreign policy—promoting commercial
interests abroad—has been made obsolete by its very success.
The powerful bureaucracy that charted postwar development
with a bold industrial policy is now in a state of near-paralysis."[9]
Widespread lack of confidence in political leaders contributes
to financial anxieties so great they nearly crashed Japan's financial markets in 1992.

Collapse of the Thinking Paradigm

History indicates that Japan will find creative solutions to its
current identity crisis. And few would argue that America has
not demonstrated historical resilience in confronting and solving
its problems. In truth, both countries have different strengths.
Thus, both have much to learn from each other.

Some of these mutually profitable lessons are obvious. For
example, in Japan, says author James Fallows, it is all but impossible for professional workers to change from one large
company to another after their mid-20s or for women to find a
place in the corporate world. Thus, Japan could no doubt
profit from a measure of American individual flexibility and
professional mobility. For their part, Americans might do well
to adopt a modicum of Japan's highly valued social discipline.
Whether or not it pleases the individual Japanese worker,
Fallows notes, the rigid system has undeniably been useful in
building Japan's trade surpluses. Factories certainly run more
smoothly when no one dreams of challenging the boss.[10]

But more than from any other cultural interchange, Japanese and Americans both could profit from adopting the most successful aspects of each other's *ways of thinking* (not each other's ways of organizing or manufacturing or education or health care delivery).

Japanese-American marketing expert Sheridan Tatsuno explains that the Japanese way of creating is unlike Western creativity, but that both are equally powerful. Japanese creativity, he notes, is a cycle of innovation—"creative fusion" based on group dynamics. Western-style creativity tends to be more individualistic and linear—"creative fission." Japan is strong on recycling (finding new uses for existing ideas) and refinement (improving and adapting ideas to the changing environment). The West is strong on exploration (searching for new ideas when existing ones are inadequate) and generation (experiencing breakthroughs). Both cultures excel at nurturing (seeding and incubating new ideas). Taken together, says Tatsuno, these five phases define the holistic "mandala of creativity."[11]

Unfortunately, as writer Robert Collins notes in his book *Japan-Think, Ameri-Think: An Irreverent Guide to Understanding the Cultural Differences Between Us,* "There are probably no two nations on earth with citizens more inept at speaking a language other than their own."[12]

The fact that both the U.S. and the Japanese societies have been so successful in applying technology—and so aggressive in exporting their own successful systems and solutions—in large part explains why developing countries sometimes create problems for themselves when they intend to find solutions. Too often, developing countries make the mistake of adopting technologies and organizational arrangements inappropriate for their own specialized situations.

Developed societies tend lately to find costly and complex ways to do what was once simple and inexpensive. Moreover, they have become so enamored of technology that they apply it inappropriately in developing countries. As a result, today billions of dollars worth of rusting and inappropriate equipment is strewn across the fields of the Third World.

It would be far better for manufacturers in Kenya, for example, to improve productivity not by importing Japanese tools and techniques designed to address assembly tasks in Japan, but rather by asking the purposes of their own unique company, in their own unique society in the context of their own cultural traditions, at their own level of technological development and supporting infrastructure.

The resulting solution found would no doubt seem "low-tech" indeed to Japanese, American, or German consultants. Yet it might well be a significant advance for Kenyans and far more appropriate to the unique problems they face. Following the purposes, uniqueness, and people-design principles of Full-Spectrum Thinking, such a purpose-based "home-grown" solution is invariably better than any prepackaged imported model.

Although technology is often considered a product of science, mathematics, and engineering, any piece of hardware is part of a larger system that includes the individuals and organizations that apply the science and engineering, build and operate the machinery, ensure a smooth flow of input to and output from the system, and determine the strategic importance of the desired change to the organization, whether it be improved productivity, reduced costs, or better service delivery. Technology is fundamentally an organizational and human endeavor that links what is theoretically possible to what happens in the laboratory, the design shop, the operating room, the office, or on the plant floor.

In the Western industrialized world, implementing new technology has most often been explained and shaped by theories in which work was divided into small tasks with clearly defined responsibilities and standards of acceptable performance based on low levels of employee skill and motivation. Management roles were highly specialized, and authority was reinforced through sharp status hierarchies. Labor and management relations have for the most part been hostile.

Today, however, people increasingly recognize that the successful introduction of technology is tied to the understanding of existing organizational structures, as well as to employee perceptions and expectations. Underlying these changes is a shift in basic assumptions about people, from limit and control to trust and cooperation.

Another example illustrates how Conventional Thinking for finding solutions fails not only in developed countries, but also in developing regions. Physicist Freeman Dyson recounts a story of the Boulou people of Cameroon in his book *From Eros to Gaia* in a chapter titled "Cautionary Tale For Scientists."

Dyson's daughter, a Peace Corps volunteer in Central Africa, observed attempts to supply water to a Boulou village. The villagers had to choose between two options: Hire a local, professional well-digger to design and construct a well, bathhouse, and laundry using local Boulou workers, or submit a competitive proposal to the distant central government requesting a massive water system using imported urban technology.

The Boulou chose the latter course. Not only were they attracted by the long-shot possibility of enormous bounty; they also were repulsed by the "low-tech" solution, which meant working for a well-digger from the low-status Fulami tribe, from whom the Boulou did not relish taking orders. As a result, the Boulou are reportedly still without a supply of water.[13]

A Full-Spectrum Approach to the Boulou people's water supply problem would have encouraged them to overcome their antipathy to working under a well-digger whom they traditionally considered inferior. They would then have almost certainly chosen the cheaper, better, faster solution to their problem, not wasted time and energy on an uncertain high-tech "solution" that never came to pass.

The critical point to note here is that the conventional approach to problem solving—a research-based analysis of apparently limited options—presented the Boulou people with only two choices—one traditionally unpalatable, the other unlikely to succeed. Full-Spectrum Thinking would have suggested a much wider variety of alternative solutions, greatly increasing their solution space and thus their chance of success in solving their problem.

The same sort of self-limiting presentation of alternatives is conventionally made in the most technologically advanced cultures and organizations. Corporate chieftains similarly present to their people severely limited alternative solutions, all too often, only one. And that one is usually copied from another company.

"We're going to do it this way," they insist, "because this way has proven to be the best way." Perhaps. In another company, at another time, with different people, utilizing different systems. But in order to solve the unique problem faced in the present moment, it is much better to examine, with those who will be involved in implementing the solution, the purposes that the solution is intended to accomplish. In addition, it may be possible to develop a major change that leaps ahead of what competitors are doing.

Even if only a single predetermined solution is presented, it helps to explain to those involved in implementing it what other solutions were considered, why the presented option was chosen, what their own roles in its implementation will be, and how they might positively modify the chosen solution. This concept is critical at all levels of an organization. For example, instead of simply presenting a recommendation for a major capital expenditure to a board of directors, a company officer should offer a list of the alternatives from which that recommendation was selected. This gives the board members a chance to understand the situation and even to use their wide varieties of experience to improve it. An inclusive approach—one that expresses confidence in the abilities of people to understand what is being done, as opposed to acting on the belief that you can make the decision—will increase the likelihood of effectively implementing the chosen solution.

Of course, it is easier to demonstrate how Full-Spectrum Thinking would discover a better solution for a relatively simple problem like the Boulou water deficit. It is more difficult to accurately trace the root cause of a four-trillion-dollar national debt.

Yet even with so overwhelming a problem as the U.S. national debt, specific parts of the larger problem, such as the "pork-barrel" allocations that add up to billions of dollars in wasted government appropriations, could obviously be better addressed by Full-Spectrum Thinking. A short-term "solution" to the problem of elected officials' ensuring their reelection by steering needless government expenditures to their own states and districts, might be the line-item veto that presidents and governors so covet. Another short-term solution might be the term limits that are currently fashionable opinion among many citizens.

A longer-term solution—which would neither upset the balance of constitutional powers, nor deny citizens of smaller states access to national influence by means of Congressional seniority—would be to address legislative appropriations with expansive Full-Spectrum Thinking. A legislator would thus be encouraged to examine his or her appropriations votes on the basis of the larger purposes of the district (which leads to the nation as a whole), rather than focus on the limited and narrow interests of local constituents. At the same time, Full-Spectrum Thinking offers a variety of alternative solutions, options that congress can use to demonstrate to voters how their narrow interests are constructively subsumed within the larger purposes for which a legislator's vote is cast.

Take the problem of health care in the United States. During the presidential election of 1992, there was general agreement that the system as then constituted was both inadequate and unjust. Widespread consensus was that "something must be done." So pervasive was the sense of failure—solution crash—for the U.S. healthcare system that even the doctors and insurance companies who most profited from the existing system realized that change was ultimately in their self-interest.

Many individual experts, politicians, organizations, and professional associations were called upon to draft the patchwork health reform plan proposed by President Clinton. That plan resulted from following Conventional Thinking's Research Approach, whereby the problem had been "studied to death." The plan tweaked the old, outmoded system while extending its coverage to the millions currently without healthcare protection. It suggested limited "solutions" such as cost controls, tax credits, and healthcare vouchers. Much like squeezing an expanding balloon so that it takes on different shapes, these "solutions" only served to move around the increasing problem and delay the inevitable explosion.

At least in the beginning of the debate, few insisted on examining the purposes to be achieved by the entire healthcare delivery system problem and then determining the best delivery systems *as if nothing yet existed.* Full-Spectrum Thinking directs the search for solutions toward an expansive purpose space, within which to develop the ideal solution—one which addresses the largest purpose to be served—as well as determine the best *achievable* solution aimed at the target "ideal." The best solution usually demands a new "balloon." This will at least serve as a guide for "patch-up" solutions. At best, it will lead to the major changes that most people recognize are required.

The solution paradigm is crashing because the *thinking* paradigm has crashed. We fail to solve our problems because we mistakenly apply Conventional Thinking. It encourages a mind-set that leads to the basic Eight Errors of solution finding mentioned in the Introduction.

For example, a much discussed problem today is the presumed shortcomings of elementary education. In this problem area, we might make the first error—*ineffective mental assumptions*—by assuming that a standardized curriculum exists. Or that, in order to succeed in each grade, a student's reading skills must reach a certain level. Or that the lists of so-called top problems of public schools—drugs, alcohol, pregnancy, suicide, rape, robbery, etc.—should be addressed for all schools, however inaccurate and incomplete the list may be.[14] Assuming an educational model in which "one size fits all" is the first error.

Or we may take an *ineffective approach* to the subject. Even if we assume, correctly, that there is no single model of an excellent educational curriculum, we are still likely to gather "all the facts" about what exists today on all aspects of education because that is what Conventional Thinking tells us to do.

This leads to asking *ineffective* or *"standard" people* to work on the situation—the researchers, statisticians, guardians of bodies of knowledge in education, psychology, sociology, and so forth. The "customer" of education, students for example, and the "customer's customer"—family, society—are not even considered; they are disenfranchised from the current system.

As a result, we will very likely address the *visible* or *wrong problem.* The actual problem may not be the specific curriculum. It may well be the learning environment; it may be the overall structure and framework of elementary education in the particular district. Working on the curriculum would not necessarily improve the specifics of classroom instruction to provide a good learning environment.

We could work on the right problem, with an effective approach and mental assumptions, yet still err in our *timing.* We may not accurately prioritize the necessary solutions. The solution we choose to act on first may not be the most critical. Or an external factor—such as a business forum report on poor preparation in reading—is not used quickly enough to take advantage of the public's attention to the opportunity to take action.

Ineffective control. Who's responsible for fixing this problem of elementary education? Who has the authority to do so? Is it the curriculum director downtown, at the district level? The school curriculum committee? The principal in the school? The teacher? Are curriculum decisions made locally, close to the individual student, within broad guidelines and parameters? Or are they made by a distant bureaucracy incapable of accurate specification?

Unfortunately accepting a false or incomplete solution. This often occurs when someone who is exceptionally articulate or has great powers of persuasion considers the alternatives then declares him- or herself in favor of a particular choice. Swept away by charisma, others acquiesce.

Inappropriately rejecting a broader and more effective solution. In this case, someone—even an articulate, persuasive, charismatic person—may offer a good solution, only to have it rejected by the group. Due to past history, others may (rightly or wrongly) be leery of that person's judgment. So they will reject whatever solution he or she may favor.

The greatest and most critical obstacle to finding solutions to our problems (or preventing them in the first place) is the *thinking process* that we employ, the set of values and modes of reasoning endemic in our society. Particularly self-defeating in the prevailing Conventional Thinking is its characteristic search for *the* answer, the *single* solution exclusive of all others, the only *right* choice.

This tendency is exemplified by the recently fashionable utopian thesis proposed by American foreign policy analyst Francis Fukuyama, who argued that liberal democracy had won the great battle of ideologies and political institutions, defeating both Fascism and Communism. With the end of the Cold War, he stated, there no longer existed any challenge to liberal democracy or market capitalism. Hence history—ideological struggle—had come to an end.[15] The *right* answer is liberal democracy.

Why does Fukuyama believe that? Because, like Karl Marx and other Conventional Research Approach thinkers, he subscribes to the Hegelian notion that ideas ultimately determine reality. But as commentators Charles Krauthammer and William Pfaff, among others, have noted, rather than invoking Hegel to support a thesis that tells people what they want to hear, Fukuyama might have paid closer attention to the 3,000 years of human history that have continually demonstrated humanity's innate potential for evil.

"If evil is inherent to human nature," notes Krauthammer, "it will inevitably find its social and political expression."[16] And as Pfaff maintains, Fascism may have failed; Marxism may be failing; but human perversity and ingenuity both continue to flourish.[17] Thus, "history" is far from over. Humanity will always know conflict, always face problems, ever remain in need of solutions.

Fukuyama's provocative if misguided thesis is a perfect illustration of how contemporary societies search continually for *the* answer. He proposes a worldview with room for only one perspective. And his argument stems directly from the limitations of the Research Approach, from which he developed his faulty analysis.

The Purpose of Science and Technology

Congressman George E. Brown, Jr., chairman of the House Committee on Science, Space, and Technology, notes with rueful candor: "The promise of science—a miracle cure—serves politicians, who always are looking for a tonic to sell to the public, and it serves scientists, who understandably seek to preserve their elevated position in our culture. But it may not serve society as advertised. Indeed, the promise of science may be at the root of our problems, because it is easier—politically, socially, scientifically—to support more research than it is to change how we behave."[18]

Critics of the way research and development expenditures are allocated issued another warning. To summarize, they make the telling point that MegaScience—for example, the now-abandoned American Superconducting Super Collider program and the virtually eliminated "Star Wars" missile defense program—threatened to "devour the rest of the world." They note that of the $100 billion price tag for the SSC program, Japan, for example, was expected to pay 20 percent. That amount ($20 billion) is twice the entire annual budget for the Japanese government science and technology support program in the ministry of education.

Scientific research, say the critics, is no doubt very important, but financial resources are increasingly limited. And meanwhile, much of the world is either undernourished or actually starving. Under these circumstances, they argue, we must strike a balance between scientific research and its practical utility. And to do so, we must first question the fundamental purposes of science and the extent to which they are actually served by its Research Approach.

In the previously noted case of the Boulou people and their water shortage, the lessons drawn by physicist Freeman Dyson reflect the weaknesses of Conventional Thinking for finding solutions. Dyson finds Boulou-like decision making in all cultures, notably in the primacy of an all-too-human desire for prestige over purposes and in choices that are politically popular but fail to produce the expected results. He too cites the Superconducting Super Collider as a prime example of "high-tech" Boulou-ery. He also notes the problem of premature choice. Dyson cites the American space shuttle as an example of the danger of "betting all your money on one horse, before you have found out whether she is lame."[19]

Science has a useful and important role to play in accomplishing *one* of the five basic purposes of human activity (Introduction and Chapter 5): to develop generalizations concerning natural phenomena. Science is uniquely qualified to perform that function extremely well.

However, another critical and distinct purpose of human beings is to *translate into practice* the knowledge derived from science and other forms of human inquiry, to apply human knowledge to create useful products, processes, and systems. Full-Spectrum Thinking is unquestionably and invariably better suited to solve these sorts of problems.

Science and its Research Approach fails when it is mistakenly extended to the solution of problems concerning the *application* of our knowledge. Enthralled by the Research Approach, human beings acquire vast quantities of knowledge about nature and natural phenomena, then fail to apply it successfully. It is precisely at this point that the solution-finding crash occurs.

Our fundamental error has been to assume that, simply because the exclusively rational, analytical Research Approach has proven so successful in developing generalizations concerning natural phenomena, we should therefore follow the same approach to find solutions to all problems. To the contrary, before we run off this road and crash, we must shift gears and take an entirely new route. Precisely at this fork in the road, a shift in thinking is essential.

One important reason we must shift our way of thinking in order to find successful solutions to most of our problems, is that the Research Approach, when used to create or restructure systems, inherently promotes adherence to a single "correct" solution. Thus, it tends to create strong confrontation between the chosen and any alternative solutions. In practice, this means competition between proponents of opposing points of view, all of whom might well be proposing solutions equally effective, at least in their potential. Obviously, this leads to the frustrating "gridlock" which plagues so many of our efforts to solve public policy problems.

The Futility of Confrontation

Confrontations between and adversarial positions based on opposing points of view no longer serve the larger interests of humanity. A global example of this reality is the sudden end of the Cold War. Though many in the market-oriented West were quick to claim "victory" in the 70-year-old ideological struggle with command-based communist economies, the larger truth may be that visionary leaders on both sides recognized the compelling necessity for accommodation and cooperation in an increasingly interdependent world.

Less dramatic but equally significant examples can be found in the feuding factions that block successful solutions to problems involving rival interest groups, or problems faced by elected representatives in parliaments and congresses around the world, or intra-organizational problems such as those reflected in insurance company cases or the multi-site hospital complex cited in the introductory chapter of this book. Increasingly, we can no longer afford the luxury of misapplying inherently confrontational Conventional Thinking to solution finding.

Particularly in the 1980s, it was fashionable among U.S. business and political leaders to claim that the solution to their country's myriad problems lay in the growth of the American economy. Growth, they asserted—growth alone—would solve everything. Perhaps they were misled by their dogmatic belief that the weight of American investment in weapons systems had finally overwhelmed the Soviet adversary.

Whether their analysis was correct or whether the collapse of the Soviet Union stemmed from internal contradictions and was largely coincidental with the ultimate spasm of American economic hegemony is an argument likely to last even longer than the Cold War. There can now be little doubt that growth alone is an insufficient solution to economic and social problems in the United States. Further evidence is the "trickle down" theory of wealth creation so popular during the Reagan/Bush era. It defied gravity and pushed wealth even higher toward the wealthy, and hardly a dewdrop trickled down.

It should come as no surprise that naive faith in utterly unrestrained competition, short-term quarterly dividends, completely unregulated markets, and self-interested "trickle down" wealth creation does not work when a nation ignores the necessity for simultaneous, tangible investment in product innovation and productivity—as America did throughout the 1980s. As Michael Schrage notes, "Growth without productivity isn't prosperity; it's coasting. Productivity is the real indicator of whether our standard of living is destined to increase or erode."[20] Yet increased productivity calls for thinking about purposes and alternative target solutions, for planning, for industrial and technology policies such as the United States was at that time unwilling to pursue.

The Inadequacy of High Speed "Solutions"

Another indication of the failure of the inherently confrontational Conventional Thinking is the increasingly negative impact of high-speed responses to market competition. Taken alone, speed of product introduction can do more harm than good, both to consumers and producers. Consumers more often question their need for the latest clever if superfluous high-tech "advance."

There is certainly a constant need to encourage new enterprises, the majority of which are destined by nature to fail. Only through such failures does the species progress. Indeed, in some cases, failure becomes the mother of successful invention. Yet even given the need to experiment with potential solutions, balance and utility are more essential than ever.

"The gains from new technologies are plentiful and real," writes *Newsweek* economics commentator Robert J.

Samuelson. "But the benefits are being crudely offset by a lot of technology-inspired waste.

"Every new technology inspires the temptation to see what it will do—no matter how inane or time-consuming the task. Old and inexpensive ways of doing things are eliminated to help pay for new and expensive methods."[21] Samuelson cites such questionable innovations as electronic books, video press-releases, and personal digital assistants.

Indeed, the practice of rapid introduction/obsolescence has now begun to undermine productivity. Today, many companies seem to care more about going faster than about understanding the direction they're heading.

"Most people are pursuing speed with absolutely no understanding of the economic basis behind it," says business consultant Donald Reinersten, one of the first experts to attempt to quantify the benefits of cycle time reduction. "It's true that six months of delay can reduce a product's life cycle profits by 33 percent. But speed in a development cycle is purchased at a certain price. You really need to know what it's worth to you."[22]

Even so successful an innovative product developer as Akio Morita, Chairman of Sony Corporation, now believes that his company may have mistaken speed (a *measure* of success) for success itself, thus confusing means with ends. One result: neither seller nor buyer finds satisfaction in a system increasingly out of control, a system focused on research and data analysis, not on fundamental purposes. It may be preferable, he suggests, to concentrate less on what will sell and more on the importance of the purpose that the product is intended to accomplish.[23]

The Necessity of a Systems Perspective

Because it reduces the whole into parts, Conventional Thinking finds "solutions" that are merely partial. Thus it tends to deny the global perspective, ignore the wholeness of the planet, the integrity of the environment, the interests of animals and other species, the imperatives of ecological balance.

The utopia it seeks is one exclusively for human beings. In an interdependent environment, Conventional Thinking is inherently self-defeating.

This particular weakness may be seen as directly responsible for many of the solution crashes that we confront in the world today. Science's astonishing success in comprehending distinct (thus partial) natural phenomena has, at the same time, unleashed a pervasive abuse of the natural world.

As writer Alan Ryan noted in his *New York Times* review of Charles Taylor's book *The Ethics of Authenticity*, "If we learn to understand the natural world as having its own voice and its own meaning—if not in the way our medieval predecessors saw it, as one of the texts by which God communicated with us, perhaps in the way Wordsworth or Emerson saw it—we are already halfway to knowing where to draw the line over the exploitation of natural resources. If we see ourselves as already deeply implicated in the common life of our society, we ought to find it easier to reanimate our democratic faith."[24]

From medieval times through the middle decades of the current century, human beings increasingly sought to escape the physically brutal, economically, intellectually, and spiritually repressive environment of rural, agricultural villages, in the hope of finding a safer, better, freer, more fulfilling lives in the city. The result: great numbers of people now experience the crash of the Research Approach to understanding Nature as they exist in largely artificial urban environments, consuming polluted air and water. Living in modern cities, further alienated from nature, human beings grow ever weaker as natural organisms.

While few among even the most avid of today's environmentalists would forego the many benefits of modern urban life to go all the way "back to the land," it is by no means clear whether we are less vulnerable to Nature's forces than in centuries past.

Once we sought to create sheltered, civilized centers of social interdependence as havens from the rigors of the savage wilderness. We placed our confidence in the "progress" certain to derive from Science and the widespread application of its Research Approach. We were certain that our well-being and standard of living would improve as Science tamed and bent Nature to our will.

Yet today we find ourselves less able to respond positively to the benefits of Nature, because we have overstressed our natural systems—our bodies—by attempting to adapt to life in the urban spaces we have created. Whether in New York or Tokyo, Sao Paolo or Mexico City, Calcutta or Kiev, the phenomena of human existence today mock our hopes and fall far short of our expectations.

The Forest and the Trees

It is easy to fall prey to despair under such disappointing and challenging circumstances. Both in number and severity, the problems we confront increase daily. It is only natural that we feel overwhelmed, that this is an age of anxiety.

Yet we must not panic. There is no cause for despair. Nor do we need to diminish the expectation that we can indeed solve the problems we confront. By applying the Full-Spectrum Approach of Breakthrough Thinking, we can find the way toward excellent solutions to our problems.

But if we consider individual problems, which are overwhelming when added up, we make two fundamental mistakes. First, we will fail to see the holistic beauty of the forest for fear of the overwhelming mass of individual trees. Secondly, even more important, if we focus with apprehension on the overwhelming mass of individual problems, we are in peril of approaching those problems with the compartmentalized perspective of Conventional Thinking.

Remember that a central element of the Conventional Thinking Approach is to break up a problem into smaller parts. At first, this seems to help us get a grip on problems; but in fact, it inevitably dooms the "solution" that we find. Peter Robinson, a speech writer for President Reagan for six years, describes the loss of reality by subdividing a whole into supposed constituent parts in his tales of spending two years pursuing an MBA degree: American education breaks practical work into academic disciplines, which produce courses of gibberish unrelated to real business.[25]

To address individual problems, then, we must consider the mass of which they are a part. And yet, secure in the knowledge that Full-Spectrum Thinking will discover excellent solutions to our problems, we will find in that forest not overwhelming fears, but rather shelter, food, and fuel, sustenance, beauty, and delight. Soon, we can face our forest of problems with hope and excitement rather than dismay and despair.

According to Haynes Johnson, Americans are concerned about the huge difficulties that we face. Johnson believes this anxiety will stimulate action, action based on a "new American spirit" and a willingness to shift from blaming others for the problems we all face toward realizing that we must be responsible for our own actions.[26]

To effect this auspicious transformation, to begin mastering our problems, to discover and implement excellent solutions, we must shift our underlying mental assumptions about how to approach problems. Our fundamental *thinking paradigm* must change.

NOTES

1. Mikhail Gorbachev, in T. Mitchel and W. G. Scott, "America's Problems and Needed Reforms: Confronting the Ethic of Personal Advantage," *Academy of Management Executive,* Vol. 4, No. 3, (1990).

2. Haynes Johnson, *Divided We Fall: Gambling with History in the Nineties* (New York: W. W. Norton, 1994).

3. David Gordon, "Here's a 6-Point Plan for Rebuilding the Fundamentals of Our Economy," *Los Angeles Times,* (December 29, 1991).

4. Jonathan Rauch, "America's Crack-Up: Government Can Wage War, Build Roads, and Desegregate Schools, But It Can't Save Us From Ourselves," *Los Angeles Times Magazine,* (July 26, 1992).

5. Lawrence E. Greiner, "Resistance To Change During Restructuring," *Journal of Management Inquiry,* Vol. 1, No. 1, (March 1992), pp. 61–62.

6. Michael Schrage, "Japan Seeks Next Management Breakthrough," *Los Angeles Times,* (October 29, 1992).

7. Ibid., (re: Ikujiro Nonaka).

8. Yoshi Noguchi, "Dropping Out of Tokyo's Rat-Race," *The New York Times,* (March 1, 1992).

9. Karl Schoenberger, "Blinded by Success, Japan Searches for a New Vision," *Los Angeles Times,* (June 19, 1990).

10. James Fallows, "Standing Up To Japan," *Los Angeles Times Magazine,* (March 12, 1989).

11. Kittredge Cherry, "Japanese Are On The Cutting Edge Of Creativity," review of Sheridan Tatsuno, *Created In Japan: From Imitators to World Class Innovators* (New York: Ballinger/Harper and Row, 1990), *Mainichi Daily News* (Tokyo, March 6, 1990).

12. Robert Collins, *Japan-Think, Ameri-Think: An Irreverent Guide to Understanding the Cultural Differences Between Us* (New York: Penguin, 1992).

13. Freeman Dyson, *From Eros to Gaia* (New York: Pantheon, 1992).

14. Barry O'Neill, "The History of a Hoax," *New York Times Magazine,* (March 6, 1994).

15. Francis Fukuyama, *The End of History and the Last Man* (New York: The Free Press/Macmillan, 1992).

16. Charles Krauthammer, "History Is Chugging Along, but Politics Is Decided," *Los Angeles Times,* (September 17, 1989).

17. William Pfaff, "'History Is Over' Is Only a Siren Song of Retreat and Disengagement," *Los Angeles Times,* (October 2, 1989).

18. George E. Brown, Jr., "It's Down to the Last Blank Check," *Los Angeles Times,* (September 8, 1992).

19. Dyson, *From Eros to Gaia.*

20. Michael Schrage, "R & D Lags, Despite Presidential Puffery," *Los Angeles Times,* (January 30, 1992).

21. Robert J. Samuelson, "Technology in Reverse," *Newsweek,* (July 20, 1992).

22. Michael Schrage (re: Donald Reinersten), "Drive to Obsolescence Needs a Brake," *Los Angeles Times,* (July 2, 1992).

23. Ibid., (re: Akio Morita).

24. Alan Ryan, "Don't Think for Yourself Unless You Can," review of Charles Taylor, *The Ethics of Authenticity* in *The New York Times,* (September 27, 1992).

25. Peter Robinson, *Snapshots from Hell: The Making of an MBA,* (New York: Warner Books, 1994).

26. Johnson, *Divided We Fall.*

Chapter 2

The Nature of Mental Assumptions and Conventional Thinking

"We must change our organization from a command-control paradigm to one of participation and lowered levels of decision-making."

"The educational paradigm of rote memorization and lecturing will be supplanted in the computer age with a paradigm of self-motivation and learning."

"Our land-use planning paradigm will have to be significantly modified to one which emphasizes conservation of forests and green areas."

Now, if these and other changes that we seek are going to occur, we must add to the clamor for "paradigm changes" the most important change of all. Yet most people do not even consider this essential change. We must change our *thinking paradigm,* the assumptions we use as we try to create or restructure solutions. Then many of those solutions will prove to be the other significant changes that we seek.

What is a Paradigm?

Paradigms exist. They must. Humans need them to live as individuals and with one another. Paradigms are neither good nor bad; they just *are*.

There are at least 41 different definitions of "paradigm." Not only does a paradigm have many meanings, but it may mean different things to different people. Even Thomas Kuhn, who first popularized the term in 1962, used the concept of paradigm in no less than 21 different ways.

Webster's Collegiate Dictionary defines paradigm as "an example, a pattern." The word derives from the Greek: "para," meaning "from," plus "deigma," meaning "example," which stems from "deiknynai," meaning "to show." Thus, in its simplest sense, a paradigm is a *pattern,* an *example,* upon which to *model* actions or thought. In most cases, children use the rules and examples of the way they were raised as the basis for their own adult actions and beliefs.

Pattern is a guide or plan to be strictly followed. *Example* suggests that which is presented as a sample or which sets a precedent for imitation, whether good or bad. *Model* refers to any person, thing, or system to be copied, followed, or imitated, presumably because of excellence or worth. For example, questioning every suggested expenditure with the guide of "Does it contribute to the growth of the company?" is the way that New Hampshire's Cabletron, Inc., a company listed on the New York Stock Exchange, keeps its overhead costs to a minimum.[1]

A paradigm so well-established that it serves as the original model for all later things of the same kind would be considered an *archetype* or *prototype*. It becomes the enduring *standard* that is used as a rule or a basis of comparison in judging quality. An archetypal paradigm embodies accepted tradition. It is the *criterion* by which all others are judged. It is considered the *exemplar,* the *ideal* that all others should emulate, the *epitome* of its sort. For example, the ideal of democracy in the United States—"life, liberty, and the pursuit of happiness"—is the basis for evaluating how decisions are made in national and international politics; and it very likely explains why the majority of those who seek to leave their native countries want to come to the United States.

Some 30 years ago, Thomas Kuhn wrote about the sort of paradigm shift that we now propose. However, in his landmark book *The Structure of Scientific Revolutions,* Kuhn referred only to paradigm shifts within science itself. He spoke of them primarily as fundamental changes in theories or explanations of natural phenomena that have occurred during the history of science, changes in the way scientists have come to view the natural world.

Kuhn's basic notion of paradigms was that they represented generally accepted traditions, such as Ptolemaic astronomy (later supplanted by Copernican), Aristotelian dynamics (supplanted by Newtonian), corpuscular optics (supplanted by wave optics), and so on. To Kuhn, such paradigms were "universally recognized scientific achievements that, for a time, provided model problems and solutions to a community of practitioners."[2]

Thus, central to Kuhn's understanding of the term is that succeeding paradigms exist as *alternative* realities. Philosophically, then, the term "paradigm" denotes an implicit or explicit view of reality, yet one that is always *subject to change.*

In contemporary, popular usage, the word has acquired a plethora of definitions. One meaning is basically *any dominant idea.* Some see it as meaning the *conventional wisdom* about how things have for a long time been done and so must continue to be done. (One way to recognize a paradigm is to hear people say: "That's just the way we do things around here.") Others define "paradigm" as a *general perspective* or *state of mind* that reflects fundamental beliefs and assumptions.

Futurist and management consultant Joel Barker defines a paradigm as a *set of rules and regulations* (written or unwritten) that does two things: (1) establishes and describes boundaries, and (2) tells you how to behave and what to do to be judged successful within those boundaries.[3]

A paradigm is a *mind set,* a *worldview* mapping the figurative terrain that we inhabit. At once guiding and limiting our thoughts and actions, paradigms so color the way we perceive facts, circumstances, and experiences that they virtually determine our responses.

The paradigm as *mental model* is another way of describing culture, which is usually defined as a set of learned, functionally related behavioral patterns, as well as the material products produced by people following those patterns. A paradigm is a *lens* through which we interpret life, the prescription that clarifies (or distorts) all that we perceive. In this sense, a paradigm can be seen to embody *myth*.

All of these definitions do not affect the basic reality that each person, family, community, organization, and even region, state (or prefecture or province), and nation *does* operate within a specific paradigm set (dominant idea, state of mind, rules, regulations, assumptions, worldview, myths, mental model) about everyday existence, policy framework, organizational structure, and personal interactions. It is these paradigms that many claim must change as the twenty-first century approaches. Our point in this book is that such paradigm changes can only be achieved effectively by changing first our paradigm of thinking.

SOME CHARACTERISTICS OF A PARADIGM

We can learn to understand paradigms better with reference to their characteristics. Management consultant Harvey Gelman offers four characteristics of paradigms: (1) Paradigms influence our perception of the world; (2) Because we get so good at using our present paradigms, we resist changing them; (3) It is the outsider who usually creates the new paradigm; (4) Those who change to a successful new paradigm gain new vision.[4]

This brings us to a central point: Whether in their most flexible and benign form (theory) or in their most calcified and malignant form (dogma), paradigms have the capacity to evolve and change. New paradigms arise even while old ones remain efficient and useful. As Kuhn relates, "Often a new paradigm emerges, at least in embryo, before a crisis has developed far or been explicitly recognized." And the new ones allow us to solve problems considered impossible under the old paradigm.[5]

As matters of personal perspective, paradigms can be (with effort) changed at will. Deliberately changing or modifying paradigms—effecting a "paradigm shift"—can free us to find solutions, to enjoy more successful and creative lives.

As physicists Alan Lightman and Owen Gingerich have noted, scientific theories change when anomalies are recognized. An anomaly is simply any deviation from the expected natural order, that is, from the existing paradigm. For example, the *Oxford English Dictionary* cited Darwin in 1873: "There is no greater anomaly in nature than a bird that cannot fly."[6]

Anomalies function as a sort of evolutionary compass that heralds paradigms shifts. They often point to the inadequacies of an old paradigm and emphasize the merits of the new. Indeed, certain scientific anomalies, for example the inadequacy of measurements for subatomic movement, are recognized only after they are given compelling explanations within a new conceptual framework—the new paradigm—quantum mechanics.

The difficulties one experiences when trying to solve problems with conventional approaches are the source of the anomaly we address in this book. After all, if the good solution ideas, such as those embodied in total quality management programs, have not produced anywhere near the expected success rate for companies that use them,[7] then it is time to question—and change—the thinking paradigm being followed.

HOW PARADIGMS PROPAGATE

Paradigms spread both through formal instruction and through individual experiences and observations. Regarding their power and necessity in formal science education, Kuhn notes that a community's paradigms are "revealed in its textbooks, lectures, and laboratory exercises."[8]

He emphasizes that "the study of paradigms . . . is what mainly prepares the student for membership in the particular scientific community with which he will later practice. Because he there joins men who learned the bases of their field from the same concrete models, his subsequent practice will seldom evoke overt disagreement over fundamentals."[9]

Indeed, one can argue that the various systems of formal education are organized primarily to provide an appropriate milieu for the transfer of [paradigmatic] ideas from one generation to the next and for the faithful replication of those paradigms.

In this light, it becomes clear that humans can be and often are formally "programmed" to address their problems—to think—in a certain way. This programming shapes our *thinking paradigm,* our basic mental assumptions.

Of course, paradigms are also established and propagated informally. They are formed and maintained (or changed) by the countless individual experiences we have, the observations we make in all the situations we confront throughout our lives.

Thus do we accept, abide by, and change the paradigms by which we guide our thoughts and actions. Moreover, the *mental assumptions* by which we live permeate each others' boundaries to affect the way we think and act and relate to others in all areas of our life experience. For example, the fundamental perspectives from which we view science and religion will impact the way we view society and politics and economics, not to mention how we interact with colleagues, friends, and loved ones.

By our definition, then, a paradigm is a funda-*mental assumption* by which we *choose* to guide our lives.

Various Paradigms

Science itself provides the most obvious examples of the sort of mental models that we are discussing. Kuhn cites many such paradigms, all of which have flourished variously during the course of the history of science. Aristotelian dynamics, phlogistic chemistry, and caloric thermodynamics, he notes, are all once-current views of nature, "neither less scientific nor more the product of human idiosyncrasy than those current today." Major turning points along the course of scientific development are associated with the names of Copernicus, Newton, Lavoisier, and Einstein.

Each of these revolutions, says Kuhn, "necessitated the community's rejection of one time-honored scientific theory in favor of another incompatible with it."[10] Countless scientific paradigms, universally accepted in their day, have nonetheless been supplanted by others found more true, which is to say more useful.

PARADIGMS OF MANAGEMENT
AND ORGANIZATION

Of course, different cultures, whether national or local, are likely to hold different paradigms. For example, different paradigms can be recognized by contrasting the mental assumptions about management in China, in Japan, and in the United States.

International Management magazine recently contrasted decision-making paradigms in those three countries. The author notes that, in Japan, the most important part of the decision-making process is understanding and analyzing the problem and developing various alternative solutions. Final authority for making a decision rests with top management, but before a proposal reaches the top executive's desk, the problem and the possible solutions have been discussed at various levels in the organizational hierarchy, so that a consensus is reached throughout the organization.

This Japanese management paradigm assures that the problem or decision is examined from different perspectives, an obvious strength. Previous consensus means that implementation can occur without complaint or delay. However, the process of decision making itself is viewed as relatively time consuming. And the sharing of power can result in no one feeling individually responsible for the results of the decision.

In typical U.S. organizations, usually only a few people have decision-making power. As a result, after the decision has been made, it has to be *sold* to others, often to people with different values and different perceptions of what the problem really is and how it should be solved.

At the beginning, this U.S. management paradigm is relatively fast; but its implementation is time consuming and often results in much greater total time used than in Japan. It also requires compromise from managers holding different viewpoints, which ultimately leads to a less than ideal solution and less effective results. While individuals feel personally responsible for the decision, this paradigm can also lead to "scapegoating" when the decision has negative results.

In U.S. companies, the decision power and the responsibility for decisions is vested in different people. In Japan, the same people share both decision power and responsibility. In Japanese companies, the emphasis is on collective responsibility and accountability. In U.S. companies, the emphasis is on individual responsibility, with efforts to clarify and make explicit who is responsible for what.

In China, major decisions are also made by people at the top, but even more strictly than in the United States. Decision making, through the central planning bureau, is under the direct control of the state. Consequently, lower-level managers have little authority to make strategic decisions. At the same time, much as in Japan, many people are involved in operational decisions.

This Chinese management paradigm leads to a lack of flexibility in implementing decisions. Despite widespread recognition of the need to change, upper-echelon managers in the state hierarchy resist reforms that would mean giving up some official privileges. Until recently, this has resulted in the worst of both worlds: the slow decision-making characteristic of the Japanese paradigm, coupled with the slow implementation characteristic of the U.S. paradigm.[11]

Commentator James Fallows notes that the practical Japanese are fundamentally more interested in outcome than in ideology. By contrast, Western nations tend to pay more attention to ideology—constitutional provisions, laws, rules, policies. In Japan, says Fallows, the result itself is more important than the rules that led to it. Principles take a back seat to pragmatism.[12]

This aspect of the Japanese management paradigm appears to have its roots in the Confucian ethic, which teaches the value of harmony but offers no universal principles on how to achieve it. Buddhism and Shintoism, widely held religious ethics in Japan as well, also lack the absolute standards of Christianity. As a result, says Japanese expert Frank Gibney, the Japanese do not have absolute values. They never make decisions based on principle alone; they always consider the practical results of a decision.[13]

Unlike their Japanese counterparts, U.S. government and business leaders often act on the basis of abstract principle alone and let the chips fall where they may. For example, the Bush administration refused government assistance to private industry in the development of high-definition television (HDTV). Based on absolute principles of market forces, they insisted that the choice of which HDTV system (analog or digital) to develop be left entirely to the free market.

Japan has shown no such distaste for forming government-business consortia to research and develop promising technologies; the HDTV government-sponsored consortia promoted only the analog system. Yet 1994 saw the Japanese disband this effort because the market-driven forces in the United States led to the selection of digital HDTV over analog as early as 1991.

The fundamental pragmatism that underlies the Japanese paradigm of management creates one of its greatest strengths: operational flexibility. By contrast, U.S. government policies often lurch unpredictably between pragmatism and idealism, the opposite polarities of the American cultural myth. The tension between these two equally valued instincts forms a large part of the basis for the altruistic yet individualistic, moralistic yet secular, fast but rigid American early decision-making paradigm.

Akio Morita, founder and chairman of Sony Corporation, observes that these different paradigms of organizational management are rooted in very different origins of community and society—on the one hand, Confucian; on the other, Judeo-Christian. Morita also emphasizes fundamental differences in the Japanese and American nations. Japanese, he notes, are born Japanese; America is a nation of immigrants. "Historically, then, Americans know that rules are created by themselves in their own interests. The Japanese mentality has not been affected by such an experience of self-government. For millennia, we have been governed by a government that has forced rules and regulations upon us."[14]

It is fascinating to consider that—perhaps in an attempt to seek balance—the resulting paradigms of management in the two countries are in direct contrast to the historical national experiences. The Japanese, historically accustomed to rule by emperors and warlords, now employ a management paradigm in which decision-making occurs largely from the bottom up. Americans, historically accustomed to individual liberty and self-rule, have chosen to employ a management paradigm in which decisions are generally imposed from the top down.

University of Southern California professor Kenyon DeGreene speculates that the traditional individualism of Americans and their proclivity for reductionism (breaking a problem into its parts) and "rational" decision-making (the Research Approach) "provide a poor fit for group designs, mutual problem solving, consensual decision making, and the shifting of authority downward. [By contrast,] Japanese cultural attributes of ambiguity, vagueness, uncertainty, and contradiction appear to be more harmonious to [successful, unsupervised group work]. Japanese culture is not nearly so deeply based on scientific rationality."[15]

DeGreene notes that similarly organized groups in Japanese and American companies similarly dedicated to the concept of Flexible Manufacturing Systems do not produce similar results. The Japanese groups consistently outperform their American counterparts. Yet the differences in performance could not be traced to differences in worker education, nor to any other relative lack of quality among American workers. Rather, the differences were a result of the management paradigm employed.

The Inherent Dynamism of Paradigms

Due to human nature, the search for truth is a constant process. The truths we find, and so the paradigms that we construct from them, are in a state of constant flux. So has it always been. So will it always be.

Of course, to follow the process of paradigm shifts over time is hardly easier than listening to the shifting of tectonic plates beneath the earth's surface. Consequently, predicting paradigm shifts is as much a science as predicting earthquakes. That is, both endeavors partake of art as much as they do of science. Even once a paradigm shift has occurred, few if any recognize immediately the change that has occurred.

WHAT IS A PARADIGM SHIFT?

Exactly what is a paradigm shift? First of all, in the larger "social" sphere, it is a rare event. In science, perhaps less so. Yet in the entire history of Western Civilization, states social historian W. Kirk MacNulty, only three social changes sufficiently fundamental to be considered paradigm shifts have occurred.

MacNulty lists these changes in the fundamental assumptions governing Western society: (1) the shift that occurred in Greece about 400 years before the Christian era and related to the decline of the pantheon of gods and the rise of the city-state as the central institution in society; (2) the shift that occurred in Medieval Europe during the period between A.D. 1350 and 1660, known as the Renaissance and Reformation/Counter Reformation, change from a theocratic to a humanistic/mystical/ scientific paradigm; and (3) the shift from a basically agrarian to a technological/ industrial paradigm, which occurred widely in Europe about 1800.[16]

During the many centuries within each stage, members of society generally agreed on the story that made sense of their world. People shared a common perspective and were usually satisfied to view the world through that lens. Even great conflicts, terrible difficulties, and horrible brutalities were and are accepted by society, as long as they are effectively explained by the existing paradigm.

According to Kuhn, the differences between successive [scientific] paradigms are both necessary and irreconcilable. "Since new paradigms are born from old ones," he writes, "they ordinarily incorporate much of the vocabulary and apparatus . . . that the traditional paradigm had previously employed. But they seldom employ these borrowed elements in quite the traditional way. Communication across the revolutionary divide [caused by a new paradigm] is inevitably partial."[17]

Kuhn offers the examples of laymen who scoffed at Einstein's general theory of relativity because, in their understanding of the term "space," it obviously could not, as Einstein asserted, be "curved." Again, says Kuhn, consider those who called Copernicus mad for saying that the earth moved. Yet the "earth" that these men knew clearly could not be moved; indeed, it embodied the notion of a fixed position.

While neither Kuhn nor MacNulty would consider these examples sufficiently fundamental to warrant use of the term "paradigm shift," Barker's understanding of paradigm shifts includes them among the following dramatic changes that have occurred in the industrialized world since 1960:

- Environmentalism;
- Consumerism;
- The American civil rights movement;
- Instantaneous world communications;
- Widespread use of personal computers;
- Political terrorism as an everyday activity;
- Deregulation of U.S. banking, airlines, telecommunications, trucking;
- Higher energy prices and new pricing forces;
- Energy conservation as the norm;
- Growth of participatory management;
- The emergence of information as a key resource;
- The loss of the U.S. position as the world's leading manufacturer;
- Japan as a producer of the highest quality products [18]

As this list indicates, Barker believes that a paradigm shift occurs simply whenever "the rules" change, thereby changing the way to be successful. Significantly, all of these shifts were largely unpredictable. But they happened. And they caused people to view the world in a new and different way. That is the popular understanding of a paradigm shift.

Paradigm shifts generally include and are composed of many individual trends, none of which are sufficiently fundamental to be considered paradigm shifts. For example, trends in the industrial- to service-based economy shift would include:

(1) the U.S. industrial-based economy reached its peak around 1945 when employment was 39 percent of the total workforce; (2) by 1985, it had shrunk to 21 percent; (3) it is expected to shrink to 5 percent by the turn of the century; and (4) in terms of gross national product, American industry contributed 35 percent of GNP in 1945, 28 percent in 1985, and is expected to fall to 24 percent in the year 2001.

Women-in-management writer Sally Helgesen, commenting on the ways in which particularly female characteristics of leadership are contributing to new management models, notes that a paradigm shift is occurring, away from pyramidal structures and hierarchical processes to web-like structures and circular processes.

"Until recently," she writes, "the hierarchical pyramid was considered the very model of organizational efficiency; and for heavy industry, this may have been true. But as today's companies attempt to restructure in response to the very different needs of the information age, the value of the old pyramid is being questioned: Didn't hierarchy give birth to slow-moving bureaucracy? The old military model chain-of-command increasingly is seen as too lumbering and muscle-bound for a fast-changing global economy—and far too expensive as well. Progressive companies are trying out new structures. And it is in this restructuring that the web of inclusion—that product of the female psyche—has a contribution to make."[19]

Consultant and professor Joseph McCann lists seven emerging paradigm shifts that set the new ground rules for corporate innovation today: a shift from "machine age" thinking to organic thinking; from monolithic models to pluralistic; from competition to collaboration; from structure to process; from occasional, predictable technology "programs" to constantly recurring, largely unpredictable technology "pulses"; from national organizations to transnational; and from short-term thinking to long-term.

McCann writes: "The first fundamental shift is from viewing the universe as a well-ordered machine to that of a highly organic system of dynamic, integrally related parts. It is a shift from reductionism [read: Conventional Thinking] to systems thinking [read: Full-Spectrum Thinking]. . . . Basic to this shift is the recognition that problems need to be understood in terms of their larger context, not reduced to constituent parts that in themselves give no perspective on the entire problem. You gain understanding of a problem by placing it in its larger context."[20]

A paradigm shift with wide-ranging impact has occurred in the fundamental assumptions of computer software programs. Computer consultant Ron Lane notes that, during its first 25 years, the computer industry mainly regarded information in terms of entities—data—to be processed. This data was further compartmentalized into bits, bytes, fields, records, and files. A program dealt with only one entity at a time—reading, processing, and writing. Then, says Lane, with the advent of the relational theory developed by E. F. Codd at IBM, software writers realized that it is much more efficient to focus on the relationships between data than on the data itself.

The new programming, Lane explains, "is based on the principle that a program should be composed of parts that work cooperatively. The relationships between the data . . . should be understood, and then pieces of the program can be written that are based on global understanding of how the data relates and how the parts of the program relate."[21]

Cooperative data processing now seeks to harness the power of personal computers and workstations and have them work cooperatively with mainframe computers. Lane notes that relationships among data, routines, and machines are of primary importance. Thus, this change in data processing is a fundamental shift.

HOW DO PARADIGM SHIFTS OCCUR?

The consequences of true paradigm shifts—such as Copernicus' feat of "removing" the Earth from the center of the universe—are always profound and often cataclysmic. Everyone is at risk. Many, especially those who fail to anticipate or refuse to recognize the shift, get burned. A commonly cited example of the dangers inherent to paradigm shifts is the poignant case of Freddie the Frog.

By some quirk of nature, frogs respond differently to precisely the same situation. If you drop a frog into boiling water—

revolutionize the situation—he will sensibly and abruptly hop right out again. However, if you place the same frog in a pot of cool water and only gradually raise the temperature—evolve the situation by degrees—the frog will blissfully and ignorantly sit there until boiled to death. Like most human beings, Freddy the Frog ignores a crucial, if gradual, change in environment. He fails to recognize an evolutionary paradigm shift.

Paradigm shifts can be evolutionary or revolutionary. But one thing is certain: as a consequence of a genuine paradigm shift, no one maintains his or her original position in the scheme of things.

According to MacNulty, paradigm shifts occur when polarizations appear "along the major axis or principal dimension" of the paradigm. For example, in the medieval paradigm of a theocratic society, polarization (conflicting worldviews) occurred mainly within the Church. It developed over the issue of clerical immorality—from the neglect of pastoral duties, to the selling of indulgences, to the ignoring of the vow of celibacy— all of which were addressed by Martin Luther and others.[22]

To Kuhn, competition is the engine that drives paradigm shifts. "Competition between segments of the scientific community is the only historical process that ever actually results in the rejection of one previously accepted theory or in the adoption of another."

Moreover, since human nature fears the void, established paradigms are never frivolously rejected. "Once [a scientific theory] has achieved the status of paradigm, [it] is declared invalid only if an alternate candidate is available to take its place." The old rules fail, creating a prerequisite "sense of malfunction that can lead to crisis."

Kuhn notes: "During the transition period, there will be a large but never complete overlap between the problems that can be solved by the old and by the new paradigm. But there will also be a decisive difference in the modes of solution. When the transition is complete, the profession will have changed its view of the field, its methods, and its goals."[23]

Michael Schrage observes that paradigm shifts in the application of technology are often driven by the frustration that

many companies experience when their technology investments fail to produce the results they had hoped to achieve.
Such companies become increasingly curious about and open
to shifts in the fundamental assumptions underlying the technology they use. This has been particularly evident, says
Schrage, in the field of information technology, as the actual results of these investments have lagged behind the productivity
gains expected.

An excellent example of failed technological expectation
becoming the engine for a shift in fundamental assumptions
can be found in the success of Steve Jobs and Steve Wozniak.
These two outsiders came up with a new and different way to
create and use computer hardware and software. The result:
Apple Computer forced giants like IBM to accept a paradigm
shift.[24]

Of course, anticipating a paradigm shift is central to business success. Barker notes that the Japanese—transistor radios,
quartz crystal watches, video cassette recorders, fuzzy logic—
are perhaps the most successful of the "paradigm pioneers"
who follow the "outsiders" who discover and first propose paradigm shifts. While others resist change, these pioneers will
take a risk and invest in a novel idea based on a new fundamental assumption. Soon, the global competitive pressures that result from such paradigm shifts contribute to the ultimate
triumph of the new paradigm.[25]

DeGreene notes that hardly anyone actively seeks a paradigm shift. "Indeed, such change is forced upon people. The
old paradigm stays alive and well until enough anomalies
mount up to a scandal, and the evidence for the new paradigm
becomes overwhelming. People are basically conservative because the unknown and the uncertain beget anxiety. Most people prefer to work within the accepted paradigm."[26]

Particularly within hierarchical structures such as business and the military, initial widespread acceptance of paradigm shifts demands their direction from the top. Examples
within the armed forces include the commander-in-chief directed policies promoting racial integration (President Tru-

man) and attempting to ban discrimination on the basis of sexual-orientation (President Clinton).

In business, says management consultants Noel Tichy and Ram Charan, "there has to be divine discontent with the status quo at the very top, and the courage to do something about it." Such dramatic successes as the creation of the minivan (Chrysler) and the desktop laser printer (Hewlett-Packard) demanded the rejection of existing paradigms, not only in terms of the ultimate product, but also in terms of the process by which the product was developed. These shifts may be driven by the search for profit (Federal Express) or the desire to meet an engineering challenge (Apple computers).[27]

Directed paradigm shifts also occur as a result of civilian governmental decisions based on political, social, and economic factors. One such example is the recent shift in U.S. governmental and insurance industry attitudes regarding health care. The political funding process especially can have a major impact on paradigm shifts. As U.S. Representative George Brown notes concerning research in Big Science: "Research trajectories are highly dependent on the momentum of history, and changing these trajectories can be difficult; often, change is accomplished through political means—especially by shifting funding priorities—rather than through the play of unfettered scientific inquiry."[28]

A key truth to remember is that—at least on the smaller level—paradigm shifts are constant. Since anticipation is crucial, both to take advantage of shifts as they occur and to avoid becoming overwhelmed by them, the question arises: how do I know when a shift is occurring?

One way for scientists to recognize paradigm shifts, Kuhn suggests, is to pay close attention to the details of scientific literature. This is, of course, good advice in any field of professional endeavor. When the authorities cited begin to change, fundamental assumptions are shifting. Systematic quantification and retrieval of such data is increasingly possible. But for the individual, noticing fundamental change is likely to forever remain more art than science. Perhaps the one requirement remains, as ever, intuition, along with the courage to trust in it.

The Collapse of Solutions

What has led to the collapse of our solutions paradigms? Generally, the collapse can be traced to a confluence of technological and scientific developments with existing social, economic, and intellectual conditions—that is, with urgent human needs.

For example, widespread professional notice of discrepancy between the accepted calendar and the actual position of the planets led to a revolutionary paradigm shift in planetary astronomy: Copernicus' discovery that the earth is not the center of the universe; instead, all planets revolve around the sun.

By the early sixteenth century, an increasing number of Europe's best astronomers recognized that the astronomical paradigm was failing when applied to the problems it was traditionally supposed to solve. According to Kuhn, that recognition was an essential prerequisite to Copernicus' rejection of the Ptolemaic paradigm and his search for a new one.

When the Ptolemaic system was first developed, Kuhn explains, it was admirably successful in predicting the changing positions of both stars and planets. Yet with respect both to planetary position and to precession of the equinoxes, predictions made with Ptolemy's system never quite conformed with the best available observations.

Given a particular discrepancy, astronomers were always able to eliminate it by making some particular adjustment in Ptolemy's system. But as time went on, it became clear that astronomy's complexity was increasing far more rapidly than its accuracy and that a discrepancy corrected in one place was likely to show up in another. Copernicus himself wrote that the astronomical tradition he inherited had finally created only a monster.[29]

A stark contemporary example of the confluence between technical/scientific developments and urgent human needs is provided by the U.S. Food and Drug Administration's response to the AIDS crisis in public health. Professor Stephen

Gould notes the distinction between generally docile terminal cancer patients and HIV-positive patients, who are much more likely to take an active role in seeking out and practicing alternative therapeutic methods:

> AIDS patients' demands center not only on new drug innovation, but also on speeding up the diffusion process for new drugs. It has been argued that it is immoral and inhumane to limit the availability of experimental AIDS drugs, pending final proof of safety and efficacy, since by that time many AIDS victims may already have died.
>
> The AIDS Consumer Movement is in the early stages of transforming the way Americans view treatment for chronic disease. It has also focused public attention on the healthcare regulatory system and its central dilemma of balancing individual choice with consumer protection. The dramatic changes of the last few years in healthcare policy, while too slow for some, still have come to represent a "revolution" in thinking to others. The result is that we may be on the verge or in the middle of a paradigm shift in healthcare treatment and research policy, which has been precipitated by a consumer movement.[30]

According to DeGreene, paradigms need to match their times. When they no longer do so, paradigms are ripe for change. They shift to the new paradigm to match the needs of the time.

Particularly, says DeGreene, the behavioral and social sciences, which have utilized essentially the same dominant paradigm since the turn of the twentieth century, when the classical Newtonian paradigm was borrowed from physics, may now be most in need of radical paradigm change.[31]

Various factors contribute to the failure of contemporary solution paradigms, but three obvious factors can be tracked over time. The first is shifting structures within individual lives, society, and organizations. Second is the compression of time, due primarily to increased transmission speed of electronic communications. Third is the global reach of those communications—a growth in their quantity and their increasing accessibility.

CHANGES IN EXISTING STRUCTURES

Toffler observes that new wealth creation systems force new companies to restructure. Increasing access to data means that more people are empowered to make decisions. This is in stark contrast to the hierarchical, rigidly controlled organizations we have known for most of the twentieth century.[32]

For example, the web structure of organization, which Helgesen identifies as inclusive and characteristically female, today exists in contrast to the exclusive, characteristically male model of hierarchical organization. "The advantages of the web structure are many," she writes. "For one thing, because it is not primarily concerned with where people stand or how they are ranked, it permits flexibility without lowering morale. Another advantage of the web structure is that it permits a greater flow of information, because there are more points of connection or contact. This feminine method of management is more appropriate to today's environment than a model first developed to serve the needs of Caesar's army." [33]

Yet another significant structural shift has been noted by McCann: the fact that new technologies no longer reside primarily where they are first developed. "The important point is that there are many new technologies which simply do not have national allegiances. In the never-ending search for comparative advantage, we have postured technological innovation as a 'them versus us' contest among the largest industrialized countries. [But] as the technological infrastructure of some rapidly industrializing countries and newly industrialized countries develops, the action-packed game of technological competition in the next century will welcome a potentially much expanded set of players."[34]

Such paradigm shifts in organizational structure involve not only the changes in contemporary communism (whether these are considered evolutionary or revolutionary); they also extend to modern capitalism. Despite the reemergence of financial capitalism during the 1980s and a related rise in entrepreneurial endeavors, managerial capitalism is still largely responsible for the administration, coordination, and allocation necessary to run the multi-unit enterprises that have come to dominate, first the United States, and now all the Western economies.

Unfortunately, DeGreene reminds us, there is considerable evidence that, as organizations grow to large scale—as they did under the gigantic state-owned enterprises of Soviet communism—and innovation and problem solving decrease, "the functions of the dominant [managerial] coalition may degrade to individual self-enhancement and self-preservation and to a preoccupation with preservation of the [existing] power structure."[35]

INCREASED SPEED OF COMMUNICATIONS

Another factor contributing to the collapse of current solution paradigms is the increasing compression of time, due primarily to the rapidly increasing speed of global communications. Thus, changes in one market demand changes in another, a new ideology in one country (particularly a large and economically or militarily powerful one) can foment similar or complementary changes in many others. Witness the student rebellions of 1968: first in Prague, then Paris, then New York, then Chicago, then Mexico City. Witness the domino effect in Eastern Europe of recent ideological changes in the former Soviet Union. Or the global impact of supply side economic policies in the United States during the 1980s.

Because things happen so quickly today, with such widespread impact, many of the safety mechanisms that solution paradigms count on become outmoded all too quickly. Thus, the solution paradigms themselves suddenly become precarious, teeter, and soon collapse.

Toffler notes that the growing volatility of the world capital market, dramatized by huge swings and punctuated by recent stock-market collapses and recoveries in both the United States and Japan, is a sign that the old system is increasingly going out of control. "The Savings and Loan crisis and the crisis in banking and insurance similarly tell us that old safety mechanisms, designed to maintain financial stability in a world of self-contained national economies, are as obsolete as the rust-belt world they were designed to protect."[36]

Under such pressures of time compression, McCann emphasizes the futility of rigid organizational structures. "The pace of technological and industry change makes the erection of structures of any kind comparable to creating the Maginot Line in anticipation of World War II. The flexible, adaptive, fast company is the one that wins in today's markets. Maneuverability and the ability to have maximum impact at a chosen point in the market can count more than scale."[37] Evidently, despite the well-known obsession of corporate leaders with military strategy, American management particularly has failed to heed a fundamental lesson of modern warfare.

Tuomo Sarkikoski states the case even more succinctly: "Technical developments and changes in world trade structures have become so rapid that traditional social adaptation mechanisms are incapable of reacting to them. In the long run, societies cannot stand this uncertainty. The question now is whether the old technological paradigms are adequate any longer, when new, socially sensitive, and flexibly reactive technologies have to be created."[38]

INCREASED ACCESS TO COMMUNICATIONS
Adding to the disorientation of shifting organizational structures and the pressures of time compression is the fact that increasing numbers of people (of disparate rank) have increasing access to increasingly powerful and rapid means of communication. Toffler offers two potent examples:

> In the streets of Prague, [during the 1989 "Velvet Revolution" that displaced monopolistic communist government,] students set up TV monitors on street corners and played videotapes showing the brutality of Czech authorities trying to suppress anti-government street rallies. Chinese students in America faxed news of Tiananmen Square back to the [pro-democracy] student demonstrators all across China.[39]

In another example of the power of "underground" communications, Gould notes that the AIDS-related consumer movement has fostered a "gray market" for experimental drugs to combat the deadly disease. "These patients have taken matters into their own hands by making use of available lists of drugs and diagnostic procedures under clinical trial and investigational status [by the U.S. Food and Drug Administration]. In many respects, they have had de facto FDA approval for this approach because FDA has ignored these efforts." [40]

Communications via satellites, fiber optics, and cellular radio is undergoing a revolution by providing a large increase in usable effective communications bandwidth available to each person. Information services riding on the computer and communications waves are also undergoing a rapid revolution. The world is becoming increasingly connected, on-line, and digital, as reflected by military and consumer products.

And Csanyi and Kampis remind us that, even before the advent of contemporary mass communications, certain ideas, replicated merely by spoken language, could spread and propagate very quickly. A good joke could, even then, reach millions of people in a city in a couple of days. Mass communication has made idea replication even faster.[41]

Most Paradigms Need to Change

For all the benefits that they provide, paradigms are in constant evolution. At any given moment, most paradigms require change.

At this moment in human history, we maintain, the paradigm most in need of change is our thinking paradigm, by which the analytical methods of Conventional Thinking are systematically misapplied.

As MacNulty has noted, "[Our contemporary,] materialistic worldview is the predictable result of a phenomenally successful, rigorously materialistic physical science which has dominated life in the industrial societies for nearly 150 years, through the agency of a well-implemented and highly successful technology.

"People's lives are defined, their problems are [addressed], their governments' decisions are guided, and in some cases their political systems themselves are devised, by the application of the scientific method, which was developed for the study of physical phenomena."[42]

THE DIFFICULTY OF CHANGE

Realizations such as these, which in our view are based upon an embryonic understanding of the need for a new thinking paradigm, have led U.S. Representative George Brown and other political leaders to call for a new contract between science and the citizenry.

"The current debates over issues such as global climate change; energy production, consumption, and conservation; endangered species and disposal of hazardous waste," writes Brown, "all hinge on the expectation that science will provide the data and the technologies needed to overcome these challenges, many of which were caused by technological innovation in the first place.

"But there has never in human history been a long-term technological fix; there have merely been bridges to the next level of societal stress and crisis. Society needs to negotiate a new contract with the scientific community. A new contract will require an increased emphasis on exploring humankind's relationship with the surrounding world, through research in the oft-maligned disciplines of the social and interdisciplinary sciences."[43]

Barker identifies two warning signals that indicate a paradigm has outlived its utility. The first warning is that the time between problems solved starts to extend significantly. The second is that the cost per problem solved suddenly starts going up.[44]

Both red flags are waved at once in the failure of our current Conventional Thinking paradigm for creating and restructuring solutions. Why then are we surprised to find that our solution paradigms increasingly fail us?

RESISTANCE TO CHANGE

And yet, however failed the solution paradigm, however obvious the need for change, resistance to change is a phenomenon Conventional Thinking says should always be expected during a paradigm shift. But our contention is that using Conventional Thinking to finding solutions causes human beings to resist change.

It is true that individuals and organizations have no control over the scientific and technological quantum paradigm shifts that do occur—steam power, electricity, plastics, computers. As Barker notes, "All your investments in your position, your power, your expertise, and your credibility just disappear. Here you are, someone with significant leverage—then the paradigm shifts, and you find all the things you are good at are irrelevant."[45]

However, organizational changes developed with Conventional Thinking produce predictable resistance. As management consultant Tom Terez writes, "managers know that any kind of change—new ideas, new methods, new programs, new technologies—stirs resistance. If it is allowed to build, this resistance soon forms a strong wall protecting the status quo.

"Employees have their own reasons to be dubious about change. Too often, word comes down from the higher-ups that 'from now on, this is how things are going to be.' Just when everyone seems accustomed to the company's way of doing things, management marches in with some new approach, expecting everyone to fall in line and adopt the change as their own."[46]

Why should needed change be so hard to realize? In addition to the resistance generated by Conventional Thinking used to create or restructure societal and organizational solutions, because the status quo is considered fundamental to our essential character in the face of the quantum paradigm shifts.

Economic consultant Krowitz points out that the old guard naturally has a stake in safeguarding the status quo. Thus, decision makers convinced of the need for reform face the problem of persuading their constituencies to give up personal benefits for improved prospects of general betterment.

New information to change the decision-making process is not so much lacking, says Krowitz, as it is ignored, precisely because it is at odds with the existing paradigm and the self-interest and beliefs of elite groups, who benefit from the old way of doing things. As John Maynard Keynes wrote more than 50 years ago, "The difficulty lies, not in the new ideas, but in escaping from the old ones, which ramify, from those brought up as most of us have been, into every corner of our minds."[47]

There can be no doubt that human beings naturally resist paradigm shifts. Seeing the world one way—the old way—people find themselves almost unable to change their orientation. The old mind-set is so embedded in their consciousness that it is difficult to supplant it with a new paradigm.

Certainly the most dangerous recent example of this resistance to paradigm shifts was evidenced during the long years of the Cold War's "balance of terror." As DeGreene notes, "Strategic policymakers are often extremely resistant to changes in belief structures, and their seemingly rational thinking may be a superficial expression of deep emotional conflict.

"S. Kull interviewed high-level U.S. and Soviet defense policymakers. He identified a number of inconsistencies in their responses and an overall attempt to maintain consistency. For example, there was a strong tendency to ignore the realities of nuclear weaponry, and therefore national vulnerability, and to apply traditional prenuclear military logic to the nuclear situation.

"When Kull pointed out these inconsistencies," says DeGreene, "the policymakers responded with an elaborate and convoluted hierarchy of rationalizations. Many of the rationalizations camouflaged deep-seated conflicts and emotional needs for status, prestige, and alleviating fear. The emotional resistance to recognizing nuclear reality arose because such recognition was perceived as interfering with significant personal needs."[48]

Similar resistance can be expected among powerful civilians. Discussing the problems currently confronting U.S. business and industry, and the paradigm shifts necessary to the solution of those problems, professors of economics R. Florida and M. Kenney emphasize that "if we are to transcend the [current] economy, it will be necessary to transform many existing institutions and organizations and to create completely new ones. We will have to uproot many of the ways we structure our society if we are to accomplish such a major shift in our existing economic and social institutions."[49]

THE INTERRELATION OF PARADIGMS

A further obstacle to the acceptance of paradigm shifts is that existing paradigms are often interrelated in an ecology of fundamental assumptions. Consequently, a shift in one existing paradigm will affect many others; and all those who have a stake in the affected paradigms can be counted on to contribute to the general inertia resisting change.

Only when a "critical mass" of awareness is reached concerning the need for change will fundamental shifts occur. For the same reason, once the impetus for shift tilts over the edge, the new paradigm is likely to prove irresistible.

Robert Waterman has written: "Organizations, like people, are creatures of habit. For organizations, the habits are existing norms, systems, procedures, written and unwritten rules—'the way we do things around here.' Over time, these habits become embedded like rocks in a glacial moraine."[50]

Just as glaciers move slowly but inexorably, so slowly that their motion is hardly distinguishable, so inexorably that they cannot ultimately be resisted, so too with paradigm shifts. They require many alterations in traditional habits, comfortable ways of thinking. They affect everything around them. Thus they will be mightily opposed.

No Successful Future Can Be Found by Following the Past

The fact that solution paradigms shift continuously—and succeed one another with increasing rapidity and impact—should serve to make clear that no future can exist along the same line as the past. Yet we persist in depending on the demonstrably insufficient methods of quantitative data collection, analysis, and general prediction that derive from the pervasive influence of Conventional Thinking. It's "push" thinking from the past. Yet it is clear that "pull" thinking lets us learn from the future.

Actually, endless information is more likely to drown than to buoy the individual, group, or organization that struggles to survive and strives to flourish. Abundant information alone is not knowledge. Vast knowledge alone is not power. What is necessary is knowing *how* to convert information to knowledge, *how* to transform knowledge into power. What is essential is knowing how to think, how to approach the problems that we seek to solve.

THE INSUFFICIENCY OF QUANTITATIVE METHODS

As Donald Christiansen has noted, quantification of data is essential to science and engineering, but it can also quell the intuitive spirit while the quest for new (quantified) insight is carried to cautious extremes. Christiansen rightly asks: How would a visionary entrepreneur such as David Sarnoff behave today? "Would he make the decision to invest millions in color television on the basis of the scant information he then had? Or would he call for extensive technical and market studies, some of which might have delayed or altered the courageous decision Sarnoff made to proceed?"[51]

Certainly, it is now evident that overreliance on the then-existing paradigm of the U.S. automobile industry—extensive data collection and market research—caused Ford and General Motors to lose out to the intuitive, paradigm-shattering approach taken by Chrysler to develop the minivan market.

Unfortunately, not only do many individuals not trust their intuition, most business leaders do not know how to deal with any information but "hard"—that is, quantified, numerical—data. Moreover, the quantitative data collection Research Approach to problem solving creates inherent traps and dangers.

All of this data—cheaply stored and potentially accessible—can easily be misused, can stymie as well as motivate and support action. The plethora of data available becomes seductive, inviting us to seek correlations that may or may not exist. As more people increase their ability to acquire and process data, the divisions of responsibility and authority erode. We are tempted to do jobs other than our own, to find fault as well as to control.

THE PROBLEM WITH "SCIENTIFIC" RESEARCH

When appropriately limited and directed, information and knowledge—combined with a clear sense of purposes and the uniqueness of any given problem—are certainly valuable assets. Yet one problem with information-gathering for its own sake in planning or in solution finding is that it rarely pays for itself. Moreover, it fails to address the big picture. That demands intuition, which is to say vision and courage. Yet many of our leaders prefer to rely on the questionable predictions of consultants who have little more to recommend than does Madame Rosa the Fortune Teller.

Iconoclastic commentator Harry Shearer plants the barb: "Futurism and megatrendism are only the most pretentious versions of the pseudo-scientific hand-holding to which this country's decision makers are addicted. For short-range decisions, such as what TV shows to crank out or how tasteless a beer to brew, executives turn to the variety of psychics who peer into focus groups rather than crystal balls; we call them market researchers. Just on sheer percentage of accurate predictions, Madame Rosa can give these guys a good run for our money."[52] Forecasting, statistical correlations, and simulation modeling produce what McGill University Professor of Management Henry Mintzberg, in his eloquent book *The Rise and Fall of Strategic Planning*, calls the "Fallacy of Predetermination."[53]

As economist Edward Krowitz has written, "The real issue does not concern doubts about the positive contributions that can be made to economic reasoning [by mathematical data] but relates to the worries about the negative effect, in the form of exclusion, that overconcentration on standard mathematical methods tends to produce.

"Continuous, accurate information processing is essential for the growth of a dynamic system. But each system has a fixed capacity for transmission, reception, and processing. The breaking point occurs when the time available for processing information is less than the average reaction time for processing the information. Beyond this point, a state of confusion ensues."[54]

And this confusion leads to the inertia of complacency, which may in fact only mask the fear to risk. If we allow this inertia to prevail, the ultimate result is paralysis, absolute incapacity to take positive action.

Christiansen points out that excessive capacities for data collection, storage, and retrieval foster excessive conservatism. In business, for example, the ease of re-researching, acquiring, and processing data encourages the apparently endless formation of committees, task forces, and study groups, all of which follow each others footsteps through apparently endless phases of discovery, analysis, and recommendation.[55]

Genius, it is often said, recognizes the obvious. Similarly, great innovators such as Thomas Edison know well that, if you don't try it, you'll never know whether or not it works. No doubt, by today's standards, Edison lacked "sufficient" data. But he knew what his purpose was; and he had enough data to know that a solution to his problem might well be at hand. So he tried it. Ever since, Edison's incandescent light bulb has provided the universal symbol for a "stroke of genius," an inherently brilliant idea.

By contrast, despite the promise of science, the yield of its Research Approach has been disappointing relative to expectations. Arguing for a different approach that addresses purposes, U.S. Representative George Brown writes: "The promise of science—a miracle cure—serves politicians, who always are looking for a tonic to sell to the public, and it serves scientists, who understandably seek to preserve their elevated position in our culture. But it may not serve society as advertised. Indeed, the promise of science may be at the root of our problems, because it is easier—politically, economically, socially, scientifically—to support more research than it is to change how we behave."[56]

In part, this is a predictable result of inherently narrow thinking. In Kuhn's phrase, much of the Research Approach consists of "a strenuous and devoted attempt to force nature into the conceptual boxes supplied by professional education [in the sciences]."[57]

Whether consciously or not, by their very method, scientists deliberately put on blinders before tackling a problem in the course of their research. "The decision to employ a particular piece of apparatus and to use it in a particular way," says

Kuhn, "carries an assumption that only certain sorts of circumstances will arise." Such assumptions and other requirements of the Research Approach lead to "an immense restriction of the scientist's vision and to a considerable resistance to paradigm change."[58]

As regards general sociotechnical systems theory and practice, Professor DeGreene states the case even more emphatically: "Much laboratory-style research may be irrelevant, misleading, or downright wrong. The concept of clearly definable and correlatable independent, intervening, and dependent variables may be completely inappropriate in a dynamic, mutually causal world."[59]

FAILINGS OF THE CASE STUDY METHOD

The educational straitjacket into which we thrust our legal and business professionals is every bit as constraining as it is for engineers and scientists. Why? Because it is based on precisely the same principles as the Research Approach.

The case study method so favored in schools of law and business examines existing examples and attempts to extrapolate from history general principles that are then proposed as paradigms within the field. In short, it slavishly imitates the pervasive "positivistic" paradigms of scientific education.

Despite recent arguments that have undermined every one of its tenets, positivism is still the dominant ideology of academia. Consequently, business schools have jumped on the positivist [read: Conventional Thinking] bandwagon in the desire to attain academic respectability.

In fact, the case study method is only one possible solution paradigm for the problem of how to teach and learn about law or business. When things changed at a slower pace, the method had its benefits and could claim a certain relative success. Case studies do provide a more realistic study of the subject than can be gained solely from textbooks. They offer "relevant" but always incomplete detail on situations that existed in the past, even the present. Where they fail is in the future—precisely where students will spend their professional lives.

A fundamental weakness of the case study method is that it forces students to view different situations through a lens that makes them appear similar. A related weakness, notes professor Gary Hamel of the London Business School, is that the case study method "offers students an exercise in slow-motion replay, when what they need is the ability to make decisions in fast-forward."[60]

No two businesses should be designed and operated the same way, particularly when they spring from different technologies and are targeted toward different markets. In fact, no two business problems are ever exactly alike. Therefore, no two business solutions will have the same specifics. Imitative strategies seldom, if ever, succeed. Yet the cloning of solutions is precisely the assumption upon which the case study method of American business education is based.

Science and its Research Approach are so pervasive that even the humanities are now mimicking science. Witness the analytical deconstruction movement in academic departments of language, now bent upon the atomization of texts of literature, a fragmentation so complete as to deliberately render even the most stellar prose "meaningless."

Business management especially seeks to associate itself with science. Witness the "scientific management" of Taylor's day and the "management science" of today. But as John Hendry, director of the MBA program at The Judge Institute of Management Studies, University of Cambridge, England, notes, "Management is about working with other people to do a job effectively. It is inherently practical, and while analysis is important, it accounts for perhaps 10% of a manager's work. The other 90% is about implementation, about making things happen. [Yet] industrialists continue to pay premium prices for the graduates of these schools, for people whose training, even in the best schools, has been 90% analysis and 10% implementation. No wonder they are disappointed."[61]

An emerging paradigm shift is finally occurring as U.S. business schools contend with the failure of the case study method as educational paradigm. As Henry Mintzberg, professor of management at Canada's McGill University wrote to the *Harvard*

Business Review, "Business school education as it currently stands is undermining U. S. business." Mintzberg continues:

> I am increasingly convinced that the more Harvard and similar business schools succeed, the more U.S. business fails. That is because these schools confer important advantages on the wrong people. They parachute inexperienced people with mercenary pretensions into important positions. For the most part, these people are committed to no company and no industry, but only to personal success, which they pursue based on academic credentials that are almost exclusively analytic, devoid of in-depth experience, tacit knowledge, or intuition.
>
> Stanford takes people, many with a minimum of experience, and pumps them full of theory, which they cannot possibly understand in context, because there is no context, neither personal nor in the classroom nor in the professor's head. That is bad enough. But Harvard goes one step further.
>
> [Harvard] takes people who know nothing about a particular company and then insists—based on 20 pages of verbalized and numerical abstractions—that they pronounce on it in the classroom. The students have never met any of the company's customers, never seen the factories, never touched the products.
>
> But because good managers are decisive, good Harvard Business School students must take a stand. After you have done this several hundred times, what kind of a manager do you become? Glib and quick-witted, to be sure, just the kind to race up the fast track. But to what effect?
>
> Why should anyone be surprised at what has been happening in U.S. businesses these past years? Let's stop pretending to train non-managers to be managers through the use of detached case studies and disconnected theories.[62]

The need for change in our paradigms does not, however, in itself, mean that the ways we used to do things were themselves wrong in their time. For example, the ideas of such once-favored theoreticians of industrial production as Frederick Taylor and Henry Ford are no longer useful to us. Yet, in their day, quantifications of industrial production efficiency (Taylor) and reduction of industrial production labor into repeated, replaceable parts (Ford) were both recognized as great advances in productivity. The new paradigms these pioneers of the early twentieth century introduced prevailed over prior paradigms of individual craftsmanship.

It is worth noting that the solution paradigms offered by Taylor and Ford—efficient organization of labor and assembly line production—were both based on the Conventional Thinking paradigm of the Research Approach. Now, almost a hundred years later, as a Full-Spectrum Thinking is increasingly demanded by the problems that we need to solve, the solutions offered by Taylor and Ford have simply outlived their usefulness.

The devastating impact of the pervasive influence and misapplication of Conventional Thinking has been examined by MIT researcher Peter Senge. Through the lens of so-called chaos theory, Senge and others view organizations as complex and integrated organisms, not infinitely divisible machines. According to Senge, our current inability to cope with complexity is a direct result of traditional scientific approaches to management—the reductionism of nineteenth-century science, on which Taylor and Ford based their no longer successful solution paradigms.

"From a very early age," Senge notes, "we are taught to break apart problems, to fragment the world. This apparently makes complex tasks and subjects more manageable, but we pay a hidden, enormous price. We can no longer see the consequences of our actions; we lose our intrinsic sense of connection to a larger whole."[63]

The human mind, it should be noted, is aptly compared to a parachute. It only works when it is fully open.

No doubt that is one reason why "creativity consultants" such as Ann McGee-Cooper now earn substantial fees for bringing top managers together with outgoing children for training sessions where the adults vent their business problems. Children, she notes, have "fresh brains." Adult experts can claim expertise only in relation to existing paradigms. By startling contrast, children know nothing of the old rules and verities.[64]

Especially in entrepreneurial activities—where the greatest financial success is most often realized—those fully open minds called "paradigm pioneers" abound. Invariably, they flourish on the basis of insufficient data.

In order to achieve success, says Barker, these pioneers must first convince themselves, then others, that they are pursuing the right course. In such risk-filled and exceptionally successful enterprises, there is only one certainty: Sufficient data *never* exist. The paradigm pioneer can never honestly state: "I can prove that I am doing the right thing."[65]

The Conventional Solution-Finding Paradigm

The Conventional Thinking approach to finding solutions may be said to comprise the following steps: define the problem, formulate the problem, gather data about the problem, analyze the data, develop models of the data with techniques others have used, explore alternatives, select and detail a solution, sell the solution to others, implement the solution. (The number of steps stated in the literature varies from four to twelve, or more.) Thus, any attempt to solve a problem by means of Conventional Thinking will focus on analysis of the problem, not on the potential solution.

This conventional Research Approach permeates all fields. It is such an overwhelming, pervasive paradigm that, even today, after decades of increasing failure to solve most problems, it dominates almost everyone's thinking and life experience. The Research Approach of Conventional Thinking has by now become so entrenched for creating and restructuring solutions as to qualify for Barker's category of "unchallenged dogma."

WHY THE CONVENTIONAL APPROACH IS INSUFFICIENT

Beyond our questioning of the Research Approach in Conventional Thinking for creating or restructuring solutions, researchers outside of the physical and natural sciences are claiming the Research Approach itself is inappropriate for their investigations. As Professor Orlando Behling notes, "Research methods similar to those used in the natural sciences have long been the norm in organizational behavior and organization theory. However, several writers have questioned their appropriateness for the study of organizations and the groups and individuals who make them up . . . [which] differ from phenomena of interest to the natural sciences in ways that make natural science methods inappropriate for their study."[66]

Business and policy professors Ian Mitroff and L. R. Pondy expand this thought: "Looser, non-testable, non-generalizable descriptions . . . of social facts are equally legitimate forms of representation and, perhaps, even more appropriate forms of inquiry than the normal model of science. Perhaps 'science' is the wrong strategy for understanding social phenomena."[67]

Among the objections to applying the Research Approach to the social sciences that Behling identifies are (1) the uniqueness of the groups being studied and (2) the instability of quantified data.[68]

Each organization, group, and person differs to some degree from all others. The development of *precise* and *predictive* general laws in organizational behavior and organization theory is thus impossible. No organization, group, or individual can represent any other, much less a broad class. If each class is unique, the idea of useful general laws is meaningless.

In contrast to the relatively stable natural sciences, the phenomena of interest to researchers in organizational behavior and organization theory are transitory. Natural science research is poorly equipped to capture these fleeting phenomena of the social sciences. Not only do the "facts" of social events change with time, but the "laws" governing them change as well, making it extremely difficult to combine data obtained at different times, in order to arrive at general laws.

As Mitroff and Pondy put it, "The phenomenon will never be completely described or understood before it vanishes and some new phenomenon supplants it. That is the guts of our conjecture that science is the wrong enquiring system for the social 'sciences'; it converges too slowly relative to the rate of decay and evolution of social phenomena."[69]

In addition, Conventional Thinking for finding solutions and changes relies upon basic beliefs and assumptions that are inappropriate in a dynamic, global, cyclical world. Conventional Thinking is linear, that is, it moves only from a particular past to a specific change, with no thought given to the future of that change. It is based on the perspective of experts who are not themselves part of the system being changed. It assumes the ability to isolate what is to be changed from its surroundings, while the disequilibrium of a change or solution-finding effort is generally caused by shortsighted, non-visionary people within the system being changed.

RESULTS OF THE CONVENTIONAL APPROACH

Quantified market research as varied as advertising and automobiles, motion pictures and microchips pervades (and often paralyzes) U.S. industries. This research borrows the mantle of "scientific knowledge"—proven truth—to promote a product that is certain to be outmoded soon, sometimes before it can even be applied. Political pollsters now offer "tracking polls" that claim to monitor electoral mood swings on a daily basis: the ultimate variable masquerading as axiomatic truth.

Almost everywhere we turn, from education to business and industry, from government to volunteer efforts, from sports to the military, even art to literature, over the last 50 years, we have witnessed an ever more encroaching tendency to quantify and measure human experience, all in a futile effort to infuse it with predictability, and thus control. Whatever our endeavor, we have been increasingly compelled to do it "by the numbers." No wonder, then, that modern life feels increasingly devoid of "poetry."

We must now acknowledge what for centuries we have known: human beings are not numbers. We are flesh and blood.

Even the best-intentioned corporate attempts to humanize their structures, streamline their processes, and increase productivity—for example, the implementation of Total Quality Management programs (the latest/most popular solution paradigm)—often run afoul of the pervasive influence of the current Conventional Thinking paradigm, which is inherently antithetical to the changes now required for corporate success. Solution paradigms developed exclusively with Conventional Thinking will only continue to fail.

Yet even successful companies today are obsessively concerned with the latest quick fix "alphabet program." They are willing to try almost anything, whether it be "just-in-time" or "bench marking" or "Business Process Reengineering" or "Total Quality Management." Meanwhile, they are drowning in this "alphabet soup" of false solution paradigms.

WHAT TO DO

When what has been successful before increasingly fails, when previously heralded solution paradigms collapse all around us, we must be truly creative in addressing this pervasive problem. The antithesis of true creativity is to fail to notice that every new "solution" tried seems to succeed less and less, to fail faster and faster.

Our solution paradigms have collapsed as the direct result of an even more basic failure: the collapse of our thinking paradigm. In this crisis, it is folly not to agree with Einstein that what we need now is a radically different way of approaching our problems, an entirely new fundamental assumption about thinking, a shift in our paradigm of thinking.

Perceptions, habits, traditions, and assumptions form our paradigms and determine the way we view the world. By shifting our focus of attention—by focusing on our thinking process and the practice of solution-*finding,* rather than on the solution we seek—we allow for, we encourage, indeed we guarantee precisely the sort of paradigm shifts in changes and solutions that have so long evaded our best efforts and intentions.

NOTES

1. Craig Benson, "Setting a Tone With Battered Desks," *The New York Times,* (September 29, 1991).

2. Thomas H. Kuhn, *The Structure of Scientific Revolutions* (Chicago, IL: University of Chicago Press, 1970).

3. Joel Barker, *Discovering the Future: The Business of Paradigms* (Burnsville, MN: Charthouse Learning Corporation, 1989).

4. Harvey Gelman, "Knowledge Workers: It's Your Choice," *Business Quarterly*, Vol. 50, No. 3, (Autumn 1985), pp. 45–50.

5. Kuhn, *Structure of Scientific Revolutions.*

6. Alan Lightman and Owen Gingerich, "When Do Anomalies Begin?" *Science,* Vol. 255, No. 5045, (February 7, 1992), pp. 690–695.

7. Fred R. Bleakley, "The Best-Laid Plans: Many Companies Try Management Fads, Only To See Them Flop," *Wall Street Journal,* (July 6, 1993), p.1.

8. Kuhn, *Structure of Scientific Revolutions.*

9. Ibid.

10. Ibid.

11. Heinz Weinrich, "Management Practices in the United States, Japan, and the People's Republic of China," *Industrial Management,* Vol. 32, No. 2, (March/April 1990), pp. 3–7.

12. James Fallows, "Looking at the Sun," *Atlantic Monthly,* Vol. 272, No. 5, (November 1993), p. 69.

13. Frank Gibney, *Japan: The Fragile Super Power,* (Tokyo/Rutledge, VT: Charles E. Tuttle, 1975).

14. Akio Morita with Edwin M. Reingold and Mitsuko Shimomura, *Made in Japan: Akio Morita and Sony* (New York: Dutton, 1986).

15. Kenyon B. DeGreene, "Rigidity and Fragility of Large Sociotechnical Systems: Advanced Information Technology, The Dominant Coalition, and Paradigm Shift at the End of the 20th Century," *Behavioral Science,* Vol. 36, (1991), pp. 64–79.

16. W. Kirk MacNulty, "The Paradigm Perspective," *Futures Research Quarterly*, Vol. 5, No. 3, (Fall 1989), pp. 35–53.

17. Kuhn, *Structure of Scientific Revolutions.*

18. Barker, *Discovering the Future.*

19. Sally Helgesen,"Breakthrough! How to Get Into Your Company's Inner Circle: What Does It Take To Make Partner Today?" *Working Woman,* Vol. 6, No. 6, (June 1991), p. 74.

20. Joseph McCann, "Design Principles for an Innovating Company," *Academy of Management Executive,* Vol. 5, No. 2, (1991), pp. 76–93.

21. Ron Lane, "Learning To Relate," *Software Magazine,* (April 1991).

22. MacNulty, "The Paradigm Perspective."

23. Kuhn, *Structure of Scientific Revolutions.*

24. Michael Schrage, "Information Technology, the Key Is Good Relationships," *Wall Street Journal* (Marcj 19, 1990)

25. Barker, *Discovering the Future.*

26. DeGreene, "Rigidity and Fragility of Large Sociotechnical Systems."

27. Noel Tichy and Ram Charan, "Speed, Simplicity, Self-Confidence: An Interview with Jack Welch," *Harvard Business Review,* Vol. 67, No. 5, (September-October 1989), pp. 112–120.

28. George E. Brown, Jr., "It's Down to the Last Blank Check," *Los Angeles Times,* (September 8, 1992).

29. Kuhn, *Structure of Scientific Revolutions.*

30. Stephen Gould, "The AIDS Consumer Movement and the FDA: A Potential Paradigm Shift in Health Care Policy," *Journal of Public Policy and Marketing,* Vol. 8, (1989), pp. 40–52.

31. DeGreene, "Rigidity and Fragility of Large Sociotechnical Systems."

32. Alvin Toffler and Heidi Toffler, *War and Anti-War. Survival at the Dawn of the 21st Century,* (Boston, MA: Little, Brown, 1993).

33. Helgesen, "Breakthrough! How to get into Your Company's Inner Circle."

34. McCann, "Design Principles for an Innovating Company."

35. DeGreene, "Rigidity and Fragility of Large Sociotechnical Systems."

36. Toffler and Toffler, *War and Anti-War.*

37. McCann, "Design Principles for an Innovating Company."

38. Tuomo Sarkikoski, "Re-orientation in Systems Thinking?—Some Remarks on the Methodological and Ideological Traits of Technological Reproduction," *European Journal of Engineering Education,* Vol. 13, No. 3, (1988), pp. 341–349.

39. Toffler and Toffler, *War and Anti-War.*

40. Gould, "AIDS Consumer Movement and the FDA."

41. V. Csanyi and G. Kampis, "Modeling Society: Dynamical Replicative Systems," *Cybernetics and Systems. An International Journal,* Vol. 18, (1987), p. 40.

42. MacNulty, "The Paradigm Perspective."

43. Brown, "It's Down to the Last Blank Check."

44. Barker, *Discovering the Future.*

45. Ibid.

46. Tom Terez, "A Manager's Guidelines for Implementing Successful Operational Changes," *Industrial Management,* Vol. 32, No. 4, (July-August 1990), pp. 18–20.

47. John Maynard Keynes, Collected Writings (New York: St Martin's Press, for the Royal Economic Society, 1971–89).

48. DeGreene, "Rigidity and Fragility of Large Sociotechnical Systems."

49. R. Florida and M. Kenney, *Corporate America's Failure to Move from Innovation to Mass Production* (New York: Basic Books, 1990).

50. Robert H. Waterman, *The Renewal Factor: How the Best Get and Keep the Competitive Edge* (New York: Bantam Books, 1987).

51. Donald Christiansen, "The Measurement Explosion," *IEEE Spectrum*, (January 1992).

52. Harry Shearer, "A Poll Apart," *Los Angeles Magazine* (December 22, 1991).

53. Henry Mintzberg, *The Rise and Fall of Strategic Planning* (New York: The Free Press/Macmillan, 1994).

54. Edward Krowitz, "Economic Development, Cognitive Dissonance, and Use Theory of Changes," *Systems Research,* Vol. 8, No. 1, (1991), pp. 41–58.

55. Christiansen, "The Measurement Explosion."

56. Brown, "It's Down to the Last Blank Check."

57. Kuhn, *Structure of Scientific Revolutions.*

58. Ibid.

59. DeGreene, "Rigidity and Fragility of Large Sociotechnical Systems."

60. Gary Hamel, "Corporate Imagination and Expeditionary Marketing," *Harvard Business Review,* Vol. 69, No. 4, (July-August 1991), pp. 79–91.

61. John Hendry, "Debate," *Harvard Business Review*, (November-December, 1992).

62. Mintzberg, *Rise and Fall of Strategic Planning.*

63. Peter Senge, "Learning Organizations," *Executive Excellence,* (September 1991), pp. 7–8.

64. Ann McGee-Cooper, cited in Marc Hequet, "Creativity Training Gets Creative," *Training,* (February 1992).

65. Barker, *Discovering the Future.*

66. Orlando Behling, "The Case for the Natural Science Model for Research in Organizational Behavior and Organization Theory," *Acad-*

emy of Management Review, Vol. 5, No. 4, (October 1980), pp. 483–490.

67. Ian I. Mitroff and Lois R. Pondy, "Afterthought on the Leadership Conference," in M.W. McCall and M.M. Lombardo, *Leadership: Where Else Can We Go?* (Durham, NC: Duke University Press, 1978), pp. 145–149.

68. Behling, "Case for the Natural Science Model."

69. Mitroff and Pondy, "Afterthought on the Leadership Conference."

Chapter 3

The Importance of a Shift in Mental Assumptions About Thinking

*T*he prevailing thinking paradigm for creating or restructuring solutions has led us seriously astray. Yet in attempting to change so profoundly and widely held a paradigm, we are "shadow boxing in the dark," grappling with a force so powerful and so pervasive that it represents what we don't know we don't know.

Consider, for example, what happened in a very large commercial insurance company. A team was developing a cost allocation procedure; but the regional managers, promoting one method, were "feuding" with the home office people who proposed another method. A Full-Spectrum Thinking manager from another area suggested the team be facilitated with a new thinking process. Only then did the team quickly recommend and implement a system that everyone agreed was much better than what either group had previously proposed. A secondary benefit of the new process paradigm, Breakthrough Thinking, a company executive proclaimed, was its capability as "a powerful team-building agent."

Today, a predictable, pervasive paradigm collapse has occurred in individual lives, economies, and societies throughout the world. Proposed "solutions" everywhere are failing to solve problems. When people are in trouble, they tend to scramble frantically and grasp at straws. They hire consultants at an increasing rate. Thus, the current plethora of failed "solutions." The result: a desperate search for ever more "creative" solutions, which can be relied upon only to fail in their turn.

This constant introduction of fashionable "solutions," the latest quick-fix fad, breeds skepticism that increases resistance to change. That is one reason why, rather than proposing still other major shifts in solutions, a shift in the underlying and most fundamental assumptions—the thinking paradigm—is now essential.

The reality, effectiveness, truth, and concepts of the mental assumptions of Conventional Thinking, as used to create or restructure solutions, have been taken for granted far too long, both in our civilization at large, and on all levels of formal education.

Precisely because all paradigm shifts elicit resistance and cause displacement and distress, what is needed now—as we face an increasing number of increasingly intractable problems occurring with increasing frequency—is a difference not in the solutions offered, but in the thinking process that leads to those possible solutions. Until such a shift in thinking is successfully undertaken, our solutions will continue to fail.

The Process of Change and the Paradigm of Thinking

One would have to be a literal hermit not to notice that the world is changing. In this Holonic (holistic and electronic) Age, people everywhere are calling for greater collaboration, more appropriate technology, the sharing of information, and responsibility.

Almost all people want to change, or know that change is coming, or continually talk about change; but they seldom consider the steps necessary to effect such change. The first step is to change one's way of thinking.

If you really want to change, you must realize that the way you think, and thus the way you approach a problem, profoundly influences the results that you achieve. You may want to change, but if you go about trying to effect change based on the conventional way of thinking, you are in fact denying yourself the opportunity to be successful.

You must break the habit of seeking outmoded "solutions" by changing your way of thinking. Such a change in thinking would provide a new "common language," one that would enable you to cut through all the many inadequate solution paradigms and adopt the best parts of each.

The Need for Change

We certainly are not alone in recognizing that the current way of thinking needs to change. Many others who realize the shortcomings of Conventional Thinking have raised questions concerning how human beings go about the process of thinking. Particularly in political life, the tendency of Conventional Thinking to promote endless analysis has often been questioned.

James Fallows, Washington editor of the *Atlantic* magazine, is only one who has noted the inherent distinction between misplaced analysis and the effective solution of our most pressing problems. Yet he provides convincing evidence of the widespread perception that we need to change our way of thinking.

> Robert S. McNamara, Herbert Hoover, David A. Stockman, Richard G. Darman—men like these, plus [President] Carter himself, are among the smartest analysts to have served during this century. They have not been our finest leaders. Analysis means reveling in subtle distinctions and immersing yourself in details. Leadership sometimes means ignoring the subtleties, leaving the details to others, and stressing large, oversimplified truths.
>
> Indeed, analysis is at inherent odds with action. The ideal leader would have both abilities: a mastery of detail, so as to come up with the wisest policies, and a capacity to overlook detail, so as to persuade the public to embrace the plans.

A President should know when to stop worrying about finding the best solution to a problem and start working to put some solution in place. The policy issues a President must 'resolve' are, almost by definition, irresolvable.[1]

Fortunately, we need neither the resources nor the burdens of the American presidency to become effective leaders. Each of us can be a leader in our activities, regardless of whether or not we command legions of followers. How we think, how we behave in trying to find solutions, is tied directly to the actions we take. We can lead if we simply refuse to analyze our problems endlessly. Instead, we must always keep our focus on the bigger picture as the guide to *acting now.*

In business as in politics, most self-anointed experts are quick to offer attractive "solutions" to the shortcomings they perceive. As Ken Shelton, executive editor of the U.S. magazine *Executive Excellence,* has noted, it is nothing short of amazing to observe the number of "creativity gurus hawking their wares, all in the sacrosanct name of corporate training and development."[2]

One contribution to the study of thinking is the work of Edward de Bono. He too emphasizes that, today, everything is changing and everything needs to change.

"Each of the four mainstays of management thinking is being re-considered," says de Bono. *"Efficiency* is no longer enough; we need effectiveness. *Problem-solving* is limited; we now need design [read: creating and restructuring solutions]. *Information analysis* will not by itself yield the new ideas that are needed. Even *competition* is seen to be insufficient, since it only provides the baseline."[3]

The shift away from technology and production toward concepts is going to be tough on U.S. business, de Bono predicts. U.S. business, he notes, is less at ease with concepts than are business leaders in almost any other industrial nation. Short-term thinking emphasizes quick action and favors me-too developments in a tested market, rather than new concepts.

But in order to surpass their competitors, U.S. corporations will have to treat concept development as seriously as they now treat technical development, de Bono insists. And the necessary concept development is going to demand serious creativity—Full-Spectrum Creativity, as we term it.

Moreover, the extensive data gathering, analysis, and modeling of the past and present that are required by the conventional Baconian and Descartian Research Approach, as currently used to create or restructure solutions, ignore the hypothesis that no future is on the same line as the past. Business world leaders are panicking because they realize they cannot approach the future with the same thinking they used in the past, yet they do not yet know what solution-finding approach to follow instead. They know change is needed but are unable to see the "wholeness" of a new approach.

The absurdity of discovering a "final theory" in any field of understanding should be obvious. Certainly, it is generally recognized that *the* single answer for the design of any system or the solution of any other problem simply does not exist.

Yet even scientists—who should know better, having watched paradigms continually come and go—continue to search for *the* answer, the single correct solution, the elegant, constant, and final understanding. Those so enamored with the scientific method as to be blinded to its shortcomings continue to praise reductionism.

Conspicuous among those who praise reductionism, are the scientists who championed the now-canceled eight billion dollar superconducting Super Collider, a machine of staggering size and complexity, designed to illuminate the predicted existence of the fundamental, ultimate particle of Nature. In such a particle, we are told, humankind may glimpse the "face of the Creator." Or perhaps not.

Faced with such compelling yet supremely costly and far from certain ventures, we must ask ourselves, even if the "fundamental laws" of the universe were to be found, would science (and scientists) then somehow disappear? Of course not. There will always be more to learn, new laws to discover, problems to solve.

Writing in *Science* magazine, deputy editor Philip Abelson commends the view of Harold Shapiro, president of

Princeton University: "The debate [concerning the impact of higher education on economic development] is . . . long on wishful thinking regarding the potential impact of new science and technology on economic growth, and short on credible analysis of . . . factors capable of driving a country to a position of economic leadership."

Noting the gap between rich and poor countries, Shapiro asks: "Is the material affluence of certain countries due to their nationality, diligence, intelligence, natural abilities in science and technology, and hard work, or some other set of factors?"

Abelson reports Shapiro's assertion that technical progress has been among the most potent forces in our history and that science and technology will remain of vital importance to the health of our society. A relatively advanced capacity in science and technology, Shapiro indicates, may be a necessary but *not sufficient* condition for productivity and economic leadership. Technological progress in advanced countries, he says, depends on many cultural and environmental factors, including public policy, political stability, values and attitudes, . . . and attitudes toward risk and openness or resistance to change.

"We have failed," Shapiro emphasizes, "not in science and advanced training, but elsewhere in our national life. The critical issue for our country is which of the major elements has been lacking in more recent years and what this portends for the future."[4]

Most such exhortations to change find a ready audience among American corporate leaders who are rightly focused on the necessity to compete effectively with more productive firms in the global economy. As management consultant Tom Peters puts it, "Competitive practices required to survive in the '90s—pursuit of 'six sigma quality' (99.9997 percent perfect, a Motorola goal touted even in its ads), shrinking innovation and order cycles by orders of magnitude, the use of team-based organizations everywhere, and the subcontracting of anything to anyone from anywhere—are downstream links in a chain of immutable forces sweeping the world's economy."

Peters notes that successful companies today embrace the need for change; indeed they see change as the only constant, and they reward those who cope effectively with change by means of creative solutions. Peters writes:

> "We eat change for breakfast," says Harry Quadracci, chairman of innovative Quad/Graphics, a half-billion dollar revenue printing firm. "Our workers see change as survival," he adds. Dick Liebhaber, executive VP of $6 billion MCI, chimes in: "We don't shoot people who make mistakes; we shoot people who don't take risks."
>
> Behaving in a "button-down" fashion, "keeping one's nose clean," and acting as a "steward" were once the hallmarks of the climb up the corporate career ladder. Forget it. Firms that change—fast, constantly, and from bottom to top—have a chance at survival. Those that resist disorder and change don't.[5]

McGill's Bronfman Professor of Management Henry Mintzberg shows how the analytical processes of conventional thinking have caused strategic planning to fail—it is reductionist; it isn't possible to do the conventional analysis of strengths, weaknesses, opportunities, and threats (so-called SWOT analysis); and it causes people to look for the key "where the light is, not where it was lost."[6]

Scholars of organizational change raise the change questions about both the solutions and the thinking used to develop those solutions. For example, Harvard University professor Michael Beer challenges professors and business organizations alike with three questions that echo the theme of this chapter: *"How* should [managers] think about the problem? . . . *How* should they redesign the organization structure and management process to become more competitive? . . . *How* should [they] go about managing the change?"[7] (Emphasis added.)

And yet change—or even feeling empowered to stay the same—requires two things, notes psychologist Ellen Langer: first, learning to think about old situations in new ways; second, opening and enlarging one's frame of reference. Langer calls the fresh approach to life that this new style of thinking creates the attitude of "mindfulness."

" 'Mindlessness,' on the other hand, is the psychological roadblock to change," says Langer. "When we act mindlessly, we behave like automatons, and change becomes impossible. When we're trapped by old mind-sets, clinging to them regardless of circumstances, we behave like the fire horses who kept returning to the scene of a blaze long since extinguished.

"Because they lock us into one interpretation of a bit of information, mind-sets prevent choice. And without choice, change becomes difficult. Before we can make important changes in our lives, we need to reexamine our old mind-sets."[8]

Foremost among several common psychological tendencies from which mindless behavior springs, says Langer, is the search for certainty. Americans especially confuse certainty with confidence. Confidence is useful when it gives us the faith that we can solve problems if we try. Yet certainty can close our eyes to new opportunities and better ways of doing things.

By cultivating creative uncertainty, says Langer, we can stay tuned to the present and alert to changes we must make to function at our best. That goal becomes attainable when we broaden our perspective.

Precisely the breadth of perspective Langer calls for is assured by application of purpose-based Full-Spectrum Thinking. In part, this is because Full-Spectrum Thinking—while entirely realistic—rejects a slavish devotion to the supposed necessity of gathering endless (largely useless) data in the process of solving problems.

And yet, almost all of the literature on change dwells on overcoming resistance to change. It then compounds the difficulties of using Conventional Thinking to seek solutions to problems of change by using that same approach to seek solutions to the problems of resistance to change that Conventional Thinking helps generate—analyzing people problems, probing for psychological explanations, micro-analyzing human behavior, finding causes of the behavior, and so forth.

Professor Neil Postman, chair of the Department of Communication Arts and Sciences at New York University, supports this essential distinction between Conventional Thinking and the more broadly useful Full-Spectrum Thinking:

> Technopoly is the word I use to describe technology's new domination of our culture and society. Technology is a great servant, but a terrible master. Yet without even noticing it, most of us have begun to think and act in ways that serve the ever-growing demands of technology, rather than the needs of humanity . . . machines rather than people.
>
> Technopoly involves techniques as well as machinery. People give undue power to technopoly when they place blind faith in 'facts' expounded by practitioners of such techniques as statistics or the social sciences. Statistics are valuable when they are used with good judgment in those applications for which they were designed—finding patterns in large amounts of data. But like all technologies, statistics must be watched and controlled, so that they are servants and not masters to the people who use them.[9]

In many ways, Postman argues, computers have only made things worse. People used to think that the vast quantity of additional information generated by computer technology would help us make better choices. To our dismay we've learned that, all too often, we are paralyzed in our effort to make sensible choices, because in fact we have *too much* information.

What can individuals do about the information glut? Postman rightly insists that we must simply accept the fact that some information is useless and that too much information can be harmful. "We must give up one of our cherished modern beliefs and learn that it is vital to 'destroy' information that is of no help to us."

Yet all these new ideas—most of them useful are far as they go—are promoted as solution paradigms, when what is actually needed is an entirely new way of thinking, one that leads to the expansion of purposes that characterizes Full-Spectrum Thinking.

Collaboration versus Competition

In recent years, business theory and practice has modified in many ways. One significant shift regards changing attitudes toward competition. In the old perspective, not only did the customer have to be won, but everyone was treated on a competitive, zero-sum basis. For example, suppliers and manufacturers considered themselves at odds with one another, each vying to wrest the best deal. Suppliers competed to provide the lowest price, and purchasers chose the supplier who did so.

Today, collaboration is the order of the day. Increasingly, both sides in the profit equation seek to establish a relationship, to understand (and help to solve) each other's problems. Today, manufacturers seek to lower costs, but not necessarily to offer the lowest price or to purchase from the supplier who offers the lowest. More important is involving the supplier in the broader picture, so that the supplier will naturally seek better, company-specific ways to supply the manufacturer.

Joseph McCann emphasizes the current pressing need for a shift away from what he calls "machine age" thinking to "organic" thinking. "The first fundamental shift is from viewing the universe as a well-ordered machine [as does Conventional Thinking] to viewing it as a highly organic system of dynamic, integrally related parts [as does Full-Spectrum Thinking]. Basic to this shift is recognizing that problems need to be understood in terms of their larger context, not reduced to constituent parts that, in themselves, give no perspective on the entire problem.

"The shift to more organic, systems thinking has several practical implications," adds McCann. "First, organic thinking deemphasizes analytic skills, which stress finding a single right answer, to appreciative skills, which emphasize asking the right question. In a world of infinite information and maximum uncertainty, asking the right question may be more important in directing energies and effort."[10]

Michael Schrage emphasizes that information collection (a by-product of Conventional Thinking) without regard to relationships (a key aspect of Full-Spectrum Thinking) is insufficient. "Information technology only addresses a small part of the organizational challenge," he insists. "Organizations don't run on information. They run on relationships—relationships with customers and suppliers, relationships between peers and colleagues. Yes, information matters; but it's the quality of relationships that primarily determine how successful companies can be."[11]

Such an extension of purposes allows us to put ourselves in one another's shoes. Our relationships become no longer antagonistic. The supplier no longer looks at the manufacturer as someone to exploit. Instead, today's successful supplier tries to do a better job for his customer so that both companies prosper.

"Scientific" versus Holistic Medicine

Medical thinking (if not yet training) is also evolving from treating parts of the patient to treating the whole. Clearly, the direction today is away from the compartmentalization and separation of the Research Approach, to the larger perspective of purposes and systems. And yet, even though changes are already taking place among practitioners, medicine is still being taught according to outmoded methods. Even advanced medical practitioners and educators are promoting holistic medicine simply as a solution paradigm. They still have not changed their fundamental way of thinking about solving problems.

In psychology and psychotherapy, however, the current professional literature includes "solution focused therapy," which is contrasted to the previous methods of "problem analysis therapy." The former concentrates on helping patients find those attitudes and actions that might work to solve their problems, as opposed to endless analysis of the psychological problems themselves.

What each individual assumes about solution-finding and does (or fails to do) in his or her thinking about problems significantly affects the solutions achieved and the impact of his or her work in teams, groups, and larger organizations. Recognizing this is crucial.

However much we may desire to change or reengineer systems and solutions, we cannot ignore the defining impact, the deeply held assumptions, the inherent limitations and capacities of the thinking paradigm that we employ. A change for the better in our fundamental assumptions about thinking begins with each individual; only then can it expand into teams, groups, and other human organizations.

Mental Assumptions and Where They Come From

Individuals are raised and educated differently in different countries. Even within large and diverse countries, such as the United States, Canada, and the former Soviet Union, different ethnic and religious groups provide different educational settings and values for their youth. Yet the one prevailing and pervasive pattern is the way that all of us are taught to think about creating and restructuring solutions, the way we are taught to solve problems, the way we obtain "deeply-held assumptions about how organizational members ought to think, feel, and act," as Michael Beer puts it.[12]

Later in life, organizational culture similarly affects paradigms of thinking. For example, a certain sort of autocratic organizational culture is reflected in the whimsical statement "I'm the boss. Do it my way. Don't ask why." Such an organizational culture automatically creates the framework for severely constrained thinking. And it is often based upon the collection and hoarding of data by top executives and managers whose attitude toward employees tends to be: "You're paid to work, not to think." Most such businesses and executives fail.

Why Our Thinking Fails Us

Why are so many personal lives in disarray? Why are quality, productivity, competitiveness, timeliness, and innovation in the workplace stalled? Why is government treated with greater skepticism than ever before? Why are so many companies working on the wrong problems, experiencing low morale, getting mired in irrelevant details and organizational chaos, overlooking creative options, and making incremental or piece-meal changes at best?

Because our organizations represent conventional wisdom, and our leaders use Conventional Thinking. How can we expect to make paradigm changes in our structure, systems, style, relationships, and patterns of activity without first making major shifts in our thinking?

The theme of this book is that each of us and our organizations needs a paradigm shift in thinking to develop the significant changes we seek in our personal lives and our organizational structures, products, and systems. Such a shift in fundamental assumptions about thinking can make personal lives more ful-filling and provide business with strategic advantage.

Until we make that fundamental shift, how we think about converting goals to practices, and how (or whether) we choose to use a given technique will remain based on conventional assumptions that are doomed to fail. Consequently, these conventional assumptions must be challenged.

An extensive study of professionals (planners, executives, architects, engineers, etc.) conducted by James Peterson at the University of Wisconsin in Madison showed that less effective people address their problems with Conventional Thinking. Such people

- are technique-oriented for the problem as stated
- insist on hard data
- seek data about what exists in the problem area
- try to solve their problems alone or with just a few people
- insist on a firm statement of work and firm specifications
- deal only in the context of the problem area

Effective professionals have intuitive characteristics on which they base Full-Spectrum Thinking. They

- are purpose-oriented to find the right problem
- cope with soft data

- seek needed information from a variety of sources
- involve many other people
- are tolerant of ambiguity
- deal with visions of solutions-after-next[13]

Applying Full-Spectrum Thinking demonstrates that the way you think about accomplishing the worthy values and goals you pursue significantly affects the quality and quantity of the results you obtain. It shows the way toward achieving much better solutions.

Oved Friedman's study of 48 midwestern manufacturing companies, 24 of which used Full-Spectrum Thinking, showed that Full-Spectrum Thinking produces over twice the benefits (measured by savings as a percent of sales) of Conventional Thinking. One person using the total approach produces the same economic benefits as two people using conventional reasoning.[14]

Why then is Conventional Thinking still so common? Because scientism—the basis of Conventional Thinking—is taught throughout our formal education and subsequently reinforced in work organizations.

In this period of rapid change, some people intuitively use Full-Spectrum Thinking. Some people and organizations adapt quickly and move ahead brilliantly by developing effective and productive answers. Because of their extraordinary success, these people and organizations often gain influence and achieve good solutions. Books and articles are written describing their successes, and everyone races to read them and imitate the solutions they proclaim. Their *solutions* are promoted, copied widely, and usually fail elsewhere. Meanwhile, the *thinking process* by which they reached successful solutions to specific problems is largely ignored.

Unfortunately, adopting solutions directly doesn't work. What works for one person or organization will not work for another. Nor will simply emulating the "best of the best." Their ideas, however clever or insightful, are limited to their own specific situations. Besides, the real leaders, the best of the best, are already coming up with new ideas.

The gap we have to overcome, then, is how to convert all our technology, knowledge, values, goals, and "good ideas" into practice. Just proclaiming it to be done is far from enough. We can truly bridge the gap only by accomplishing a paradigm shift in thinking.

Full-Spectrum Thinking is not a solution—it is a paradigm shift in thinking, one that replaces conventional wisdom about processes for planning, designing, improving, and problem solving.

Conceptual Perspectives

Someone once estimated that the average person makes 50,000 decisions in a day. The number might be much higher if we consider that the choice of each word we speak or write represents a selection from among several alternatives. The number would be far lower if we agree that a decision relates only to "important" choices.

In any event, a decision is the choice from alternatives (at least two are always present—use the idea or word or solution versus do nothing or stay with what exists). Regardless of how many decisions a person makes each day, a decision must relate to what precedes the choice (the problem or need that generated alternatives) and to the impact of or the results that follow the selection.

All decisions are based on the problems, purposes, needs, or desires that are to be met, and on an assessment of the consequences that are likely to occur. All aspects of the process need to be considered if one is to achieve the desired results. And all aspects should be considered regardless of the number of decisions in a day, even for deciding on the next word or sentence that one speaks to a colleague or employee, an executive or spouse. These considerations show why making a decision is not really a rational or even consistent choice, but is highly related to individual and group thinking processes and values and to the perceived outcomes.

In solving problems, our aim is often to restructure or create the solutions, systems, products, services, and work of our organizations, so as to achieve the goals we have identified and the values that we hold. This means that it is necessary to improve the effectiveness and creativity of thinking about each aspect of the process for each problem or need where a decision is made: What is the problem to work on? Who should be involved? What are the measures of effectiveness? How are alternatives generated? What information is needed for sketching out and assessing each alternative? How is the choice to be made? How is the selection to be detailed? How will the recommendation be installed?

One should always explore these kinds of questions, rather than simply respond to each problem with an ideologically generated answer. The idea that a single, correct answer—*the* answer—exists for any given situation, is a major cause of many collapsed solutions that we confront today.

Thinking itself—the thinking paradigm with which we approach problems—is an issue most ignore. People assume that thinking is simply a human characteristic that some naturally do better than others. However, people also tend to assume the thinking approach they learned in school is sufficient to solve any and all types of problems. That is a false and dangerous assumption. In truth, the types of problems, the types of needs and desires we have, require our using different modes of thinking to reach the most effective solution.

The Conventional Thinking Approach to finding solutions—the thinking paradigm that we were taught in school and now instinctively use most of the time—embodies the current assumptions about thinking. It represents the concepts, values, perceptions, and practices of thinking that have prevailed in Western culture—unquestioned, seldom discussed, persistent, and passed down through the generations—for the last 400 years.

J. R. Searle states: "The Western intellectual tradition . . . involves a very particular conception of truth, reason, reality, rationality, logic, knowledge, evidence, and proof. . . . Most practicing scientists simply take it for granted."[15]

The gamut of problems each individual and organization faces is infinite. In its simplest definition, a problem, need, or desire is a condition or set of circumstances that a person or group *thinks* should be changed. Problems are the product of human dissatisfactions and aspirations.

This is not to say that problems are only a matter of perception. Many are intensely tangible—a flat tire on the freeway, a dread disease, an erupting volcano, a military attack. But *how we approach* any problem, how we consider it, is plainly a mental process—and a crucial one.

It is the thinking *process* that is paramount. *How* we look at any problem shapes the way we deal with it. *How* we approach an individual problem or a problem facing humanity, *how* we come to grips with it, determines whether we will end up with a thoroughly successful solution, an indifferent result, or possibly bigger trouble. A poor solution may leave us with multiple problems in place of the original one.

Enumerating just the *types* of problems that a person may encounter would be an endless exercise. So Chapter 5 describes only major areas in which problems arise and defines them in terms of the basic purpose that a particular person or organization seeks to achieve: to operate and supervise, to create or restructure a solution (planning and design), to develop generalizations, to evaluate, and to learn. We fail to achieve four of these five major purposes when we mistakenly apply Conventional Thinking. "Scientism" is a type of thinking that successfully addresses only one of the five problem types—developing generalizations.

The fact that each type of problem has a different purpose is obvious. For example, achieving the purpose of developing a generalization about atomic structure (research) will require a different mode of thinking than will achieving the purposes of restructuring or creating an order-filling system for a manufacturing company (planning and design).

Different Types of Thinking
for Different Types of Problems

Probably the simplest problem is typified by a jigsaw puzzle. Solving one is largely a matter of trial and error, an exercise even young children can perform.

Unfortunately, the trial-and-error method is applied too often to complex problems that call for a reasoned approach. We have an atavistic urge—perhaps inherited from our cavemen ancestors' confrontations with predatory animals—to lunge at a problem and seize the first solution that we find. When that doesn't work, we grab another, then another, only to wind up in confusion and frustration, which may be only slightly worse than succumbing to the tiger's fangs.

Of course, most problems have a number of possible solutions, so the odds of hitting the optimal one on the first stab are simply not good. We then try other approaches, but the human track record on problem solving—whether in government, business, or personal lives—is increasingly a tale of horrors. This is particularly true as Americans compare their performance in education, health care, transportation, finance, and many other sectors of society and organizations with the performance of other people in other countries.

The vital link between the perception of a problem and implemented change is the solution-finding approach, the mode of thinking used to find solutions. The decision to do something about a problem automatically gives rise to the question of how to do this something. The key word here is *how*—how to proceed, how to formulate a problem, how to seek and implement solutions.

Answering the question of *how* means offering explicit and predictive methods, not simply a set of exhortations. It means providing, for example, specific processes for transforming a problem as stated into a statement of the right problem to solve. It does not mean merely proclaiming: "Be sure you formulate the problem correctly."

Answering the question of *how* must address all aspects of an approach: determining the problem type and locus, the timing sequence for problem-solving activities, who should be involved, what group of techniques will be most effective, methods of ensuring continual solution change and improvement, developing the transition and installation plans, and so on.

In truth, many solution-finding approaches are possible. But all are variations on four basic approaches: do-nothing, chance, affective, and rational.

The first approach, *do-nothing,* we must dismiss, since we assume that people do want to solve their problems. The *chance* approach, which includes the trial-and-error method, focuses on the accidental in problem-solving and life in general. *Affective* approaches stress intuition, insight, feelings, and divergent thinking. *Rational* approaches are characterized by structured, systematic, methodical "scientific" processes.

Each of the latter three approaches has merit, and each has serious flaws. Some are more applicable to specific types of problems than are others. What is important to remember is that each approach leads to different types of solutions, as a result of providing different kinds of information. At the same time, each problem requires a different mind-set and method of inquiry to achieve a successful solution, because the ends and values of each *type* of problem are different.

For example, *develop generalizations*—where the rational, scientific Conventional Thinking is used—requires detachment, objectivity, piercing questions, rigid methodology, and the challenge of old dogmas, as well as new ideas. The "doubting game" of Conventional Thinking assures that new theories are based on evidence, and that the status quo is not summarily rejected.

Sarkikoski aptly relates both the need for and the benefit derived from the current Conventional Thinking paradigm, as well as its limitations: "We cannot deny the importance in technical problem-solving of positivistic methods and of accurate facts about natural phenomena. Technical science is an exact science as far as its natural scientific basis is concerned. But this is only one side of the matter. It has become extremely important that the social dimensions of technology be taken into account in technical solutions. We could argue that the largest technological problems are no longer technical but social in their character."[16]

Operate/supervise and *evaluate* usually require a similar "doubting game" approach. For example, maintaining a smooth-

ly operating bus system demands anticipation of where difficulties are likely to arise. Evaluation without doubting and
probing would be mere "window dressing." But evaluation
can begin by designing the ideal system ("believing game"),
then comparing ("doubting game") what currently exists to
the ideal.[17]

A compelling example of the failure of Conventional
Thinking in solving problems of evaluation may be found in
the startling success of Emmitt Smith, an outstanding football
player for the two-time Super Bowl champion Dallas Cowboys.
For all his well-analyzed physical shortcomings, Smith has
come to be recognized as the leading running back in the National Football League. Why? Because of idiosyncratic, specific,
qualitative virtues that do not lend themselves to the "objective," generalized, quantitative analysis of the conventional approach.

By conventional standards, Smith should have proven a
journeyman player at best. But he has great leg power and an
unusually low center of gravity; he has extreme quickness
within a confined space and consequent durability; he rarely
fumbles the ball, and for a celebrated professional athlete, he
has relative humility.

"It's not that I didn't like him," says the personnel director
of a competing team that could have chosen Smith for its ros-
ter. "But he didn't have stopwatch speed. He was undersized,
had average hands and left school early. Our mistake was that
we based our decision too much on the numbers, and not
enough on performance."[18]

The "believing game" mind-set is most effective for creating or restructuring a situation-specific solution—that is, for
problems of *planning and design*—and for *learning* a skill or
field of knowledge.

In order to solve problems of planning and design, you
need the "believing game's" commitment to projection, willingness to explore what is new, flexibility, subjective involvement, deep experiencing, dedication to searching for how an
idea *could* work, determination of how to be larger and more

encompassing, and willingness to work with other people and to listen to and incorporate their ideas.

Learning is also aided by the "believing game." It enables us to change or add to our existing knowledge base. Continually believing in the learning process is likely to result in far greater retention and synthesis of knowledge.

A Good Idea Gone Astray

Unfortunately, in Western society Conventional Thinking has become standard for *all types* of problems and needs. It is mindlessly preferred for connecting what we perceive needs to be achieved with how we go about achieving it, *regardless of its actual utility or the effectiveness of the solutions it provides.*

This pervasive yet severely limited approach directs that we:

1. *Define the problem.* Select what appears to be a high priority difficulty or need from those that are available.

2. *Formulate the problem.* Compose a clear-cut statement of what is to be solved and achieve agreement that it is to be worked on.

3. *Gather data about the problem.* Analyze what appears to have signaled the need or problem, get the facts, observe the situation, apply techniques, subdivide, partition, break down, reduce the problem to discrete components, factor, and otherwise gather information.

4. *Analyze the data.* Review with others to assure completeness and accuracy.

5. *Develop models of the data.* Find out "what's wrong," identify the difficulty, ask what is going on, whose fault it is, and otherwise diagnose the problem situation.

6. *Explore alternatives.* Find out how to correct what's wrong, seek ideas to eliminate difficulties, use creativity techniques, and otherwise seek solutions for the troubles.

7. *Select and detail a solution.* Use decision-making process-es, such as decision trees, behavioral decision making, se-lecting the first alternative that appears to work, utility and value theory, and statistical decision processes. As-semble the facts into specifications.

8. *Sell the solution.* Present recommendations to those who must approve the solution and devise plans to convince those who will have to use the solution to agree to it.

9. *Implement the solution.* Many Conventional Thinking strategies do not include this step, presumably because of the assumption that someone else will implement the "ob-viously" good solution.

Whether stated in three or nine or fourteen steps, these steps (which will be detailed in the following chapter) seem reasonable enough. But it is precisely their breadth and gener-ality that constitute a major shortcoming of Conventional Thinking. These steps describe, but do not make operational, the fundamental process. With all such conventional strategies, the questions remain: *How* do you formulate the right prob-lem? *Why* gather data about what exists? *How* can any person be objective? *How* are creative solutions generated? *How* should alternative solutions be evaluated to select the most ef-fective one? *How* is implementation to be assured?

This Conventional Thinking pattern for creating and re-structuring solutions is just *assumed* to be the way to do it. The process is almost always supplemented by exhortations to "get all the facts" or "be sure you know what is happening now" or "make an organizational audit" or "study the present system." Its prime emphasis follows Conventional Thinking as established by science to develop generalizations about natural phenomena. As an almost inevitable result, people look only for what is possible within the very limited bounds of their cur-rent situation. They settle for *good enough* solutions, rather than strive for what might be the *best possible* solution.

As professor and marketing expert Theodore Levitt notes, "Much of the clutter which surrounds change is unnecessary confusion. Change requires a clear view into the future, rather than an evaluation of the past."[19]

Moreover, we suggest that the huge literature (research, books, and newspaper articles) about the alienation of people in work and families, separation from one another, and division of people into parts ("How does this person suit my needs? How can I *use* this person?") is mainly the result of using Conventional Thinking for finding solutions. It causes us to overlook the full spectrum of a person's abilities and humanity by focusing on what is obvious. This often abuses that person and needlessly hampers our own possibility of achieving success. It leads to alienation and needless competition, rather than mutual respect and productive collaboration.

Clearly, given the evolving needs and pressures in today's societies, the times demand a change in our fundamental assumptions about thinking.

What the World Needs Now

What we need now is to shift to a mode of thinking that integrates the situation-specific truths essential to successful planning, design, and solution finding with the generalizations regarding natural phenomena that are the hallmark and particular strength of Conventional Thinking.

To effect a paradigm shift of this magnitude, Austin insists, diplomacy is essential. "Instituting real change requires that you be sensitive to, but not enslaved by, the 'way we do things around here.' That means that a genuine paradigm shifter must be able to speak in the soothing language of the status quo, as well as with the quiet voice of change. Don't attack the pitifully shortsighted boors who run the place," she advises. "Accentuate the positive dimensions of your proposal instead."[20]

In other words, especially in times of change, it pays to remember that diplomacy has been aptly defined as "the ability to tell people to go to hell, in such a way that they look forward to the trip."

We Know It When We See It

The great paradox in proposing a paradigm shift in thinking for creating and restructuring solutions is that almost everyone intuitively recognizes that such a change is imperative. Indeed, people often state what a paradigm shift in thinking might accomplish, how it might proceed, what it might produce, even what it might "sound" like, "feel" like, "taste" like, and what human reactions it might cause.

The new approach that people in many of our audiences state they prefer, has been described as flexible, long-term, warm, challenge-motivated, visionary, integral, innovative, non-restrictive, free, excited, open, competitive, change-oriented, multiple, and intuitive.

By contrast, these same participants describe Conventional Thinking as linear, control-based, data-intensive, defensive, bureaucratic, old, conservative, producing analysis-paralysis, opposing change, creating boundaries, relying on power, and diminishing downward.

In other words, most people know *what* they ought to be thinking as they plan, design, improve, and find solutions. The missing link, the gap that must be filled, still requires principles of *how* to do that sort of exceptionally productive thinking.

Based on our own 30 years of investigating thinking and the intuitive approach to problem solving highly successful problem solvers use, as well as on the research and observations of numerous other investigators in the field, we propose a set of characteristics and factors that a paradigm shift in thinking must include:

- identify the uniqueness of each project or problem
- treat each part of the project as a problem
- investigate the problem-as-stated to determine the problem-to-work-on
- expand the solution space
- define the quality and the result measures that are important
- determine what information really needs to be collected

- get people to participate and develop their own buy-in
- bring people from many disciplines and departments together
- build in the concept of continual change
- lead from the beginning to plans for implementation
- show environmental impacts of solution ideas

These desired process characteristics should also serve as criteria to evaluate principles to be synthesized from studies reporting on the thinking process.

The Age of Thinking Productivity

This raises a crucial question: How effective is our thinking process? How successful are we in achieving the *productivity of thinking,* that is, the number of effective results achieved per time and energy expended. Effectiveness, quality, timeliness—today, we must learn to apply these and similar measures to the productivity of thinking itself.

Many experts today seek to enhance creativity. Their assumption is that, by increasing creativity, we will naturally increase productivity. Obviously, some correlation does exist. But Marshall Fisher, whose computer program "IdeaFisher"[21] provides some 705,000 words and phrases to stimulate creativity, notes that "real world" needs go beyond mere idea creativity. A total approach goes beyond; it identifies what we need to be creative about and shows how to implement creative ideas, how to translate them into practice. Although you may become extremely productive in generating creative ideas, that alone falls far short of the "full-spectrum creativity" of the new paradigm of thinking.

While we have greatly reduced human effort, movement, time, dangerous jobs, and at the same time increased production, our productivity has been growing at a declining rate. Since 1970, in the United States productivity has increased only about one percent per year. (The 1993 rate surprised many by reaching approximately 4 percent.) Prior to 1970, the annual rate was more than 2 percent. In other words, our net output is growing less than half as fast as it once did.

Productivity is generally measured by the ratio of outputs to inputs. The more outputs you get for the inputs you expend, the more productive you are. In manufacturing, inputs include raw materials, labor, capital, technology—everything it takes to make the product. Typically, labor has been squeezed to increase productivity. Other ways to increase productivity include finding alternative, cheaper materials or developing new technologies that reduce costs and labor.

An important indicator today of thinking productivity in modern industry is the "lead time" needed for development of a new product or service. For example, Ford Motor Company developed its Neon car in 33 months. Five years had been considered normal before, but now Toyota is trying to develop a car in 18 months. A very large Japanese candy maker used Breakthrough Thinking to develop a new rice cracker snack in just six months (the usual time is 18 months), and the product increased the company's market share.

The productivity or effectiveness of a solution-finding thinking paradigm is not usually easy to determine. Some studies noted earlier (and others to be described in Chapters 6 and 9) show that it is possible. The need to improve productivity (or creativity or effectiveness or quality) of thinking has been made clear by the increasing number of problems for which the "solutions" found are only marginally, if at all, better than the existing problem situation. Japanese books, such as *Strategy for Creation* by T. Murakami and T. Nishiwaki,[22] portray this need in Japan as well, just as Chapter 1 pointed out the many, seemingly intractable problems that exist around the world.

The Limits to Automation of Thinking

While productivity is theoretically limitless in potential, much increase depends on technology. However, despite high hopes to the contrary, increasing our productivity of *thinking* by means of new technologies such as computers is significantly limited.

For example, General Motors spent $40 billion automating its manufacturing operations, then simply assumed that automation alone would enable them to compete successfully. Such wholesale automation is one more solution paradigm foisted on needy companies and desperate managers. No single answer will serve all situations, solve all problems.

GM should have instead determined the most effective way to accomplish its operations before deciding which could best be automated. Even such reengineering, useful as it may be as a tool for organization, is based on outmoded Conventional Thinking. What is needed are new fundamental assumptions about finding solutions, a new paradigm of human thinking.

Even with such new technologies as Computer Assisted Design (CAD), Computer Assisted Manufacturing (CAM), and Concurrent Engineering (CE), the biggest block to increasing productivity remains the individual human person. As a result, many companies experiment endlessly with ways to make their employees more creative, assuming this will automatically make them more productive. A legion of creativity gurus accrue fortunes promoting their latest scheme to help people come up with brilliant (or even good) ideas.

What organizations forget is that human beings frequently make minute decisions as they use, say, a computer program to specify design details of a gear. *How* they do this—based on techniques or on purposes in a total framework—significantly affects the quality and productivity of the results.

For example, at Lockheed Aircraft Corporation—where the promotion of advanced technologies is evident everywhere—the president insists that Lockheed most needs imaginative people who will take initiative, take risks, and be open-minded, decisive, good at rapid approximations, have an interdisciplinary orientation, stay current technically, and be committed to the future.[23] No computer can provide what Lockheed and other corporations most need—more humans with characteristics that increase productivity. Human beings who understand Full-Spectrum Creativity can achieve the gains in thinking productivity that are so urgently needed.

However good computers become, however advanced the automation technology may be, the greatest need remains greater productivity in thinking. In Japan, some years ago, in the most automated factory in the world, a plant so automated that robots manufactured robots, a visitor could observe signs exhorting people to "Cut Costs Thirty Percent." Robots cannot consciously cut costs, automation equipment cannot do it, flexible manufacturing units cannot do it, only thinking human beings can.

What Now?

We are not alone in calling for a reassessment of thinking. Today, expert and layman alike recognize that theories about intelligence, thinking, and mental processes need reexamination because current assumptions are incomplete, ineffective, cause failures, and do not reflect reality. The current plethora of different solution paradigms indicates the urgent need to change. However, few relate these changes to essential changes in thinking principles and processes for solution finding, planning, and design. Some, such as consultant and business school professor Charles Hardy, say that organizations need to find new ways of thinking to cope with discontinuous change[24] without describing how the new way of thinking is done.

We go further. We call for a change in fundamental assumptions about thinking itself. We urge a paradigm shift to the Full-Spectrum Thinking. We believe that claims, beliefs, and assumptions concerning the applicability of Conventional Thinking, as used to create or restructure solutions, must be subjected to "the magnifying glass of rationality, logic, and evidence"[25]—the precise purpose of this book.

In order to solve innovatively, coherently, and openly the problems that exist today—and the problems certain to make themselves known tomorrow—we must achieve nothing less than a metamorphosis in our fundamental assumptions about thinking.

NOTES

1. James Fallows, "The President Who Knew Too Much," *Los Angeles Times,* (February 14, 1993).

2. Ken Shelton, "New Ways To Make Bread," *Executive Excellence,* (August 1991).

3. Edward de Bono, "Taking Creativity More Seriously," *Executive Excellence,* (August 1991).

4. Harold Shapiro, quoted by Philip H. Abelson, in "The Willingness To Risk Failure," *Science,* Vol. 250, No. 4981, (November 2, 1990).

5. Tom Peters, "Prometheus Barely Unbound," *Academy of Management Executive,* Vol. 4, No. 4, (1990).

6. Henry Mintzberg, *The Rise and Fall of Strategic Planning,* (New York: The Free Press/Macmillan, 1994).

7. Michael Beer, "Strategic-Change Research," *Journal of Management Inquiry,* Vol. 1, No. 2, (June 1992), pp. 111-116.

8. Ellen J. Langer, "Mindfulness," *American Health,* (March 1990).

9. Neil Postman, "How to Protect Yourself Against the Technology Epidemic," *Bottom Line/Personal,* (August 15, 1992).

10. Joseph E. McCann, "Design Principles for an Innovating Company," *Academy of Management Executive,* Vol. 5, No. 2, (1991), pp. 76-93.

11. Michael Schrage, "In Information Technology, the Key Is Good Relationships," *Wall Street Journal,* (March 19, 1990).

12. Michael Beer, "Strategic Change Research."

13. James G. Peterson, "Personal Qualities and Job Characteristics of Expert Engineers and Planners," Ph.D. dissertation, University of Wisconsin, 1985.

14. Gerald Nadler, "Design Processes and Their Results," *Design Studies,* Vol. 10, No. 2, (April 1989), pp. 124-127.

15. J. P. Searle, "Rationality and Realism: What Is At Stake," *Daedalus,* Vol. 122, No. 4, (Fall 1993).

16. Tuomo Sarkikoski, "Re-orientation in Systems Thinking?—Some Remarks on the Methodological and Ideological Traits of Technological Reproduction," *European Journal of Engineering Education,* Vol. 13, No. 3, (1988), pp. 341-349.

17. Peter Elbow, "The Doubting Game and the Believing Game," Appendix essay in P. Elbow, *Writing Without Teachers* (New York: Oxford University Press, 1973).

18. Randy Harvey, "Excellence Without Ego," *Los Angeles Times,* (January 28, 1993).

19. Theodore Levitt, *Thinking About Management* (New York: The Free Press/Macmillan, 1991).

20. Nancy K. Austin, "Movers and Shakers: The New Breed," *Working Woman,* Vol. 17, No. 5, (May 1992), pp. 41–43.

21. Marshall Fisher, "IdeaFisher: Generate Great Ideas Quickly and Easily," (Irvine, CA: IdeaFisher Systems, Inc., 1994).

22. T. Murakami and T. Nishiwaki, *Strategy for Creation* (Cambridge, England: Woodhead, 1991).

23. Sherman N. Mullen, "Lockheed Skunkworks Product Development in the 21st Century," Lecture, 50th Anniversary of Industrial and Systems Engineering Dept., University of Southern California, November 10, 1992.

24. Charles Hardy, *The Age of Paradox,* (Boston: Harvard Business School Press, 1994).

25. Ibid.

The History of Thinking and Solution Finding

Chapter 4

The Rise of Science and The Research Approach

*I*n Part I, we stressed the importance of shifting mental assumptions about thinking. Chapter 3 presented a generalized version of Conventional Thinking for solution finding.

We suspect you instinctively nodded your head: "Yes, of course. That *is* it. Everybody knows that's the way to solve problems. Even though the difficulties described in Chapters 1 and 2 are real, I can't believe that there could be any other way to find solutions."

Part II will show how wrong this supposition is. Not only will we describe the background leading to Full-Spectrum Thinking, we will also show that paradigms other than Conventional Thinking actually *preceded* it.

To do this, we turn to the history of thinking paradigms to consider how and why the Research Approach has come to prevail as today's fundamental assumption of thinking for creating and restructuring solutions.

Let us clarify, however, that our expertise does not lie in the history of thinking for solution finding. The historical table we present is derived from sources more knowledgeable in that field. It is based especially on the work of W. S. Fowler, late scholar of Queen's College, Oxford, particularly from his book: *The Development of Scientific Method.*[1]

Thus, the historical perspective offered here is best regarded as one interpretation of the available literature on a subject whose vast breadth and depth would otherwise render it overwhelming and incomprehensible. Moreover, we recognize that the views expressed in the literature were held by perhaps one percent of the population at the times of fundamental change discussed—that exclusive elite of expansive intellects identified by MacNulty as directly involved in and aware of a paradigm shift as it is occurring.[2] In the phrase of Michael Adas, the "articulate classes."[3]

We emphasize that the historical table we propose is not a formal study in the history of thinking for solution finding. Nonetheless, we are confident that it is both useful and enlightening. Certainly, it provides understanding of how the Research Approach came to prevail as today's paradigm of thinking for creating and restructuring solutions.

Professor George Kneller views science as a succession of movements within the greater historical movement of civilization:

> History reveals not one science, but several. In every civilization, certain men have thought systematically about the natural world and have sought the causes of phenomenal change in nature itself, rather than in human or suprahuman volition.
>
> Glancing through history, we find that nature has been studied for a variety of reasons. In Aristotle's Lyceum, it was studied to enlighten and improve the seeker of knowledge; in Renaissance Europe, to display God's design in His creation; in modern times, to advance knowledge, both for its own sake and for its social and technical uses.
>
> But these grand purposes seem to have inspired scientists less than two primal emotions—wonder and fear. Early man was largely at the mercy of nature. Perhaps his strongest motive for natural inquiry was to attain peace of mind, through having some plausible explanation of nat-

ural disasters. He wanted to find out what caused earth-quakes, floods, fire, and disease.[4]

Our own interpretation of Western intellectual history suggests six distinct phases or periods, based on six different though somewhat related paradigms of thinking about solution finding. These periods of history we call (1) Primitive, (2) Early Greek, (3) Classical Greek, (4) God Thinking (or Christian Theocracy), (5) Scientific Revolution, and (6) Established Science.

Each respective thinking paradigm grew out of the immediately preceding paradigm and stemmed directly from the inherent contradictions of its precursor. Once leading thinkers recognize these contradictions, then realize that the old fundamental assumptions no longer adequately explain observed phenomena or solve existing problems, they develop a new set of assumptions. In time, this new paradigm will dominate, as did the old.

Table 4-1, "A History of Thinking Paradigms," identifies what appear to be the human motives or the intellectual driver behind the activities of each period, the thinking process generally applied during that period, the resulting doctrine or thinking paradigm, the practical outcome of that paradigm's prevalence, and its effect on the current prevalence of Conventional Thinking for creating and restructuring solutions (scientism).

We recognize that others propose many categories of eras or time periods. For example, Martin-Marietta Company Chairman and CEO Norman Augustine proposes five "distinct engineering ages," each with "a beginning and no end." Interestingly, the second and later ages occur after the paradigm shift in science reasoning in approximately A.D. 1600. The five ages proposed are "structural" (from 2900 B.C.), "mechanical" (from mid-1700s), "electrical" (from 1879), "information" (from 1906), and "socioengineering" (from 1979). Augustine's socioengineering age corresponds to our own call for a paradigm shift in thinking. Implementing the fifth age without a paradigm shift in thinking for creating and restructuring solutions will be difficult if not impossible.[5]

Table 4-1. A History of Thinking Paradigms.*

Period	Intellectual Driver	Thinking Process	Resulting Doctrine	Outcome	Effect on/Contribution to Scientism
Primitive < 600 B.C.	-survival (person centered) -control/modification of nature	-intuitive, reactive	Animism—Personification of great natural forces; material items (such as the Sun) are animated by spirits.	-Appeasement of nature via placations, taboos, myths, (etc.).	-None
Early Greek 600–400 B.C.	-explanation of nature -universe centered	-correlative, reason-based, inductive -based on the observation of phenomena	Organism—The whole universe is dynamic; it possesses some kind of life analogous to human life.	-Derivation of "Basic Elements" (i.e., fire, water, air, earth) as a basis for all being. -General theories based only on superficial observation, for example, the Basic Elements Theory.	-An early basis for Scientism—"rediscovered" in the 1600s.
Classical Greek (Socrates, Plato, Aristotle) 400 B.C.–Christianity	-explaining the nature of reality -satisfaction of human needs and desires -universe and person centered at the same time	-inquisitive, deductive -assumed mathematics to be the instrument of knowledge	Syllogism—A deductive scheme of a formal argument consisting of a major premise, a minor premise, and a conclusion.	-Established a form of reasoning (syllogism) that held until the beginning of the twentieth century. -Promoted the development of theories which were unscientific in the sense that hypothesis far outran observation, experiment, or proof.	-"Elucidation" of precise revelations between fact, theory, experiments and hypothesis. -Established a formal framework for scientific discovery and explanation. -Denounced "experimentation" (in the lab) as "artificial" because the world is ever changing, always in flux.

God Thinking Up through A.D. 1600	-personal salvation	-interpretive, normative -faith-based -authoritative	Creationism—God, as stated in the Bible, is the force behind humanity, nature, the universe, etc. . . .	-Clerical scholars became powerful agents in the nurturing and direction of schools of thought.	-Inescapably tied Scientism and scientific education to religious philosophy/theology.
Scientific Revolution (Bacon, Newton, Galileo)	-causes behind the occurrences of physical phenomena	-abduction (drawing away from the center) -experiment-based -investigative	Discoveryism—The discovery of the effects (causes) of physical phenomena is what leads to knowledge and hence truth.	-Method for concluding a material fact based on another fact (typically with no aesthetic or moral values). -Tangentially freed philosophy, art, drama, etc., from bounds of previous paradigm.	-Asserted experimental confirmation of theories as the basis for scientific investigations. -Appreciation of the problem of induction.
Established Science (Descartes) Up through today . . .	-causes behind the occurrences of physical phenomena	-analytical -method-based	Scientism—Everything can be divided into components. Any part can be replaced. Solution of partial problems can solve the entire problem. The whole is the sum of its parts.	-Five-step "Scientific Method" for problem solving: Observe pattern or possible relationship of factors. State hypothesis. Find facts. Analyze facts. Test results against hypothesis. -Established a research tradition. -Generation, cumulation, and legitimization of knowledge about natural world.	-The start of formal, so-called value-free, problem-solving thinking.

*With acknowledgment to Tom Pieronek

What We Mean by "Thinking"

Although *Webster's* provides some 20 different definitions of the verb "to think," our particular interest, professional endeavor, and theory relate to a limited number of its meanings. Generally, we equate "thinking" to thought processes and mental organization.

We do not concern ourselves with the motor functions of the human brain. Nor do we mean the color sensing or spatial relationship capacities of the brain. These and other functions are undeniably useful in problem solving, important to planning and design, often essential in creating and restructuring systems and solutions. The thinking part of the brain, as we mean it, relies and draws upon all these capacities, but such physical phenomena are not what we mean by "thinking."

When we refer to thinking, our particular focus is set on creating and restructuring solutions, what is often called planning and design. We are not, in this book, concerned about thinking as it relates to, for example, the appreciation of artistry, passion, or desire. We *are* concerned with philosophy, but mainly that portion of philosophy known as praxiology, the theory of action essential to the successful implementation of solutions. Thinking to us is an activity related to accomplishment, not just an activity in itself.

From our point of view, to "think" means especially to establish a course of action, a set of ordered questions and series of steps, that lead you or your group to the most effective recommendations for solutions and systems (policies, structures, products, devices) that *achieve your purposes,* and that lead to the implementation of those solutions, which is to say, *solve problems.*

Primitive Thinking

The thoughts of primitive humans were instinctively self-centered and motivated almost exclusively by their fundamental interest in survival. This demanded, above all, that human beings control or modify the forces of nature they observed and feared. The primitive thinking process was largely intuitive and reactive, associative and subjective.

The prevailing doctrine among primitive humans was usually animism—the belief that great natural forces were personified in material objects (for example, the sun, the moon, a tree, a river), which were animated by spirits, both benevolent and malevolent. The outcome of this perspective was ritual appeasement of those spirits, the attempt to placate natural forces by means of offerings and sacrifices, the faithful honoring of myths, and fearful observance of taboos. The pyramids and temples of the early Egyptians illustrate the resulting manifestations. The contribution of primitive thinking to the development of the Research Approach was effectively non-existent.

It should be noted that significant modifications in certain aspects of primitive thinking were found among the Greeks as early as the time of the Trojan Wars (about 1,100 B.C.) and as early as 2,000 B.C. among the Jews, whose God was purely conceptual, understood as unitary and intangible.

Early Greek Thinking

Between about 600 and 400 B.C., the ancient Greeks were moved by curiosity to attempt not only to control and modify, but actually to understand the forces of nature. Their thinking moved beyond self-centered to universe-centered intellectual endeavor. They made a practice of observing natural phenomena and, on the basis of inductive reasoning, attempted to correlate their understanding of Nature with such observations.

The doctrine that ancient Greeks espoused was that of organism: the belief that the entire universe is dynamic and possesses some sort of life analogous to human life. The result of this perspective was the derivation of what these Greeks considered the four basic elements of the universe: earth, air, fire, and water. These elements were believed to provide the basis for all life and being.

Their theories were general, not specific, and based on superficial observation, not rigorous and repeatable experimentation. However, the ancient Greek dedication to the observation of natural phenomena led in the direction of the Research Approach.

In accordance with the thinking paradigm of ancient Greece—the mental assumption known as "semiotica"—Greeks assumed that, in order to solve problems effectively, human beings should follow the thread of purpose. Consequently, the Greeks sought first to answer the question of purpose to solve a problem. Their constant guide was: "What are we trying to accomplish?" In rough translation, the word "semiotica" means "what should we do?"

In ancient Greece, philosophy was considered the highest form of intellectual endeavor, the most worthy work. Greeks developed the idea of a *theory*. As philosophy was the most worthy endeavor, the practice of *semiotica* was reserved for free men. By contrast, slaves were reduced to reliance upon *matematica,* the root word of mathematics, which is to say quantification. Some 20 centuries later, with the rise of science, this relationship of quality and quantity turned on its head. As problem-solving lost sight of purposes, the role of *semiotica* grew ever smaller, and the quantified analysis of *matematica* prevailed.

Classical Greek Thinking

The period of classical Greek thinking extends from about 400 B.C. through the era of Roman ascendency and decline, to the beginning of the Christian Era in A.D. 333, when the Roman emperor Flavius Valerius Aurelius Constantinus, later known as Constantine the Great, abjured the polytheistic Greco/Roman religion and accepted monotheistic Christianity as the official religion of what came to be the Holy Roman Empire. During this 700-year period the motivation of intellectual endeavor fostered by the Greeks changed from the explanation of natural phenomena to a far broader focus: explaining the nature of a presupposed existence of an independent reality. At the same time, the Greek belief in man as reflection of the gods led to another motivation for thinking: the satisfaction of the more refined human needs and desires.

Thus, the thought of this era was both person- *and* universe-centered. The thinking process was inquisitive and inductive. That is, generalizations were inferred from a variety of known facts.

*In*duction may be defined as reasoning from particular facts or individual cases to a general conclusion. Scientists arrive at their hypotheses and theories by means of inductive reasoning. Inductions *lead to* general laws or principles based on specific observations. Einstein induced his theory of relativity.

By contrast, *de*duction may be defined as reasoning from a premise, a known principle, or a generalization to a specific solution. Solutions, artifacts, systems result from creative deduction from general principles and specific statements of needs and purposes. Detectives solve crimes by means of deductive reasoning. Deductions *proceed from* general laws or principles to a logical conclusion. For example, Sherlock Holmes deduced the identity of the murderer from the clues.

A third form of reasoning—called "abduction"—has recently been identified. It may be understood as a form of reasoning that attempts to combine the methods and benefits of induction and deduction. Abduction is literally defined as "a drawing away from the center." It can assume a solution then determine the principles from which that solution arose, or it can assume the principles and then develop possible solutions based on those principles.

In contrast with early Greek thought, classical Greek thought came to accept mathematics as a worthy instrument for ascertaining the nature of reality and thus acquiring knowledge. The doctrine that resulted nonetheless remained largely one of logical enquiry: the syllogism. This thinking paradigm required and proposed a deductive scheme for a formal argument, consisting of a major premise (stone is tough, firm, and durable), a minor premise (houses can be built with stones), and a conclusion (stone houses are tough, firm, and durable). Inquiry and argument proceeded on the fundamental assumption that if A is true (mammals bear live young), and B is true (dolphins are mammals), then C must deductively be true (dolphins bear live young). Remarkably, this form of reasoning and logic held sway, to a greater or lesser degree, until the beginning of the twentieth century.

The outcome it promoted was the development of theories that were unscientific, in the sense that their hypotheses tended to far outstrip actual observation, experiment, or proofs. (*Webster's New World Dictionary* even gives one definition of syllogism as "subtle, tricky, or specious reasoning.") Its impact on the development of the Research Approach was mixed. On one hand, it elucidated the precise relations between fact, theory, experiment, and hypothesis; and it established a formal framework for scientific discovery and explanation. On the other hand, classical Greek thinking denounced laboratory experimentation as artificial, since Greeks considered the world to be ever-changing, in a constant state of flux. Moreover, Greek intellectuals maintained a fundamental aversion to the physical labor essential to practical experimentation, since such labor was thought to tarnish and demean the soul of man.

Two towering classical Greek intellectuals were Plato (427–347 B.C.) and Aristotle (384–322 B.C.)—the latter a disciple of the former. Both roamed the entire area of human culture within their horizons. Seitz notes that Plato—himself a follower of Socrates—expressed in his younger days the common view that results obtained by hands-on experimentation were not to be trusted, relative to the speculations of the unrestrained human mind, which the classical Greeks regarded as more refined and trustworthy.

Indeed, except for astronomical observations and the experiments of Archimedes (287–212 B.C.) with levers and with bodies immersed in liquids, hard-core experimentation did not underpin classical Greek science at its most critical stage. In our view, this Greek rejection of "laboratory" experimentation, on the grounds that the world is dynamic, not static, may be seen as supporting, if for a completely different purpose, our own contention that initial analysis of the problem is not an effective method of creating and restructuring solutions.

Greek thought and its thinking paradigm have proven the dominant intellectual influence over most of Western history.

Frederick Seitz notes with interest the fact that "Aristotle's work held such a prominent place in six great cultures (Greek, Egyptian, Roman, Jewish, Arabic, and Christian) for over two thousand years. Indeed . . . Aristotle's physics continued to be central to the teaching of that subject at the University of Copenhagen well into the eighteenth century."[6]

God-Thinking (Theocratic Dogma)

Between the currently prevailing hegemony of science (*matematica*) and the age of purpose-based thought (*semiotica*) in Greece, another thinking paradigm prevailed. This fundamental assumption, upon which all Western problem-solving was based for more than a thousand years, can generally be described as "God-thinking," that is, Christian theocratic dogma. Over much the same period of time, Islamic theocracy also took hold, resulting in many wars between these two forms of interpreting "God-thinking."

The motivation for thought during this 1,000-year period was personal, spiritual salvation. Its thinking processes were interpretive, normative, and based on faith. The resulting doctrine was dogmatic and held that the Christian unitary yet tri-partite God (or the Islamic unitary Allah) was the sole progenitor and explanation of the entire universe, including all humanity and all of Nature.

During this period of prevailing theocracy in Western thought, for example, the answer to any problem was to be found by recourse to the supposed will of God. His will was held to be revealed in Biblical writings (the work of men inspired by God) and interpreted by priests of the Catholic Church, who provided the fundamental dogma that guided and underlay all human life, consequently, all human problem-solving.

Clerical scholars such as Augustine and Thomas Aquinas became powerful agents in the nurture and direction of various schools of thought, all of which were nonetheless required to support the fundamental Christian dogma. Its impact on the development of science and scientific education was to tie it inescapably to Christian religious philosophy and theology. This dogma prevailed in most of the Western world for some 10 to 15 centuries.

As Muḥammad's followers swept out of the Arabian Peninsula in the seventh century A.D. and took over large portions of the Roman world both east and west, the Arabs displayed considerable tolerance for the dispersed religious groups and their learning and reached out for advanced knowledge, not in conflict with the precepts of Muḥammad that had previously been unknown to them. They welcomed both foreign scholars and their science texts wherever they found them. Many of the books were rapidly translated into Arabic.

By contrast, "the early Christian attitude was based on the view that natural phenomena were relatively unimportant," notes historian Lynn Townsend White, Jr. "Only spiritual values had significance. The natural world deserved attention solely because God used it to communicate specific messages to the faithful.

"By the 12th century A.D., however, this attitude began to change. In the 13th century, St. Francis of Assisi supplemented the doctrine that material things convey messages from God [much like the Greeks and Romans thought] with the new idea that natural phenomena are important in themselves: all things are fellow creatures praising God in their own ways, as men do in theirs. This new notion opened a door to natural science."[7]

White observes that the accompanying concept of natural theology urged late-Medieval men to move beyond their accustomed role as passive recipients of spiritual messages through natural phenomena to become active seekers for an understanding of the Divine nature, as reflected in the pattern of creation.

"Natural theology," he asserts, "was unquestionably a major underpinning of Western science. From about 1250 to 1600 every major scientist considered himself primarily a theologian: Leibnitz and Newton are notable examples. The importance to science of the religious devotion which these men gave their work cannot be exaggerated."[8]

Seitz also comments on the fact that all of the major contributors of science, up to the period which includes Newton (A.D. 1642–1727), were deeply religious. In one way or another, he notes, they regarded their work as part of the process of divine revelation. For example, when the Inquisition began to attack Galileo for his belief that the earth rotated and revolved around the sun, he insisted that he was only revealing the handiwork of the Creator.[9]

The social [read "thinking"] paradigm in Medieval Europe, notes MacNulty, was that "God had created the universe (at the center of which was Earth) and the whole hierarchy of angelic, animal, and human beings, of which the last was His chief interest. The business of people was twofold: first, humankind was to cause the Earth to reflect the heavenly hierarchy through the Pope (and the Church), Christ's representative on Earth and the Holy Roman Emperor, and his hierarchy of feudal lords; secondly, one was to live life in such a way as to earn for one's soul a place of eternal bliss in heaven (and to avoid the similar consignment of one's soul to hell).

"That was the Medieval Paradigm. . . . It worked smoothly for almost 12 centuries."[10]

About A.D. 1350, however, primarily in Italy and particularly in the city of Florence, a small number of individuals, inspired first by the Italian lyric poet and scholar Petrarch, then by the Byzantine scholar Chrysolarus, began to study the surviving texts and artifacts of Greece and Rome. Their goal was to find in these long-ignored treasures of their pagan forebears, some principles to guide their contemporary life—especially its "thinking," its intellectual and artistic endeavor, its understanding of the natural world and the place of humankind within it.

In part to overcome (at least, avoid) the suspicion of powerful theocrats, these early humanists and scientists limited their inquiry. They did not ask, openly, the large questions of philosophy reserved for the learned scholars of the Church. Instead, they focused on a smaller matter: "how things worked." Of necessity, the questions that these pioneering innovators sought to answer were on the micro-, not the macro-level.

Their questions, and so their answers, were intended to be limited and partial, not universal, holistic, and all-encompassing.

In the fifteenth century, such early Renaissance humanists as the Florentine scholar/chancellors Leonardo Bruni and Coluccio Salutati, architects Filippo Brunelleschi and Gianbattista Alberti, mathematician Paolo Toscanelli (whose theories informed the nautical exploits of the Genoese admiral Cristoforo Colombo), and philosophical/artistic/scientific polymath Leonardo da Vinci sought to achieve and master limited, practical knowledge of natural phenomena. In the beginning, their efforts were often in the service of the Church, whose theocratic dogma remained the prevailing thinking paradigm.

Later, as the discoveries of early Renaissance innovators were elaborated by their successors—such as Nicolas Copernicus and Galileo Galilei—and spread north to less temperate European climes, the rudiments of a new paradigm of thinking took hold, both informing and being strengthened by the protestant passion for religious reform. Finally, by the late 1500s, the principles of scientific enquiry had overtaken theocratic dogma as the prevailing paradigm of human thought.

Sachs notes, however, that extreme dogmatism—a last gasp of Medieval theocracy—arose in response to the success of the new paradigm. "In Spain and the Middle East, the intellectually exciting developments of Islamic and Jewish science, mathematics, and philosophy were truly stagnated. Later, in Western Europe, the Copernican revolution in science was severely pressured by the Inquisition to stop its free thinking and experimentation in science—most notably the attack of the Christian Church on Galileo."[11]

Similarly, at more or less this same time, in both the Hindu and the Moslem worlds, religious dogma stultified the search for knowledge concerning the material world. Adas notes that "the early promise of Indian scientific discoveries had not been fulfilled. Like Indian technological innovation, Hindu scientific thinking had stagnated, become mired in superstition and mythology."[12]

Seitz remarks that "the Moslem world . . . played an enormously important role during its peak centuries, say between

A.D. 700 and 1400, by consolidating the scientific knowledge of the known world, ranging from India to the Mediterranean, and placing its own remarkable imprint upon the fusion. Moreover, Moslem scholars through cultural transfer sparked the Scientific Revolution which emerged in Europe in the late Middle Ages and Renaissance. Unfortunately, Islam . . . suffered setbacks in the intervening period which . . . caused its intellectuals to retreat to a considerable degree from the scientific stage."[13]

It was precisely such stagnation, within the prevailing paradigm of Christian theocratic dogma, that the humanists of the early Italian Renaissance sought to overcome. Paradoxically, considering the outcome of the journey on which they embarked, their efforts were all intended to contribute "to the greater glory of God."

Strangely, to the modern observer, humanism at this time came to be allied with mysticism, and (stranger yet) mysticism with science. Only later, with the institutionalization of the Research Approach, did science reject its original comrades in the struggle to throw off the shackles of dogmatic theocracy.

Prior to the sixteenth century in Europe, the prevailing paradigm of thinking was the concept of absolutism embodied in the theocratic dogma of the Church. If an individual faced a problem, the Church provided the answer. The authority of God, interpreted by ordained priests, was considered sufficient response to all human needs. Individual human beings were not encouraged to attempt to find solutions on their own.

But this theologically oriented "God-thinking" was increasingly confronted by inherent contradictions. In Kuhn's phrase, its anomalies became apparent to ever greater numbers of astute individuals. This was particularly so in its attempts to understand and explain natural phenomena. After 1492, few persons of intelligence could any longer claim the Earth was flat or that God's sun revolved around our blessed human orb.

Obviously, theocratic dogma was mistaken. Its failures— or at least its limitations—had become evident. A new paradigm of thinking was needed to explain the world of human experience. New fundamental assumptions were called for, sought, discovered, and developed.

As described by John R. Searle, professor of philosophy at the University of California, Berkeley, the "basic tenets of the Western Rationalistic Tradition," the "new set of propositions," were: "Reality exists independently of human representations, [a] function of language is to communicate meanings from speakers to hearers, [even in reference] to objects and states of affairs . . . that exist independently of language, truth is a matter of accuracy of representation, knowledge is objective, logic and rationality are formal, [and] intellectual standards are not up for grabs [because] there are both objectively and inter-subjectively valid criteria of intellectual achievement and excellence."[14]

In the stead of theocratic dogma rose the method of observation, quantification, and analysis toward understanding that has come to be known as the Research Approach.

René Descartes and the Research Approach

This new paradigm of thinking—the Research Approach—was epitomized by the work of the French mathematician and philosopher René Descartes (A.D. 1596–1650), perhaps best known for his elegantly self-conscious postulation of the certainty of his own existence: *"Cogito. Ergo, sum."* ("I think. Therefore, I am.")

"Among other things," notes Seitz, "Descartes was probably the first true popularizer of science in the best sense of the word since, through lectures and essays, he inspired many others to become involved in research."[15]

"By the 'scientific method' [read: Research Approach]," explains Kneller, "we mean the rational structure of those scientific investigations in which hypotheses are formed and tested. This structure is much like that of everyday thoughtful problem-solving. Hypothesis, inference, test, and feedback are the core of the structure.

"The scientific method [read: Research Approach] is not only intrinsically rational," says Kneller, "it is a refinement of everyday reasoning. The scientist has received a more specialized training than the layman, but his thinking is not fundamentally different."[16]

The method of Descartes and his colleagues—notably, the English philosopher Francis Bacon (1561-1626) and the English philosopher and mathematician Isaac Newton (1642-1727)—was to state a hypothesis, find obvious facts, analyze these facts, test the results against the hypothesis, and thus arrive at Truth concerning a natural phenomenon—a single, irrefutable generalization—a Truth that not even the Church could reasonably deny. In this way, they sought to overcome the barriers to the growth of human knowledge imposed by theocratic dogma.

Note that they did not seek to batter down the walls of theocratic dogma, nor directly to challenge the authority of the Church in spiritual matters. They chose instead to outflank the Church, to go around the walls its dogma raised. How? By devising and promoting an entirely new paradigm of thinking, by proposing and effecting new fundamental assumptions concerning human intellectual enquiry. Faith, they asserted, was (by itself) no longer sufficient. Reason must also play its part.

The Research Approach they developed (known in Japan as "Descartes Thinking") is itself based on four assumptions: First, everything can be divided into its component parts. Second, any of those parts can be replaced. Third, solution of the partial problem can solve the entire problem. Fourth, the whole is nothing more than the sum of its parts.

Unfortunately, exclusive application of the Research Approach as thinking paradigm for *all* solution-finding leads inevitably to viewing the human being as an infinitely divisible machine, simply the sum of its parts, which can (given sufficient knowledge) be replaced. Modern Western medical science is based on this approach. Find out what's wrong and fix it. If the heart is failing, replace the heart. The kidneys. The liver. According to this view, health is defined as the curing, ultimately the replacement, of any diseased part. The whole is defined as the sum of its parts. Nothing more.

The logical positivism thinking paradigm fostered by Descartes and his compatriots had a dramatic effect on Western society, an impact that, for good and ill, continues to this day. The Research Approach provided the foundation of the Scientific Revolution. In turn, this led to the Industrial Revolution and modern rationalism (reductionism and analysis).

Realized variously in different countries (and still being realized today), the Industrial Revolution led to tremendous political and social upheavals, notably that of the apparently competitive but fundamentally similar systems of socio/economic organization known as Capitalism and Communism. Although seemingly at odds, and certainly often in conflict, both are founded on principles of quantification and materialism that stem directly from the Scientific and Industrial Revolutions, especially from the Research Approach that created those revolutions.

THE DOMINANCE OF THE
RESEARCH APPROACH

Since Descartes and his contemporary colleagues developed the Research Approach, it has become so dominant that today it is generally believed that there is simply no other way to think effectively about any type of solution finding or purposeful activity.

There is no doubt that science has contributed greatly to an understanding of the material world and that the knowledge it provides has been effectively applied to create useful technologies. Indeed, as Seitz points out, "Science has provided us with a new light with which to view the world in which we live and to illuminate the path along which we travel. Perhaps this is the greatest gift of science to technology. Indeed, the revelations of science undoubtedly encouraged the development of new attitudes in many other areas of human endeavor."[17]

Yet the sword of science is obviously double-edged. According to Sarkikoski, social development in the modern world has become a function of technological logic: "Technology and the whole industrial ideology can be considered as the most effective and essential factors in the development of modern societies. This means that technological rationality guides both national and international productions strategies."[18]

Perhaps the dominance of the Research Approach, despite its obvious limitations, can be explained by the fact that it pretends to be (for a moment) as close to absolute as human beings can come. As Sarkikoski points out, when you use the Research Approach, you feel that your picture of the world is correct.

"The idea of a totally controllable system is implicitly adopted: If we can only find connections between observed (and scientifically identified) phenomena, we feel able to place our trust in the correctness of our picture of the world."[19]

Defined by science, the world took on an "absolute character" that, "mimicked the older Christian truth . . . unprejudiced, dispassionate, all-seeing."[20]

As MacNulty reminds us, "People's lives [today] are defined, their problems are solved, their governments' decisions are guided, and in some cases their political systems themselves are devised, by the application of the scientific method, which was developed for the study of physical phenomena."[21]

Unfortunately, science is based upon the assumption that all reality can be quantified, measured, and explained mathematically. And in the 1930s, the Czech mathematician Kurt Godel demonstrated that certain key elements of mathematics cannot be proved true or false by using the rules of its own logic. Nonetheless, science persists in its reductionism, attempting with an increasing sense of urgency to develop an ultimately elegant "universal field theory," one that would mathematically describe the reality of everything.[22]

This was Einstein's quest. And, at least with regard to the physical universe, science and its Research Approach offer us the best method yet devised to approach comprehension of material reality. Yet the most important point to note here is that, as Einstein himself asserted, problems cannot be solved by applying the same type of thinking that created them.[23] To solve problems, the thinking paradigm and process must change. One obvious example: Christopher Columbus could not have discovered the New World had he chosen to be bound by the thinking paradigms of theocratic dogma.

The Formalization of the Research Approach to Thinking

The formal beginning of the scientific method may be traced to Descartes' four assumptions, noted above. But even prior to Descartes publication of his famous *Discourse on Method* in 1637, Francis Bacon (1561–1626) had in 1620 published *Novum Organum,* the second volume of a larger work called *The Great Instauration.* According to Fowler, "Bacon realized that *psychological* as well as *logical* influences bore upon the discovery of truth in Nature. . . . Bacon's most important contribution to scientific method was, however, his appreciation of the problem of *induction*: how is it ever possible to conclude a material fact from another material fact?

"The speculative philosophers," Fowler explains, "had relied upon a minimum of observation and the maximum of reasoning and hypothesis—they had considered that a great amount of truth about the physical world could be arrived at by the exercise of reason upon a few observed facts. In contrast to this view, Bacon maintained that in the world of Nature, facts must constantly be checked by reference to other facts and, at every stage of reasoning, experiments must be made which would be crucial for the line of reasoning which was being adopted.

"The weakness of the Baconian system lay in the fact that, although Bacon was able to demonstrate what processes in fact would lead to scientific discovery, he failed to perceive that in practice it is impossible to test every possibility, or even to be aware of every possibility."[24]

ENVIRONMENTAL AND HISTORICAL FACTORS

"Far from being predestined," writes Kneller, "modern science seems to have arisen in Europe out of a fortuitous combination of historical conditions. The Renaissance, for instance, fostered individualism and an interest in *this* world, rather than the next. The Reformation and Counter Reformation weakened the hold of established religion and reduced religious opposition to secular enterprises. Capitalism created a class with an appetite for new knowledge, a sympathy with experimentation, and a belief in the exploitation of nature. Voyages of discovery enlarged the known world and revealed a wealth of novel phenomena."[25]

According to Seitz, science "could emerge and develop only after civilization had progressed to a stage where individuals could exercise their innate curiosity concerning nature freely and had both the freedom and the inclination to do so. From its start in the special climate provided by the Athenian state for about two-and-a-half centuries, [science] tended to have a life of its own and to flourish differently in different civilizations."[26]

Moreover, Seitz notes, at the same time that the Research Approach was developed, so was the printing press and publishing. Relatively widespread access to the method and to the results of experiments helped the Research Approach to spread quickly and be adopted by many people in many different occupations and professions.[27]

Adas points out that limited access to education and the high cost of books at first kept the audience for scholarly scientific works small. "Yet the publication of relatively inexpensive popular encyclopedias that sold in the hundreds of thousands, the establishment of lending libraries, and the proliferation of literary societies, as well as salons and the better sort of coffeehouses, which became centers for intellectual exchange, spread the new learning to a readership that expanded remarkably over the course of the century.

"At this time in northern Europe, physicians, philosophers, and writers conversed in the same salons and debated in the same societies, exploring realms, posing questions, and gaining knowledge of the natural world that would have been unimaginable for the priests and scholar-administrators of other civilizations."[28]

Two major reasons can be given for the initial and continuing acceptance of the method espoused by Descartes and his colleagues: (a) the scholarly way its authors communicated their position; and (b) the logic implied in their position. The Research Approach also grew in part because it provided a formal, teachable, and repeatable way to address practical and human needs, nourish national pride, and respond to global problems such as widespread disease.

MacNulty comments, "Science and the Research Approach in fact, emerged in part from a body of mystical tradition, condemned as heresy by the Roman Church, which explains much concerning the relative lack of scientific development in Latin Europe after the mid-seventeenth century.

"Perhaps we need not be too surprised by this. The Hermetic/Kabbalistic tradition encouraged an attitude of inquiry and personal independence. Carl Jung has indicated that Renaissance mysticism in general should be interpreted, at least in part, as containing procedures designed for achieving psychological integration."[29]

Eastern Philosophies and Modes of Thinking

Since the time of the ancient Greeks, notes science writer Lee Dembart,[30] Western thought has focused on clear-cut distinctions in the natural world. It has looked for and thus found the nights and days, paying scant attention to the twilights. From the perspective of formal, Western logic, a statement is either true or false. The logic finds an exclusive, *fundamental* truth. It cannot be both true and false at the same time.

As a result, today, when questions are asked of Western students, they almost never take the time to ponder before responding. Instead, most seek to immediately provide "the answer." In the business world as well, corporate executives and managers expect (and are expected) to quickly give "the answer." Today, both student and businessperson are rewarded for speed, seldom for profundity. Thus, few initially question purposes.

In contrast to most Western thought, Eastern thought tends to reflect reality more accurately, in that it is more inclusive and more sensitive to nuance, vagueness, and uncertainty. Eastern philosophies and religions such as Buddhism often maintain that wisdom lies in paradox. In the East, reality is seen as normally encompassing more than one truth at a time. The East is the land of both-at-once. The Eastern tradition is to amplify reality to achieve inclusive, *comprehensive* truth.

Boznak and Decker relate the fundamental difference in the way Western and Eastern cultures experience the world. "Perhaps these differences are the results of teaching and learning that began 2,500 years ago in ancient Greece," they suggest. "The [Greek] physician Hippocrates proposed a theory that a physical body was a holistic entity. He stressed a functional relationship between the parts and the whole, working in harmony and balance, creating an inner strength or well being.

"Hippocrates was opposed by a contemporary, Democratis, who believed that man, as well as the universe, is nothing more than a composition of minute particles (atoms). Democratis taught that by treating these individual atoms, a physical body could experience strength and well being. These two opposing philosophies have become known as 'vitalism' and 'atomism.'

"Eastern cultures have never abandoned the philosophy of vitalism, also called 'Chi' (chee). The West [on the other hand] has continued to pursue the more 'scientifically respectable' philosophy of atomism. As an example, western scientists and engineers tend to study how the world works by analyzing the parts of a phenomenon of interest that are small enough to be understood separately. They then attempt to integrate this detailed knowledge into a description of the whole. [By contrast,] their eastern counterparts first create a vision of the whole, then decompose the vision into smaller and smaller parts to allow greater study and understanding."[31]

THE CHINESE

Despite the adoption of his oath as the foundation of Western medicine, Hippocrates lost out to Democratis in the adoption of his fundamental perspective. In fact, Hippocrates' holism was adopted not by his Western successors, but rather by succeeding Eastern philosophers and scientists, notably, the Chinese.

Needham points out that the Chinese fundamental assumption was one of organic wholeness, the continuous wave motion of opposing natural forces, Yin and Yang, a universe in which everything was interrelated and interconnected.

"The organicist conception, in which every phenomenon was connected with every other according to a hierarchical order, was universal among Chinese thinkers. [The Chinese were] already convinced that there was an organic wholeness in the cosmos itself."[32]

"During the first fifteen centuries of the Christian era, Chinese science was the equal of any and Chinese technology was probably superior to all," Kneller asserts. "Certain sciences—astronomy, mathematics, hydraulic engineering—were supported by the state bureaucracy, which was imbued with the teaching of Confucianism. This philosophy studies man as a social being and proposes principles for the wise management of society."[33]

In his book, *The Lever of Riches,* economist Joel Mokyr also addresses the question of why medieval China failed to build on its technological superiority to effect an industrial revolution, as the West was to do later. Mokyr's answer focuses on the Chinese fundamental interest in continuity, both in their view of the natural world and in their social values. [34]

THE MOSLEMS

No other culture contributed so much to the early advance of science in the West as did that of Islam. As Fowler writes, "With the death of Augustine and the destruction of the Roman Empire by the Vandals, Goths, and Huns, we enter the period of the Dark Ages in the West (A.D. 500–1000) and the rise of Arab power in the Middle East.

"By A.D. 750, a vigorous Moslem empire had established itself, stretching from Spain to Egypt, Arabia, and Persia. With this return to settled conditions, the academic nucleus at Alexandria began to revive, and fresh ideas were germinated in the physical, medical, and mathematical sciences."[35]

The Arabs welcomed both foreign scholars and their science texts wherever they found them. Seitz notes that "both Moslem Mesopotamia and Moslem Spain soon generated great centers of what might be termed international Islamic culture. What was inherited from the Greco-Roman world as well as from Persia and India was enhanced by major additions."[36]

During some four centuries, from roughly A.D. 750 to 1150, Islam held the lead in scientific activity. Moreover, its scholars translated, protected, codified, and preserved the best of all the philosophy and science throughout most of the then-known world. Original scientific work began appearing in Arabic by the late ninth century, especially in mathematics, optics, astronomy, and medicine.

As White notes, "The Arabic-speaking civilization knew what science was and was proficient in it. For 400 years, science was one of its major concerns. But a crystallization of other values occurred in the late eleventh century, which shifted the whole focus of Islamic culture. Science was abandoned, and abandoned deliberately."[37]

"In spite of the brilliance of Islamic civilization," Seitz laments, "Islamic scholars seemed to be acting under almost invisible constraints, probably arising from the all-pervading influence of religious doctrines. Again, there is no evidence that any systematic experiments were carried out in support of [the concepts and theories Islamic scholars developed]."[38]

THE HINDUS

India was a major contributor to the advancement of early science, well before the rise of Islam. Indian achievements in mathematical analysis and astronomy are especially note-worthy and were greatly admired by eighteenth- and nineteenth-century Europeans.

In contrast to the results of investigations in China, European study of Indian scientific learning generally enhanced India's standing in the eyes of European thinkers. But according to Adas, the European exploration of Indian learning concentrated on literary and philosophical works, particularly those of Hindu rather than Moslem origin. And the learning admired by

Europeans was associated with ancient Hindu civilization, not with contemporary Indian society.[39]

"Indian achievements in many areas of scientific inquiry," writes Adas, "convinced the Orientalists that the ancient Hindus had attained a high level of civilization. [Robertson] judged that India's ancient scientific discoveries alone were sufficient to warrant regarding it as one of man's greatest early civilizations."[40]

THE EAST'S REJECTION OF THE RESEARCH APPROACH

Despite the many mathematical and scientific achievements of Hindus and Moslems, despite the myriad technological marvels accomplished by the Chinese, none of these great cultures developed and relied upon—or even particularly valued—the Research Approach, as did the seventeenth-century Europeans. Relative to Europe, all three cultures were more scientifically and technologically advanced, at least through the thirteenth century, and in the case of China, for at least two centuries more. Why then did Europe come to outstrip them all in science?

Adas notes that India's supposed stagnation in the sciences, as well as its general decline was sometimes attributed to India's historic isolation and the Brahmin castes' secretiveness and indifference or open hostility to European scientific instruments and techniques. The Brahmins sought to monopolize India's ancient learning, and discouraged critical and creative thinking and, consequently, advances in scientific knowledge.[41]

As for China, various European observers nearly always qualified their praise for its society and culture. This was particularly the case as it became evident that, between the sixteenth and nineteenth centuries, Chinese capacity in science and technology had actually declined.

Adas points out that Parennin, writing about the Chinese history of science, "faulted the Chinese for failing to probe beyond specific findings to underlying principles and for disregarding the necessity of 'exactitude' in observation and investigation. Above all, he stressed the Chinese attachment to ancient customs and teachings and hostility toward innovation as key impediments to advances in the sciences. He argued that . . . the Chinese valued and rewarded veneration for tradition, while original thinking and attempts to challenge long-accepted views in astronomy or geography met with disapproval, dismissal, or, in extreme cases, official repression."[42]

Du Halde, on the other hand, extolled the long-standing commitment of the Chinese to scientific investigation and learning in general "reflected in their 'magnificent libraries,' their 'vast number' of doctors and colleges, and the extensive education of their elite classes. Yet he concurred with . . . Parennin that, despite their dedication to the sciences for such a long period of time, the Chinese had not 'brought to perfection' any of the 'speculative sciences,' which required 'penetrating' and 'subtle' minds."[43]

Despite the presumption of these European observations, it is worth speculating as to why the Western mind began to raise and probe these fundamental questions, whereas other, more generally advanced societies did not. It is possible that, in societies where, due to the certainty of established religious dogma or rigid social stratification, the human mind is relieved of intense curiosity as to the meaning and origins of life, these deeper questions—already irrefutably, eternally answered—are not asked as often, if at all.

In answer to the question of why the Chinese, in more than a millennium of inquiry, failed to discover and utilize the Research Approach, a number of other answers have been proposed.

"It has been suggested," writes Kneller, "that the enormous Chinese bureaucracy with its Confucian ethos frustrated scientific innovation.

"Another proposal is that the Chinese lacked the idea of a 'divine lawmaker' and so never realized that nature has laws. There is no doubt that this idea lent self-confidence to European science. If the universe is divinely designed, it is comprehensible and can be analyzed like a piece of machinery to see how it works."[44]

It seems to us worth noting that, much like the Western "Protestant ethic," Confucianism also maintains that hard work leads to success. This may well explain why expatriate Chinese have often become so financially successful outside of their Chinese homeland. In China itself, by contrast, social, political, and economic repression by centralized government or local power-brokers has been the historical norm.

Whether suppressed by imperial bureaucracies, by war-lords and dictators, or by the Communist Party, the Confucian ethic was seldom allowed to function fully and flourish. Inter-estingly, with the current relaxation of Communist economic (if not political) repression, the standard of living for mainland Chinese is rapidly increasing.

The Sixteenth-Century Paradigm Shift in Thinking

As Table 4-1 indicates, four major paradigm shifts in thinking have occurred in the Western world. The intuitive/reactive thinking of primitive humans gave way to the correlative/inductive thinking of the early Greeks, which then gave way to classical Greek thought, which was inquisitive and came to ac-cept mathematics as a worthy instrument of knowledge. With the fall of the Roman empire, Greek thinking paradigms gave way to dogmatic God thinking, which, in the sixteenth cen-tury, gave rise to science and its Research Approach.

Through all these epochs—on the basis of the prevailing paradigm—systems, objects, and products were developed and restructured. Our own studies (described in Chapters 6 and 9) indicate that roughly eight percent of human beings today intu-itively follow a process of effective thinking to create or re-structure solutions, and we thus surmise that, at any time in history, a similar percentage of human beings thought differ-ently—and more effectively—than their contemporaries.

We believe they intuitively used Full-Spectrum Thinking. They were the innovators, designers, changers, builders. We surmise that, especially during the so-called Dark Ages, even these intuitives, whoever they were, were not able to convert much of their intuition to action. Due to the overwhelming weight of the prevailing paradigm, their thinking and all it might have contributed to human life, were largely repressed. Similarly, during the last 100 years or so, human thought about processes for creating and restructuring solutions has been repressed by the assumption that the Research Approach is the only way to find solutions.

Those who are most innovative and creative were, and are, usually ostracized, at least initially. Without them, however, we would never have the buildings, bridges, products, systems, and solutions that we now enjoy. For example, someone, some individual, had to discover and convert to practice the fact that fire melted things. No doubt, however useful the discovery, the person who thought of it first—even when the efficacy of the idea could readily be demonstrated—was feared and scorned. Or worse.

The same human instinct is reflected in modern anthropological studies of tribes living in the wild. Almost invariably, they instinctively reject the opportunity to change. "It's our tradition. The way we do things." And yet, some people in those tribes are certain to know a better way to do things.

WHAT WAS THE SHIFT?

In the fourteenth century, the evolutionary paradigm shift that ultimately led away from theocratic dogma to the Research Approach, which so dominates our own thinking to this day, slowly began.

MacNulty elaborates: "The . . . paradigm shift occurred in Europe during the somewhat arbitrarily-defined period between 1350 and 1660, that is, during the Renaissance and Reformation/Counter Reformation. During this more recent paradigm shift, Western Civilization entered the period as Christendom, an other-worldly, religiously-oriented society in which the purpose of human endeavor was the salvation of the human soul. It emerged as Europe, a pragmatic, materialistic society in which the purpose of human endeavor was the satisfaction of physical needs."[45]

The scheme of scientific discovery devised by Francis Bacon (1561–1626) is reported by Fowler. Bacon's aphorisms from his book, the *Novum Organum*, include the following:

" 'There are and can be only two ways of searching into and discovering truth. The one flies from the senses and particulars to the most general axioms, and from these principles, the truth of which it takes for settled and immovable, proceeds to judgment and to the discovery of middle axioms. And this way is now in fashion. The other derives axioms from the sense and particulars, rising by a gradual and unbroken ascent, so that it arrives at the most general axioms last of all. This is the true way, but as yet untried.' "[46]

As Kenyon De Greene has noted, during a paradigm shift, those who are most invested in the prevailing paradigm are called upon to defend it against the new thinking. "The dominant coalition consists of the top management, the key decision makers of the organization. [In this case, the Catholic Church.] The main functions of the dominant coalition [during a time of paradigm shift] are to perceive challenges, opportunities, and crises developing in the external environment, reconcile these developments with organizational purpose, mission, and goals, and devise strategies for external action and internal design."[47]

In sixteenth-century Europe, the Catholic Church responded to the perceived threat of Protestant Reformers and the emerging paradigm of the Research Approach, which was then challenging the doctrine of an Earth-centered universe, by subjecting all those under its temporal control to the intellectual and spiritual repressions of the Inquisition.

WHAT CAUSED THE SHIFT?

As with all shifts in fundamental assumptions, deficiencies in the prevailing method cause anomalies to be recognized. Interestingly, the quarrel of the scientists who succeeded the early Renaissance humanists was less with the prevailing paradigm—the theocratic dogma of the Catholic Church—than it was with the deficiencies they discovered in the 1,500-year-old science of the classical Greeks. In particular, it had to do with the lack of experimentation by which Greek theories might be verified. In fact, until the sixteenth century in Europe, experimentation was evidently not a part of any previously existing paradigm of thought.

This new concept—proof by experimentation—an essential feature of the modern Research Approach, helped force the development of a new paradigm. Francis Bacon especially found the paradigm of the day inadequate and promoted experimentation as a requirement for the advancement of science.

Fowler reports that "Bacon saw clearly that the . . . methods of the traditional formal logic could never, by themselves, lead to the advancement of science. [He] realized that psychological as well as logical influences bore upon the discovery of truth in Nature . . ."[48]

THE REFORMATION

The Protestant Reformation—based on opposition to corrupt and authoritarian practices within the Roman Catholic clergy and the papacy, as well as the primacy of mercantile values over agrarian—provided major impetus to the new thinking paradigm. Emancipation from the Roman Church meant freedom from the more repressive aspects of theocratic dogma. A religious Reformation that was itself based on the questioning of fundamental assumptions could not legitimately continue to repress human thinking.

Nor did its chief proponents, members of the rising merchant class of Northern Europe, find it in their self-interest to limit ideas. European merchants had a financial interest in technological invention. They believed in the freedom necessary for scientific debate. Moreover, being ready to work with their hands, they recognized the importance of experimentation.

Seitz notes: "The rapid spread of the Reformation proposed by Martin Luther in 1522, which gained the support of the powerful nobles in large segments in Northern Europe, caused great panic in the [Roman] church and led it to become militant, as well as highly reactionary.

"Actually, some of the early Protestant reformers, including Martin Luther, were skeptical about the revolutionary concepts arising from science. For example, Luther . . . opposed the publication of Copernicus' main work in Wittenberg in the mid-sixteenth century. This mood was a transient one, however. Presumably the noble and merchant classes were anxious to benefit from the advantages associated with relative freedom from the church and access to new knowledge of all kinds. They determined the actual course of events, encouraging science, technology, and trade."[49]

The Universality of the Research Approach

THE RATIONAL DREAM

Professor Roald Hoffman, Newman professor of science at Cornell University, comments on the unfaltering belief in the Research Approach, especially among scientists: "If only the scientific approach were applied to the way countries are governed, it is supposed, the world's problems would vanish. Scientists typically define for themselves a universe of study in which the outcome may be intricate and surprising but in which there is no doubt that an analysis is possible: Complexity is simplified by decomposition, and there is always a solution."[50]

Indeed, the power of the Research Approach seems so dazzling that it is all too easy to believe that, given sufficient resources, all the secrets of the universe might be revealed. Moreover, whatever is ascertained as deriving from science, that is, from the rigorous application of the Research Approach, is considered irrefutably true.

Science, we have come to believe, will always find "The Truth." And truth, we are assured, will "set us free." As Sarkikoski reminds us, "The whole history of technology has been a refinement of the idea of the new natural science: the mastery of man over nature.

"The fact that the traditional paradigm has proved to be successful in so many ways in society has encouraged people to strengthen it further. It is still believed that only an intensified technological capability can enable us to hinder or to relieve disadvantages which have been produced by technological operations."[51]

SCIENCE AS THE PATH TO PROGRESS

"All of us today" writes historian Lynn White, "take for granted that humanity is progressing from bondage to mastery of the natural environment, from superstition to knowledge, from darkness to light. It is axiomatic that science is the exploration of an endless frontier and that its processes cannot be reversed or even seriously interrupted. Every American or European, every Asian or African deeply influenced by Western culture, has implicit trust in the inevitability and rightness of this onward sweep of science."[52]

"Civilization was not [considered to be] a state," Adas explains, "it was a process. Individuals who through education and hard work had risen above their modest family origins placed a high premium on improvement, a term that is ubiquitous in nineteenth-century writings on colonial areas. Change was not only good; it was essential for the civilized. Stagnation and decadence were associated with barbarians; 'primitive' and poorly developed material culture with savages. The history of civilized peoples was a tale of progress, of continuous advance; that of barbarians, a dreary chronology of endless cycles of decline and recovery."[53]

Science was viewed as the impartial rationality that would save humanity—eliminate poverty and diseases, discover our origins, provide unlimited power, indeed eradicate all human suffering.

In early twentieth-century America, Adas writes, "Henry Ford was widely regarded as the prophet of a new age of 'heroic optimism,' in which science and invention were hailed as the key to American prosperity and the best solution for social ills."[54] He further comments on the period after the First World War: "A greatly heightened European interest in the scientific management procedures by which Frederick Taylor and his disciples proposed to increase plant efficiency and the mass production techniques pioneered by . . . Ford reflected a growing conviction that Europe's salvation could best be won by emulating America's technological successes."[55]

This attitude has, until recently, pervaded engineering education. The approach pioneered by Frederick Taylor, notes professor of industrial engineering John E. Gibson, "seems so obvious that it is universal. We begin with the simplest mechanisms and equations, then proceed step-by-step to more complex devices and mathematics, in a bottom-up manner.

"Thus, without words, the budding engineer learns to accept engineering reality as susceptible to decomposition into simpler sub-units best handled in isolation, a hierarchical management approach with professors as 'bosses' who 'think' and students as 'workers' who 'do,' and an absence of discussion of goals, except for questions that are meant to elicit what the boss wants."[56]

Our own perspective is fundamentally different. We see "progress" not only in strictly quantifiable terms, but also as essentially value-oriented. For any society, we believe, "progress" may best be defined as a relatively smooth upward movement along a spiral that includes human dignity, individual betterment, effectiveness, and quality of life.

Even those who would agree with our definition, seem to turn instinctively to science for solutions. For example, in the depths of the Great Depression, U.S. President Franklin Roosevelt, as one of his first official actions, called upon the National Academy of Sciences to convene a Science Advisory Board to offer counsel to the president. Not surprisingly, the advisory board emerged in 1935 with a series of recommendations for government support of programs in science and engineering. Its successor panel serves to this day.

THEN AGAIN . . . MAYBE NOT

Despite 400 years of habitual belief, if not obsessive faith, in the methods of science and its Research Approach, today there is growing realization that it cannot solve all our problems. This awareness registers with particular chagrin in the annals of technologically optimistic, twentieth-century American social and political history.

As historian Arthur Schlesinger, Jr., wrote: "The besetting illusion of the New Deal and the New Frontier was that every problem had a solution. [In truth,] few problems can be finally solved. Many, however, can be usefully mitigated when the time is ripe."[57]

Articles like "What Ever Happened to the American Dream," "Why Things Don't Work Anymore," and "Engineering Failure and Technological Overkill in Developing Countries" represent the vast literature detailing how newly proposed or installed solutions fail to even minimally achieve user objectives.

"This wishful thinking is beginning to be revealed in its true light," proposes Sarkikoski. "The social and ethical aspects of science and technology have become topical debates due to obvious disturbances in technological societies . . . The result has been a reassessment of the ethical principles of scientific thinking and the political character of technology."[58]

Sarkikoski further observes that the traditional paradigm of technology—the Research Approach—seems to have some systematic or ideological factor that prevents interdisciplinary ideas from being realized.[59] Though widely practiced, indeed all but revered, the Research Approach has come to be recognized as too culturally narrow to deal with most problems today. Especially in a business and organizational context, McCann emphasizes, the key to effective thinking is not knowing the right answer, but rather asking the right question: "Organic thinking places a new product into a larger cultural context of social, political, and economic conditions and forces that determine how it will be used and valued."[60]

Even in investigating the purely physical world, where it excels as a paradigm of thinking, the Research Approach has come up short, says MacNulty: "At the philosophical level, if one peels away the experimental jargon and condenses a vast body of research, the essential conclusions of contemporary work in physics suggest . . . that *objectivism* (one must stand apart from one's experiment and observe it without 'participating' in it), *reductionism* (the only way to understand something is to disassemble it into its ultimate components and understand them), and *positivism* (the only things which can be studied at all are those phenomena which can be measured by multiple, independent observers) are insufficient to explain the physical world."[61]

GLOBAL DOMINATION OF THE
RESEARCH APPROACH

Obviously, one reason that Western thinking dominates today's global frame of reference is that the West physically colonized and politically dominated the world beginning in the eighteenth and nineteenth centuries. With colonization came the notion—too readily accepted by both victor and vanquished—that the ways of thinking the colonizing nations employed must be the best.

Japan, for example, adopted the scientism and industrialization of Western society in 1868 when Emperor Meiji decreed the change from Japan's feudal heritage. These Western approaches succeeded so well that the ambiguities of Japan's Shinto and Confucian culture led the country into copying the militaristic patterns as well as industrialization of Western society, starting in the early 1900s. The same ambiguities and the concept that whoever wins the war must be "right" led Japan to wholeheartedly adopt the Western Research Approach to solve problems (as illustrated by the statistical quality control techniques such people as Deming and Juran taught to the Japanese). By tempering the rigidity of the Research Approach with its own cultural perspectives of group search for "what really needs to be accomplished" and "consider many alternatives to serve as guides," Japan was immensely successful. But now, in the '90s, Japan is searching for a new paradigm of thinking to more effectively combine their culture with others yet still increase creativity and innovation in developing and restructuring solutions.

THE RELATIONSHIP OF THE RESEARCH
APPROACH TO OTHER CULTURES

Although for some 300 years Europeans and Americans assumed that Western culture was naturally paramount, in the twentieth century Western observers find it increasingly difficult to believe in the inherent superiority of the Research Approach.

Francis Fukuyama has observed that "the suicidal self-destructiveness of the European state system in two world wars gave lie to the notion of superior Western rationality, while the distinction between civilized and barbarian that was instinctive to Europeans in the nineteenth century was much harder to make after the Nazi death camps."[62]

And yet, the West continues to promote and maintain almost exclusive use of the Research Approach in thinking because, viewing the world from within this paradigm, the West is still able to consider itself superior to others. Similarly, it is worth noting, men may continue to consider themselves superior to women on the basis of their facility and power within the Research Approach.

Reason was considered a powerful weapon in the search for truth. The truths discovered by the Research Approach, it was argued, would set free peoples long enslaved both by religious superstition and by the power of entrenched plutocracies. At the same time, increased productivity would create a larger economic pie to share. In large measure, in the West, science did indeed have the salutary effect of advancing spiritual and political (if not always economic) democracy—witness the proliferating environmental pollution and Chernobyl-like discharges.

To the extent that it develops widely available data and information, science certainly seems to advance democratic values. Effectively disseminated, such information can be a powerful educational tool for a wide variety of people. When more information exists, and more people have access to it, democracy is likely to advance.

However, the resulting applications of scientific knowledge, especially when manifested in costly technology, have generally been controlled by states. Whether directed by Nazis, Communists, or other types of "corporativist" government, technology has often been used to repress human beings.

Thus, the argument can be made that, even in a democratic society, the more expensive fruits of the Research Approach—costly technological applications of scientific knowledge—do not necessarily free human beings. At least not when governments or corporate interests maintain effective control over that technology. Yet there can be little doubt that, from the first, Western political and philosophical ideals have advanced in tandem with the progress made by science.

Syndromes, Pitfalls, and Errors of the Research Approach

Over several centuries in Europe, a number of different planning and design professions (architecture, engineering, government planning, land-use planning, etc.) emerged from earlier crafts. Each had its own jealously guarded techniques and standards. In the nineteenth century, these professions wholeheartedly embraced both scientific knowledge and the Research Approach. Indeed, these professions viewed themselves as "applied sciences."

The assumption was that the Research Approach, tremendously successful in generating scientific knowledge, was equally applicable to creating and restructuring products, urban areas, and systems. Equally pervasive was the notion that scientific discovery preceded innovations in planning and design. Ironically, historical case studies (Egyptian and Native American pyramids, Roman aqueducts and roads, Gothic cathedrals, gold jewelry) have proved this assumption incorrect. Planning and design denied its own rich heritage and became the stepchild of the sciences.

Originally, adoption of the Research Approach made sense, largely because problems were definable, understandable, and consensual. Indeed, the results were spectacular. Streets were laid out, roads paved, homes built, dread diseases eliminated, indoor plumbing installed, and hospitals and schools built to serve every locale. But by the mid-twentieth century, neither science nor planning and design could promise ever rosier futures. Hiroshima, environmental disaster, diminishing resources, and exploding populations inaugurated an era of infinitely more complex and unmanageable problems, problems that are not definable, understandable, nor consensual. Conflict resolution, implementation in highly politicized environments, and multiple impacts pose difficulties less amenable to the Research Approach. Postindustrial society that deals mainly with information and services poses similar difficulties. As the substantive problems have multiplied, so too have the methodological.

DIFFICULTIES AND ERRORS

In the case of machines, the fundamental hypotheses of the Research Approach are often appropriate and acceptable. However, they are not always appropriate or correct in the "organic" world, such as a human society. Particularly, they tend to lead to the sort of "analysis paralysis" that most corporations and governments confront today.

As Hoffman notices, "Much of the real world out there is not amenable to simplistic (or complex) scientific analysis. When it comes to the resolution of personal and societal problems, a clear statement of issues, alternatives, and consequences can help, but the existence of unique rational solutions is just a dream. We've recently witnessed the failure of one such technocrat-run dream—Marxism. Ironically, in the Soviet Union and China, that theory was largely implemented by men and women trained in science and engineering."[63]

Fowler also comments on the nature of the scientific method, which has "proved far more successful in the sphere of things than in the sphere of life. [For example,] we are still ignorant of the answer to such a relatively minor question as 'Can a computer be regarded as a brain?'

"This dichotomy between the living and the dead," speculates Fowler, "raises again the two fundamental problems of scientific method: (1) Are there any 'patterns of discovery,' any general methods of experimental enquiry, which can be said to be likely to yield fruitful results, or constitute a specific 'scientific method?' and (2) Does the human mind impose uniformities *on* Nature or discover them *in* Nature? In other words, are the 'laws of thought' also 'laws of things?' "[64]

Moreover, as Adas points out, modernization theory, that is, the widespread, exclusive application of the Research Approach, is fundamentally flawed because it cannot account for "the actual experiences of peoples in developing worlds. The limited cultural horizons of the theory tend to involve [practitioners] in a subtle form of 'cultural imperialism,' an imperialism of values which superimposes . . . Western cultural choices upon other societies, as in the tendency to subordinate all other considerations (save political stability perhaps) to the technical requirements of economic development."[65]

McCann identifies the Research Approach as resulting in: "machine age" thinking that is monolithic, competitive, structured, technologically programmatic, nationalistic, and short-term. He favors organic thinking that is pluralistic, collaborative, process-oriented, technologically 'pulsating,' transnational, and long-term.[66]

Our reliance on the Research Approach is by now so ingrained that what was first a self-conscious method became a habit that is a blind instinct. Unfortunately, as J. L. Adams describes, "problem solving is influenced by habit. [And we] are programmed to a considerable degree in [our] thinking."[67]

We maintain that, for the last 300 years, especially the last 100 years, the "habit" of using the current Research Approach thinking paradigm for creating or restructuring solutions (which we call Conventional Thinking) has in fact *limited* our creativity. It is worth recalling MacNulty's point: "Scientific research in the field of quantum physics has demonstrated that the scientific method, as it is presently formulated, is insufficient to explain even the physical universe, let alone the problems presented by human beings."[68] So ingrained is the Research Approach as a "habit" that authors, such as management professor Henry Mintzberg, dismiss planning as reductionist and analytical in nature, when in reality it is the habit or thinking paradigm which is poor, not the needed purposes of planning.

CONSEQUENCES OF EXCLUSIVE RELIANCE ON CONVENTIONAL THINKING

Perhaps the most treacherous consequence of universal devotion to Conventional Thinking is that humans have begun to believe that the method, which they themselves devised, is somehow larger and greater than the humans who devised it. Science has come to control us, as well as free us. Our current veneration of the Research Approach may ultimately cause us harm, even set back our human progress.

"No faith can afford to reign unexamined," asserts White. "[Thus,] our habit of regarding scientific progress as inevitable may in fact be dangerous to its continuing vigor."[69]

White reminds us that "the prestige of science today sustains a common but false assumption that any robust culture must have had considerable scientific activity. Now, Rome was immensely vigorous. Languages descended from Latin are still spoken from Tijuana to Bucharest. The overwhelming mass of legal structures of the world . . . is descended from Roman law. The Romans had vast creative ability and originality; yet there was no ancient Roman science. Nothing that can be called science existed in the Latin tongue until the twelfth century."[70]

John Ralston Saul, for one, insists that the West has spent the last two centuries in the grip of a cult of reason (read: the Research Approach) that has brought it to the brink of ruin. Particularly, he proclaims the blind worship of reason—a faith mediated by expert elites—to be the original sin of the twentieth century. Saul writes:

> The philosophers of Europe, England, and America threw themselves into the arms of reason, convinced that birth would be given to new rational elites capable of building a new civilization. And yet the exercise of power, without the moderating influence of any ethical structure, rapidly became the religion of these new elites. And their reforms included an unparalleled and permanent institutionalization of state violence.
>
> Possession, use, and control of knowledge have become their central theme, the theme song of their expertise. However, their power depends not on the effect with which they use that knowledge but on the effectiveness with which they control its use.
>
> Thus, among the illusions which have invested our civilization is an absolute belief that the solution to our problems must be a more determined application of rationally organized expertise. The reality is that our problems are largely the product of that application.
>
> The illusion is that we have created the most sophisticated society in the history of man. The reality is that the

division of knowledge into feudal fiefdoms of expertise has made general understanding and coordinated action not simply impossible but despised and distrusted.

A civilization unable to differentiate between illusion and reality is usually believed to be at the tail end of its existence.[71]

The widely (mis)applied "medical metaphor" aptly illustrates the consequences of excessive reliance on Conventional Thinking. Heralded advances in understanding diseases and medical treatments have led almost everyone trying to solve problems to follow the approach used by physicians. Most change-oriented groups—for example, those working in organization design, information systems design, reengineering, and the like—even adopt the language of physicians by saying that their first effort is *diagnosis*—find causes, locate the root-source of the problem, and so forth. Yet the use of such metaphors ignores a wide range of dissimilarities between illusion and reality: the human body is not the same as the organization structure or the product design or the information system; a physician cannot create or restructure a human body; a system, artifact, or structure is developed by humans, not predetermined by nature; and so on.

At the same time, Adas argues, global dominance of the Western-based Conventional Thinking has undermined ways of thinking indigenous to other parts of the world. "Less arrogance and greater sensitivity to African and Asian thought systems, techniques of production, and patterns of social organization would . . . have enhanced the possibility of working out alternative approaches to development in non-Western areas, approaches that might have proved better suited to Third World societies than the scientific-industrial model in either its Western or its Soviet guise."[72]

De Greene writes:

The United States, which should have been developing a new paradigm during the 1970s and 1980s, instead retreated along several fronts. Although as prominent as ever in world affairs, the U.S. has shown several trends that can be viewed only as unhealthy.

These indicators of an exhausted paradigm include:
(1) an extreme obsession with money as a goal; (2) a shift
in organizations from innovation and quality production
to growth for growth's sake and the financial bottom line;
(3) an increase in scandals and corruption; (4) a focus in
government and by the news media on superficiality and
emotion-laden issues; (5) a reliance on quick fixes that
provide relief from deep thinking but almost invariably ex-
acerbate the situation; (6) an increased liaison between
government and business that emphasizes exploitation;
(7) an increasing dissolution of the social safety nets that
protect people from extreme deprivation and loss; (8) the
decay of the two-party system and balance-of-power systems long held to be among the fundamental roots of
American democracy; (9) a decay in feelings of cama-
raderie, neighborliness, and mutual obligation; and (10) a
quasi-religious but internally contradictory, almost nineteenth-century faith in the effectiveness and goodness of
the free-market system.[73]

Not everything has turned out badly. Great progress has
been made by science, particularly in terms of enhancing the
quality of human life. Indeed, few of us today would choose to
live without the benefits produced by science and its Research
Approach.

Nonetheless, our belief is that the negative indicators
noted above pervade efforts to solve problems and to create or
restructure systems because of an inappropriate reliance upon
the Conventional Thinking paradigm. The scientific analysis of
Conventional Thinking is particularly inappropriate and ineffective in the human dimension, that is, when trying to resolve
personal or societal problems, even those which arise in the
scientific domain.

"Much of the real world out there is not amenable to
simplistic (or complex) scientific analysis," opines Hoffman.
"When it comes to the resolution of personal and societal
problems, a clear statement of issues, alternatives, and consequences can help, but the existence of unique rational solutions is just a dream."[74]

In this same vein—and similarly confronting the difference between brain and mind—are the efforts now underway to devise "expert systems" and other forms of computer/electronics-based "artificial intelligence."

"Nowadays," write professors Michael Prietula and Nobel Laureate Herbert Simon, "organizations are increasingly building expert systems to retain knowledge resources. While we are learning fast how to represent and use certain types of knowledge on machines, we are still faced with the difficulties and inefficiencies of determining what the know-how of the human expert 'looks like.' In the parlance of artificial intelligence, this is the knowledge-acquisition bottleneck. Even if this hurdle is overcome, there is no guarantee that a usable system can be built. Some kinds of expertise are simply too difficult to replicate."[75]

Seitz concurs that some issues are simply beyond human comprehension, at least when addressed solely on the basis of current scientific methods.

Commenting on issues not related to the increasing cost of experimental equipment in some areas of science, he writes, "there are two possible obstacles [to the advance of science] that deserve mention. First, it is possible . . . we may face issues which are beyond treatment, even statistically, on the basis of knowledge gained from reductionist analysis—the tool which has been so powerfully useful since the dawn of science.

"Second, we undoubtedly will also face imponderable issues which are entirely beyond our comprehension, let alone our ability, to treat qualitatively. For example, . . . will we ever comprehend the qualities of the human mind, both in depth and in totality, beyond knowing the details of its molecular structure and the simpler forms of molecular interaction?"[76]

TAYLORISM AS A PROTOTYPE OF CONVENTIONAL THINKING

Frederick Taylor, the quintessential and prototypical "efficiency expert" of the late-nineteenth and early twentieth century, based his "scientific management" theories on the Research Approach and the related economic theories of Adam Smith.

Taylor's theories and methods, a major contribution to industrial development and extraordinarily successful in their day,
sought to increase productivity by reducing work to its simplest, replaceable components. Today Taylor's ideas are generally ineffective in our complex environment, only rarely
successful in such services as fast-food restaurants.

Engineer John E. Gibson charts the following seven elements as essential and critical to "Tayloristic" engineering practice.

1. An analytic, bottom-up approach, "analytic" being used in
   the classical sense of 'breaking into component parts or elements'
2. The absence of the goal-definition phase in normal engineering design process
3. The practice of engineering in a vacuum, without regard
   to human factors
4. A hierarchical, non-professional style of engineering
5. The fantasy of 'value-free' design
6. The traditional practice of separating thinking from doing
7. A strong emphasis on individual reward for individual effort

"Analogous to Taylor's procedure of breaking down the
manufacturing process into elemental steps," Gibson explains,
"the first step in the engineering design process is the careful
division of the overall task into simple sub-elements and assign-
ing these parts to individuals or teams for detailed design. This
is so simple and obvious, and it works so well in certain practical design tasks and in engineering design education, that we
may fail to understand the deeper implications of this step.
One of the implications of this minute subdivision of tasks
is . . . that the Taylor process works best if the boundaries of
the sub-units are sharp and well-defined and interconnections
are clear and separable."[77]

Sarkikoski takes a more critical view of the Tayloristic
management philosophy: "Taylorian management philosophy
can be seen as a formalization and scientification of the use of

the labor force in ways similar to earlier exploitations of natural resources. This may also be seen as a good example of how the whole history of the social sciences manifests the prevalent antagonism of nature and society."[78]

American industry was and remains particularly susceptible to the seduction of Taylor's theories. As R. Florida and M. Kenney point out: "U.S. manufacturers treat automated manufacturing as if it were just another set of machines for high-volume, standardized production—which is precisely what it is not.

"Captive to old-fashioned Taylorism and its principle of scientific management, these executives separated the establishment of procedures from their execution, replaced skilled blue-collar machinists with trained operators, and emphasized machine uptime and productivity. In short, they mastered narrow-purpose production on expensive [new] technology designed for high-powered, flexible usage. Certainly, Frederick W. Taylor's work still applies—but not to this environment. Managing a flexible manufacturing system as if it were the old Ford plant at River Rouge is worse than wrong; it is paralyzing."[79]

Confronting the Syndromes of Scientism

Today, as we face the problematic results of misapplying the Research Approach, organizations and societies try to protect the existing paradigm of Conventional Thinking by responding in one or more of four ways. Unfortunately, none of these ways—which are all, to some degree or other, based on the same approach that caused the problems—effectively responds to the problems we face.

APPLY CONVENTIONAL THINKING MORE RIGOROUSLY

The first, and most ill-advised, response is to try more of the same. Some promotions of the Research Approach (or, as some call it, the Scientific Method) try to make it more palatable by expanding the number of steps in the process—detail each with many techniques, identify more measurements to use, exhort with "outstanding" examples of *scientific* results, and advise on developing better personal characteristics and behaviors.

This response assumes that we are not doing all we can within the existing paradigm. The prescription: more studies, more data-collection, more analysis. The result: more paralysis.

TWEAKING THE METHOD

The premise of this response is that the method is fundamentally sound, but not quite right. Instead of abandoning it, this attitude assumes, we should simply adjust it. This response is characterized by methods that propose X, Y, or Z number of steps in problem-solving, all of which recommend data collection and analysis of the current problem as the primary steps. Or by "psychobabble" about how everything should be viewed as "selling something" through research, analyzing your "customer," discovering the "hot button" of the customer, and handling objections.

MacNulty gives an example of this response: "Science, which has had such a profound influence in shaping the Industrial Paradigm, will certainly adapt its role to the [emerging] Consciousness Paradigm. As conservative as scientists are when it comes to changing their methods, they form a group which is probably unique in the world's history—a very large group dedicated to understanding things as they are, regardless of personal cost. This integrity will require—and enable—science to introduce the sort of *changes into the scientific method* [emphasis added] which will be required by the findings in disciplines such as consciousness research."[80]

SUGGESTING "LIBERAL ARTS BASED" ALTERNATIVES

The premise of this response is that other disciplines may be able to avoid or overcome the pitfalls of Conventional Thinking. The shortcoming of this attitude is that the reader is seldom told exactly how to use these "soft" methods to solve real problems.

An example of this response can by found in Hoffman's otherwise laudable suggestion: "Where should the capacity to deal with the real, partially coherent world come from? In large part, from the ethical, literary, historical, artistic realm. From the arts and humanities. Not just salve on mental pain, the arts and humanities leaven and enrich. As they make us think, they make us feel at one with the terrible and beautiful world. And they prompt us to step outside of ourselves, to empathize."[81]

Similarly, Sarkikoski proposes addressing the social dimensions of technical problem-solving education and methodologies. But he does not specify how to integrate and use this new dimension.

"A certain specific disciplinarity is surely fruitful for new research findings and practical innovations," he writes. "But if technical science is going to persist solely in its positivistic orientation, it will miss its opportunity to integrate the analysis of its own social dimensions into technical problem-solving. Technical and social problems may seem different in nature, but the need to solve them together is increasing continuously."[82]

RESIGNATION

This response assumes that nothing can be done. No alternatives are offered to the current impasse. Its outlook, however, is not, entirely bleak.

As Timothy Ferris has pointed out, "[The fact] that no one theory of the universe can deservedly gain permanent hegemony," writes Ferris, "does not mean that all theories are equally valid. On the contrary: to understand the limitations of science (and art, and philosophy) can be a source of strength, emboldening us to renew our search for the objectively real, even though we understand that the search will never end."[83]

Saul concludes that, in order to overcome the impasse we have reached as a result of the limitations of science, "we must alter our civilization from one of answers to one which feels satisfaction, not anxiety, when doubt is established."[84]

Ultimately, Lane suggests, the most important realization is that science and its Research Approach are indeed specific remedies, limited in their power. "It is important for us to be aware of what we are up against. How we respond to the problem should be a matter of discussion. The answer is not clear. But it is important for us to understand the problem, in order to develop a strategy for dealing with it effectively."[85]

The Breakthrough Needed

As should by now be abundantly clear, we cannot respond effectively to the syndromes of scientism with the thinking of scientism.

Sarkikoski writes of this sort of virulent technology based on the syndromes of scientism: "The general tendency is that national competitiveness in technological capacity and in all other dimensions is underlined. The profitability of different sectors of social reproduction is emphasized along with the needs of the changed productive circumstances, in a paradoxical attempt to cure the disease by using its own causes as the panacea.

"Now, clearly," he asserts, "instead of strengthening the methods which have been proved to be imperfect or inadequate, the insane elements of the theory should be found and replaced by better ones. A necessary (but not sufficient) condition for this would be a reformation of technological rationality itself: a socially more comprehensive paradigm should be created."[86]

THINKING DIFFERENTLY

In order to respond effectively to the syndromes of scientism, we must accept the need for, learn, and practice an entirely different way of thinking.

The new thinking paradigm that we present in Part III involves considerably more than simply intuition, but it surely values intuition and provides for its realization in the process based on its seven principles. It recognizes that the future solutions we seek to develop are not full of data to be "collected" and "analyzed." It holds that there is no future on the path of the past, and that a *broad* "systems" view must prevail throughout solution finding.

Greeno points out that creativity can be enhanced by altering the way people formulate problems: "The main issue in discussions of creativity involves flexibility of thinking and restructuring of understanding in innovative ways. In most discussions, a creative achievement is characterized as an occurrence in an isolated mind, almost by definition.

"[For example] Getzels and Csikszentmihaly (1976) gave tests and observed the activities of students at the School of the Art Institute of Chicago. The most striking findings involved observations of the students' concern for problem formulation, including the extent to which they explored alternative arrangements of materials before they started a drawing, changes in structure during work on the drawing, and concern for discovery during formulation of the problem. [In short,] creativity involves a restructuring of one's relation to a situation."[87]

Even scientists may well benefit from the sort of restructured, purposes-based problem formulation perspective presented in Part III. Indeed, the most creative among them are already calling for just such a change in perspective. No less than the rest of humans, and probably more so, scientists today need to rely on and draw from a wide variety of thinking skills and processes.

In his book *The Art of Science: A Practical Guide to Experiments, Observations, and Handling Data,* Joseph J. Carr asks, "Should the scientist be monological or multilogical? Should the scientist be reductionist or holist? Should the scientist be inductivist or deductivist: lateralist or verticalist? In a word: Yes.

"As a thinking person, the scientist needs to be able to draw on all of these thinking skills, or risk being little more than a technician with a lab coat. Perhaps the best metaphor is the zoom lenses used on cameras. You need a Zoom Mind that can change focal length from wide angle to long distance with, of course, a high degree of close-up macro capability (and equipped with special filters for discerning intellectual traps)."[88]

CHANGING THE CULTURE

Why must we change our paradigm of thinking for creating and restructuring solutions? Why are we engaged in what conventional thinkers may perceive as blasphemous activities? Because we are again facing a paralysis of problem solving similar to that which was resolved 400 years ago by the rise of science and its Research Approach. Again, the anomalies in the prevailing paradigm have become apparent. Again, human problems seem intractable and so insoluble and will remain so as long as we rely on assumptions about thinking that no longer serve our needs.

Sometime during the seventeenth century, explains Saul, "Reason began, abruptly, to separate itself from and to outdistance the other more or less recognized human characteristics—spirit, appetite, faith and emotion, but also intuition, will and, most important, experience. This gradual encroachment on the foreground continues today. It has reached a degree of imbalance so extreme that the mythological importance of reason [read: the Research Approach] obscures all else and has driven the other elements into the marginal frontiers of doubtful respectability. Our unquenchable thirst for answers," Saul observes, "has become one of the obvious characteristics of the West in the second half of the twentieth century."[89]

Saul points out that, in the last 400 years, Western thinking has taken only one clear step forward—away from the divine revelation and absolute power of church and state. All the rest of Western thought, he states, has been merely fiddling with the details, as knowledge has been ever more minutely subdivided and compartmentalized. Meanwhile, flouting the original intent of Descartes, Voltaire, and their contemporaries, the self-perpetuating elites ensconced and values enshrined by exclusive reliance on the Research Approach have become not only established, but ossified.

"Thus, the Age of Reason," Saul laments, "has turned out to be the Age of Structure. A time when, in the absence of purpose, the drive for power as a value in itself has become the principal indicator of social approval. And the winning of power has become the measure of social merit.

"In general terms," he points out, "this means that management methods are being mistaken for solutions and so, as if in some sophisticated game, the problem is pushed on with a long rational stick from point to point around the field."[90]

Professor of business and leadership expert Warren Bennis suggests that to influence the way people think is to influence how they behave. In order to change a culture—and its paradigm of thinking—both changes are essential.[91]

Such a fundamental change does not, however, happen overnight. Nor does it occur first on the macro-level of a larger culture, whether societal or corporate. Instead, culture of any sort begins and ends with individuals. As Sarkikoski comments, "Those who reproduce technological ideas and structures, i.e. the producers and users of technological knowledge, also formulate patterns of social conditions and consciousness."[92]

Particularly in American corporations and institutions, it is generally assumed that the latest, most recently popular "program" or fad can change a given culture, make it more open, more creative, more flexible, more productive, more competitive. Managers seek novelty, however superficial, through such fads. In fact, professors D. Scott Sink and Thomas Tuttle state, the "organization of the future" is not created in so haphazard a fashion. "You don't need another program if you truly want to become the organization of the future. You need a *process* that is an integral part of your culture, the way you do business."[93]

Business strategy and business culture drive each other, says McCann. "The implicit assumption today is that the company's strategy drives its culture. Culture is increasingly seen as a variable changed to support the execution of major shifts in corporate strategy. Neither strategy nor culture totally drives the other; they are actively managed to make sure that they reinforce each other."[94]

In truth, all human action and organization has an emergent, experimental, holistic, unpredictable, pragmatic, and non-rational quality and is always specific to time and place. Consequently, individuals making individual choices, trying to convert their knowledge and specialization into practice, invariably effect cultural change more than a given culture changes an individual. An effective theory of action[95] must address the paradigm of thinking as a major thrust. If individuals such as you are willing to and learn to think with a new paradigm, a new culture can emerge.

NOTES

1. W. S. Fowler, *The Development of Scientific Method,* (New York: Macmillan, 1962).

2. W. Kirk MacNulty, "The Paradigm Perspective," *Futures Research Quarterly,* Vol. 5, No. 3, (Fall 1989), pp. 35-53.

3. Michael Adas, *Machines as the Measure of Men: Science, Technology, and Ideologies of Western Dominance* (Ithaca, NY: Cornell University Press, 1989).

4. George Kneller, *Science as a Human Endeavor* (New York: Columbia University Press, 1978).

5. N. R. Augustine, "Preparing for the Socioengineering Age," *ASEE Prism,* (February 1994), pp. 24-26.

6. Frederick Seitz, *The Science Matrix: The Journeys, Travails, Triumphs* (New York: Springer-Verlag, 1992).

7. Lynn Townsend White, Jr., "Science, Scientists, and Politics," in Alexander Vavoulis and A. Wayne Culver, eds., *Science and Society: Selected Essays* (San Francisco: Holden-Day, 1966), p. 71.

8. Ibid.

9. Seitz, *Science Matrix,* pp. 34, 37.

10. MacNulty, "Paradigm Perspective," p. 36.

11. M. Sachs, "Einstein and the Evolution of Twentieth Century Physics," *Annales de la Fondation Louis de Broglie,* Vol. 16, No. 2, (1991), p. 246.

12. Adas, *Machines as the Measure of Men.*

13. Seitz, *Science Matrix,* p. 75.

14. John R. Searle, "Rationality and Realism: What Is At Stake," *Daedalus,* Vol. 122, No. 4, (Fall 1993), pp. 55-83.

15. Seitz, *Science Matrix.*

16. Kneller, *Science as a Human Endeavor,* pp. 118-119.

17. Seitz, *Science Matrix,* p. 11.

18. Tuomo Sarkikoski, "Re-orientation in Systems Thinking?—Some Remarks on the Methodological and Ideological Traits of Technological Reproduction," *European Journal of Engineering Education,* Vol. 13, No. 3, (1988), p. 343.

19. Ibid., p. 342.

20. Joyce Appleby, Lynn Hart, and Margaret Jacob, *Telling the Truth About History* (New York: W.W. Norton, 1994).

21. MacNulty, "Paradigm Perspective," p. 49.

22. Sharon Begley, "Math Has π On Its Face," *Newsweek,* (November 30, 1992).

23. Albert Einstein, "Telegram to Prominent Americans," *The New York Times,* (May 25, 1946).

24. Fowler, *Development of Scientific Method.*

25. Kneller, *Science as a Human Endeavor,* pp. 9, 10.

26. Seitz, *Science Matrix,* p. 10.

27. Ibid., pp. 73, 123.

28. Adas, *Machines as the Measure of Men,* p. 73.

29. MacNulty, "Paradigm Perspective," p. 39.

30. Lee Dembart, "Bringing Fuzzy Logic Into Focus," review of Daniel McNeill and Paul Freiberger, *Fuzzy Logic: The Discovery of a Revolutionary Computer Technology—And How It Is Changing Our World* in *Los Angeles Times,* (February 26,1993).

31. Rudolph G. Boznak and Audrey K. Decker, *Competitive Product Development: A Quality Approach to Succeeding in the '90s and Beyond,* manuscript in progress, pp. 15–17.

32. Joseph Needham, *Science In Traditional China: A Comparative Perspective* (Cambridge, MA: Harvard University Press, 1981), pp. 11–14.

33. Kneller, *Science as a Human Endeavor,* pp. 5–7.

34. David S. Landes, "Rewarding the Better Mousetrap," review of Joel Mokyr, *The Lever of Riches: Technological Creativity and Economic Progress* (New York: Oxford University Press, 1990), *The New York Times Book Review* (January 6, 1991), p. 15.

35. Fowler, *Development of Scientific Method,* p. 32.

36. Seitz, *Science Matrix,* p. 23.

37. White, "Science, Scientists, and Politics," pp. 70–71.

38. Seitz, *Science Matrix,* p. 23.

39. Adas, *Machines as the Measure of Men,* p. 97.

40. Ibid., p. 104.

41. Ibid., pp. 99–102.

42. Ibid., p. 81.

43. Ibid., pp. 86–87.

44. Kneller, *Science as a Human Endeavor.*

45. MacNulty, "Paradigm Perspective," pp. 35–38.

46. Fowler, *Development of Scientific Method,* p. 43.

47. Kenyon B. De Greene, "Rigidity and Fragility of Large Sociotechnical Systems: Advanced Information Technology, The Dominant Coalition, and Paradigm Shift at the End of the Twentieth Century," *Behavioral Science,* Vol. 36, (1991), p. 67.

48. Fowler, *Development of Scientific Method,* pp. 41–42.

49. Seitz, *Science Matrix,* p. 32.

50. Roald Hoffman, "Why Scientists Shouldn't Run The World," *Issues of Science and Technology,* (Winter 1990-91), pp. 38–39.

51. Sarkikoski, "Re-orientation in Systems Thinking?"

52. White, "Science, Scientists, and Politics," p. 69.

53. Adas, *Machines as the Measure of Men,* p. 196.

54. Ibid., p. 409.

55. Ibid., p. 381.

56. John E. Gibson, "Taylorism and Professional Education," *THE BENT of Tau Beta Phi,* Vol. LXXXII, No. 4, (Fall 1991), p. 15.

57. Arthur M. Schlesinger, Jr., "Memo to the 1993 Crowd: Believe in Yourselves," *Newsweek,* (January 11, 1993).

58. Sarkikoski, "Re-orientation in Systems Thinking?" p. 343.

59. Ibid., p. 344.

60. Joseph E. McCann, "Design Principles for an Innovating Company," *Academy of Management Executive,* Vol. 5, No. 2, (1991), p. 78.

61. MacNulty, "Paradigm Perspective," p. 46.

62. Francis Fukuyama, *The End of History and the Last Man* (New York: The Free Press, 1992).

63. Hoffman, "Why Scientists Shouldn't Run The World," pp. 38–39.

64. Fowler, *Development of Scientific Method,* pp. 93–102.

65. Adas, *Machines as Measures of Men,* p. 415.

66. McCann, "Design Principles," p. 78.

67. J. L. Adams, *The Care and Feeding of Ideas: A Guide to Encouraging Creativity* (Reading, MA: Addison-Wesley, 1986).

68. MacNulty, "Paradigm Perspective," p. 49.

69. White, "Science, Scientists, and Politics."

70. Ibid.

71. John Ralston Saul, *Voltaire's Bastards: The Dictatorship of Reason in the West* (New York: The Free Press/Macmillan, 1992), p. 7.

72. Adas, *Machines as the Measure of Men*, p. 16.

73. De Greene, "Rigidity and Fragility," p. 77.

74. Hoffman, "Why Scientists Shouldn't Run the World," p. 38.

75. Michael J. Prietula and Herbert A. Simon, "The Experts in Your Midst," *Harvard Business Review,* (January-February 1989), pp. 120–124.

76. Seitz, *Science Matrix,* p. 81.

77. Gibson, "Taylorism and Professional Education."

78. Sarkikoski, "Re-orientation in Systems Thinking?" p. 343.

79. R. Florida and M. Kenney, *Corporate America's Failure to Move from Innovation to Mass Production* (New York: Basic Books, 1990).

80. MacNulty, "Paradigm Perspective," p. 51.

81. Hoffman, "Why Scientists Shouldn't Run The World," p. 39.

82. Sarkikoski, "Re-orientation in Systems Thinking?" pp. 343–347.

83. Timothy Ferris, *The Mind's Sky: Human Intelligence in a Cosmic Context* (New York: Bantam Books, 1992).

84. Saul, *Voltaire's Bastards.*

85. Ron Lane, "Learning To Relate," *Software Magazine,* (April 1991).

86. Sarkikoski, "Re-orientation in Systems Thinking?" p. 345.

87. James C. Greeno, "A Perspective on Thinking," *American Psychologist,* (February 1989), pp. 134–141.

88. Joseph J. Carr, *The Art of Science: A Practical Guide to Experiments, Observations, and Handling Data* (Solana Beach, CA: High Text Publications, 1992).

89. Saul, *Voltaire's Bastards,* p. 15.

90. Ibid., p. 16.

91. Tom Rubython, "Warren Bennis: The Man Who Made John Harvey-Jones," *Business Age,* (July 1992).

92. Sarkikoski, "Re-orientation in Systems Thinking?" p. 342.

93. D. Scott Sink and Thomas C. Tuttle, "The Performance Management Question in the Organization of the Future," *IM,* (January/February 1990), p. 12.

94. McCann, "Design Principles," p. 87.

95. Talcott Parson, *Toward a General Theory of Action* (New York: Harper & Row, 1962); T. Kotarbinski, *Praxiology: An Introduction to the Sciences of Efficient Action* (New York: Pergamon, 1965).

Chapter 5

What We Think About: Different Types of Problems

All living organisms face problems. Luckily for them, nonhuman organisms encounter a limited range of problems; and their resolution is most often the result of genetic programming.

Conversely, human beings constantly confront a baffling array of problems and unmet needs, from the simple to the complex: What to eat? Where to live? When to marry? Which career? When to sleep? Moreover, humans form innumerable groups, each with its own particular problems. The resolution of human problems is seldom programmed or simple, depending instead on human intelligence, attitude, knowledge, and thinking.

But what exactly is a "problem"? And what types of problems are there? We listed quite a few in Chapter 1, but now we probe the nature and characteristics of "problem" or "opportunity" or "issue" or "policy" or "activity" or "need" (and even "want") to find what thinking paradigms might be most effective. We will use the word "problem" henceforth to represent all of these situations for which solutions are sought.

Actually, there is no such thing as an "objective" problem—not in the same tangible way that there are chairs, computers, tornadoes, mountains. A problem exists only when some thing or situation is *perceived by a human* as a problem or an unmet need. In other words, a thing or situation becomes a problem or need only when humans identify it as one. Problems exist solely because of human purposes, motivations, and aspirations.

As discussed in Chapters Three and Four, different thinking patterns and problem-solving approaches have existed during human history. Each may be considered more or less appropriate to solving different types of problems. For example, the early Greeks applied their philosophical thinking in order to discover truth for all types of problems, while people in the God-thinking era evaluated all problems in terms of the presumed standards of "the word." Thus, in any solution-finding situation, the structure of the solution-finding approach determines the way the problem is defined and will critically impact its solution.

In fact, the primary task of the solution-finder is to formulate exactly what the problem is more than to determine a solution. The quality of a solution is significantly affected by the way a problem is formulated. This chapter establishes a framework for the essential understanding of what a problem is. In turn, the framework established will lead to selecting the particular thinking pattern most effective for its corresponding problem type.

Problems: Different Definitions

The dictionary defines a problem as a substantive matter about which there is concern. A substantive matter may be a question, situation, policy, phenomenon, person, or issue. A concern may be an uncertainty, obstacle, desire, difficulty, or doubt.

Educator Dewey calls a problem a "felt difficulty."[1] For psychologist Davis, it is a "stimulus situation for which an organism doesn't have a ready response."[2] For creativity specialist deBono, "a difference between what one has and what one wants."[3] Generic ideas include a gap, a dissatisfaction, an obstacle. Whatever the formulation, a problem remains something that causes concern.

As practitioners and scholars seek solutions, they tend to classify problems. Ironically, classification both leads to and reflects solution approaches. Classifications range from the minimal—since there is only one problem-solving approach (Conventional Thinking), there is no need to classify problems—to the mind boggling. *The Futurist*, the magazine of the World Future Society, at one time identified 2,653 problems that humanity faces, ranging from nuclear war to art forgery.[4]

Generally, classifications include:

Classification by problem type.   Business tends to classify problems in the categories of finance, sales personnel, marketing, manufacturing, distribution administration, human resources, and product development. Japanese engineer Tomo Sugiyama has identified three types of problems that arise in the workplace. His categorization comprises problems of irrationality, problems of inconsistency, and problems of waste.[5]

Management consultant Theodore Levitt divides problems into those that pertain to the purposes of an organization and the directions in which it must be led; problems regarding the need to foster and manage change; and problems regarding the need to conduct operations so that the organization and its people function effectively and efficiently.[6]

Rosabeth Moss Kanter, Barry Stein, and Todd Jick, writing about *The Challenge of Organizational Change*, categorize those challenges into problems of emergent change, problems of forced change, and problems of engineered change.[7]

Historians usually categorize problems as ones of art, religion, economics, science, politics, or language. Problems can be arranged by interest groups or estates: political, professional, administrative, and scientific. Often problems are classified by discipline: engineering, astrophysics, sociology, and so on.

Smith suggests each of the Research Approach-type steps—goal setting, diagnosis, design, description, research, alternative generation, prediction, evaluation, and persuasion—could be viewed as problem types.[8] Taylor preferred resource specification, goal specification, creative, and well-structured as problem types.[9] Maier and Hoffman found three categories of problem types: high acceptance requirement and low quality; high acceptance requirement and high quality; low acceptance requirement and high quality.[10]

Several sources say problems can be categorized in "people" domains—pay, incentives, security, learning, "ownership" of work, cross-training, group skills, involvement in decision-making, and so on.

Classification by solution-finding approach.   In these formats, problems are not really differentiated. All are simply subsumed under a single method, usually a variant of the Research Approach. Some illustrations include the seven analysis tools of Total Quality Management, Management by Objectives, and the systems approach. These approaches all delve into the causes and components of a problem, whatever the label attached to them.

Classification by analytical technique.   This is a variant of classification by solution-finding approach. It admits that not all problems can be solved by the same technique but claims that problems can be categorized according to the specific technique *assumed* to solve them, such as linear programming, cost-benefit analysis, family counseling, statistical inferences, client-server networks, or work measurement.

Ackoff and Rivett categorized organizational problems by basic structures: queueing, inventory, allocation, scheduling and routing, replacement and maintenance, search, and competition.[11]

Classification by analogy.   Although similar to classification by problem type, classification by analogy is particularly susceptible to the errors in judgment that result from drawing false and misleading "parallels" between historical and current problem situations. In government and business, bad historical analogies make for bad policy.

As Harvard University historian Ernest May points out, most policy makers tend to use history badly. They seize upon the first analogy that comes to mind and then see only those facts that conform to their preconceived notions of the problem at hand.[12]

In personal life as well, we tend to view inherently distinct people and unique situations in terms of our previous experience with apparently (but never actually) similar people and situations. False analogies can blind us to the realities of our own time and circumstances.

Classification by the way people view the world.   Psychologist and designer Will McWhinney proposes four alternative realities—sensory, social, unitary, and mythic—according to which one different people use to view the world.

Sensory: The foundation of being is the physical reality—"that which we touch, smell, see—that which is sensed—is what is real. It presumes [a] natural environment that represent[s] the 'certain ways' of the world. . . . It is the espoused belief system of the educated American, certainly of natural scientists and, oddly, also of social scientists and psychologists."

Social: The objective world is the shared consensus among the perceptions and feelings of a population. "Social reality," says McWhinney, "is a humanistic view of mankind, an acceptance of different viewpoints, histories, [feelings, values] and moral codes as well as of the conflicts that such acceptances engender. In the extreme, a person who holds fully to this worldview would say, 'If it does not matter to someone, it does not exist.' "

Unitary: Roles are established, organizations and political states formed, actions authorized and forbidden, and dogma interpreted. It is the reality we associate with authoritarianism and with disciples. "It is the reality that underlies the processes by which human kind regulates itself, . . . the spirit and ritual, religion and law, mathematics and the theoretical sciences. In the pure extreme, we find the blissful world of romantic idylls [or] the world of . . . holocausts called down by Inquisitors to enforce the unique "truth" of religious and political movements."

Mythic: Personal experience and creation are indistinguishable, so that which exists does so because an individual person gives it meaning by force of will. "The 'mythic' is the creator of symbols, of ideas, unhindered by the limits of what already is present for persons of the other reality beliefs. [Such] people act as though each sees him- or herself as the only existing being. Certainly, the great leaders of the world—the charismatics, the painters and architects, the impresarios, the movie moguls, and the megalomaniacs—hold strongly to the mythic worldview."[13]

As these various categories and classifications demonstrate, most typologies focus on technique categories, previous solutions, current organizational activities, or abstract definitions. But do *effective* people actually think in terms of any of these typologies?

Now What?

The problems that "walk in" a manager's or anyone else's door seldom if ever present themselves in terms of such typologies. Instead, we suggest, they more likely present themselves in terms, often unstated, of the purposes that people are trying to achieve. Consequently, using any of the relatively esoteric problem typologies takes us down the wrong track at high speed, especially if we want to talk the language of real people who face and must solve real problems in the real world every day.

Indeed, there are so many ways of defining and classifying problems—none intrinsically wrong, yet all limiting—that the only way to not remain restrictive is to classify them according to the legitimate purposes that humans seek to achieve by finding a solution, irrespective of their worldview or reality perspective. Otherwise, we build walls against our ability to comprehend the holistic nature of these various, interrelated problems. Above all, the uniqueness of each problem.

It is thoroughly human, of course, to avoid confronting problems, to act as if our problems didn't exist. Particularly within organizations, Harvard School of Business professor and consultant Chris Argyris claims, managers and executives tend to avoid the embarrassment or threat that might result if they were to discuss their concerns openly. Moreover, with the best intentions, they tend to act as though they are *not* avoiding problems by indulging in what Argyris has recognized as *organizational* defensive routines. These work in many ways but are usually evidenced by rigid adherence to commonly accepted practices, including the traditional classification of problems and problem types.[14]

Thus, even when people and organizations overcome their tendency to avoid problems, they often classify problems—and thus their solutions—in preexisting, one-size-fits-all terms. One reason people have developed these various, limiting frameworks for classifying problems is that humans dislike the anxiety of the uncertain. Conversely, they very much like the sense of (false) security that comes with adhering to what they already know, whether "solutions" or techniques with which they have worked in the past.

The initial rationale for adopting existing solutions and techniques is that such classification saves time, energy, and effort. People assume they will come out ahead by not "reinventing the wheel" or having to learn different techniques every time. In fact, they end up spending more time and more money. In most cases, twice as much.

Remember, however, that focusing on the uniqueness of every problem situation is simply a way to *begin* solving your problem. It does not mean that, ultimately, you might not end up "importing" an existing solution or technique. Before you made that decision, however, you would know whether or not your chosen solution or technique was in fact appropriate to *your particular purposes*. In effect, then, problem classification always leads back to purposes.

With the notable exception of a purpose-based classification, all of the various schemes of problem classification noted above relate more closely to Conventional Thinking than to Full-Spectrum Thinking. All characteristically seek to quantify objects and experiences. For good and ill, quantification, measurement, classification, and objectification are the gifts of the Research Approach. Since it has worked spectacularly well in some cases, we now tend to apply it across the board.

Yet certainly, human beings made important advances prior to the advent of science. After all, technology first developed some 5,000 years ago. How did it develop? It was not based on random curiosity but on fundamental human purposes and needs.

Way back when one of our ancestors said, in effect: "You know, it's cold out here in the rain. What can I do to keep out of the rain?" Many animals, of course, apparently are content to sleep out in the rain. But the human being decided to stop shivering with cold and fear, to take shelter in a cave, and to fight the bear for possession.

Later, needing to move about in search of food, our ancestors sought a way to take their "cave" with them. Based on this need, they created and developed the idea of portable shelters. At first, these were probably no more than a stick and an animal skin. Over time, they discovered that a certain type of skin or one that had been treated in a certain way was less permeable than another and provided better, more effective shelter. Their temporary shelters were improved. As human civilization became agriculturally based, our ancestors came to build permanent shelters. The creative idea of "shelter"—whether portable or permanent—was constantly improved upon, developed, and refined. It is still being improved today. Indeed, much of human history can be viewed as a continual process of creating and restructuring products, solutions, and systems to achieve human purposes.

Naturally, prior to the development of science, people would also have used whatever approach to problem solving they had previously used successfully. For instance, how did people 5,000 years ago solve problems of creating and restructuring—building a house, improving a road? What led them to try?

Part of the answer is surely that they were looking for something to do. Another likely reason is that they noticed something unusual, something extraordinary, happen. They then asked themselves how they might benefit from that phenomenon. For example, how could they use the phenomenon of fire? The existence of wind? To what end?

Note that these fundamental reasons for trying to solve problems are purpose-based. Indeed, it seems that our early ancestors were more purpose-focused than not.

If these early humans built a house, for example, they were quite unlikely to make such an effort out of simple curiosity. Instead, they would first have asked themselves why they wanted to build a house, what the purpose of their activity was. Answer: "I want protection from the weather and from predators. I want to have a roof over my head, walls around me. I want to stay warm (or cool) and dry. I want to be safe."

For thousands of years, people have been developing ever more effective ways to achieve their purposes. Indeed, it seems that, as humans, we have an innate need to create and restructure systems. Evidently, creating and restructuring solutions is one of the basic purposeful activities in which we naturally engage.

From the dawn of the human race, we have perceived difficulties and shortcomings—dissatisfactions—that have led us to create and restructure. At the same time, though rather less so, it would seem, we have been curious. Why, we would wonder, does the sun always rise over there? Why does it set every day over there? In such innate curiosity lay the seeds of the Research Approach. After all, if you don't observe the sun a great deal and take note of your observations, you will probably never discover how or why or when the sun rises and sets. But the finding of such facts seems to be another human purpose.

All problem classifications that are not based upon human purposes have serious deficiencies. And the result is often ineffective solution finding.

First, few other proposed formats point to a specific way of seeking the most effective solution. What does it mean if a problem is characterized as "analogy" or "irrationality" or "emergent change" or "unitary" or "marketing"? Each then focuses on a single "correct" approach or solution. Yet the existence of many "correct" solutions suggests that exclusive reliance on any one of them may be risky. Specifically, it is likely to lead to one or more of the eight basic errors in problem solving: ineffective mental assumptions, ineffective approach, ineffective or "standard" people, inappropriate focus on the visible or wrong problem, inappropriate timing, ineffective control, inappropriate acceptance of an ineffective "solution," inappropriate rejection of a broader and more effective solution.

Second, formats based on analytical techniques lead to deterministic thinking and rigid definitions of problems. For instance, long lines at bus stops are subsumed under the rubric of a "queueing theory problem." The tendency is for the problem solver to reach for a technique rather than grapple with larger issues outside his or her specialty or issues too messy to quantify. The existence of analytic techniques may even create "made" problems, for example, attempts to define problems to fit the parameters of new computer systems. As a result, the possibility of working on the wrong problem increases dramatically.

Finally, classification by type tends to be based on physical and structural ("This is a product distribution logistics problem") or analogical ("This training problem is like educating ninth graders") similarities, rather than on purposes. Physical and structural categories engender little understanding of what to do about the actual problem, especially the people, purposes, and new technology for the uniqueness involved. Analogical similarities are constructed on the basis of an assumed direct mapping of "comparable" circumstances and consequences, which can never be correct. Also, these categories are based on existing problems, that is, they are constructed on the basis of hindsight. Particularly for problems of planning and design, hindsight is hardly the way to determine the type or nature of new problems and solutions.

These deficiencies in problem classification mandate a different perspective on problems. We believe that such a new perspective should meet the following criteria:

- Categories should minimally overlap but still encompass all the problems associated with all activities in which humans engage.

- Categories should, while identifying problems, focus on the purposes with which humans confront a situation rather than on the problems themselves. To do otherwise unnecessarily restricts the solution-finding space. Philosophers and psychologists have noted that a focus on *the problems* indicates that a society is ill and is "going downhill."

- Categories should produce a prescriptive understanding of what to do about the problem, that is, they should suggest a methodology for moving toward solution.

- Categories should enhance the probability of working on the right problem and developing creativity in solution finding.

The following classification organizes problems on the basis of human purposeful activities, that is, on the repertoire of needs leading to the behavior we exhibit day in and day out in the process of living. This classification emerges from the imperatives of the preceding criteria.

HUMAN PURPOSEFUL ACTIVITIES: THE MOST APPROPRIATE DEFINITION

Because everything comes back to purposes, the most effective way to define problems is in terms of the purposes humans seek to achieve. Every other way of classifying problems results in constructing artificial "silos," containment devices that limit our understanding of a problem and, therefore, the possibility of finding an effective solution. Whether the proposed classification refers to a particular path to change, a particular sector of a company or society, or a specific academic discipline, if it is not grounded in purposes, it will result in one or more solution errors. The key question to ask in defining a problem is always—and first of all—"What are we trying to accomplish?"

Philosopher Michel de Montaigne put it well: "The great and glorious masterpiece of man is to know how to live to purpose."[15]

Purpose implies aim or intention. Activities are the behaviors and action steps associated with aim or intention. A review of the vast literature concerning what historians, sociologists, anthropologists, and others say are the aims, intentions, mission, and primary concerns humans seek to accomplish prompts us to propose the following fundamental human purposeful activities. Values, beliefs, and goals related to each purposeful activity will be shown later.

The seven fundamental human purposeful activities are:

To assure self-preservation and survival of the species:
   Self-preservation

To operate and supervise—control the effectiveness of an existing "good" solution or system:
   Operate and supervise

To create or restructure a situation-specific solution or system:
  Plan and design

To develop generalizations:
  Research

To evaluate the performance of previous solutions or of other
  purposeful activities:
  Evaluate

To gain skills or acquire knowledge about existing information
  and generalizations:
  Learn

To engage in leisure:
  Leisure

Unlike other classifications by type, this one does not focus on an issue or object. For example, the need for food, as a problem, could be associated with all seven purposeful human activities. The types we propose enable you to identify whether food in a specific situation poses a problem of self-preservation, operation and supervision, planning and design, evaluation, learning, leisure, or research. At the same time, these problem types are not mutually exclusive: each may be involved with, and depend on, any other. For example, successful planning and design frequently requires, at various points in a project, re-search, evaluation, learning, and operation and supervision.

TWO ASPECTS OF ALL PROBLEMS: SUBSTANCE AND VALUES

Any problem or need has two separate aspects—a values aspect (the "concern" of the dictionary definition) and a substantive aspect. The values aspect of a problem includes the beliefs, desires, and goals implicit in human purposeful activities and those specific to a particular problem situation (or locus). The substantive aspect includes both the purposeful type of problem—operate and supervise, research, plan and design, learn, or evaluate—and the unique, specific problem situation (or locus). For instance, the operate and supervise purpose of preparing a meal needs to be achieved billions of times every day throughout the world, but the substantive problem is incomplete without reference to the specific locus (*your* kitchen).

While we originally identified seven human purposeful activities, we now refer mainly to only five. For the sake of simplicity, we have chosen to subsume two of the seven purposeful activities originally identified (self-preservation and leisure) within the five listed above.

For example, even though you may want to achieve the purpose "to engage in leisure," the purpose you may have could be to create or restructure (plan and design) your leisure or to operate and supervise your self-considered effective leisure "system," or to evaluate the effectiveness of your current leisure solutions, and so on.

The locus of a given problem is the particular "what, where, when, and who" unique to each problem situation.

Thus, the substantive aspect of a problem is broadly defined as the five purposeful activities. Criteria for determining which broad purposeful activity is being pursued (and the specific purposes to fit the locus) will be provided later. The locus is identified by the particular problem situation (organization, home, school, city department, etc.) being addressed. For example, the substantive aspect of a problem might be to design a pharmaceutical delivery system for hospital ABC.

The values aspect primarily concerns the doubt, uncertainty, perplexity, difficulty, or desire that most often is the motivation for addressing the substantive situation. The values aspect has three components—the societal, local, and personal beliefs (which we call values), the goals (which indicate the broad measures of success and effectiveness—cost, time, quality, satisfaction, and so on), and the objectives (which provide the specific "amounts" of the goals) that are sought by the effort made to work on the problem.

For example, the values of developing your career plan (a purposeful activity of planning and design) might be: attaining economic self-sufficiency, enhancing personal interests, experiencing tranquility, enhancing personal dignity, encouraging individual betterment, attaining a good quality of life, and maintaining physical and emotional health.

Your goals might be: to increase your income, increase the time spent with your family, decrease the time spent on searching for misplaced papers, improve specific job-related skills, maximize the caloric amount of foods you eat, minimize the number of sick days you take, maintain your house so that it remains saleable, improve your job satisfaction, and maximize the amount of your retirement money.

Your related objectives might then be: to obtain a 10 percent per year salary increase within two years, to take your family to one artistic event or athletic match per month by next April, to reduce by 50 pecent within six months the number of times you search for needed papers, to take one continuing education course per quarter, to find and follow the appropriate dietary balance of foods by January, to reduce the number of sick days taken to one per quarter beginning the first quarter of the year, to spend one day per month identifying and fixing items that need to be repaired or upgraded in your house, to reduce to no more than two days per month the times that you bring home "sad" stories from work.

Consider the positive benefits to actual problem solving that derive from classifying problems in the context of human purposeful activities:

- Defining the substantive aspect of a particular problem assures that an appropriate methodology will be used. For example, a particular situation may pose a problem of planning and design. If it is instead approached as a research problem, the end product is likely to be a series of "studies," not an operational solution. Strict attention to problem type and locus significantly reduces the possibility of erroneously finding the "perfect" solution to the wrong problem.

- A clear idea of a problem's locus centers the solution-finding effort on the specifics of each unique situation. Rather than a solution being transferred from another situation (for example, an evaluation of a procedure), each solution is tailored to specific needs, values, and resources. The abysmal failure of attempts to transfer American agricultural solutions to Third World countries underscores this point.

• Designating a problem's values aspect places solution-finding squarely in the context of human aspirations and needs and societal goals. This forestalls the unhappy tendency of professionals to become specialists with a limited sense of ethical responsibility, whereby it is too often assumed that problems will be defined simply to fit into available techniques and that solutions will reflect normative concerns. Swift's "modest proposal"—eat children to end both overpopulation and hunger—is clearly satirical, yet it evokes the specter of solutions that presume to ignore values.

THE SUBSTANTIVE ASPECT: HUMAN PURPOSES, LOCUS

Some further explanation of each purposeful activity will be based on the substantive and the values aspects of any problem.

Assure Self-Preservation and Survival of the Species

These are paramount purposes shared by humans and animals. Included are all life support systems: food, shelter, safety, and procreation. Studies with animals as well as humans suggest that love, belonging, and self-esteem are necessary to survival. Self-preservation may also depend on satisfaction of social and creative needs.

The scope and type of these activities vary with the dictates of history and environment. The civil rights and women's liberation movements can be considered in a very real sense to be self-preservation activities.

Yet each aspect of the purposeful activity of self-preservation may be translated almost immediately into one of the five fundamental purposeful activities, which is why we shall omit future reference to this purposeful activity. For example, to determine the source of food that others find (operate and supervise/control); to develop coping skills if homeless (learning), and so on.

Operate and Supervise an Existing "Good" Solution or System

Human capabilities enable us to change aspects of our environment. These changes then require operation and supervision to maintain their structure and function. Everyone engages in operation and supervision.

A father and mother operate and supervise a family, a student a study schedule, a mayor a city. The activities of operation and supervision, which is to say control, range from those of a janitor operating and supervising a building to a minister operating and supervising the religious system, to those of bureaucrats and business managers. Operation and supervision concerns the generally effective systems and solutions that people participate in routinely, expecting fairly standardized results (clean teeth, air travel, telephone, cook dinner). A society without such systems would be in chaos.

Ironically, this purposeful activity poses a real threat to our society: the exponential growth of bureaucracy. People operating bureaucracies often fail to understand the purpose of the system and even its larger purposes. Consequently, the system may be operating beautifully and simultaneously yet be counterproductive to the new (and often the original) purposes for which it was established.

For example, the bureaucracies of the finance and trade ministries in Japan were successful in developing policies for the purpose of attaining economic recovery (build industry and exports while levying high taxes on its citizens to hold down consumption) until the early 1980s. After that time, however, they were powerfully resistant to any new purposes and policies the country needed.

Create or Restructure a Situation-Specific Solution or System
Human history is the story of innovative solutions: plows, Roman aqueducts, the U.S. Constitution, computer systems. Throughout the ages, individuals with the gift of imagination have emerged.

Planning and design activities result in custom-made solutions, policies, and specifications that restructure existing systems or create new ones (the Constitution of the United States or the arrangement of your closet). As a purposeful activity, planning and design is concerned with inventing the specifics of how a particular locus ought to be arranged. Good planning and design develops those specifics to satisfy as much as possible the desires and values motivating the effort. They provide a format—a plan, a design, a set of solution specifications—that reflect the priorities and ways of using resources (time, people, materials, money) for the organization, group, or individual.

To plan and design is to imagine, specify, and implement new and restructured systems and solutions; to operate and supervise is to maintain them. The latter stresses standardization and routine, the former flexibility and innovation. Imagination and foresight are planning and design hallmarks. Planning and design provides informed recommendations about decisions affecting the future. This purposeful activity also encourages the support and buy-in of others to reach the outcomes and purposes being sought (a new product, an installed information system, your enrollment in a class identified in your career plan, the completed remodeling of your home, and so on).

Search for Generalizations
The desire for explanation, the urge to explore and discover, is universal. We want to know how the world was created, how it developed and brought forth humankind, how it will one day end. This boundless human curiosity flowered into science and other bodies of systematic thought. Frequently, the result of this activity is new knowledge in the form of laws and theories explaining the relationships among, and the characteristics of, phenomena and events. As philosopher of science Philip Kitcher describes it, science is an efficient way to investigate and determine "truths" about Nature.[16]

Pure research develops generalizations for their own sake; applied research meets the needs of other purposeful activities. There is a certain tension between those who seek truth for itself and those who believe, like Francis Bacon, that "knowledge is not to be sought for the pleasure of the mind . . . but for the benefit and use of life."[17]

Developing generalizations is not the exclusive domain of "intellectually pure" philosophers, scientists, and the myriad professionals engaged in research. Even the weekend gardener testing the relationship of certain types of fertilizer to lawn health is doing research.

The reliability and utility of generalizations vary with the phenomena where connections are sought. The physical and natural sciences produce the most reliable (although not always noncontroversial) generalizations, religion the least. Obviously, the importance of generalizations is not solely a function of "objective predictability."

Evaluate Performance of Previous Solutions or Other Purposeful Activities

How well did a solution work? Did it achieve its purpose? These are questions posed in an evaluation. The aim of evaluation or auditing is to provide information about performance, assure accountability, and lead to improvement. It occurs at all levels, at the level of the individual class session or the entire course you attend, of one individual patient or of total hospital care. Evaluation occurs in relationship to every other purposeful activity. For example, a board of directors' evaluation of capital expenditure paybacks and assessment of compliance with employment regulations occur in the process of operating a particular system. Or an evaluation of a pilot project is frequently an integral feature of planning and design.

Gain Skills or Acquire Knowledge

If everyone were forced to rediscover all knowledge and skills previously developed, civilization would be in sad shape. Learning is the purposeful activity by which knowledge and techniques are transmitted. Learning takes place in a variety of structured and unstructured situations. Its results vary from the development of analytic and predictive ability to the development of the capacity for synthesis, decision making, and insights. Successful accomplishment of other purposeful activities depends on people who know the appropriate generalizations and techniques.

Experience Leisure

Leisure provides relaxation or recreation. It represents demand-free time for self-determined activities and pleasures. Leisure ranges from doing absolutely nothing to highly structured endeavors often resembling "work." Many forms of leisure may actually be another purposeful activity. Painting, composing, and sculpting clearly involve planning and design. Leisure and the problems associated with it underscore the notion that problems are not merely the result of avoiding noxious stimuli (as is common to most psychological problem models), but are also a result of seeking pleasurable stimuli.

Secondary Purposeful Activities
The primary purposeful activities include a number of secondary ones, which are not exclusive to any single primary activity but occur frequently in all. Secondary purposeful activities include but are not limited to the following: make a decision (select a choice from among alternatives), maintain a standard of achievement, resolve a conflict, make a model of or abstract a phenomenon, develop creative ideas, establish priorities, practice and exercise, and motivate individual efforts.

The fundamental, primary purposeful activity sets the context for these secondary activities. You make a decision about what—operate and supervise, or plan and design a solution? You resolve a conflict about what—evaluation or learning? You develop creative ideas . . . about what? You model a situation . . . for what purpose? You establish priorities . . . for what reason? You practice a skill . . . to what end? You motivate people . . . to accomplish what purpose? The primary purposeful activities spell out the alternatives about which a decision is to be made, the characteristics of the phenomenon to be modeled, and the categories to be prioritized.

THE VALUES ASPECT: VALUES, GOALS, OBJECTIVES

Why does something become a problem? Why do humans seek to better the world and themselves? What does "better" actually mean? Where do human aspirations and ideals come from? Such questions are essentially unanswerable. But even if we cannot know the causes of human motivations and values, we can assess, albeit incompletely and inaccurately, their expression. What follows is a clarification of the values, goals, and objectives that form the "why" aspect of a problem. It should be noted that these values reflect a Western bias.

Contemporary theorists argue that values, ethics, and motivation stem from human instincts, wants, and desires for certainty and security. The nature of these "needs" has been explored by various authors including Abraham Maslow whose needs hierarchy is one of the best known. It delineates the multifaceted aspect of "needs" and acknowledges a wide variety of human behaviors.

The Maslow hierarchy of needs, from basic to highest levels, is (1) physiological existence, (2) security needs, (3) social and affiliative needs, (4) esteem and reputation, (5) autonomy and independence, and (6) self-actualization. Maslow initially suggested two other needs but did not rigidly include them: (7) the cognitive need to learn and understand, and (8) aesthetic needs. As a person's needs are met at one level, Maslow suggests, they are likely to seek the next.[18]

In discussing human motivations to take actions that better the human condition, it is helpful to define the word *better. Better* never reflects a single desire or need but can have many meanings. For example, a better understanding of rain (the search for generalizations concerning that natural phenomenon) means concern for accuracy, precision, completeness, level of water supply, impacts, and so forth. When the desire for "better" is directed toward some thing or situation, it can be expressed on three levels: as values, as goals, and as objectives. In the preceding example, "better" embraces *the values* of "learning for its own sake" and the desire to apply knowledge about rain to meet human needs.

Values are also beliefs, desired end states, societal and individual aspirations and desiderata. For example, safety, convenient schedules, and passengers' comfort are values in a city mass transit system. These values are then expressed in specific goals and objectives. *Goals* are the criteria or measurement categories for determining how well a particular value for a purposeful activity is achieved (accident rate, time between buses, rider complaints). *Objectives* are the performance levels or amount of a goal to be attained within specified time and cost limits (reduce accident rate by two percentage points in one year, maintain current 10 minutes between buses, reduce complaints by 50 percent in six months).

Only the desire for "better," as expressed in the values and measures of human purposeful activities, makes "a problem" of a particular phenomenon. An effective solution will reflect and deliver more values than were present when the "problem" was first recognized. Goals and objectives make values operational for a specific locus.

Recognizing the following values aspects of a problem has important implications for creating or restructuring solutions.

1. Developing clearly stated values, objectives, and goals in a specific situation clarifies decision making. Trade-offs can be shown and their impacts understood.

2. Understanding that the idea of values includes objectives and goals will move planning and design from vague "parenthood and apple pie" type statements toward specific criteria and measurable objectives render basic values operational.

3. Clarifying values enables those who participate in an effort to create or restructure solutions to understand one another better, thus reducing the disruptive potential of hidden agendas. It leads toward a collective sense of the purposes of a particular effort, significantly influencing both solution and implementation.

4. Acknowledging the values aspect precludes the stance of "objectivity" adopted by any planning and design expert. It incorporates subjectivity and human concerns, removes efforts to create or restructure solutions from the realm of narrow disciplines and techniques, and forces the solution measures to transcend the merely quantifiable and to incorporate critical subjective factors. Because planning and design solutions affect so many people, as well as the environment, it is crucial that solutions reflect larger social values.

THE RELATION OF PROBLEMS
TO SOCIETAL VALUES

Why do we strive to achieve the fundamental purposes of human beings? We are driven by our own needs and virtues as individuals, as well as by the needs and values of our societies, that is, the culture that surrounds us.

The values of a society reflect those of the individuals and groups composing it, both now and in the past. It is virtually impossible for people to agree on a single formulation of values, but the high degree of similarity among various value systems is striking. Most societal value systems reflect a belief in the values of the past; acceptance of the worth of economic and technological growth; expanding the knowledge base; the character qualities of fortitude, temperence, prudence, and justice to guide human actions; and the intrinsic importance of life.

The desire for "better" is the basis for these societal values. What does "better" entail in this context? One component is the desire to achieve greater effectiveness (economic self-sufficiency, personal survival, quality, productivity, an acceptable inflation rate, the accomplishment of larger purposes). Greater effectiveness is largely concerned with harnessing limited natural and human resources to do more. Although this could be a sufficient value in itself, inquiry into its result or larger value reveals another component of "better."

The result of seeking greater effectiveness is attainment of a higher quality of life. The values associated with such attainment are concerned primarily with the physical goals of life (stay healthy, achieve security and safety, physical comfort, domestic and foreign tranquility). Overemphasizing them engenders a materialistic attitude, which may be detrimental to other values. Again, a higher quality of life could be a sufficient value in itself. But doesn't it result in the enhancement of human dignity? Consider individual civil liberties, labor mobility, social well-being, community service, the incidence of divorce, the unemployment rate.

Even though human dignity could be a sufficient value in itself, what is the result of enhancing it? Its result is individual betterment. This value recognizes that people are equal, have the self-actualization capacity to grow and choose a unique path in life. Protection of individual rights and encouragement of individual development are the cornerstones, for example, of American democracy. America's dynamism is largely due to the values of social mobility, individual responsibility, and egalitarianism, above all, to the determination to invest in human beings, especially through the promotion of education.

As with the other values, the desire for individual betterment could be a sufficient value in itself. But if we ask "what is its result?" the answer seems to be to enable societies and individuals to achieve greater effectiveness. In effect, the relationship of these four societal value connotations of "better" can be expressed in a circular fashion. That is, the result of achieving greater effectiveness is attaining a higher quality of life, the result of which is enhancing human dignity, the result of which is developing individual betterment, the result of which is achieving greater effectiveness, the result of which is. . . .

Any one of the four fundamental societal values—individual betterment, effectiveness, quality of life, human dignity—could be selected as a starting point. But the continual search for a "better" condition in the other three values always leads back to the first.

This circularity means that concentration on any one value affects, intentionally or not, the entire set. All four are critical; one alone is insufficient. Overemphasis on one may be detrimental to the others. For example, in the Industrial Revolution, emphasis on greater effectiveness resulted, temporarily at least, in the diminishing of human dignity. Many external factors—economic conditions, social beliefs, technological breakthrough, and so on—can create this imbalance.

The circular values can further be portrayed with time as a third dimension. Assume that an upward improvement produces the spiral effect shown in Figure 5-1. Of course, a historically accurate spiral would show an unevenness of progress along the spiral. Trade-offs and imbalances among values are, historical facts. But the spiral suggests that both the definition and realization of values expand over time. The amount of a single value, human longevity for instance, is greater now than

150 years ago. "Progress" for any society may in fact be defined as a relatively smooth upward movement along the spiral.

The values aspect of a problem includes the values, goals, and objectives *unique* to its substantive aspect, that is, to each purposeful activity and each specific problem situation (or locus). A solution finder must understand that the values, goals, and objectives associated with each purposeful activity pursued and each specific problem situation will differ from those of any other situation. At the same time, note that what is a value in one situation may be a goal or objective in another.

For example, creating cultural opportunities may be the guiding value of a city repertory theater. But it is only one objective of a city council concerned with overall public health, safety, and welfare. And the city's values are only objectives from the perspective of the four basic societal values. The dividing lines among values, objectives, and goals are fuzzy. Most of the fuzziness disappears, however, when they are identified with reference to a specific purposeful activity for a specific locus.

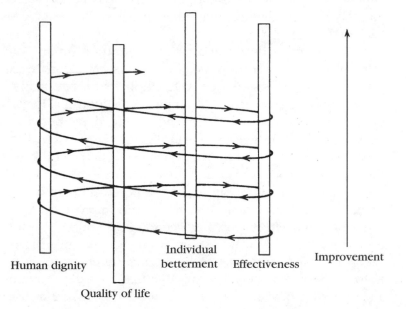

Figure 5-1.   The Spiral Nature of Societal Values.

FROM PROBLEMS TO PURPOSES: IDENTIFYING THE CORRECT PROBLEM

The single, most important reason to define problems in terms of purposes is that doing so will maximize the likelihood of identifying (and solving) the correct problem. Otherwise, as Paul Nutt suggests, analysis of a problem according to organizational categories tends to imply a certain type of solution. "For instance, morale problems imply a morale-type solution, cost problems a cost-type solution, and marketing problems a market-based solution. A solution is implied by the problem, compared to target processes that are open to any solution that has favorable performance."[19]

In practice, many people make statements that seem to define a given problem. For example: "We have to reduce waste." Or: "We have to increase sales." Or: "The loading dock is a mess." In fact, such statements may well miss the actual problem altogether. And by focusing attention and problem-solving efforts too narrowly, too soon, they limit the "solution space" available.

By contrast, when attention is paid to all five components of a problem (purposeful activity substance, locus, values, goals, objectives), and problems are defined in terms of (usually) one of the five purposeful human activities, the possible solutions to a given problem are both expanded and integrated into a successful solution.

This is one of the major reasons to avoid the use of medical metaphors in defining a problem or the way of thinking about solving it. Indiscriminate use of the medical metaphor ignores the insights gained by reviewing what human purposeful activity is involved. The approach followed by physicians to keep the "human body system" operating well (the purposeful activity of physicians) is not the best approach to create or restructure a system. Why? Because professionals in planning, design, and change do not deal with any system as fixed as the human body. Thus, to approach their tasks on the basis of medical metaphors is patently foolish. Advances in medical technology are in fact the results of creating and restructuring the *tools* that can help "operate and supervise" the human body system.

By constantly asking purposes, and expanding those purposes as far as possible, you learn what actually needs to be done to solve the problem at hand. As you expand your awareness of the purposes served in solving a given problem—its substantive aspect—you automatically expand your awareness of a problem's other four component parts—its locus, values, goals, and objectives. Ultimately, the solution you choose will prove both different and better than it would have if you had defined the problem in any other way.

THE UNIVERSAL PURPOSE:
TO CREATE OR RESTRUCTURE

Regardless of whether the human purposeful activity you want to accomplish is to develop a generalization, to maintain and operate a system, to learn, or to evaluate, each time you attempt one of those purposeful activities, you, in effect, create or restructure a system. Why? Because creating and restructuring is the most fundamental of all the human purposeful activities, the five problem types. As a result, it gives you the opportunity to determine what you need to accomplish, even when the actual problem is one of evaluation, of learning, of research, or of operation and supervision.

For example, you may confront what you assume is a research problem. But if you start collecting data right away, without first addressing the fundamental human purpose of your efforts, you may discover that you're pursuing a solution in the wrong way. Even if it is in fact a research problem you confront, you may choose the wrong method of data collection.

In the activity of creating or restructuring, you first examine the purposes of solving *any* problem. If the purpose of solving a problem, as you expand the purpose, proves to be to maintain and operate an effective system, then, at that point, you should go into the maintain and operate mode. But do so only after you have identified that particular human purposeful activity as the one you are pursuing, as what actually needs to be done.

For example, if you approach a problem-solving project assuming the problem you face is lack of productivity, then you're almost certain to come up with an answer that relates solely to productivity, such as automation. However, if you then ask the purpose of automation—not just what kinds of robots are available, but what purposes are served by the various robots available—you'll be better able to focus on the actual problem to be solved. The most important advantage of defining any problem in terms of purposes is that it helps you focus on what really needs to be done.

There's another reason to focus on purposes, to use the create/ restructure mode first, regardless of which human purposeful activity is under consideration. Theoretically, if not always in practice, one can *design the process* by which the other purposeful activities are undertaken.

THE UNIVERSAL ACTIVITY:
TO PLAN AND DESIGN

Plan and design is the label assigned to the purposeful activity of creating or restructuring a situation-specific solution. According to the *Oxford English Dictionary*, a plan is a scheme of action, a project—particularly, the way to carry out some proceeding. A plan proposes a method of action.

To plan, then, is to arrange something beforehand, to devise something to be done, some action to be carried out in the future. A plan is prompted by unsolved problems, unmet needs and aspirations, or existing systems requiring change or improvement. In this sense, to design is to form a plan or scheme of your work, to conceive and arrange in your mind, to contrive. To have in mind a design is to have in mind a purpose or intention; it is to mean a system or solution to serve your purpose, to fulfill your plan.

Professionals in the field tend to assume that "planning" and "design" are different activities. In point of fact, however, the two seek similar ends. What may differ among projects, rather than between the two concepts, is their scale, scope, complexity, specificity, and time horizons. Table 5-1 illustrates this overlapping relationship by placing some characteristics of planning and design efforts on a series of continua.

PROBLEMS AND SOLUTIONS IN CREATING AND RESTRUCTURING

Anything that the human mind can identify as needing a new or restructured situation-specific solution becomes the source or locus of a substantive planning and design problem. "Anything" can be physical, social, organizational, conceptual, local, or global in nature. "Needing" is, of course, in the eyes of the beholder. Poisonous snakes, for example, pose a safety problem in Dallas, but are the solution to the rat problem in Malaysia.

Problems can vary in size and scope, ranging from the need for a national health policy to the need for a "better mousetrap." The emerging awareness that preparing for the future will by necessity be interdisciplinary and even global in nature has significantly expanded the sources and loci of planning and design problems.

For example, 50 years ago, urban planners could control land use at the city level. Today, however, diminishing resources and urban sprawl require a county, regional, and national focus.

Values and objectives associated with bettering the human condition also foster "needs" and thus efforts to plan and design. Dislike of hard work and a desire for leisure, for instance, have generated literally thousands of "labor-saving" devices created or restructured over many centuries.

There are as many planning and design solutions as there are problems. They vary in resource commitment, complexity, time horizons and can be of any size and scope. (Size and scope refer to the number of components and people required.) National health insurance is clearly larger in size and scope than a design for a patient healthcare unit in a hospital. Resource commitments concern the amounts of money, time, person-hours, and types of personnel a solution requires. Complexity and time horizons vary with the problem's purposes, scale, scope, and implementation environment. For example, a company's product development plan may have a three- or

Table 5-1. Frequently Used Descriptions of Planning and Design*

Planning	Design
Larger Scope	Smaller Scope
Open-ended	Specific
Low potential to model the solution accurately	High potential to model the solution accurately
Continuing process over time	Limited to a short time period
Ends are variable	Ends are given
Abstract/social	Physical/individual
Program-oriented	Project-oriented
Deals with future needs	Deals with immediate needs
Mixed technical and non-technical	Technical
Longer time horizon (> 3 years)	Shorter time horizon (< 3 years)
Time- and process-oriented	Space- and artifact-oriented
Innovative	Allocative
Larger number of people affected	Smaller number of people affected
Higher risk associated with decisions	Lower risk associated with with decisions
Policy and strategic organizational levels	Tactical and operational organizational levels
Fewer well-defined outcomes	More well-defined outcomes

*Each line of description respresents the two opposite perspectives on a continuum.

four-year time horizon. An actual product program may be obsolete in two years.

All of these factors reflect the level at which an effort to plan and design is carried out. These levels may be geographical—home, neighborhood, state, region, nation, the world.

More commonly, however, these levels are described as those of policies, strategies, tactics, and operations. Policies are clearly larger in size and scope than tactics. Table 5-2 suggests the characteristics of each level.

GOALS IN CREATING AND RESTRUCTURING SYSTEMS AND SOLUTIONS

The *sine qua non* of successful efforts to plan and design is to "better" the four values that all human beings and most societies seek: individual betterment, effectiveness, quality of life, and human dignity. A variety of additional planning and design values can be summarized in terms of the following three goals:

The first goal of creating or restructuring systems and solutions is *to maximize the effectiveness of recommended solutions.* There are many definitions of what characterizes an effective solution, ranging from Plato's cardinal virtues of comprehensiveness, economy, practicality, and ethicality to "shared values and flexibility." A more contemporary definition might include the ideas of innovation, breakthrough, and creativity. Other descriptions frequently encountered are reliability, adaptability, environmental and social soundness, a pluralistic element, client or customer satisfaction, high benefit/cost ratio, efficiency, and simplicity.

Indeed, this first goal seeks to achieve the largest amount of "effectiveness" possible from the effort to plan and design. In Chapter 9, we will review the results of many efforts in solution-finding projects using Conventional Thinking and compare these to projects that instead addressed a problem by means of Full-Spectrum Thinking.

The second goal of creating or restructuring systems and solutions is *to maximize the likelihood of implemented solutions.* Getting results in the real world is basic to the effort to plan and design. Failure to implement the recommended solutions, however brilliant they may be, is evidence that something went wrong in the process of creating or restructuring. Truly effective solutions are the product of the *quality of solution × implementation.* Even if the solution quality is 100, non-

Table 5-2. Characteristics of Different Levels of Planning and Design (P&D)

Level	Characteristics
Policy	Statements of purposes and objectives, guidelines for specific actions and plans at other levels (5 to 7)*
Strategical	Broad plans or courses of action that represent a means of accomplishing a particular purpose within the policy guidelines (3 to 5)*
Tactical	Specific plans or designs that are usually the implementation, transition, and intercommunication links between strategic plans and operational designs (1 to 3)*
Operational	Detailed design that prescribe specific actions of specific people at specific points in time (0 to 1)*

*Relative time spans of discretion. A company board of directors may do P&D on a basis of 5 to 7 years, top management 3 to 5 years, middle management 1 to 3 years, and first-line people 0 to 1 years. What the board considers operational P&D, the first-line supervisor will consider policies of 5 to 7 months, the foreman 3 to 5 months, the lead person 1 to 3 months, and the worker 0 to 1 months. A homemaker may consider food policies on a 5- to 7-week basis, the family shopping trip on a 3- to 5-week basis, the fill-in shopping 1 to 3 weeks, and daily meal schedule 0 to 1 week.

implementation (zero) produces a zero measure of solution effectiveness.

The third goal of creating or restructuring systems and solutions is *to maximize the effectiveness of the resources used to plan and design.* With unlimited amounts of time, people, and money, many problems might be solved. But it is highly unlikely that any organization (family, company, government agency) would or could commit to vast expenditures. Limits on time, people, and money imposed by the real world demand maximizing the synergy, effectiveness, and efficiency of efforts to plan and design—that is, increasing the productivity of thinking (shorten lead times from the beginning of a plan and design project to the availability of the product or service outcome).

DIFFERENT APPROACHES FOR DIFFERENT PURPOSES

Achieving different purposes obviously requires different approaches. For example, the attempt to define different types of problems, as we have in this chapter, seeks to achieve the human purposeful activity of *developing generalizations*. Note that the approach we used to achieve that purpose led us, in this chapter, to follow the Research Approach—identify the problem, gather data about phenomena, analyze the data, and so forth.

If different types of problems are best defined and classified in terms of the five purposeful human activities, it becomes evident that solving problems requires more than simply one conventional approach. Universal application of the limited Research Approach is not only insufficient; it is counterproductive. What is required then is a new paradigm of thinking, one that *includes but is not limited to* the Research Approach.

Next, we will explain the background and results of various investigations into thinking. You will see that, to achieve the most effective results, you must tailor the way that you think in solving a problem to the specific type of human purposeful activity you are pursuing. Knowing the type of problem you confront and how best to address that type of problem will enable you to become an effective, multi-thinking solution-finder.

NOTES

1. John Dewey, *Problems of Men,* (New York: Philosophical Library, 1946).

2. G. A. Davis, *Psychology of Problem Solving: Theory and Practice* (New York: Basic Books, 1973).

3. Edward deBono, *Lateral Thinking: Creativity Step by Step* (New York: Harper & Row, 1970).

4. "Outlook Report: 1985," *The Futurist,* November–December, 1984.

5. Tomo Sugiyama, *The Improvement Book: Creating the Problem-Free Workplace* (Cambridge, MA: Productivity Press, 1991).

6. Theodore Levitt, *Thinking About Management* (New York: The Free Press/Macmillan, 1991).

7. Rosabeth Moss Kanter, Barry Stein, and Todd Jick, *The Challenge of Organizational Change: How People Experience It and Manage It,* (New York: The Free Press/Macmillan, 1992).

8. Gerald Smith, "Towards a Heuristic Theory of Problem Structuring," *Management Science,* Vol. 34, 1988, pp. 1489-1506.

9. Gerald Nadler, *The Planning and Design Approach,* (New York: John Wiley and Sons, 1981).

10. N. R. F. Maier and L. R. Hoffman, "Types of Problems Confronting Managers," *Personnel Psychology,* Vol. 17, 1964, pp. 261-269.

11. R. L. Ackoff and B. H. P. Rivett, *A Manager's Guide To Operations Research,* (New York: John Wiley and Sons, 1963).

12. Ernest May, *Lessons of the Past: The Use and Misuse of History in American Foreign Policy* (New York: Oxford University Press, 1972) cited by Janny Scott, "Patrols by 'History Police' Urged," (*Los Angeles Times,* April 20, 1993).

13. Will McWhinney, *Paths of Change: Strategic Choices for Organizations and Society* (Newbury Park, CA: Sage, 1992).

14. Chris Argyris, "Strategy Implementation: An Experience in Learning," *Organizational Dynamics,* Vol. 18, No. 2, (Autumn, 1989) pp. 5-15.

15. Michel de Montaigne, *Essays* (New York: Penguin, 1958).

16. Philip Kitcher, *The Advancement of Science: Science Without Legend, Objectivity Without Illusions* (New York: Oxford University Press, 1993).

17. Francis Bacon, *The Physical and Metaphysical Works of Lord Bacon,* including The Advancement of Learning *and* Novum Organum (St. Clair Shores, MI: Scholarly Press/Regent, 1976).

18. Abraham Maslow, *Toward a Psychology of Being,* (Princeton, NJ: VanNorstrand, 1962).

19. Paul C. Nutt, *Managing Planned Change* (New York: MacMillan, 1992), p. 122.

Chapter 6

Investigating Thinking

*I*f we are to change our way of thinking, our fundamental assumptions about creating or restructuring solutions
and solving problems, we must begin at the source of all
thought: the human brain.

Some 2,500 years ago, Aristotle believed that the main
purpose of the brain was to cool the blood. It was clear to him
that the heart was "the source of the sensitive soul."[1] Today, we
know somewhat better.

Particularly over the last 20 years or so, significant
progress has been made in our understanding of the brain and
how it functions. And yet, the truly remarkable fact is that, despite years of study, despite all that we have come to learn
about the brain itself, we know relatively little about the human
mind and its most basic artifact: the process of thinking that
transpires inside the brain.

This book does not seek to explain the biological operations involved in thinking. Such matters are not essential to our
enquiry and, in any case, lie beyond our expertise.

Let us simply state then that, based on our reading of the
literature, we consider the human brain far more a biological
entity than a machine. Although myriad biochemical reactions
certainly do occur in the brain, and these reactions are essential
to thinking processes, we believe the brain is not merely a collection of such reactions. It can be understood and appreci-

ated, even in a limited fashion, only by means of a holistic view, one that surpasses the strictly mechanistic.

THE HUMAN BRAIN IS NOT A MACHINE

We also doubt the mind can be replicated in a computer. Indeed, this perspective is to some extent supported by even so articulate and influential an advocate of the computer model of the brain as Daniel Dennett, director of the Center for Cognitive Studies at Tufts University. Dennett, who has spent some 30 years studying thinking, maintains that, despite the extent to which the brain may be considered to resemble a machine, despite the validity and virtues of the computer model—and despite the $100,000 prize offered—no computer now existing or likely to exist in the foreseeable future can pass the so-called Turing Test, one that demands fooling a panel of judges into thinking a computer is actually human.[2]

Unlike the human mind, the so-called expert systems that attempt to create "artificial intelligence" in the form of a "thinking machine" computer have proven unable to cope well with novelty.[3] A computer may be programmed to solve rule-based puzzles, such as chess, but is not even remotely close to being programmed for relationship and context games, such as crossword puzzles, let alone real-life decision making, which depends on all the senses and emotions.

In our view, although the biological and chemical interaction between brain synapses and neurons is certainly essential to thinking, it is by no means the whole of thinking, nor does it accurately and fully describe the human thinking process. Context matters. The nature of the task matters. The person's life experience and learning matter.

Over the next century, biochemical research will certainly find many new "truths" about what happens during the thinking process. In the present and near future, however, it will not be of much (if any) help in describing actual thinking to create or restructure solutions.

Thinking about Thinking

Just as it is beyond the scope of this book to address the biological and neurological aspects of thinking, neither will we try to define the mind or that remarkably elusive phenomenon known as consciousness, much less to "solve" the age-old problem that is at the base of human psychology. Instead, we offer here an eclectic overview—by no means exhaustive but, we trust, comprehensive—of what others have thought about thinking.

The new paradigm of thinking that we believe this overview supports will be presented in Chapters Seven and Eight. It consists of seven principles or fundamental assumptions directly related to a specific practical process that produces significant improvements in creating or restructuring solutions. We will explain how to achieve a productive integration of the various modes of thinking that others recommend generically in this chapter.

We begin with perhaps the two most seminal thinkers and most influential modern perspectives on the subject, both of which are rooted in the Western, Judeo-Christian tradition of Europe, approximately 100 years ago, at the turn of the twentieth century.

CLASSICAL MODELS

Sigmund Freud, the progenitor of psychoanalysis, proposed that two distinct patterns of thinking exist. The first, which he called "primary process" thinking, arises from the frustration of the drive brought about by the absence of the mother. Swedish psychoanalyst Eva Basche-Kahre explains that this sort of thinking arises in infancy, "when the child hallucinates the satisfaction of his desire, that is, the presence of the mother. Out of this first representation, primary process thinking develops."[4]

The second pattern of thinking Freud identified, "secondary process" thinking, he defined as the language of conscious and preconscious thinking. According to Basche-Kahre, "it is characterized by logic, concepts of time and space, and by verbal representation." This is the sort of thinking that is generally considered self-evident in normal adults.[5]

Over time, Basche-Kahre herself and many others have challenged and amplified Freud's perspective, both to refine its assertions and to posit the existence of other patterns of thought.

Chief among these was Freud's one-time disciple, Carl Jung, who proposed a wholly different perspective on thinking, based on his theory of personality types. In 1923, Jung suggested that four psychological functions—sensing, intuition, thinking, and feeling—comprise the basic attitudes that affect conscious behavior.

According to Jung, people develop dominant preferences for certain types of data in their thinking, preferences for either sensation or intuition. Sensation-dominant people prefer precise, specific data; they see themselves as realists concerned with immediate problems. In contrast, intuition-dominant people seek holistic information that describes possibilities; their decisions use more general data.

Jung also found two dominant ways that people reach decisions: by thinking or by feeling. Thinking-dominant people emphasize logic and formal modes of reasoning; they generalize and make abstractions. Feeling-dominant people form personal value judgments; they explain things in human terms and emphasize affective and personal processes in making decisions.

On the basis of the two ways people obtain data and the two ways in which they evaluate data, Jung defined four personality types: (1) Sensing-Thinking; (2) Intuition-Thinking; (3) Sensing-Feeling; and (4) Intuition-Feeling. In perceiving and judging, many people exhibit all four personality types at different times. Most people, however, have a dominant, preferred style. This is the style that they use more often than the others, across a variety of situations, particularly in situations that are fluid and not firmly structured.

Sensing-Thinking types stress systematic decision-making and hard data. They try to establish order, control, and certainty. They focus on tasks and structured information. They take fewer risks than other types.

Intuition-Thinking types tend to ignore specific, detailed information. They prefer to study patterns in data. Their thought takes bolder leaps into the unknown. They emphasize longer-range plans and new possibilities.

Sensing-Feeling types stress harmony, personal communication, and other people's opinions. Facts about people are more important than facts about things. They focus on short-term problems, with human implications.

Intuition-Feeling types rely on their own judgment and experience, often portraying personal views as facts. They prefer holistic, intuitive perceptions over rules in decision-making. They focus on broad themes and long-term goals.[6]

From Jung's classic treatise, *Psychological Types,* evolved the Myers-Briggs Type Indicator (MBTI), the test used to measure one's problem-solving style. According to Myers and Briggs, those who are primarily sensing personality types tend to be patient, practical, realistic, and good with facts and details. Those who are primarily intuitive types tend to be impatient, oriented toward theories and ideas, creative, and holistic. The Myers-Briggs test suggests that sensing types account for about 75 percent of the U.S. population; intuitive types about 25 percent.[7]

MODERN CONCEPTUAL PERSPECTIVES

As might be expected, the exponential growth in research in many cognitive sciences—psychology, sociology, anthropology, learning, psychotherapy—has produced a variety of models of thinking. We mention many of them, pausing to expand on only a few, as they appear to be factors to consider in the Full-Spectrum Thinking synthesis presented in Parts III and IV.

- Attempting to explain human consciousness, Daniel Dennett proposes the existence of what he calls a "Joycean machine," a mental operating system that controls the mind much like computer-operating programs such as Windows or MS-DOS control computer hardware. This operating software, says Dennett, is not innate to human beings. It is an accretion of learned behaviors developed for recruiting teams of highly specialized, narrowly task-focused "facts" or data—all utterly dependent on one another—to deal with deliberative processes that the brain is otherwise ill-equipped to handle. Dennett proposes that it is thanks to this mental software that we can not only think, but reflect on our own thinking.[8]

- T. Murakami and T. Nishiwaki of Japan's Nomura Research Institute relate the work of the outstanding early cognitive psychologist J. P. Guilford. "Placing memory at the core of thought," they explain, "Guilford distinguishes two mnemonic segments, one being the reservoir of concentrated (logical) knowledge, and the other, of diffuse (empirical) knowledge. In addition, he links these respective segments to the concentrated [recognize the problem, commit the problem to memory with related problems] and diffuse [free consideration of the problem] operations. . . ."[9]

According to Guilford, concentrated thought is exemplified by the thinking typically used in numerical calculation. Diffuse thought is more creative; it includes the kind of thought that generates ideas for new product development.

- Murakami and Nishiwaki also note the work of Japanese mathematician Heisuke Hironaka, whose own research experience has led him to propose the concept of "variable thought" as a key factor in creativity. Hironaka also distinguishes between needs and wants. He defines "need" as existing in a certain time and place, dictated by external circumstances, and based on past experience, knowledge, and analysis of the present. "Want," however, is essentially removed from time and place; it is dictated by the individual's sentiments or aspirations for the future. Consequently, Hironaka interprets the "necessity" in Edison's famous phrase, "Necessity is the mother of invention," as referring more to wants than to needs.[10]

- On the basis of a 25-year longitudinal study of Massachusetts Institute of Technology students, psychiatry professor Benson Snyder concluded that two distinct modes of thinking exist. He identifies these as "numeracy" (Mode One) and "literacy" (Mode Two), the two ways of thinking most often learned in formal educational contexts, which may sustain one or the other of these modes of thought, seldom both.[11]

  Snyder first determined which students used which model(s) as MIT undergraduates. The early preference among more than two-thirds of the subjects—a preference reinforced by both the formal and the informal curriculum on that campus during the early 1960s—was to practice Mode One thinking.

Some 20 years later, however, he found that those former students who were most successful and effective had come to develop and consciously employ both modes of thinking, which they now viewed as complementary, in both their personal and professional lives. Both modes of thinking had become "essential to their efforts to understand and deal with a variety of technical and human concerns."[12]

• Stanford University educational psychologist James G. Greeno notes that research on general thinking abilities—productive, higher order, critical, and creative thinking—has progressed slowly compared with the rapid progress made in the study of cognitive structures and procedures. If we are to make significant progress toward an adequate understanding of thinking and creativity, says Greeno, we should significantly alter the "framing assumptions" with which research in the field of thinking has been conducted.

Greeno proposes the following three new assumptions:

Situated Cognition. Thinking is situated in physical and social contexts. Cognition, including thinking, knowing, and learning, can be considered as a relation involving an agent in a situation, rather than as an activity in an individual's mind.

Personal and Social Epistemologies. Thinking and learning are situated in contexts of beliefs and understandings about cognition that differ between individuals and social groups, and fundamental properties of thinking and learning are determined by these contexts.

Conceptual Competence. Children have strong potential capabilities for cognitive growth that enable complex and subtle processes of construction of knowledge and thinking skills. Thinking, learning, and cognitive growth are activities in which children elaborate and reorganize their knowledge and understanding, rather than simply applying and acquiring cognitive structures and procedures.

If we think about thinking in these [new] terms, we will probably ask different questions about thinking and look for different kinds of phenomena. A theory of thinking, in these terms, would view it as activity in physical and social contexts and would consider the individual's intuitive conceptual understanding and beliefs about knowledge, learning, and intelligence as important background factors for thinking activity.[13]

University of Amsterdam social scientists Jacobijn Sandberg and Bob Wielinga further interpret Greeno's perspective: "Knowledge evolves continually as it is being used. Indeed, there is ample evidence that memory is reconstructive. The central point is that—there being no 'fixed,' internal representations—knowledge is fluid. Learning goes on all the time; learning entails creating new representations in speaking and acting and is part of everyday life. Knowledge can never be simply transferred, because it does not exist in transferable form."[14]

- Eva Basche-Kahre has adapted and expanded Freud's thinking patterns—primary and secondary—from two to four. Based on her clinical studies, Basche-Kahre has been able to delineate four "clearly distinguishable" patterns of thinking, which she has found helpful in conceptualizing what occurs in the analytic process. Basche-Kahre calls these patterns (1) chaotic functioning, (2) operational thinking, (3) emotional sensorimotor thinking, and (4) primary process thinking. She suggests that what Freud called adult secondary process thinking develops through integration of the four patterns she has identified.[15]

- A fundamental premise of most research in cognitive psychology has been that cognition can be meaningfully investigated in the laboratory by simulating critical aspects of the phenomenon in question. Increasingly, however, some researchers, the proponents of "everyday cognition," maintain that research results obtained from sterile, artificial, and contrived laboratory situations may not generalize to less constrained, more natural environments.

  These researchers include Leonard Poon, David Rubin, and Barbara Wilson, who believe that cognitive functioning in natural settings is likely to involve processes that differ, either quantitatively or qualitatively, from those that occur in psychological laboratories. The subject's level of motivation, prior experience, relevant knowledge, and personal goals are a major cause of the differences.[16]

• In 1967, P. M. Fitts and M. I. Posner outlined three stages of skill developed through experience along a continuous learning curve. The first phase, called "cognitive," occurs when active attention to all cues and significant reasoning is required. The second stage, they called "associative." In this stage, errors are eliminated and elements of behavior are joined together to develop procedures. The third stage, called "autonomous," results in highly automated procedures.[17]

In 1978, D. E. Rumelhart and D. A. Norman,[18] and, in 1982, J .R. Anderson[19] extended the last phase identified by Fitts and Posner. They included a "tuning" function, in which the automated procedures are made more general or more specific for increasingly targeted and precise application in various circumstances.

In 1986, J. Rasmussen also identified three levels of cognitive behavior, which coincide with those of Fitts and Posner. Rasmussen defined these levels as (1) skill-based activity, which is characterized by smooth, autonomous functions; (2) rule-based activity, where procedures are consciously controlled by a rule; and (3) knowledge-based activity, which occurs in unfamiliar domains, when rules or procedures cannot be recalled.[20]

• Jonathan King, associate professor of management at Oregon State University, relates Richard Bernstein's "three faces of thinking." According to Bernstein, "the obsession with transforming social studies into natural sciences obscures, distorts, and suppresses the legitimacy of issues vital for theorizing about political and social life." King notes that Bernstein argues that adequate theories of human endeavor must have empirical, interpretive, and evaluative dimensions.

"We understand the empirical face of thinking well enough," writes King, "for we have developed empirical methods [read: Research Approach] for over two hundred years. We do not have comparable understanding of the interpretive and evaluative faces of thinking, yet it is precisely with these that the humanities make a difference."[21]

- Professors of business management Usha Haley and Stephen Stumpf point out that "theorists often adopt either prescriptive or descriptive approaches toward managerial decision processes. Prescriptive approaches assume that managers can make optimal choices; they emphasize techniques for information collection, alternative generation, and alternative evaluation. Descriptive approaches note that managers rarely make optimal choices; actual decisions flow from cognitive limitations, political processes, routines and environmental constraints. Both these approaches sidestep subjective differences in decision-making."[22] Haley and Stumpf conclude that management decisions are in fact more complex and that different managers seem to use different, distinctive rules-of-thumb to gather data and to generate and evaluate alternatives.

- With regard to another context, Robert Glass, whose company consults and educates concerning software engineering, relates the results of investigations conducted by computer software researchers Bill Curtis and Elliot Soloway. According to Glass, after examining the thought processes of software designers who were interviewed during the process of design, the researchers concluded that the essence of that form of thinking called "design" consists of four discernible mental processes or phenomena: (a) constructing a mental model of a proposed solution to the problem; (b) mentally executing the model—in essence, running a simulation of it—to see if it solved the problem; (c) finding that it did not solve the problem, usually because the model was too simple; playing back the inadequate model to compare it with those parts of the problem to see where it failed; and then enhancing the model in those areas; and (d) repeating the three steps until they had a model that appeared to solve the problem.

"[It is] a mental process—a very rapid, iterative process—of fast trial and error. The mind forms a solution to the problem, all the while knowing that it will be inadequate, because the mind is not yet able to fully grasp all the facets of the problem.

"The essence of design, then," Glass concludes, "is rapid mental modeling and simulation. A key factor in design is the ability to propose solutions and allow them to fail."[23]

- "Science and objective thinking are unnatural activities [because] the mind wasn't designed to study physics" is the presumably controversial claim of Northwestern University physicist Alan Cromer. He argues that math and science thinking is abnormal, rather than a natural development as claimed by psychologist Jean Piaget.

    "Our minds," Cromer contends, "make us believe we are intuitively connected to what we observe as an explanation for the world. That is why people thought the Earth was flat for so many centuries. Thinking that there is a reality beyond oneself requires abandonment of the arrogant belief that each of us knows the world interrelationships."[24] Western society alone developed the logical positivism and rationality of the Research Approach. Many great civilizations flowered without it, although they did develop "hard" technologies—bronze, gunpowder, sculpture, paper, etc.—which did not require abstract thinking.

- The effects of information on decision-making, particularly in businesses and other organizations, and the subsequent impact on performance have been analyzed extensively. This analysis has evolved considerably and embraced at least three distinct perspectives in the course of its development. As enumerated by business and management scholars Rashi Glazer, Joel Steckel, and Russell Winer, these perspectives include (1) the traditional rational economic view, in which individuals are seen as *perfect information processors,* for whom additional information is always of value; (2) the bounded rationality perspective, in which individuals are seen as *limited information processors,* for whom additional information may be unnecessary; and (3) the recent emphasis on cognitive errors and biases, according to which individuals are seen as *fallible information processors,* for whom additional information may be harmful if it leads to mistakes in judgment.[25]

Studies indicate that this third category is correct. Often ignoring pertinent factors, effective people focus on those aspects of a decision model most clearly addressed by the information. This tendency leads to sub-optimal answers even as the decision process seems "locally rational."

• Edward DeBono has devised a scheme of thinking that proposes six categories, based in part on the emotions at play in each type of thought. To each of these proposed types, DeBono assigns an imaginary colored hat, which he suggests can be worn or removed at will. DeBono's Six-Hats theory proposes the color white for thinking based on objective information, red for thinking based on hunches and intuition, black for cautionary "logical negatives" (difficulties and dangers), yellow for "logical-positive" thoughts (benefits and savings), green for creativity, and blue for an objective overview of which hat to wear when.

The Six-Hats theory, DeBono claims, encourages groups of people to think together in parallel, not at cross purposes, about a new idea. The approach is reputed to overcome the predictable gridlock that occurs between eternal optimists and perpetual naysayers.[26]

At this point, we are compelled to note that the question of *how* to think about each of the various types of thinking DeBono identifies is critical. Even given DeBono's blue hat, the supposedly objective overview, which "hat" to wear in relation to which purposeful human activity remains unclear. Moreover, since each human being is unique, "objective" reality can seldom if ever be precisely gauged.

• Much like the psychiatrist Snyder, Peter Elbow, director of Writing Programs at the State University of New York at Stony Brook, proposes two types of thinking: "first order," which is intuitive, creative, and free; and "second order," which is conscious, directed, and controlled. Each type offers characteristic strengths and weaknesses, and both are essential to powerful writing. In this sense, says Elbow, to teach writing is to teach thinking.[27]

Elbow notes: "Advocates of reason and logic tend to criticize all relaxations of critical vigilance. If we would see clearly the truth about thinking and writing," he asserts, "we would see that the situation is not either/or, it's both/ and. . . . It's a matter of learning to work on opposites one at a time in a spirit of mutual reinforcement, rather than in a spirit of fearful combat."[28]

MODES OF THINKING

Clearly, almost since the earliest recorded history, a wide variety of thinkers, in a wide variety of disciplines, have posited the existence of a variety of thinking modes. Too often, these thinkers have tended to present the modes of thinking they identify as contradictory pairs. In our view, such a presentation is at best insufficient. Like almost everything else, thinking is not an either/or activity. To present alternative modes in pairs, as if passengers on Noah's Ark, is a flawed concept, far too simplistic and limiting.

Here are 20 different modes of thinking identified by various researchers, each followed by a brief précis of its defining characteristics. We suggest that the existence of these different modes of thinking implies that different problems must be approached in different ways.

Analysis   Analysis dissects a whole into its component parts. It seeks to discover the characteristics of those parts and their relationship to each other and to the whole.[29] The analytic approach is microscopic.[30] It is the basis of the Research Approach.

Synthesis   Synthesis puts together parts into a whole. The purpose of synthesis is to achieve a construct that satisfies a goal.[31] Synthesis is the mode of thinking that is the kernel of the process of design. In this sense, it is reasoning that proceeds from statements concerning the purpose of a new artifact to statements about its form and use.[32] Whereas analysis can be an enemy of vision, synthesis is supposed to be its ally.

Holistic   Holistic thinking takes the position that even if each part is perfect, the whole may not be perfect.[33] Holistic thinking is based on the following assumptions: (1) The whole is more than the sum of the parts; (2) The whole determines the nature of the parts; (3) The parts cannot be understood if considered in isolation from the whole; (4) The parts are dynamically interrelated or interdependent.[34]

Systems   General Systems Theory, an alternative to the analytical-mechanical conceptual schemes, arose in response to the need to investigate and understand living, open systems. It urges people to "look at all factors" or perspectives; but it still tends toward the dissection and decomposition of Conventional Thinking. Systems thinking is closely allied with holistic thinking.[35]

Dialectical   Dialectical thinking evolves from an established thesis to an antithesis and thence, if successful, to a resolving synthesis. The synthesis can be viewed as a solution to a problem or merely a resolving stage in an unending cycle of dialectical evolution. The dialectic begins with the awareness of a potential split, a denial of the established convention. It assumes polarity, a conflict between two defined positions. It is undertaken to settle a dispute.[36]

Integrative   Integrative thinking frames differences and problems so that practitioners and group participants focus on what is to be gained, rather than what is to be lost, by following a particular path of action. It further emphasizes that the identified gains can be accomplished only by working together.[37]

Heuristic   Heuristics are intuitive responses, based on past experience. They are the "various learned shortcuts"[38] that humans tend to apply in stressful or complex decision-making situations.[39] Heuristic thinking proceeds "off-the-cuff." It is founded on "intuition as distilled experience."[40]

Critical   Critical thinking can be defined as rationally deciding what to do or believe in a particular context.[41] It is conscious, directed, controlled thinking, in which each link in a chain of reason [read: Research Approach] is closely scrutinized to assess the validity of each inference. It is committed to accuracy and strives for logic and control.[42]

Divergent   As originally defined by Guilford in 1950, divergent thinking refers to an individual's ability to generate multiple potential solutions to a problem. It is typically measured by presenting individuals with an open-ended stimulus problem to which they are required to generate as many solutions, ideas, concepts, and approaches as possible.[43] The greater number of alternatives generated results in a greater probability of a better, more creative solution.[44]

Convergent   Convergent thinking focuses on an answer, a solution. It is used when solving problems such as long-division and calculating income tax. Convergent thinking techniques eliminate uncertainty, simplify complexity, and enhance decision-making ability.[45]

Conscious   Conscious thinking is regimented. It deals with abstractions of reality. It proceeds in "real" time, receiving information both from the senses and from memory. Conscious thinking is linear and single-channel. It is occupied by one topic until it switches to another. Conscious thinking prefers complete information and is limited by the nature of the information processing involved.[46]

Unconscious   Unconscious thinking is uninhibited, faster and more flexible than conscious. It is better able to deal with uncertainty and able to operate in non-linear, multi-channel modes. It is powerful in discovery, invention, innovation, and accommodation to change.[47] Incorporating previous experience to foster new insights, unconscious thinking is the well-spring of intuition and the foundation of the elusive quality known as "judgment."[48] Unconscious thinking fosters creativity by allowing unconscious ideas and associations to flow into consciousness, thereby providing a basis for the integration and redirection of thought.[49]

Deductive   Deductive thinking reasons from the general to the specific. It proceeds from existing theories and facts to specific facts or solutions. For example, given that a computer can compare data sets, have the information system match orders received with the mailing list to determine percentage response. In mathematics, it reasons from a set of assumptions to an answer. It is often used in education or in applying a technique. In science and mathematics, deductive thinking is oriented toward arriving at the "right" answer or answers that develop from a theory. In design, it is oriented toward arriving at a solution that can be used.[50]

Inductive   Inductive thinking reasons from the specific to the general. It is the way that scientific theories are created. It responds to the fact that adequate theory does not exist to explain most of life. Inductive thinking tries to arrive at a single, broad generalization that includes and adequately explains many specific observations in a realm of interest. For example, if 90 percent of families with tall parents have all tall children, then tall parents are very likely to have all tall children.

Abductive   Abductive thinking reasons from the result and a generalization to propose a specific case. It is more closely aligned with deductive than with inductive thinking. It involves both at times and tends to be used in finding causes, as well as in fields of inquiry such as artificial intelligence. For example, because the children on my block are tall (result) and tall parents have tall children (generalization), then the children of my tall neighbors will most likely be tall.

The "Doubting Game"   This approach to problem solving emphasizes argument and a rigidly reductive method of rational-

ity: problem definition, problem analysis, presentation and evaluation of alternatives, detailing of solutions. The doubting game
forces one to poke holes in ideas, tear apart assertions, probe
continually, and be analytical. Careful development of generalizations in research requires an emphasis on the doubting
game. Its view of rationality makes a person feel "rigorous, dis-
ciplined, tough minded." Conversely, if a person refrains from
playing the doubting game, he or she feels "unintellectual, irra-
tional, sloppy."[51]

The "Believing Game"   In this approach to problem solving,
the first rule is to refrain from doubting. It initially believes all
assertions, so as to see further into them. Effective planning
and design require the believing game, in order to engender
"breakthrough" solutions. The believing game is complementary, not contradictory, to the doubting game. That is, successful solution finding requires use of both approaches. Yet the
believing and doubting games cannot be played simultaneously.
Each must be employed at different times in the solution-
finding process.[52]

Automatic   Automatic thinking occurs without conscious
thought. It enables people to act swiftly and effectively in a
wide variety of situations, on the basis of relatively permanent
cognitive structures known variously as mental maps, scripts,
schemata, belief structures, or theories of action. Yet the very
advantages of automatic thinking for dealing with routine situations [for example, operation and supervision] are likely to become disadvantages in the face of change and uncertainty.
Automatic thinking leads people to see only what they already
know, to ignore crucial information, and rely on standard behavioral repertoires when change is necessary. Learning from
experience requires switching to a more conscious, reflective
mode; yet researchers have noted that people often resist making this switch, precisely when it is most called for.[53]

Reflective   Reflective thinking is an active, contemplative
mode of serious thought. It helps in learning and in the judi-
cious consideration of various alternatives. As noted by Chris

Argyris and Donald Schon, conscious, reflective thinking is quite useful under conditions of ambiguity and threat.[54]

Active   Active thinking enables people to see situations differently and to experiment with novel responses. It enables them to become aware of how they select, interpret, and act on information about themselves and the contexts in which they act. Schon has used the term "reflection-in-action" to describe a particular kind of active thinking that enables people to question the assumption-structure behind their actions.[55]

Intelligence, Creativity, and Intuition

Just as the brain is the *source* of thinking, the *product* of thinking can only be considered with reference to cognitive characteristics such as intelligence, creativity, and intuition. These concepts describe the relative levels at which human beings are able to think, whether their thinking is expressed in verbal, visual, schematic, musical, or mathematical terms.

INTELLIGENCE

In the relatively recent past, formal intelligence was often limited to "book-learning." Today, however, most people recognize that formal intelligence extends far beyond the merely academic. Certainly, beyond what can be measured by standard "intelligence" tests, which are now generally considered to be too bound by white, Western culture and neglectful of certain kinds of intellectual achievement.

In fact, humans have many and various types of intelligence. All of them—from verbal ability, to spatial perception, to relation/connection recognition, to "street smarts"—are necessary for contemporary solution finding. Thus, all the various types of intelligence need to be developed. And all can, in fact, be augmented by processes that build on and enhance the existing levels of intelligence, whether innate or developed.

For example, our late 1970s study, reported in *Student-Planned Acquisition of Required Knowledge,* showed that learning was enhanced and made easier by students' contextual awareness. When students examined the purposes of learning required subjects and were then themselves involved in planning their own methods of translating the required reading material to convey knowledge to others, they gained increased understanding of educational subject matter at an increased rate.[56]

WHAT CONSTITUTES INTELLIGENCE?

American novelist and story-writer F. Scott Fitzgerald once observed that "the test of a first-rate intelligence is the ability to hold two opposed ideas in the mind at the same time, and still retain the ability to function."[57]

Intelligence has to do with a person's accumulated knowledge. Thinking has to do with how a person applies that knowledge. Or as our old *cher ami* René Descartes once put it: "It is not enough to have a good mind. The main thing is to use it well."[58]

Perhaps the most insidious myth about thinking is that the ability to think effectively is related directly and solely to analytic intelligence. "Those who believe it," notes psychologist and consultant Eric Bienstock, "are willing to let others . . . experts, do their thinking for them. Certainly, these experts possess a great deal of intelligence (much of which is the accumulation of a substantial amount of knowledge in a particular field). But this accumulation of knowledge has little to do with their ability to think—to make good decisions, understand another person's point of view, have a clear sense of priorities, be able to suspend judgment temporarily, or be willing to explore different alternatives."[59]

Another definition of intelligence is offered by the *American Heritage Dictionary:* "the capacity to acquire and apply knowledge." In turn, knowledge is defined as "familiarity, awareness, or understanding gained through experience or study." Intelligence depends on context.

While admitting that many ambiguities exist with respect to a definition of intelligence, psychologists Michael Mumford and Sigrid Gustafson suggest that "general intelligence represents an individual's ability to formulate and use abstract concepts. This observation," they note, "finds substantial support in the many studies reporting moderate positive relations between indexes of intelligence and creative production among artists, scientists, and professionals, but weak or insignificant relations in lower level occupations."[60]

Campbell reports the view of Herbert Simon—who, in 1956, coinvented with Alan Newell what is generally considered the first "thinking machine":

"Simon maintained that a core criterion of intelligence, whether in a human or in a machine, is the ability to reduce the complexity of the choices confronting the mind when it is considering a problem. Certainly, Newell and Simon did not believe in an 'intelligence principle,' a single idea that accounts for thinking in all its manifestations. But they did insist that there is no intelligence without symbols."[61]

Campbell himself concludes that "if . . . the essence of human intelligence [were to be] compressed into a single word, that word would probably be *worldliness.*"[62]

Intelligence, he suggests, is composed of various aspects including, but by no means limited to, perception, memory, reasoning, intention, generation of action, and attention.[63] These aspects can, however, be sorted into two distinct styles of intelligence: (1) the deliberate ordering of thoughts with full awareness—the style of intelligence reflected in conscious thinking; and (2) the thoughts that well up into consciousness without disclosing when they came or how they were formed—the style reflected in unconscious thinking.[64]

THE VARIETY OF INTELLIGENCES

Research into human intelligence has relatively recently shifted its own paradigm of thinking to recognize the variety of intelligences that are now considered to exist. In our view, this recognition of multiple types of intelligence leads almost inevitably to a general recognition of a multiplicity of thinking patterns, thus to the need to approach different types of problems in different ways.

To cognitive scientist Robert Sternberg, IBM professor of psychology and education at Yale University, the *combination* of analytical thinking, creative thinking (the ability to combine areas of knowledge and come up with new ideas or approaches), and contextual thinking (the ability to make practical use of this knowledge) is what constitutes intelligence. Yet Sternberg maintains that the most important aspect of intelligence is balance—not simply possessing these abilities, but knowing which is which and when to use them.[65]

Educational psychologist Howard Gardner defines intelligence as a "relatively autonomous human intellectual competence" and claims there are seven distinct types of intelligence: (1) linguistic; (2) logical-mathematical; (3) spatial; (4) musical; (5) bodily-kinesthetic; (6) inter-personal; and (7) intra-personal.[66]

Gardner has been criticized for including musical and bodily-kinesthetic activities under the rubric of intelligence. However, according to psychologist Anima Sen of the University of Delhi, India, neuro-physiological evidence "unequivocally subscribes to the notion that learning and perfecting these faculties do involve mental or cerebral processes that are generally assumed to be intelligence."[67]

Sen herself has focused on the cultural and economic biases of most tests that have purported to measure intelligence. In response, she proposes three "bias-independent" techniques for measuring intelligence: (1) information processing speed/reaction time; (2) inspection time; and (3) iconic image duration.[68]

Sen concludes that "it is possible to tap intelligence, irrespective of one's background or special experience or training. [Such] a more reliable index of intellectual capacity [is] less likely to be affected by cultural bias and similar other problems."[69]

With reference to Gardner's work, management consultant and educator Stephen Covey notes that "virtually every person rates very high in at least one of those seven categories."[70]

Educational psychologist Richard Sinatra also notes that most standard intelligence tests fail to measure fully the intelligence of those who reveal the ability to plan, will, and hypothesize through nonverbal modes. "There is enough evidence from a number of sources—psychological, artistic, educational, and cultural—that there are unique individuals, not particularly gifted in the written literacy mode, who excel in nonverbal, visuospatial thought modes.

"That this possibility can exist neurologically has been affirmed by Sperry (1973). He noted that the differential strengths of left and right [brain] processing modes allow for a spectrum of individual variations in human intellect—from the mechanical or artistic geniuses who exhibit difficulty in expression through the verbal mode to the highly articulate who think almost entirely in verbal terms."[71]

CREATIVITY

The characteristic of thinking that most of us would like to enhance is creativity, the generation of unusual and innovative ideas, as most people define it today. So the question becomes: Are there modes of thinking that either inhibit or encourage creativity? Obviously, the exclusive practice of analytical thinking—exclusive reliance on Conventional Thinking to find solutions—while possibly increasing factual knowledge, will inhibit the creation of new ideas, answers, products, and systems, as well as the intuition that is essential to the realization of creativity. At the same time, a person who believes completely in Conventional Thinking and practices it exclusively might nonetheless be "creative" in developing new analytical tools and techniques, thus displaying the elusive ambiguity that envelops the entire notion of "creativity."

Ever since the discoveries of California Institute of Technology neurologist and Nobel Laureate Roger Sperry, who first postulated the dedication of different hemispheres of the human brain to different sorts of reasoning, the type of intelligence called creativity has, in our view, been too often oversimplified. It is actually a complicated matter, more complicated than most studies of the very real left-brain/right-brain dichotomies report.

As described by Sperry (and briefly summarized in Table 6-1), there appear to be "two modes of thinking, verbal and nonverbal, represented rather separately in the left and right

Table 6-1. Characteristics of Left- and Right-Brain Thinking.

Left-Brain	Right-Brain
Intellectual	Intuitive
Convergent	Divergent
Digital	Analogical
Propositional	Imaginative
Linear	Nonlinear
Rational	Affective
Sequential	Multiple
Analytical	Holistic
Objective	Subjective

brain respectively." The left hemisphere appears to operate in a logical, analytical, computer-like fashion. Its language is inadequate to the complex synthesis readily achieved by the right. The forebrain combines the capacities of both left- and right-brain in the process of decision making.[72]

On the basis of Sperry's discoveries, several taxonomies of parallel ways of knowing have been developed. One of these is particularly interesting because it coincides almost exactly with the difference between affective and rational approaches to problem solving.[73]

As Sinatra reports, "The issue of brain functioning in creativity and giftedness is more complicated than that based on hemispheric considerations alone. As mental processing increases due to task complexity, the more likely it is that both brain hemispheres will be called into play to generate a solution to the task.[74]

Sinatra defines creative behavior, often based on the thinking of synthesis and representational images, as "making original and unique mental connections."[75] His view is close to that of Sprinthall and Sprinthall, who define creative thinking as "thinking in divergent modes, as arriving at numerous novel or unique meanings or new and original thought, and as departing from the conventional or usual in idea."[76]

Sinatra refers to Gallagher's four-stage model of the creative process: preparation, incubation, illumination, and verification.

"In his model of the different stages of the creative process," writes Sinatra, "Gallagher (1975) adds that after the preparation stage of sustained study, in which cognitive memory is the predominant mode of thinking, the stages of incubation and illumination are expected to occur. In these stages, intellectual freedom, risk taking, and tolerance of failure and ambiguity are learning style characteristics required by the learner."[77]

At this point, we would again interject that the question of *how* to think about each of these four stages is critical. For example, how to approach preparation and about what to be prepared. How to incubate about the "what" of preparation: the people involved, the solution-after-next, illumination, and so on. Consequently, simply stating these four stages without reference to questions of *how* is insufficient. It may be too limiting or even reversed. For example, incubation may be a much more critical stage, especially as regards understanding purposes and their larger contexts, and may well occur *prior to* preparation.

Creativity must be tapped at all stages of the solution-finding process, not simply when trying to generate new ideas. We have to be creative about problem identification, problem selection, preparation, as well as about innovative ideas and solutions, as well as about how to install and implement the chosen solution. That is why we characterize Breakthrough Thinking as "Full-Spectrum Creativity."

Joseph V. Anderson, professor of marketing at Rollins College, identifies three broad types of creativity: that which makes things, that which combines things, and that which changes things.

"Creation is the activity we usually think of when someone says creativity," Anderson writes. "It is the act of making something out of nothing." He specifies that this sort is the creativity of Beethoven, Shakespeare, and the Wright Brothers. "Creation is, without question, creativity. But it is not the whole, nor is it even the most important type.

"Synthesis is the act of relating two or more previously unrelated phenomena. The first wheel was the product of creation. So was the first axle and the first box. But until someone came along and synthesized them into the cart, mankind didn't get much good out of the three components. Synthesis is the core of society's advancement. Creation is nice, but synthesis is the real engine of survival and prosperity.

"Modification," Anderson explains, "is the act of altering something that already exists, so that it can: (a) perform its function better, (b) perform a new function, (c) perform in a different setting, or (d) be used by someone new."[78]

IDENTIFYING CREATIVITY

While we may be able variously to define creativity, how do we identify it? How do we know who has it, or better put, who has it when? Beyond "knowing it when we see it," can we recognize and measure creativity *before* it manifests itself? This proves to be not an easy matter.

Greeno and his fellow proponents of "situated cognition" maintain that creativity occurs naturally when one's situation is restructured. Changes in the environment, they argue, can cause a reorganization of "conceptual structures."[79]

"The assumption of situated cognition says that all of our cognitive activity is connected with situations," Greeno explains. "Creativity, in this view, involves reorganizing the connection the person has with a situation, rather than a reorganization that occurs within the person's mind. The situation with which one's connections are reorganized can be physical, social, or conceptual."[80]

Mumford and Gustafson claim there are multiple definitions of creative behavior. Nonetheless, in nearly all studies of creativity, researchers use criterion measures drawn from only one of three basic categories.

"The first category consists of overt production criteria, such as publication counts or patent awards. These measures assess creativity in terms of the frequency with which individuals generate innovative products having acknowledged social worth or the quality of these products. Second, professional recognition criteria assess creativity in terms of the awards given individuals for the production of new ideas or products held to be of some value in an occupational field. Third, when social recognition criteria are used, the judgments of knowledgeable others, such as peers or supervisors, afford a basis for assessing the value of an individual's novel contribution in some area. Although these criteria differ in many ways, they seem bound together by their common concern with the production of novel, socially valued products."[81]

Daniel Goleman, cowriter of the PBS television series *The Creative Spirit,* highlights three major new theories of creativity. The first "focuses on the role of the sheer pleasures of creation during the inspired moment." This state is characterized by an elastic sense of time in which time itself seems to dissolve and a day passes like an hour. This single-minded immersion is what psychologists call the "flow" state, an altered awareness found in people performing at their peak on a project in which their skills are perfectly balanced with the demands and challenges of the task at hand.

A second theory of creativity examines the forces at work in the lives of creative geniuses like Eliot and Picasso, Einstein and Gandhi, people who not only rose to the top of their form, but moved beyond previous formal limits to recreate the form itself.

A third theory assesses the social forces that give rise to a renaissance, a time of burgeoning creativity across an entire society. Dean Keith Simonton, a psychologist at the University of California at Davis, has asked the question: Over the last 2,500 years of human history, what accounts for the rise and fall of "golden ages" of creativity?

Simonton concludes that political fragmentation is the best social predictor of great surges in creativity. Italy during the Renaissance was not a single nation, but a cacophony of city-states, all vying for financial power, political influence, and artistic recognition. The Germany that produced Goethe, Hegel, Schiller, Mozart, and Beethoven was composed of numerous small states cut adrift when the Holy Roman Empire collapsed. (Will creativity flourish in the new independent republics formed when the Soviet Union collapsed?) Indeed, monolithic states tend to squelch creativity. At the same time, while wealth does not breed creativity, abject poverty surely tends to prevent it.[82]

Japanese observers Murakami and Nishiwaki make the intriguing point that Japanese research into creativity tends to focus on organizations or groups, while Western research focuses on the enhancement of individual creativity. The overall trend they project is a drift toward the investigation of corporate creativity.[83] Among the investigations they cite are those conducted by Akira Onda, Shinichi Nakayama, and Suichi Kato.

Onda's research focuses on "Japanese-style" creativity, examined from a psychological and philosophical perspective. Studying subjects who were educators and developers, Onda's inquiries have ranged widely to include studies of creativity development, the relationship between dreams and creation, creativity among the Japanese, and education for creativity. "The common thread running through all his work," note the authors, "is an exploration of the connection of Zen, Buddhism in general, and other branches of Oriental thought with creativity. He sees in origami a means of fostering in children the power of concentration and intuition needed for creation, and suggests Zen meditation as a means of doing the same for adults."[84]

Cognitive psychologist Shinichi Nakayama studied developers to examine the relationship between personality and creativity. He proposes that the link between the two is a desire to think—the motivation toward thought. Thus, Nakayama treats creativity as a function of the desire to attain a certain goal.[85]

Perhaps the most telling measure is found in Snyder's 25-year-study of MIT graduates. He discovered that creativity was dramatically associated with the use of both modes of thinking.

Snyder developed a set of criteria for creativity that included significantly reformulating a concept or design, initiating successful innovations, or making major original contributions in any field. Of the ten individuals in his population whose achievements fit these criteria, five of them came from a group of 13 who used both analytical and intuitive modes of thinking, both in college and later. The other five came from a group of 20 who had as undergraduates relied solely on analytical thinking but had expanded their thinking after college to include use of both modes. Snyder found that none of his subjects who had continued to rely solely on analytical thinking after college later met his criteria for creative achievement.[86]

ENHANCING CREATIVITY

Can creativity be enhanced? There seems to be widespread agreement that the answer is "yes."

Moreover, it is apparent that creativity—more precisely in terms of today's definition, the ability to generate unusual and innovative ideas—can be both learned and enhanced at almost any age. The younger, the better.

In this regard, Anderson suggests that the best way to enhance creativity is by getting people to *practice* it. "[If we] sit back and content ourselves with [merely] identifying creativity, rather than practicing it . . . that makes us as useless as a drama critique . . . all talk and no action."[87]

Adams emphasizes that "perhaps the most common inhibition to creativity is our usual reliance upon traditional problem-solving routines and the fantasy that creative problem-solving should be easier, rather than more difficult, than producing answers to routine problems. . . . Conscious effort is both able and necessary to pursue new directions. Perspiration is, in fact, an excellent investment."[88]

Based on their 15 years experience in the field, management consultants and creativity trainers Ted Coulson and Alison Strickland suggest three ways to develop creativity and foster innovation.

First, they recommend that a person recognize the creativity within and around him or her. Second, in order to overcome the inhibition and fear that repress creativity, they suggest that one should call himself or herself a creative person, because it helps one to perform creatively. Third, they assert that creativity can be purposefully and systematically developed, because it comes from learnable traits. These include thinking skills, communication skills, and problem-solving process. . . . People often get stuck by focusing all their efforts on trying to fix what's wrong instead of working toward what they truly want.

"Creative people think flexibly. They know how to look at issues from many points of view. State your problem in as many different ways as you can. Look at the issue from [many] view-point[s]. . . ."[89]

INTUITION

What exactly is that mental "leap of faith" creative people seem to make with such apparent ease? What is it that allows bold, visionary leaders to make decisions regardless of the information available or based on obviously insufficient data? Sometimes, to act in direct contradiction to "conventional wisdom," which is to say, a tepid gruel of all the "leading indicators." Can we define—at least, describe—that compelling, fearsome, powerful characteristic of intelligence we know as "intuition"?

Yes, intuition can be defined. Can it be taught? Possibly. Can it be ignored? Never.

Intuition—the essence of creativity—has been described as "the wellspring of vision. In fact," say Kouzes and Posner, "by definition, intuition and vision are directly connected. Intuition has as its root the Latin word meaning 'to look at.' It has to do with our abilities to picture and to imagine."[90]

Daniel Isenberg, professor of business administration at Harvard Graduate School of Business Administration, lists five ways that intuition is used by senior managers:

"First, they intuitively sense when a problem exists. Second, managers rely on intuition to perform well-learned behavior patterns rapidly. A third function of intuition is to synthesize isolated bits of data and experience into an integrated picture, often in an 'aha!' experience. Fourth, some managers use intuition as a check (a belt-and-suspenders approach) on the results of more rational analysis. Fifth, managers can use intuition to bypass in-depth analysis and move rapidly to come up with a plausible solution."[91]

Yet intuition does not mean merely coming up with answers to pressing questions. Rather, it more effectively focuses on the types of questions asked.

As Peter Drucker has noted, "When approaching a business problem, don't try to come up with the answer. Focus on what the problems are. If you get the wrong answer to the right question, you usually have a chance to fix it. But if you get the right answer to the wrong question, you're sunk."[92] Intuition is neither the opposite of quantitative analysis, nor an attempt to eliminate quantitative analysis. Rather, they are complementary cognitive strengths and powerful tandem tools in decision making. It becomes necessary to understand and rely on intuition because very few important decisions can ever be made on the basis of complete, accurate, and timely information.

Our understanding of the nature of intuition, though not its power, is handicapped by a variety of factors. Among these, according to Bowling Green State University professors Orlando Behling and Norman Eckel, is the fact that popular, as opposed to academic, writers on the subject conceive of intuition in six different ways: as a paranormal power or sixth sense; as a personality trait; as an unconscious process; as a set of actions; as distilled experience; and as a residual category.

Behling and Eckel note that some popular authors even skip back and forth between the six conceptualizations in the course of a single book or article. They argue that this lack of an agreed-upon definition of intuition should cause executives to treat claims about its efficacy as a basis for managerial decision making with "considerable caution."[93]

Clearly, such "amateur" challenges to the notion of management as a science based on numerical analysis does not sit well with many academic researchers. But some have begun to submit assertions about the value of intuition in executive decision making to the probing research and rigorous quantifiable analysis on which academics professionally rely.

Whatever cautions may be in order as regards primary or exclusive reliance on intuition in decision making, we agree with researchers W. J. Pelton, S. Sackmann, and R. Boguslaw, who state in their book *Tough Choices: The Decision Styles of America's Top 50 CEOs:* "The empirical evidence leads us to believe that there is a strong correlation between intuitive capability and effectiveness in the face of tough choices."[94]

IMPROVING INTUITION

Skepticism exists as to whether intuition can be developed. What can surely be developed, perhaps more than intuition itself, is the willingness to listen to one's inner voice, to be enlightened by the "mind's eye" vision, and the courage to be guided by that intuition which all human beings possess.

Harper explains: "One of the best ways to tap the power of the subconscious is to incorporate the idea of mental incubation . . . the process of giving the subconscious time to run free. . . . Whether it is called letting one sleep on it or giving the ideas a chance to jell before making a decision, intuitive executives have learned the value of utilizing their subconscious."[95]

After all, informed decisions arc made only on the basis of understanding that is fully informed about the right questions, as Drucker noted. Such information must naturally include not just the needed knowledge we can readily quantify in the present and expand through purposes into the future, but also all we have already learned, and learned so well as to have had the knowledge filter to the very roots of our intelligence, in the subconscious mind.

"The ideal in learning," note Gloria Barczak, Charles Smith, and David Wilemon, "is the integration of external reality with an internal vision—a match between what is seen and what is known. Whether it be called 'intuition' or 'talent' there is an evolutionary quality to learning that captures the essence of experience and imparts the organizational vision."[96]

Using intuition to arrive at creative solutions to personal and organizational problems demands the breaking of old thinking habits, the following of new patterns of thought. These are the new thinking patterns characteristic of those innovators who change things, who generate novel ideas, who experiment, who make a fundamental difference.

DIFFERENT THINKING PATTERNS FOR DIFFERENT PURPOSEFUL ACTIVITIES

To solve problems effectively, human beings need to use different thinking patterns at different times. As we made clear in the previous chapter, which pattern of thinking to use at which time can best be discerned by defining the problems that we face in terms of the purposeful activities that they reflect. Different thinking patterns best address different purposeful activities, thus different types of problems.

According to Sternberg, whose research into applied intelligence combines the perspectives of psychology and education, some intellectual styles prove more effective in certain fields than do others. He writes: "I've discovered three intellectual styles:

"Executive. Although these people may be very smart, they want to be told what to do. They then do it very well. They are good thinkers within a given framework.

"Legislative. They are interested in generating projects and ideas and in seeing situations in new ways . . . setting up new parameters.

"Judicial. They would rather judge and evaluate. Successful editors are judicial types."[97]

As we see it, the important aspect of Sternberg's work is that he identifies and illuminates different ways of thinking. While we may not agree with his categorization, Sternberg's research clearly indicates that there is more than one way to think. It is significant, however, that his categories of intellectual styles, while interesting and no doubt useful, lack any reference to the purposeful activities of human beings.

This reservation notwithstanding, Sternberg correctly stresses the impossibility of accomplishing creative, original research while relying solely on the analytical perspective of Conventional Thinking. Postulating the existence of a "triarchic" theory of intelligence, he notes that analytic types falter when they are called upon to start putting things together by themselves, to do creative, original research.

This sort of analytic intelligence, which Sternberg calls "internal," is usually the only kind measured by intelligence tests. Such tests, he asserts, fail to measure adequately (or at all) the "experiential" intelligence that allows for creative achievement or "contextual" intelligence, the street-smarts that allow one to function effectively in the world.[98]

"One of the implications of the intuitive nature of executive action," notes Isenberg, "is that 'thinking' is inseparable from acting. Since managers often 'know' what is right before they can analyze and explain it, they frequently act first and think later. Thinking is inextricably tied to action in what I call thinking/acting cycles, in which managers develop thoughts about their companies and organizations not by analyzing a problematic situation and then acting, but by thinking and acting in close concert. Many of the managers I studied were quite facile at using thinking to inform action and vice versa."[99]

Emotions, feelings, intuitions, and hunches are ingredients of what we call "affective" reasoning. This is the sort of thinking commonly associated in the public mind with "genius." Affective problem solvers tend to do whatever comes spontaneously to mind, rather than follow a preestablished approach structure. Affective reasoning is highly related to intuition. The mind-set and methods of an affective approach differ from person to person and are difficult to define.

We trust it is becoming increasingly clear that, in order to reach effective solutions, different problems require different approaches, different patterns of thinking.

DeBono's technique of "Six-Hat Thinking" is perhaps the most obvious example. He suggests that the method allows people, particularly people in groups, to focus successfully on only one particular element (or pattern) of thinking at a time. DeBono proposes that thinking about only one element at a time may be a way for people to solve problems which appear deadlocked.[100]

Indeed, thinking is so complex a process, comprised of so many different possible modes and patterns, that it often seems utterly inexplicable that any system of education claiming to be "rational" would willingly choose to restrict itself to only one mode of thought.

Barczak, Smith, and Wilemon make the point that different patterns are needed, not just at different times but over time as well. "With some effort," they write, "we could learn to cope with very high-speed change that flowed along a reasonably predictable course. We'd have to work faster, probably harder, and definitely smarter, but we could handle it.

"The greater challenge, by far, is to cope with high-speed change that is subject to frequent alternations in direction. More difficult still is to cope with change that follows an apparently random course where the linkages between cause and effect are obscure. Those are the kinds of unsettling changes we all face more frequently with each passing day. In such a world, behavior that has been reinforced by yesterday's successes can become a liability tomorrow."[101]

The concept of the Creation Society (see Chapter 4) is likely to come to pass during the twenty-first century. What would that mean about how we think as we address human purposeful activities? If society "changes the rules," what type of thinking patterns will then be needed and effective? We submit that what will be required is a type of thinking that employs one or more of the many thinking patterns here identified, in order to solve problems that are defined in terms of the purposes that humans seek to achieve.

Reflecting this approach in the field of psychology is "Solution-Oriented Brief Therapy," a concept that concentrates on finding solutions to people's psychic distress, not on the problems perceived to cause the distress. It has proven effective in the treatment of a wide variety of psychological ailments, including those affecting married couples.

"When a couple comes to see me," says psychologist Michele Weiner-Davis, "I immediately ask what their goal is. [Note that Davis consciously chooses to define the problem in terms of the human purposes that its solution would serve.] In traditional therapy, that might not happen for some time.

"I have been very successful helping people save their marriages—85% of the couples I counsel stay together. [The] key to that success [is] new technologies. I use *solution-oriented* brief therapy. This is a method that helps people come up with solutions quickly. It doesn't require long introspective journeys into the past, which often are just back-peddling. Instead, I help people identify where the trouble [that is, what the problem] really is.

"This method is based on the work of Milton Erickson . . . [who] was not at all interested in how problems developed. He was interested in how *solutions* developed. He would look for the glimmer of hope and expand on that."[102]

Snyder notes a weakness inherent to the analytical approach when applied to situations other than the investigation of physical reality—the world of mathematics and the physical sciences. This was reflected in the comments of one of his former research subjects years after graduating from MIT, where he had been one of the group who had then relied exclusively on the analytical approach. Twenty years into life in the "real world," his perspective had changed markedly to include modes of thinking that do not rely on quantification.

"I think there's definitely a weakness to the analytical style that relates to a fundamental distrust of intuition," Snyder's subject told him. "So many times, in dealing with people, you're never really sure what the answer is, at least in any absolute sense. People just don't correspond to actual exact answers. You just sort of have to wing it and see what happens. That sort of runs directly counter to what I've termed the analytical approach, where you can calculate and evaluate and you're very precise about everything."[103]

Indeed, twenty-five years after leaving MIT, 76 percent of Snyder's subjects were found to be using both ways of knowing/thinking. We can infer that these students found that thinking patterns other than Mode 1 are needed at different times.[104] Snyder concluded that "Mode One alone is not sufficient for dealing with the ambiguity and complexity of the human condition."[105]

As Charles Garfield reports, "Albert Einstein liked to underscore the micro/macro partnership [in effective thinking] with a remark from Sir George Pickering that he chalked on the blackboard in his office at the Institute for Advanced Studies at Princeton: 'Not everything that counts can be counted, and not everything that can be counted counts.' "[106]

JAPAN AND THE WEST: HOLISTIC THINKING MEETS ANALYTICAL THINKING

Fortunately, the human mind is infinitely adaptive. It can learn to think differently. Anyone who doubts this truth need look no further than to Japan and its extraordinary success in adapting its traditional Eastern way of thinking to succeed in meeting (and surpassing) the demands of Western markets. Indeed, in this case, the fusion of distinct patterns of thinking led directly to the creation of new standards of excellence.

In relation to four areas of business, California State University professor of statistics Kosaku Yoshida comments on the effects of the analytical approach so fundamental to thinking in the United States as opposed to Japan's holistic approach.

"The Japanese have had centuries of experience with the holistic viewpoint, but they have had considerably less training in the analytic approach. For Americans, the situation has been the exact opposite. Since their initial encounter with Western civilization about 110 years ago, the Japanese have studied and learned the skills involved in the analytic approach, so that in Japan a well-balanced combination of the holistic and analytic approaches has been achieved and is being maintained."[107]

Yoshida goes on to enumerate four areas of contrast between the two national cultures—and thinking patterns—as reflected in their respective, generic corporate cultures.

Quality Control   "The quality of products is not necessarily improved by a mass inspection system [common in America] involving acceptance and rejection types of decision-making. . . . Each worker must strive toward becoming the best worker, rather than settling for being a marginally acceptable worker. The Japanese practice this principle by establishing, reciting, and referring frequently to company philosophy [or fundamental purposes]."

Personal Review Systems   "In the United States, the performance of executives is sometimes evaluated by the quarterly dividend. American managers are also evaluated in terms of how many decisions they make. Often, the manager who makes a number of quick decisions will be promoted quickly, while the manager who makes only a far-reaching decision every ten years has no chance of surviving. However, in Japanese companies, generally managers are evaluated according to long-run performance, including future potential."

Replacement   "Replacement [whether of machines, workers, managers, or executives] is a fundamental idea in American management. [It] is a strategy practiced only when management conceives of a corporation as a whole that is made up of separable or replaceable parts. That is, replacement occurs only within the governing analytic concept of Western business. Within the holistic viewpoint, however, each portion of a corporation is perceived as belonging to an organic entity, wherein no part can be replaced without substantial damage to the whole structure. One effect of replacement is that employees become short-term oriented, motivated solely toward looking well in the quarterly evaluations of performance."

Competition and Cooperation   "Each division or department of the typical American corporation operates and functions according to well-defined operational procedures. Often, these autonomous divisions are in competition with each other. [Thus], all too often, departments within U.S. firms take the following attitude: 'If they win, we lose.'

"[Japanese companies take the attitude that] the most important question should not be 'Who is responsible for this project or error?' but rather 'What is the corporate objective [read: "purpose"], and do we need to cooperate or compete with other departments in achieving [it]?'"

Rudolph Boznak and Audrey Decker compare holistic and analytic approaches in the context of product development strategies. Their fundamental point of reference is the dichotomy between the two approaches to medicine of the two classical Greek physicians Hippocrates (atomism) and Democratis (vitalism). These two opposing perspectives came to inform respectively Western and Eastern philosophical attitudes generally, and management styles in particular.

"Western scientists and engineers," write Boznak and Decker, "tend to study how the world works by analyzing the parts of a phenomenon of interest that are small enough to be understood separately."[108]

(At the least, western scientists and engineers assume that parts of a phenomenon can be understood separately. For example, Philips Co., the giant Dutch electronics company, set up a team in the early '80s to determine the cognitive or thinking processes in work activities. It devised 25 conceptual operations that comprised quality work. Each one was called a "thunk," and the "taxonomy of thought" was divided into three driving forces: "Judge what is the correct thinking to do, describe the truth, [and] generate new ideas."[109])

These two fundamentally different approaches—the atomism of the West and the vitalism of the East—are vividly reflected in the priorities attributed to various product development initiatives by Japanese auto-manufacturers and their American counterparts,[110] as shown in Table 6-2.

"The Japanese approach," Boznak and Decker conclude, "conforms to their adoption of the principle of vitalism. Their holistic product development approach began with a thorough understanding of the 'wants' of their customers. They then focused on the development and implementation of initiatives to satisfy those wants—high quality, low cost products, and rapid response.

"In contrast, U.S. manufacturers followed a predictable subconscious atomistic philosophy. This is evident by early emphasis upon computerized design (1) and manufacturing automation (2, 3). However, despite investing billions of dollars in

Table 6-2. Comparison of Japan and U.S. Automobile Manufacturer's Rank Ordering of Strategic Product Development Initiatives.

Strategic Initiative	Priority of Implementation	
	JAPAN	U.S.
Customer Needs Assessment	1	10
Statistical Process Control	2	4
Simultaneous Engineering	3	7
Just-In-Time	4	5
Customer Satisfaction	5	8
Vendor Partnering	6	6
Computer-Aided Design	7	1
Automation and Robotics	8	2
Computer-Integrated Manufacturing	9	3
Total Quality Management	10	9

such technology-oriented initiatives, U.S. companies still find themselves enmeshed within islands of automation in lieu of computer-integrated manufacturing."[111]

RESULTS FROM CHANGING PERCEPTIONS

Changing one's pattern of thinking is akin to—and to some extent depends upon—changing one's perception of reality. Simply (if not easily) looking at a problem or situation from a different perspective can so alter one's perception of it that the apparently impossible problem becomes readily solvable or even no longer a problem at all.

DeBono suggests that his Six-Hat game is effective in part because the wearing of the metaphoric hats for different types of thinking gives participants the freedom to remove their egos from the thinking process and think in many different ways.

"Wearing the hats also helps overcome ego—another big hangup in thinking. For example, if a person opposes an idea, he/she usually won't look for any points in favor of it. But if he's wearing a positive thinking hat, it becomes a game to find the positive side."[112]

And Covey also concurs that perception—what he calls frame of reference—is crucial to effective living. "How do we become more effective?" he asks. "I have found that if you want to make slow, incremental improvement, change your attitude or behavior. But if you want to improve in major ways—I mean dramatic, revolutionary, transforming ways—if you want to make quantum improvements, either as an individual or as an organization, change your frame of reference. . . . The great breakthroughs are breaks with old ways of thinking."[113]

In short, there is truth to the notion that all problems exist only in the mind. Like trees falling in the forest with no one to see or hear them, problems are really all a matter of perception. Otherwise, arguably at any rate, they do not exist.

In an experiment that assessed the effect of framing problems in different ways on a decision regarding financial allocations, researchers Dennis Duchon, Kenneth Dunegan, and Sidney Barton studied 110 engineers, scientists, and managers in a high-technology international engineering firm. They found that even very subtle changes in frame of reference have a powerful effect on decisions and perception of risk.

The subjects of the study were professionally experienced people who would be expected to be objective decision makers, and who viewed themselves as rational decision makers. Yet their decisions were influenced by very subtle informational clues. For example, they were given a hypothetical research and development project to assess for investment of limited funds. For half of the group, the last sentence of the project scenario read: "Of the projects undertaken by the team, 30 of the last 50 have been successful." For the other half of the group, the sentence was reframed to read: "Of the projects undertaken by this team, 20 of the last 50 have been unsuccessful."

Statistically, of course, the team's success ratio remained 60 percent in both cases. Nonetheless, these very subtle differences in framing not only changed the perception of objective risk in the project, but also led to differences in an inclination to fund the project.

"Different frames of reference," Duchon and his associates concluded, "can lead to different choices because different reference frames lead to different interpretations of what the facts mean. 'Facts' do not speak for themselves. Rather, the facts are interpreted in terms of a frame of reference."[114]

First among the forms of flexibility that Pelton, Sackmann, and Boguslaw found 50 top CEOs to practice is what they term "perceptual flexibility." They concluded: "Among managers who practice flexible management, the process of gathering and sorting information is not constrained by a rigid set of prior experiences. When confronted with an unprecedented situation, successful executives explore various ways of framing the problem.

"They may gather information in a new way or look for specialized data that are not generally associated with a business decision. Moreover, the more information an executive must handle, the more important perceptual flexibility becomes."[115]

As practiced by psychologist Steve de Shazer, so-called Brief Therapy is an excellent example of what can happen when people change their perspective on problems and so change their approach to problem solving.

"Most traditional forms of therapy," explains de Shazer, "are based on what seems to be a common-sense point of view about problem solving [read: Conventional Thinking]: Before a problem can be solved (or an illness cured), it is necessary to find out what is wrong. Most forms of therapy share the assumption that a rigorous analysis of the problem leads to understanding it and its underlying causes. It is generally assumed that therapy focuses on getting rid of these causes in order to solve the problem (or cure the illness).

"Interestingly, you cannot have a problem without first having the idea that a solution is possible. [So] I bypass even looking for a problem and look directly for any problem-free times. Thus, I 'ignore' the problem and work directly on developing the solution. . . . Surprisingly, therapists do not even need to know what the problem is in order to solve it, as long as they and the clients know what the goal is. . . . For me, this is best summed up with the answers to these questions: How will things be after the problem is solved? Once the problem is solved, what will the client be doing that he or she is not doing now? Who will be doing what differently?"[116]

THE NEED FOR FLEXIBILITY

Snyder makes a telling point regarding the value of flexibility: a multi-dimensional thinker is able to survive even in the most one-dimensional of thinking environments. "The 14 students who entered [MIT] with both modes [of thinking] survived the pressure and maintained both ways of knowing through graduation."[117]

"The most innovative group," he notes, "used a mix of modes to both frame problems and solve them. A central finding was the close connection between the use of both modes and the expansion of the network of enterprises. Those with only one mode were found to have more often narrowed their set of concerns and limited their network of enterprises."[118]

Pelton, Sackmann, and Boguslaw list three distinct ways that such flexibility is used by the top 50 CEOs they studied:

They are flexible in their perceptions, their analyses, and their operations. Such leaders, they write, "are responsive to change and will search for new and innovative solutions to [difficult] situations."

"The second feature is *organized flexibility*. Many of the Top 50 use an organized approach to ensure their ability to respond flexibly. They strive to demonstrate openness in perceiving and interpreting changing conditions, exploring alternatives, implementing solutions, assessing outcomes, and adjusting to new conditions. Circumstances change, but the process of confronting challenges is handled in a consistently flexible fashion."[119]

Management consultants such as Slesinski, Coulson, and Strickland agree that creativity depends upon flexibility, both in thinking and in action. "Creative people think flexibly," write Coulson and Strickland. "[They] look at an issue from the point of an analytic thinker, a procedural thinker, a people-oriented person, and an imaginative conceptual thinker. Purposefully adopting different points of view builds mental flexibility."[120]

In his study of peak performers, Garfield finds the most effective business leaders practice what he calls bi-modal thinking, combining macro and micro forms of attention.

"Micro/macro attention combines worm's-eye and bird's-eye views. A micro mode of thinking involves logical, analytical computation, seeing cause and effect in methodical steps. It is valued by those who prize attention to detail, precision, and orderly progression.

"The macro mode, the bird's-eye view, is particularly useful for shaking out themes and patterns from assortments of information. Call the macro mode intuitive or holistic or conceptual. It is good for bridging gaps. It enables us to perceive a pattern, even when some of the pieces are missing. In contrast, the logical sequences of the micro mode cannot skip over gaps.[121]

As suggested by the scope of the references already cited, a wide variety of researchers have studied various aspects of thinking as reflected in the problem-solving process. Beyond the sources we have previously noted, Murakami and Nishiwaki

offer a chart demonstrating the variety of words twelve different writers and researchers in Japan and the West use for interpretations of Conventional Thinking.[122]

The conventional paradigm of thinking, as described in
Chapters Three and Four, is clearly the basis for and profoundly
affects the meaning of certain words and phrases that appear
throughout the 12 different approaches they list. For example,
words such as "analysis," "pose problem," "set objectives,"
"study orientation," and "clarification of problem" used in almost all of the approaches for the first step make you think of
"subdivide, collect data, etc." even though the statements themselves do not say this. Each process assumes that, as a basis for
understanding a given phenomenon, you must deliberately explore it in detail, as it exists in the present moment.

Whatever their intentions to supersede outmoded ways of
thinking, the mind-set that forms the basis of the above approaches remains Conventional Thiking. "Flexibility" in using
words does not change the assumptions used by readers.

Moreover, the question remains: How closely do the
processes proposed by these writers and researchers correspond to the actual thinking processes of the most effective so-
lution-finders?

RESEARCH ON CREATING AND RESTRUCTURING SOLUTIONS: CHARACTERISTICS, HABITS, AND APPROACHES OF EFFECTIVE PEOPLE

In their study of cognitive performance of super experts, which
focused on tasks of computer program modification, Richard
Koubek and Gavriel Salvendy found that while super-expert
subjects were not faster at the top-down representation-
completion process, they performed a different type of search.
Mere experts focus on obtaining initial information related
specifically to the task at hand, while the super-expert subjects
first looked for more general, abstract features of the program.[123]

Mumford and Gustafson observe the importance of broad
intellectual interests and the capacity for visual and literal imagination among creative individuals. "Attributes of this sort," they

note, "tend to increase the probability that the individual will (a) have multiple understandings available, (b) be willing to use multiple understandings in problem-solving efforts, (c) be sensitive to information that is inconsistent with a given understanding, and (d) be willing to resolve conflicting facts or understandings."[124]

Research conducted by Stephen Norris, a professor at the Institute for Educational Research and Development at Canada's Memorial University of Newfoundland supports the finding that the initial stage of problem solution is most crucial.

"The better thinkers on our observation test," he notes, "concentrate initially on identifying the correct problem they are to solve. Poorer thinkers usually fail to identify the correct problem, may simply repeat details of the item as their response to the problem, and often become embroiled in irrelevant details of the story line, which lead them on tangents away from the real problem they are to solve. Typically, they do all of this without any apparent recognition of the fact that they are going astray."[125]

Pelton, Sackmann, and Boguslaw list five elements they found to be of primary importance to America's top 50 executives in meeting the challenge of making effective decisions of unanalyzable problems.

1. Focusing on the long term—the ability and habit of examining the long-term implications of decisions.

2. Acknowledging "the big picture"—maintaining cognizance of the range of factors affecting major decisions.

3. Employing a team of "good people"—hiring and using good people in a manner that effectively harnesses each person's contribution.

4. Retaining flexibility—throughout the decision-making and action process, recognizing that everything may be subject to change, while holding firm when necessary.

5. Imaginatively relating all strategies to "bottom lines"—recognizing that there are many varieties of bottom lines and knowing when and how to focus on each.[126]

Bray summarizes several research studies on expert designers by noting that they "exhibit greater understanding of a particular problem [read: 'purposes'], process more complete information . . . , solve a problem faster, consider more alternative approaches, [and] have a larger repertoire of solution methods."[127]

In a 1985 doctoral dissertation, James Peterson investigated the actual usage and orientations of various modes of inquiry and types of planning and problem solving, among a sample population composed of, on the one hand, effective engineers, on the other, effective planners and designers.

"In essence," writes Peterson, "all the various models were represented . . . in the orientations of the engineers and planners. Closed-mindedness, a low tolerance for ambiguity, a preference for problem decomposition, usage of technique, and isolated and routine work represent a set of operational characteristics of traditional problem solving; and we found these factors to be characteristic of engineers.

"Conversely, such characteristics as open-mindedness, a higher tolerance for ambiguity, a purpose orientation, involving others, preferring subjective or 'soft' information, and working with others are facets of the operational definition of planning and design. Through this analysis, we found that those individuals engaged in planning were characterized by these facets."[128]

From his study and observation of effective people, Covey distinguished seven habits of effective people, as well as seven converse habits of the ineffective.[129]

Seven Habits of Effective People	*Seven Habits of Ineffective People*
Be proactive	Be reactive: doubt yourself/ blame others
Begin with the end in mind	Work without any clear end in mind
Put first things first	Do the urgent thing first
Think win-win	Think win-lose
Seek first to understand . . . then to be understood	Seek first to be understood
Synergize	If you can't win, compromise
Sharpen the saw	Fear change and put off improvement

Isenberg studied successful senior managers to learn about their characteristic thinking patterns. "Two findings about how senior managers do *not* think stand out from the study," Isenberg writes. "First, it is hard to pinpoint if or when they actually make decisions about major business or organizational issues on their own. And second, they seldom think in ways that one might simplistically view as 'rational.'[130]

"In making their day-by-day and minute-by-minute tactical maneuvers, senior executives tend to rely on several general thought processes such as using intuition; managing a network of interrelated problems; dealing with ambiguity, inconsistency, novelty, and surprise; and integrating action into the process of thinking."[131]

Among the most creative, most effective problem solvers are those who challenge the status quo to create and develop alternative solutions and products. These are the risk-taking, adventurous individuals known as entrepreneurs.

In attempting to understand effective and creative thinking, many researchers have studied entrepreneurs, aptly described by San Diego State University professor Daryl Mitton as those whose fundamental mission is "to continually orchestrate change, so as to create value."[132]

Unfortunately, to our knowledge, none of these studies has probed the thinking pattern in planning, design, and solution finding exhibited by the entrepreneurial population. We include this category of research primarily to acknowledge a potential source of important data on effective thinking, an area that clearly needs further research. Particularly, we suggest, such research would do well to focus on a comparison of thinking patterns and approaches of successful entrepreneurs, as opposed to those of entrepreneurs whose business ventures fail.

What Inhibits Effective Thinking?

While we have gained increased understanding of the habits, characteristics, traits, and approaches to creating or restructuring solutions typically used by a variety of effective thinkers, a number of obstacles and inhibitions to effective problem solving must be overcome.

TEACHING STYLE AND BIASES

Perhaps the most pervasive manifestations of the hegemony of Conventional Thinking are the teaching styles and biases evident in most of contemporary education. Beyond the continual reference to some manifestation of the Research Approach as *the* way to solve all problems, these styles and biases are based on assumptions concerning the validity of results showing how students score on tests that purport to measure general intelligence, yet are able to measure accurately only a narrow band on the broad spectrum that constitutes the full scope of human intelligence. More inclusive measures of intelligence—measures considerate of differences in ethnic, cultural, and economic groups, as well as the different types of intelligence described earlier—seem appropriate if we wish to gauge effectively a person's true intellectual capacity.

"Our bias is excellence with form and expression of the printed word," writes Sinatra, "but in another culture or at another time of history, a person may have been able to flourish in artistic, constructive skills and would have been esteemed by his or her community.

"For nonverbal gifted and talented youngsters, educators could provide alternative ways through which they can learn written literacy. These ways can capitalize on the power of thinking that occurs through imagery, metaphor, and synthesis, as well as bring the emotional impact of the right-brain into play."[133]

Koubek and Salvendy find that, in order to develop super experts, training should focus on enhancing the capacity for abstract representation. "Attaining [super-expert] status," they conclude, "is more than just gaining experience on the job. Highly skilled [computer] programming [for example,] requires development of an abstract representation not found in all programmers, [even those otherwise considered expert]. Once a satisfactory level of programming performance is attained, training should focus on developing these abstract representations, rather than simply giving additional training on specific problem types."[134]

From the perspective of situated cognition, Sandberg and Wielinga argue that educating for effective thinking must involve culturally relevant, hands-on experiences. "Formal schooling does present students with a culture," they admit, "but this school culture has nothing to do with the cultures that surround the subjects to be taught. Thus, students are engaged in tasks and endeavors that have no authenticity, no real-life value.

"Students do not learn the subjects themselves, but they learn about subjects (Brown, et al., 1989). No wonder, the educators say, that formal education fails. It is no use to try to transfer isolated, decontextualized bits of knowledge. Knowledge can only be gained in authentic activity—it is not a substance, but gets constructed in action. If you want your students to learn mathematics, you have to give them the opportunity to act as mathematicians."[135]

MISCELLANEOUS IMPEDIMENTS

M. R. Montgomery, reviewing *Engineering and the Mind's Eye* by Eugene S. Ferguson for the *New York Times,* notes that modern man's apparently diminished ability to think visually greatly diminishes the effectiveness of modern thinking.

"It was the Renaissance engineer's notebook," writes Montgomery, "his accumulated drawings and calculations . . . that elevated architecture and engineering from the repetitive piling of stone upon stone in the Middle Ages to the audacity of the cathedral of Florence.

"In Filippo Brunelleschi's (1377–1446) notebooks are his plans for the crane that permitted him to build that 140-foot-diameter dome, to begin it some 100 feet above the floor of the cathedral (our national Capitol dome would easily fit inside it), and to do this all without building temporary supporting structures to hold the masonry in place during construction. His cathedral is still there; the computer-designed roof of the new Hartford Civic Center coliseum lasted three years after the building opened, until the first snow fell in the winter of 1978."[136]

Sternberg notes the importance of helping people to become aware of and remove the emotional and motivational blocks that prevent them from applying their intelligence to everyday living—lack of motivation, lack of perseverance, fear of failure.[137]

Indeed, a great inhibition to effective thinking and to Full-Spectrum Creativity is simply fear—the fear that arises naturally when we are called upon to do anything for the first time. Someone asking you to change the way you think when you seek to create or restructure solutions could cause enough fear that you would continue to suffer from the limited solutions found when you use Conventional Thinking. Fortunately, this fear can, almost as naturally—though not without effort—be overcome. Reading this book is one "effort" to eliminate this fear before a failure to find an effective solution occurs in some part of your life.

Continuing to use Conventional Thinking and even increasing the intensity of its application (get *more* facts, obtain *more* accurate measurements, do *more* studies, be *more* objective) as the means of improving the quality and quantity of solutions is perhaps the biggest inhibition to effective thinking. It reminds us of the story of the person who was looking for his lost car key by the street lamp instead of where he lost them—because that is where the light was. The studies of management professor Henry Mintzberg, reported in *The Rise and Fall of Strategic Planning*, verifies these thinking inhibitors. He calls them the "fallacy of predetermination" (forecasting and related tools cannot show what the future is going to be), the "fallacy of detachment" (it is not really possible to do the favorite analysis of strategic planning—SWOT or strengths, weaknesses, opportunities, threats), and the "fallacy of formalization" (analytical reductionism in the way to think when thinking cannot be an activity in itself but is a qualification of another activity—or purposeful activity as we described it in Chapter 5).[138]

ON ORGANIZING AND REORGANIZING BRAIN POWER

Clearly, the list of assumptions challenging the hegemony of strictly rational approaches is extensive, if not endless. It includes a variety of religions, as well as psychological and philosophical disciplines. To ask which among them should form the basis of a more inclusive solution-finding approach is an unanswerable query. Each suggests different principles and modes of action.

It makes sense, then, to take a relatively pragmatic perspective in choosing a solution-finding approach—to borrow freely from all rather than take solely from the rational approach. The necessity of enlarging the parameters of the rational approach is clear. Recent left/right brain discoveries in neurophysiology mentioned earlier lend scientific credibility to this perspective.

From our perspective, much of the research into brain hemisphere specialization, while no doubt valuable, insightful, and exciting, remains silent about how best to develop and apply principles and assumptions concerning effective thinking, about actually solving problems, about effectively creating or restructuring systems and solutions.

Clearly, a simple exhortation to use one side or other of the brain is insufficient. What is needed are specific principles and a process to access at will the characteristic strengths of either or both sides of the brain, as well as specific guidance as to when to use which side during the solution-finding process.

In this regard, the work of Betty Edwards, professor of education at California State University, Long Beach, has proven particularly successful. Edwards has trained people previously ineffective as artists to succeed in drawing realistically by using techniques that elicit and encourage right-brain functions. Through such specific, technique-oriented methods, Edwards has enabled people to consciously employ their right-brain capacities while solving other, non-artistic problems as well.[139]

TEACHING THINKING

Nowhere is the left-/right-brain debate joined more ardently, or with more ultimate impact, than in the field of education. What exactly is the best way to educate the whole brain?

Sandberg notes that "many studies—for example, in the fields of mathematics and physics problem solving—have shown that just learning the declarative subject matter is insufficient for operational use of the acquired knowledge. The main problem, however, has always been how to design teaching methods that teach both the declarative subject matter and its use . . . in a representative series of contexts.

"The established pedagogical method over most of the last 200 years might be called the transmission method. According to this technique of education, knowledge is transmitted to the supposed blank slate—Locke's *tabula rasa*—of the student's mind. The opposing argument is called constructivism."[140]

According to Greeno, constructivism means not only that children and adults have mental constructs of things, but that they go on to construct new representations based on those they have already internalized, when presented with additional outside information.[141]

"Most of what we know we have to construct for ourselves," explains Lauren Resnick, a codirector of the University of Pittsburgh's Learning Research and Development Center. "Human knowledge is not a photograph, metaphorically speaking, of something out there, not just a record of what we are told or what we see. We have to put it together in order for it to work for us."[142] Each mind has its own categories.

Yet even if teachers succeed in transmitting or constructing knowledge in such a way that students not only grasp, but seize and use it, that by no means guarantees that people will be able to use the knowledge they acquire to solve the problems they confront.

Why? Because, as Sternberg notes, "Real problems are often poorly structured and hard to define, not neat academic exercises. People should be taught how to judge a problem, decide on the steps needed to solve it, and follow it along to make sure those steps are leading to a solution. They also need to know *how* [emphasis added] to apply their knowledge and experience to the solution."[143]

By now it should be clear to you that effective thinking is not always a linear process. Indeed, humans often take advantage of abstract relations between aspects of a problem in order to quickly arrive at its solution.

Theories are themselves a kind of shortcut. As Simon notes, "the virtues of the theory are that it organizes our thinking rather precisely and it leads us to ask the right questions."[144] Of course, the questions that a theory leads us to ask are "right" only in terms of the theory itself, not necessarily in terms of the problem to which the theory is applied or the results that people seek from its solution. At the same time, theories remain valid only so long as they are able to explain the phenomena that we perceive.

Meanwhile, however, humans will, on the basis of existing theory, follow thinking patterns that reflect the existing paradigm. Once a pattern, any pattern, is established, the mind seems eager to continue following it, even though it may no longer be appropriate. Unfortunately, while the old thinking pattern persists, the new situation is likely to be entirely different from the old and so require a complete switch in perception.

THE REALITY OF INDIVIDUAL PERCEPTION

Each person displays a preferred method of understanding reality. Individuals have different operating styles. In making decisions, people vary in how much data they want, whether they rely on intuition, gut feeling, or logic, whether they play the "doubting" or the "believing" game, and in the way they arrive at conclusions. Evidence of this fact can be found in various typologies, notably that of Carl Jung, which characterizes persons in terms of how they become aware of situations, either by the logical interpretation of external sensually perceived data or by emotional, internal intuition.[145]

On the basis of their study of decision making by 110 engineers, scientists, and managers, Duchon, Dunegan, and Barton concluded that "different frames of reference can lead to different choices, because different reference frames lead to different interpretations of what the facts mean. 'Facts' do not speak for themselves. Rather, the facts are interpreted in terms of [an individual's] frame of reference."[146]

Haley notes that, given the same data, not all people see the same things: "Paine and Anderson (1977) observed that managers see varying amounts of uncertainty in similar environments. Managers' perceptions of problems affect the strategic alternatives that managers and organizations consider. Khandwalla (1976) learned that when managers perceive complex environments, managerial strategies become more complex."[147]

ARTIFICIAL INTELLIGENCE—AN OXYMORON?

As defined by Jay Liebowitz, "artificial intelligence (AI) is a field whose major thrusts are to develop intelligent computer power to supplement human brain power, and to better understand the process of thought, reason, and learning. [It may be defined as] the ability to acquire and apply an understanding gained through experience or study in order to mimic 'natural intelligence.' "[148]

Liebowitz goes on to specify six areas where expert systems are limited when compared to the human brain. These include "the ability to possess and use common sense; the development of deep-reasoning systems; the ability to vary an expert system's explanation capability; the ability to get expert systems to learn; the ability to have distributed expert systems; and the ability to easily acquire and update knowledge."[149]

In his book *Acts of Meaning*, Jerome Bruner, professor of psychology at New York University, argues that the failure of the cognitive revolution to unravel the mysteries of the workings of the human mind as the creator of meanings—whatever success has been achieved in gaining understanding of the brain—should cause psychology to return to human concerns, especially the role of culture in shaping thoughts and the language that humans use to express thoughts. He dismisses the concept of artificial intelligence as "an oxymoron (the liveliness of intelligence coupled with the flatness of artificiality)."[150]

As Campbell explains, "how we think cannot be separated from what we are thinking about, and is closely connected with what we know and how we use our knowledge. The nature of reasoning changes, sometimes drastically, when domains of knowledge change. . . . Since what they do is determined solely by internal representations, such machines are not closely linked to the external objects, events, people, to which the representations are supposed to refer."[151]

Combatting this shortcoming will not prove a simple task. After all, it has taken human beings some 2.5 million years, and living organisms generally 3.5 billion years, to learn all that they have apprehended from contact with the environments that they inhabit. "Rodney Brooks, a robotics researcher at MIT, bases a theory of intelligence on how evolution has 'spent its time' over the last 4.6 billion years," Campbell relates. "Brooks and others believe . . . that it is hopeless to try to build a machine that has general intelligence by starting at the wrong end of evolution, with types of thinking that emerged right at the end point of human development. That leads to delusion, because such a machine may give the appearance of thinking with some of the sophistication and scope of the mind, but it is apt to break down because its knowledge of the real world is actually painfully restricted and shallow."[152]

Success in the field of artificial intelligence, Campbell argues, "will mean breaking down some of the bogus distinctions between the humbler kinds of knowing, such as seeing, hearing, and remembering, which we share with other animals, and the loftier sort, like reasoning and solving problems."[153] With such AI capabilities a very long way off, we must guard against "artificial stupidity."

HOW INDIVIDUAL THINKING AFFECTS INDIVIDUAL AND GROUP PERFORMANCE

Just as all thought begins in the brain of an individual human being, so too do all individual and group decisions proceed from the thoughts of single individuals. Thus, in a very real sense, by changing your own pattern of thinking, you can change the world around you. Not only your perception of that world, but the thoughts and actions of the other human beings with whom you share the world.

In attempting to modify habits, the habits of any animal—"Sit, Fido. Down, Fido. Stay!"—or even a machine—regularly change the oil in your complaining car and it is very likely to run better—reward is essential. Similarly, modifying our own thinking patterns, thus our habitual thoughts and actions, can sometimes provide us with immediate rewards. As a result, we will be encouraged to continue the often difficult process of literally changing our mind.

"Naturally, such things as reward, punishment, and other types of motivational considerations are important in the process of habit modification," notes Adams. "Also involved are time, energy, and perhaps money. However . . . the main thing to note [about the research findings] is the centrality of the conscious in modifying habits. Not only is it effective, it is the only thing we have to modify habits."[154]

All such changes begin and end with individual human beings. You, and you alone, have the power to be more effective in your solution finding. You can enhance not only your own performance, but also the performance of any group or organization in whose thinking, decisions, and actions you take part. Fundamentally, it all comes down to you.

As Covey points out, "In a very real sense, there is no such thing as organizational behavior. There is only individual behavior. Everything else flows out of that."[155] Organizational change consultant Stanley Herman reiterates this theme in his concept (and book) of *The Force of Ones: Reclaiming Individual Power in a Time of Teams, Work Groups, and Other Crowds.*[156] In order to induce change in an organization, you must first induce change in yourself. In other words, you must lead by example. You must yourself *become,* then *be* the dream.

Although an individual's thinking and performance can significantly affect the group, excessive focus on individual goals and aspirations can damage group performance. So while the individual breaks old habits and develops new patterns of thinking, he or she must at the same time focus on the larger needs of the group or organization.

This paradox is aptly demonstrated by Yoshida, in his explanation of how American and Japanese executives might view the same business situation. "The fundamental assumption of [the holistic approach] is that the entirety is more than simply the sum of the individual parts. American [executives] might have thought that if they were given annual targets, and were evaluated in terms of the specified targets, and if each [executive] worked hard to meet his goal, then the bank would also perform well in the long run. This is a typical example of analytic thinking.

"But the Japanese [executive] might have decided that maximizing each division's measurable target or each quarter's dollar increase would not necessarily maximize the entire bank's performance. To the Japanese . . . the American . . . goals or objectives might only represent sub-optimization. Japanese might think that each [executive] should learn to identify with the superordinate objective of the [organization], and strive for the grand-optimization of the entire bank over a long time period. This is typical of holistic thinking."[157]

It is also, we note, precisely the effect realized when purposes are consciously expanded in Full-Spectrum Thinking for solution finding.

With reference to the potential impact of individual thinking—particularly visionary leadership—on corporate culture, Barczak, Smith, and Wilemon note that theorists such as Warren Bennis, Charles Kiefer, and Peter Senge have "found that successful leaders in uncertain environments maintained an ongoing vision and commitment that gave an inherent strength to their organizations.

"In large-scale change," they emphasize, "[individual] leadership plays a vital role. Leaders guide the change process by insuring the presence of visioning, experimenting, pattern breaking, and bonding, and by keeping these four elements in balance. The individual who takes full charge of a large-scale change is necessarily strong, determined, and masterful at mobilizing people around a vision."[158]

But you don't have to be the CEO to have your new way of thinking impact your organization. You just have to think differently about solution finding in all of your activities and projects.

Your new pattern of thinking is very likely to engender a new vision of your own life, as well as the life of your organization. As you develop new vision, it is essential that you communicate that vision to others around you. The individual's vision lends strength and meaning to his or her organization.

"Leaders spend considerable effort," write Kouzes and Posner, "gazing across the horizon of time, imagining what it will be like when they have arrived at their final destinations.

Some call it vision; others describe it as a purpose, mission, goal, even personal agenda. Regardless of what we call it, there is a desire to make something happen, to change the way things are, to create something that no one else has ever created before."[159]

Vision is the antithesis of Conventional Thinking. Consequently, no vision is likely to occur, no leadership likely to transpire, when analysis is relied upon exclusively to solve problems. No one has a vision of the past. We have only memories and no ability whatever to alter the events we now regret. Vision, on the other hand, is limitless in its potential. It is a beacon to the future.

Kouzes and Posner consider that vision is the word that most aptly describes exactly what it is that effective leaders do. "First of all, [vision] is a 'see' word. It evokes images and pictures. Visual metaphors are very common when we are talking about the long-range plans of an organization. Second, vision suggests a future orientation—a vision is an image of the future. Third, vision connotes a standard of excellence, an ideal. It implies a choice of values. Fourth, it also has the quality of uniqueness. Therefore, we define a vision as *an ideal and unique image of the future.*" [160]

Though they begin as images in an individual mind, impressions and abstractions, visions ultimately affect the entire organization. Visions are realized as individuals express them in increasingly concrete terms to their constituents.

Multi-Dimensional Thinking Is Best

By now, it should be obvious that fully effective solution finders employ both analysis and synthesis, convergence and divergence, deduction and induction. Research provides numerous examples where the use of each complementary pairing produces greater results.

"To use analysis or synthesis alone penalizes us," writes Adams. "In analysis where unknowns and uncertainty are present, synthesis is necessary to adapt analytical techniques to the problem. Synthesis is also benefited immeasurably by the use of analysis. Complex modern constructions such as large organizations, aircraft, sewage systems, or Christo's Running Fence could simply not be accomplished without analysis. . . . The painter and the applied mathematician, the poet and the chemist, the singer and the engineer should rely on a balance of analysis and synthesis, but they can often be found preaching the virtues of one to the exclusion of the other."[161]

What is called for is a synthesis of the best in all approaches, recognizing that each is a legitimate expression of human knowledge and experience. Given the overriding dominance of the rational approach, however, particularly in educational curricula, it may be wise to speak more specifically to the nature of this legitimacy from a philosophical and scientific perspective.

The adherents of any approach assume that their pattern of thinking, what they know and how they know it, is "true." This truth forms the underlying mind-set of their approach. Clearly, many challenges exist to any assumption of truth. The most obvious one is that there are so many brands of truth, each with its own enthusiastic advocates. None of these "truths" can be definitively proved or disproved. Even among rational approaches are uniquely different views of the nature of reality (ontologies) and different perceptions of knowledge (epistemologies).

MOVING FORWARD

Our examination of research into thinking leads us to the conclusion that—rather than passively claim that effective people are somehow different from the rest of humanity—we would do far better actively to research, teach, and use the approach to thinking and solution finding that those most effective people intuitively apply.

Moreover, continuing to teach, use, and rely exclusively upon Conventional Thinking assumes that the approximately 90 percent of people who do not intuitively use the effective Full-Spectrum Thinking simply cannot and will never become more effective. We reject this profoundly negative perspective.

The energizing truth is that all of us are both blessed with and burdened by unique backgrounds and life experiences.

These will necessarily contribute to the level of effectiveness that we achieve in life. They do not, however, in and of themselves, account for the crucial or even the most telling differences between success and failure in solving the problems that all of us confront.

That crucial difference is to be found in the thinking paradigm—the fundamental assumptions about thinking, the basic approach to problem solving—that natural leaders, naturally effective solution finders, intuitively apply.

After 35 years of observing such effective people and continuing research into the reasoning characteristics of their thinking paradigm, as well as noting the investigations reported in this chapter, we have synthesized the new paradigm, which we express in the principles and process of Breakthrough Thinking.

In our view, the inclusive, multi-faceted total approach of Breakthrough Thinking addresses and helps to solve the great majority of problems that human beings confront. In the next section of this book, we present the specific principles and process of this Full-Spectrum Thinking to effective solution finding.

NOTES

1. Anthony Gottlieb, "Brainstorming," review of Stephen Priest, *Theories of the Mind* (Boston, MA: Houghton Mifflin, 1992), *The New York Times,* (August 23, 1992).

2. George Johnson, "What Really Goes On In There?" review of Daniel C. Dennett, *Consciousness Explained* (Boston, MA: Little Brown, 1991), *The New York Times Book Review,* (November 10, 1991).

3. Jeremy Campbell, *The Improbable Machine* (New York: Simon & Schuster, 1989), p. 65.

4. Eva Basche-Kahre, "Patterns of Thinking," *International Journal of Psycho-Analysis,* Vol. 66, No. 455, (1985).

5. Ibid.

6. Carl Jung, *Psychological Types* (Princeton, NJ: Princeton University Press, 1971).

7. Katharine Briggs and Isabel Briggs Myers, *Myers-Briggs Type Indicator* (Palo Alto, CA: Consulting Psychologists Press, 1977).

8. Johnson, "What Really Goes on in There?"

9. T. Murakami and T. Nishiwaki and others, Nomura Research Institute, *Strategy for Creation* (Cambridge, England: Woodhead Publishing Ltd., 1991), p. 94.

10. Ibid., p. 162.

11. Benson R. Snyder, "Literacy and Numeracy: Two Ways of Knowing," *Daedalus,* Journal of the American Academy of Arts and Sciences, (Spring 1990), pp. 233, 237.

12. Ibid., p. 255.

13. James G. Greeno, "The Science of Learning Math and Science," *MOSAIC,* Vol. 23, No. 2, (Summer 1992), p. 41.

14. Jacobijn Sandberg and Bob Wielinga, "Situated Cognition: A Paradigm Shift?" *Journal of Artificial Intelligence in Education,* Vol. 3 (1992), pp. 133, 135.

15. Basche-Kahre, "Patterns of Thinking."

16. Leonard W. Poon, David C. Rubin, and Barbara A. Wilson, *Everyday Cognition in Adulthood and Late Life* (New York: Cambridge University Press, 1992).

17. P. M. Fitts and M. I. Posner, *Human Performance* (Belmont, CA: Brooks/Cole, 1967).

18. D.E. Rumelhart and D. A. Norman, "Accretion, Tuning and Restructuring: Three Modes of Learning," in *Semantic Factors in Cognition,* ed. J. W. Cotton and R. Klatzsky, (Hillsdale, NJ: Erlbaum, 1978).

19. J. R. Anderson, "Acquisition of Cognitive Skill," *Psychological Review,* Vol. 89, No. 4, (1982), pp. 369–406.

20. J. Rasmussen, *Information Processing and Human -Machine Interaction* (New York: North-Holland, 1986).

21. Jonathan B. King, "The Three Faces of Thinking," *Journal of Higher Education,* Vol. 57, No. 1, (January/February 1986), p. 79.

22. Usha C. V. Haley and Stephen A. Stumpf, "Cognitive Trails in Strategic Decision Making: Linking Theories of Personalities and Cognitions," *Journal of Management Studies,* Vol. 26, No. 5, (September 1989), p. 477.

23. Robert L. Glass, "Software Design: It's All in Your Mind," relating the work of Bill Curtis and Elliot Soloway, *Computer World,* Vol. 22, No. 45 (November 7, 1988), p. 107.

24. Alan Cromer, *Uncommon Sense: The Heretical Nature of Science* (New York: Oxford University Press, 1994).

25. Rashi Glazer, Joel Steckel, and Russell Winer, "Locally Rational Decision Making: The Distracting Effect of Information on Managerial Performance," *Management Science,* Vol. 38, No. 2, (February 1992).

26. Edward DeBono, "It's Time To Think," *Bottom Line/Personal,* (January 15, 1991).

27. Peter Elbow, "Teaching Thinking by Teaching Writing," *Change* (September 1983), p. 37.

28. Ibid., p. 40.

29. J. L. Adams, *The Care and Feeding of Ideas: A Guide To Encouraging Creativity* (Reading, MA: Addison-Wesley, 1986), p. 11.

30. Kosaku Yoshida, "Deming Management Philosophy: Does It Work in the U.S. As Well As in Japan?" *Columbia Journal of World Business,* (Fall 1989), p. 11.

31. J. L. Adams, *Care and Feeding of Ideas,* p. 11.

32. N. F. M. Roozenburg, "On the Pattern of Reasoning in Innovative Design," *Design Studies,* Vol. 14, No. 1, (January 1993), p. 11.

33. Yoshida, "Deming Management Philosophy," p. 11.

34. John P. Van Gigch, *Applied General Systems Theory* (New York: Harper & Row, 1974), pp. 47–49.

35. Ibid.

36. Will McWhinney, *Paths of Change* (Newbury Park, CA: Sage, 1992), p. 169.

37. James M. Kouzes and Barry Z. Posner, *The Leadership Challenge* (San Francisco: Jossey-Bass, 1987), p. 143.

38. Donald Christiansen, "Nurturing the Open Mind," *IEEE Spectrum,* (December 1991).

39. Stephen A. Stumpf and Roger L. M. Dunbar, "The Effects of Personality Type on Choices Made in Strategic Decision Situations," *Decision Sciences,* Vol. 22, (1991), p. 1047.

40. Orlando Behling and Norman L. Eckel, "Making Sense Out of Intuition," *Academy of Management Executive,* Vol. 5, No. 1, (1991), p. 49.

41. Stephen P. Norris, "Synthesis of Research on Critical Thinking," *Educational Leadership,* (May 1985), pp. 40–45.

42. Elbow, "Teaching Thinking by Teaching Writing," pp. 37, 38.

43. Michael Mumford and Sigrid Gustafson, "Creativity Syndrome: Integration, Application, and Innovation," *Psychological Bulletin,* Vol. 103, No. 1, (1988), p. 32.

44. Adams, *Care and Feeding of Ideas*, p. 11.

45. Ibid.

46. Ibid., pp. 4–5.

47. Ibid., p. 5.

48. Stephen C. Harper, "Intuition: What Separates Executives From Managers," *Business Horizons*, Vol. 31, No. 5, (September/October 1988), p. 13.

49. Mumford and Gustafson, "Creativity Syndrome," p. 33.

50. Adams, *Care and Feeding of Ideas*, p. 11.

51. Elbow, "Teaching Thinking by Teaching Writing."

52. Ibid.

53. Victor Jay Friedman and Raanan Lipshitz, "Teaching People to Shift Cognitive Gears: Overcoming Resistance on the Road to Model II," *Journal of Applied Behavioral Science*, Vol. 28, No. 1, (March 1992), pp. 118–119.

54. Ibid., pp. 119–120.

55. Friedman and Lipshitz, "Teaching People to Shift Cognitive Gears," pp. 118–119.

56. M. Norton, W. C. Bozeman, and G. Nadler, *Student-Planned Acquisition of Required Knowledge: SPARK* (Englewood Cliffs, NJ: Educational Technology Publishers, 1980).

57. F. Scott Fitzgerald, *The Crack-up* (New York: New Directions, 1945).

58. Robert J. Sternberg, quoting René Descartes, in "Think Better," *Bottom Line/Personal*, (July 30, 1987).

59. Eric Bienstock, *Thinking: A Boardroom Special Report* (New York: Boardroom Reports, 1991).

60. Mumford and Gustafson, "Creativity Syndrome," p. 32.

61. Campbell, *Improbable Machine*, p. 27.

62. Ibid., p. 274.

63. Ibid., p. 68.

64. Ibid., p. 282.

65. Sternberg, "Think Better."

66. Howard Gardner, *The Unschooled Mind* (New York: Basic Books, 1991).

67. Anima Sen, "Alternative To Psychological Testing," *Psychology and Developing Societies*, Vol. 3, No. 2, (1991).

68. Ibid., pp. 208–211.

69. Ibid., pp. 215–216.

70. Stephen R. Covey, *Principle Centered Leadership* (New York: Summit Books/Simon & Schuster, 1990).

71. Richard Sinatra, "Brain Functioning and Creative Behavior," *Roeper Review,* (September 1989), p. 49.

72. R. W. Sperry, "Lateral Specialization of Cerebral Functions in Surgically Separated Hemispheres," in F. J. McGuigan and R. A. Schoonover, eds., *The Psychology of Thinking* (New York: Academic Press, 1973), pp. 209–229.

73. Ibid.

74. Sinatra, "Brain Functioning and Creative Behavior," pp. 48–49.

75. Ibid., p. 51.

76. R. Sprinthall and D. Sprinthall, *Educational Psychology: A Developmental Approach,* 2nd. ed (Reading, MA: Addison-Wesley, 1977).

77. Sinatra, "Brain Functioning and Creative Behavior," p. 52.

78. Joseph V. Anderson, "Weirder Than Fiction: The Reality and Myths of Creativity," *Academy of Management Executive,* Vol. 6, No. 4, (1992), p. 42.

79. James G. Greeno, "A Perspective on Thinking," *American Psychologist,* Vol. 44, No. 2, (February 1989), pp. 134–141.

80. Ibid., pp. 138–140.

81. Mumford and Gustafson, "Creativity Syndrome," pp. 27–28.

82. Daniel Goleman, "Pondering the Riddle of Creativity," *The New York Times,* (March 22, 1992).

83. Murakami and Nishiwaki, *Strategy for Creation,* p. 184.

84. Ibid., p. 87.

85. Ibid.

86. Snyder, "Literacy and Numeracy," p. 252.

87. Anderson, "Weirder Than Fiction," p. 41.

88. Adams, *Care and Feeding of Ideas,* p. 6.

89. Ted Coulson and Alison Strickland, "Applied Creativity," *Executive Excellence,* (August 8, 1991), pp. 8–9.

90. Kouzes and Posner, *The Leadership Challenge,* p. 93.

91. Daniel J. Isenberg, "How Senior Managers Think," *Harvard Business Review,* (November-December 1989), pp. 85–86.

92. Harper, "Intuition," p. 14.

93. Behling and Eckel, "Making Sense Out of Intuition," p. 46.

94. W. J. Pelton, S. Sackmann, and R. Boguslaw, *Tough Choices: The Decision Styles of America's Top 50 CEOs* (Homewood, IL: Dow-Jones-Irwin, 1990), p. 27.

95. Harper, "Intuition," pp. 16–17.

96. Gloria Barczak, Charles Smith, and David Wilemon, "Managing Large-Scale Organizational Change," *Organizational Dynamics,* Vol. 16, No. 2, (Autumn 1987), p. 62.

97. Sternberg, "Think Better."

98. Ibid.

99. Isenberg, "How Senior Managers Think," p. 89.

100. DeBono, "It's Time to Think."

101. Gloria Barczak, Charles Smith, and David Wilemon, "Adaptors and Innovators—Why New Initiatives Get Blocked," *Long-Range Planning,* (April 1984), p. 57.

102. Michele Weiner-Davis, "Troubled Marriages Can Be Saved," *Bottom Line/Personal,* (April 15, 1992).

103. Snyder, "Literacy and Numeracy," p. 238.

104. Ibid., p. 248.

105. Ibid., p. 254.

106. Charles Garfield, *Peak Performers: The New Heroes of American Business* (New York: William Morrow, 1986), p. 156.

107. Kosaku Yoshida, "Deming Management Philosophy," pp. 13–15.

108. Rudolph G. Boznak and Audrey K. Decker, *Competitive Product Development: A Quality Approach to Succeeding in the '90s and Beyond,* book manuscript, work in progress, pp. 16–20.

109. B. Wiele, "Competing From The Neck Up," *Performance & Instruction,* (March 1993), pp. 10–14.

110. Boznak and Decker, *Competitive Product Development,* pp. 16–20.

111. Ibid.

112. DeBono, "It's Time to Think."

113. Covey, *Principle Centered Leadership,* p. 173.

114. Dennis Duchon, Kenneth Dunegan, and Sidney Barton, "Framing the Problem and Making Decisions: The Facts Are Not Enough," *IEEE Transactions on Engineering Management,* Vol. 36, No. 1, (February 1989), pp. 25–27.

115. Pelton, Sackmann, and Boguslaw, *Tough Choices,* p. 108.

116. Steve de Shazer, "What Is It About Brief Therapy That Works?" in J. K. Zerg and S. G. Gilligan, eds., *Brief Therapy: Myths, Methods, and Metaphors* (New York: Brunner/Mazel, 1990).

117. Snyder, "Literacy and Numeracy," p. 242.

118. Ibid., p. 244.

119. Pelton, Sackmann, and Boguslaw, *Tough Choices,* pp. 107–111.

120. Coulson and Strickland, "Applied Creativity."

121. Garfield, *Peak Performers,* pp. 41, 145.

122. Murakami and Nishiwaki, *Strategy for Creation,* p. 146.

123. Richard J. Koubek and Gavriel Salvendy, "Cognitive Performance of Super Experts on Computer Program Modification Tasks," *Ergonomics,* Vol. 34, No. 8, (1991), p. 1108.

124. Mumford and Gustafson, "Creativity Syndrome."

125. Stephen P. Norris, "Synthesis of Research on Critical Thinking," *Educational Leadership,* (May 1985), p. 43.

126. Pelton, Sackmann, and Boguslaw, *Tough Choices,* pp. 4–5.

127. Bray, "Reflections in Design Instruction," pp. 865–871.

128. James G. Peterson, "Personal Qualities and Job Characteristics of Expert Engineers and Planners," unpublished dissertation (University of Wisconsin, Madison, 1985), pp. 217–18.

129. Covey, *Principle Centered Leadership.*

130. Isenberg, "How Senior Managers Think," p. 81.

131. Ibid., p. 84.

132. Daryl G. Mitton, "The Compleat Entrepreneur," *Entrepreneurship Theory and Practice,* (Spring 1989), pp. 9–19.

133. Sinatra, "Brain Functioning and Creative Behavior," p. 53.

134. Koubek and Salvendy, "Cognitive Performance of Super Experts," p. 1110.

135. Sandberg and Wielinga, "Situated Cognition," p. 129.

136. M. R. Montgomery, review of Eugene S. Ferguson, *Engineering and the Mind's Eye* in *The New York Times Book Review,* (November 8, 1992).

137. Sternberg, "Think Better."

138. Friedman and Lipshitz, "Teaching People to Shift Cognitive Gears," p. 122.

139. Betty Edwards, *Drawing On the Right Side of the Brain* (Los Angeles: Tarcher/St. Martin's Press, 1979) and *Drawing On the Artist Within* (New York: Simon & Schuster, 1990).

140. Sandberg and Wielinga, "Situated Cognition," p. 132.

141. Greeno, "Perspective on Thinking."

142. Lauren Resnick, in "The Science of Learning Math and Science," *MOSAIC: Journal of the National Science Foundation*, Vol. 23, No. 2, (Summer 1992).

143. Sternberg, "Think Better."

144. Frank Hahn, "Bounded Economics," review of Herbert A. Simon, *Models of My Life* (New York: Basic Books, 1991), *Science*, Vol. 252, (May 17, 1991), pp. 1014–15.

145. Jung, *Psychological Times.*

146. Duchon, Dunegan, and Barton, "Framing the Problem and Making Decisions," p. 27.

147. Haley and Stumpf, "Cognitive Trails in Strategic Decision Making," p. 483.

148. Jay Liebowitz, "How Much 'Artificial Stupidity' Do Expert Systems Possess?" *Information Age*, Vol. 11, No. 4, (October 1989), p. 225.

149. Ibid., pp. 226–227.

150. Dava Sobel, review of Jerome Bruner, *Acts of Meaning* (Cambridge, MA: Harvard University Press, 1991) in *The New York Times*, (January 20, 1991).

151. Campbell, *Improbable Machine*, p. 168.

152. Ibid., p. 31.

153. Ibid., pp. 36–37.

154. Adams, *Care and Feeding of Ideas*, p. 8.

155. Covey, *Principle Centered Leadership*, p. 323.

156. Ibid., p. 31.

157. Kosaku Yoshida, "Deming Management Philosophy."

158. Barczak, Smith, and Wilemon, "Adaptors and Innovators," p. 61.

159. Kouzes and Posner, *The Leadership Challenge*, p. 9.

160. Ibid., p. 85.

161. Adams, *Care and Feeding of Ideas*, pp. 11–13.

Part III

The New Solution-Finding Paradigm: Full-Spectrum Thinking

Chapter 7

Seven New Assumptions

E xploring the nature of problems, the role of paradigms, the history of thinking, and the latest developments in solution-finding concepts and thinking lays the foundation for our next journey. Now we seek a new framework for effective solution finding, for *Full-Spectrum Creativity.*

Such a framework exists, it produces exceptional results, and is available to all. We call this total approach Breakthrough Thinking.

It is not simply a set of principles, nor just a process, nor merely another pattern of thinking. It is all these and more. It is a new and different paradigm of thinking that includes and surpasses Conventional Thinking in creating and restructuring solutions. After 400 years of that prevailing set of assumptions, the Full-Spectrum Thinking of Breakthrough Thinking leads the way to the future. Central to that future is the fact that it will continue to change its own paradigmatic assumptions and process.

A New Paradigm of Thinking

The human search for truth is a constant process. Alone among all living creatures, human beings are blessed (or cursed) with a peculiar aspiration. Not only do we have the ability to perceive dissatisfaction between the reality that we experience and our felt needs and desires, but we also possess the capacity to consciously choose a solution-finding approach, a means to close the gap, to overcome our dissatisfactions, to achieve our aspirations, to get results. In our attempt to achieve satisfaction, the truths we find—and the paradigms that we construct from these truths—are in a state of constant flux.

In Chapter 2, we explored the notion of a paradigm in detail. In its simplest sense, we noted, a paradigm is a *pattern,* an *example* upon which we *model* our own actions or thought. It is a sample that sets a precedent for imitation, a system to be copied, followed, imitated. It at once guides and limits our thoughts. It is a *lens* through which we interpret life.

In contemporary, popular usage, some see "paradigm" as meaning the *conventional wisdom* about how things have been done for a long time and so must continue to be done. We noted that most human beings today think of the Research Approach to problem solving in just such terms. It has come to be considered not just the best, but the only legitimate way to think in creating or restructuring solutions.

"Everybody knows that we must first gather data about the existing problem or situation," is what people think when beginning a solution-finding effort.

No longer.

We now realize that a paradigm represents generally accepted traditions that, *for a time,* provide model problems and solutions. Central to the understanding of the term is that succeeding paradigms exist as *alternative* realities. Thus, the term "paradigm" denotes a particular view of reality, yet one that is always *subject to change.*

New paradigms arise even while old ones remain efficient and useful. As Kuhn relates, "Often a new paradigm emerges . . . before a crisis has developed far or been explicitly recognized."[1] Unfortunately, the crisis in solution-finding is all too apparent.

Think about it.

We need a new paradigm, one that allows us to solve problems considered extremely difficult or impossible under the old paradigm. We need to supplant Conventional Thinking for creating and restructuring solutions with another approach, one found to be *more true,* which is to say, *more useful.*

According to Kuhn, the differences between successive paradigms are both necessary and irreconcilable. "Since new paradigms are born from old ones, they ordinarily incorporate much of the vocabulary and apparatus . . . that the traditional paradigm had previously employed. But they seldom employ these borrowed elements in quite the traditional way."[2] You will recognize how relevant this observation is as we describe the new paradigm.

Furthermore, people will continue to use the old paradigm and with it find some "solutions" to most problems even though a new paradigm is available. Kuhn notes: "During the transition period, there will be a large but never complete overlap between the problems that can be solved by the old and by the new paradigm. But there will also be a decisive difference in the modes of solution."[3] And, we add, in the quality and quantity of the solutions found.

OUTLINES OF THE NEW THINKING

The major theme of Breakthrough Thinking is that each of us as individuals and as part of the organizations with which we are involved needs to change our fundamental assumptions about thinking. In order to develop the paradigm shifts in life effectiveness, structures, products, and systems that we need and seek, we must accomplish "A Paradigm Shift in Thinking."

The paradigm of Breakthrough Thinking is the new "Software for the Mind" that allows you to envision where you need to be and enables you to get there, without ponderous collection of useless data.

The purpose of Breakthrough Thinking is to provide each individual—as well as each team, group, organization, community, agency, etc.—with new principles and process to significantly increase the quality and quantity of solutions created and restructured, that is, of implemented results from planning, designing, improving, reengineering, and problem-solving.

Breakthrough Thinking extends the creativity process to determine the right purposes to be accomplished, generate a large number of imaginative and original options, and develop the systems to implement effective solutions. Its "Full-Spectrum Creativity" provides both structure for the imaginative mind and freedom for the structured mind.

Research into Breakthrough Thinking conclusively demonstrates that its users arrive at significantly better solutions to almost any problem. For example, one study (reported in Chapter 9) of 48 manufacturing companies showed that company personnel using Breakthrough Thinking produced over twice the economic savings as personnel in companies using Conventional Thinking. Viewed from a different perspective, one staff person using Breakthrough Thinking could produce the same effect as two people using Conventional Thinking.[4]

Why is Breakthrough Thinking so effective? Because it provides assumptions and a process that fits the purposes of creating and restructuring solutions much better than does Conventional Thinking.

Science concerns problems involving generalization and abstraction for which the Research Approach is excellent and useful. For most other types of thinking for finding solutions, the Research Approach is, at best, relatively difficult to use. Indeed, it has become a major part of the problems themselves. While Breakthrough Thinking values and practices appropriate use of analytical thinking and research, in fact incorporating them in its Full-Spectrum Thinking, it offers seven additional fundamental assumptions. The result is an inclusive, holistic thinking process that encompasses the most cogent and useful aspects of the various alternative thinking processes and patterns proposed and examined in the previous chapter. At the same time, Breakthrough Thinking surpasses these alternatives by offering both principles and process. It doesn't simply tell you what to do; it shows you how to do it. In other words, Breakthrough Thinking embodies the total approach that a wide variety of studies concerning thinking, including our own, have indicated is essential.

Over some 30 years, we and our colleagues have studied *how* effective and successful people arrive at paradigm-shifting answers in planning and solution-finding. As noted in Chapter 9, we have identified certain characteristics and attributes that the eight to ten percent of people most effective in planning, designing, and problem solving use intuitively. These characteristics and attributes contrast markedly with those the less effective 90–92 percent of people display.

Intuitively effective thinkers, we have found, are purpose-oriented to find the right problem, cope well with soft data, seek needed information from a variety of sources, involve many other people, tolerate ambiguity, and deal with a future-focused vision of solutions-after-next. By contrast, less effective thinkers are technique-oriented to deal with the problem as stated, insist on hard data, seek data about what exists in the problem area (not the solution space), try to do it all alone or with just a few other people, insist on firm statements of work parameters and specifications, and deal with the problem only in the currently existing context.

Conventional Thinking—gather data about the problem, find the analysis technique to fit, subdivide the problem into parts, etc.—is what the vast majority of these less effective people today use. Unfortunately, it is also what schools teach as *the* way to solve problems.

To the contrary, we have found that effective solution finders address their problems very differently. They reject the conventional approach in favor of Full-Spectrum Thinking and intuitively follow many of the methods identified as effective in the research on thinking in Chapter 6.

The findings of such research has led us to synthesize seven basic assumptions based on the distinctly different fundamental thinking concepts that effective people use. Our studies show that applying these assumptions about thinking results in far more successful plans, designs, and solutions to most problems tackled.

Following are key factors that measure success using the new Full-Spectrum Thinking:

1. a significantly higher number of recommended major or innovative solutions;

2. significantly greater total value, quality, and benefits of all recommended changes or solutions;

3. a significantly larger proportion of recommendations that are actually implemented; and

4. significantly lower costs and time involved in developing and arriving at the results defined above.

The positive impact of using such Full-Spectrum Thinking goes well beyond these specific success factors for a specific solution-finding effort. The words of one senior executive illustrate these additional benefits, which will be noted throughout Part III. "Breakthrough Thinking is also a powerful team-building agent."

ASSUMPTIONS OF FULL-SPECTRUM THINKING

New mental assumptions are the principles, concepts, and insights that form the new mind-set within which all problems, plans, designs, improvements, and day-to-day activities are now considered and understood. They follow from and take advantage of the findings and insights reviewed in Chapter 6.

As you seek to find a solution, as you work on each part of a project, as you undertake each day-to-day activity (set up a committee, call a meeting, make an important telephone call, review a request for an equipment purchase), consider these seven principles:

1. **Uniqueness**

Assume initially that the problem or opportunity you now confront is different from all others. Do not initially copy existing solutions or automatically categorize a problem in terms of a technique to use in its solution. You may not want to "reinvent the wheel," but first find out if a "wheel" is what you really need.

2. **Purposes**

Explore and expand as far as possible the purposes to achieve for the area of concern. This expanded array of purposes lets you select the biggest possible purpose(s) to achieve (the real "problem" to work on within a context of larger purposes).

3. **Solution-After-Next**
   Develop many options of "ideal" solutions to achieve your selected purpose focus, how you might best achieve your larger purpose(s) if you could start all over from scratch. Consider how you will solve the problem next time— maybe three years from now—when you may have to work on it again.

4. **Systems**
   Everything is a system. In developing your solution, detail and master all interrelationships by considering it in terms of an encompassing framework. Below we propose a system matrix of eight elements defined in six dimensions.

5. **Limited Information Collection**
   What would you do with "all the information" if you had it? Clarify your purposes before collecting data. Collect mainly information that is essential to the solution, not the problem.

6. **People Design**
   Using the principles above, give everyone involved in the decision and affected by the eventual implementation of a change the opportunity to contribute to developing and selecting the solution.

7. **Betterment Timeline**
   Even while designing today's solution, schedule the next change. Install solutions that contain the seeds of future change based on the bigger purposes and solution-after-next ideas. Fix it before it breaks.

Full-Spectrum Thinking is synergistic: The whole is greater than the sum of the parts. Therefore, trying to apply one principle at a time—or one after another in a preset order—is not as effective as using all the principles at the same time. This holistic approach focuses on the total interactions (your family, group organization, etc.) rather than on problem areas only.

For example, as the president, her staff, and the board of directors of a $300 million company worked on developing a mission statement, they tried to copy, or at least use as a model, several others they liked. Then a Breakthrough Thinking consultant illuminated how the specific opportunity of developing a mission statement needed to be treated as unique, had larger purposes that needed to be defined, required a mission-after-next, was just the purposes element of the whole company system and strategic planning, should seek customer and external condition-scanning information rather than internal data, should get many people involved in contributing ideas for the mission, and should have a time-based life-cycle of, say, two years, at which time the mission statement (and other parts of strategic planning) should be reexamined and redone.

UNIQUENESS
Is it really a wheel that you need?

A prime lesson of the investigations into thinking is that each problem is unique. If the most effective solution is to be found, the problem at the outset must be treated as unique. Humans seem to prefer neat categories, even stereotypes, which is why the uniqueness assumption must be adopted first.

It is human nature to seek to simplify our lives and lighten our burdens (to avoid risk-taking or chaos) by coupling problems with apparently similar situations. Thus one of the biggest mistakes people make in solution-finding is assuming that the problem they face in the present moment can be solved by using a "prefabricated" solution because the problem is "identical" to one that a friend or another organization previously faced and solved. *It never is.* No matter how alike two problems or situations appear on the surface, they will differ in time, place, conditions, people involved, related circumstances, and the purpose of the solution being sought. More often than not, such linkages turn out to be illusory and costly—in terms of time and effectiveness as well as in monetary terms.

It is not difficult to demonstrate that no two problems can be alike. Differences in time, place, and people involved are obvious. In addition, no problem (or organization) exists in a vacuum. All are part of some inevitable web of conditions, which themselves are subject to constant change.

The distinct needs, interests, abilities, limitations, and power of all stakeholders are *always* unique to each problem. By starting *all* solution-finding efforts with the problem's uniqueness, even though solutions or "wheels" from elsewhere *may* be incorporated, you will increase the quality and effectiveness of your solution and the likelihood of implementation, while making the most effective use of time and resources.

For example, two hospitals 600 miles apart, with the same number of patient beds, types of service, community socioeconomic factors, and patient volume, each wanted to improve its medical records library system. The Breakthrough Thinking consultant did not assume that the outstanding system developed by a group in the first hospital ten months earlier would work equally well in the second. The *people,* the staff who will use the system, differ in all their myriad characteristics, their social groupings, their organizational roles, and so on. He set up a team in the second hospital to work on the project without even referring to the initial solution.

The first hospital installed an automated medical records network where physicians could enter patient information and orders on a dictation system or at a computer terminal on the patient's floor. The orders were dispatched electronically to pharmacy, radiology, or other departments, and on to patient billing and medical records. The team in the second hospital developed its own purposes (which turned out to be different from those in the first hospital) and found that its time and budget constraints and staffing problems led to a system using existing phones and some paper forms as the most effective way to accomplish their purposes. It was a "breakthrough" for them. Once the team had selected the system to use, members were delighted to adopt needed components from the system developed at the first hospital—for example, computer software to transmit charges from the pharmacy to accounts receivable—because the team "owned" the system it was recommending. Imagine the wasted time and cost, not to mention deteriorated relations among personnel, if someone had tried to force-fit the second hospital with the first hospital's solution.

Because every problem is initially unique, every problem requires a unique solution. No matter how many *available* components are integrated into the solution, they should be "pulled" in only when the need for them is identified. Directly adapting an existing solution to a seemingly similar problem (or "pushing" a technology into a situation such as trying to adopt a fashionable fad in total quality management or reengineering) can cost many times more than creating your own solution from scratch. Protect yourself from adopting technology simply for technology's sake.

Never simply copy an existing solution nor needlessly reinvent the wheel. What is important is to know if you actually *need* a wheel.

PURPOSES
The Big Picture—Purpose Expansion

There is never a single, simple purpose in creating or restructuring a solution. The initial purpose in problem solving invariably serves as only the beginning. With creative scrutiny by involved stakeholders, many more (and ever larger) purposes emerge.

The ever-expanding purposes which start with the problem-as-stated, challenge the assumptions and thinking restrictions that you or others bring to a problem. By allowing the purposes principle to guide you to expanded thinking, the expanded thinking will open the door to many more possible solutions. Visions begin with the big purposes.

By finding progressively larger purposes for each identified purpose, the original assumption/definition of a problem is likely to be discarded. Consideration is directed, in ever-broadening dimension, to *what needs to be accomplished,* to the *right* problem. In addition, the larger context of expanded purposes serves as a continuing guide to finding solutions to what needs to be accomplished.

The word "purposes" has many connotations. It can mean utility, intent, aim, mission, primary concern, end. The purposes principle encompasses all of these connotations as well as others. It goes a major dimension beyond, including the full range of motivations and possible results in seeking to change an existing condition or find a new system or product.

People tend to accept a problem as presented to them. In doing so, they almost assuredly eliminate the opportunity for a breakthrough solution. Accepting the problem as presented often leads to an "obvious solution," *not* a breakthrough but a cop-out that frequently gives rise to other problems. A *purposes* orientation helps you avoid being sold a solution to the wrong problem or fixing a system that shouldn't even exist.

Although the uniqueness principle is primarily a state of mind, the purposes concept is both a state of mind and a tool for solution-finding efforts. Your mind-set will be continually stimulated and enhanced as you search for ever-broader purposes for change.

Identifying the initial purpose is only the beginning. The following exercise will help you transform a solution-finding effort into productive change by considering purposes *at every step*.

- What is the purpose of working on this step, area, or problem?
- What are we trying to accomplish with this information?
- What function would this group of people serve on the task force?
- What is the larger purpose of this purpose?

For example, the president and several other vice-presidents and managers of a manufacturing plant spent eight months studying their problems of late deliveries, high overtime costs, decreased quality, and misplaced orders. They called a consultant to help design the new facility they decided was needed to double the factory capacity.

By asking the project group to identify the purposes of the project itself and their hierarchy, in just two hours the Breakthrough Thinking consultant led the group to the right problem: the need for management control systems! No doubt a new facility *could* have been designed and built, but it would have been a monumental and expensive mistake.

SOLUTION-AFTER-NEXT
Solve Future Problems Now

Just as your problem exists within a framework of complex interrelations among people and other systems, it also exists in the framework of time. It is not an isolated, dead-end event, but a segment on a continuum that is always subject to change and improvement.

A common failing among problem-solvers is neglecting to look beyond the immediate problem and its solution to future needs. The solution-after-next provides the ideal system for needed purposes and the larger context of purposes. Pragmatism and the conventional approach say that whatever works to solve a problem is right. Just get the job done, now. But the future implications of a short-term solution should be considered before you commit to it. Otherwise, the chosen solution may prevent you from being flexible in the short term and from being able to make a major change needed, say, two years from now. Considering future needs may make alternative solutions look more promising.

The solution-after-next principle states that the change or system you install now to achieve your focus purpose should be based on what the solution might be next time you work on the problem. In the '90s and beyond, there is no future on the line of the past. The solution-after-next concept builds on the expansion of purposes concept to provide the power to find solutions in line with the future. Designing ideal systems without a purposes orientation (without using all the principles of this new thinking paradigm) will not produce significant change.

Determining the immediate solution requires that you consider the future implications and consequences of all possible (and potentially ideal) solutions. Using each successful new product, system, or solution as the stepping stone to the next is an end sought with the solution-after-next principle. By mentally placing yourself at a point in the future when you might have to re-solve your problem, you will improve your immediate solution and incorporate adaptations designed to meet future needs. Even though many claim that systems and solutions *evolve* into changes and improvement, the purposes expansion, focus purposes, and solution-after-next aspects of Full-Spectrum Thinking encourage enhanced and more rapid "evolution."

The solution-after-next principle elevates your thinking beyond the obvious first solution that uses what you know can be done. It encourages you to envision the ideal solution—one that might not be implementable now, but one toward which you can strive. Your immediate solution becomes not an end in itself but a promising, transitional step toward a better future.

A long-term and even "ideal" solution gives direction to the near-term solutions and infuses them with larger purposes. Having several alternative solutions-after-next stimulates creativity and gets more people involved.

For example, a department store team developed an ideal solution-after-next conveyor system for receiving and marking its merchandise, assuming all came in cardboard containers. When it found that nearly 85 percent of the merchandise did arrive in cardboard containers, it was still able to install most of the conveyor system, creating a separate receiving area for wooden crates and plastic containers not suitable for the beginning part of the conveyor system.

Your solution-after-next—what you consider the ideal target solution for your future—can be implemented over time as part of an ongoing process, a natural evolution. It thus joins daily decision-making to bigger purposes. Lofty ideals and vision are essential if one is to continue enjoying outstanding results.

Think ahead—first.

SYSTEMS
No solution exists in isolation

All problems—and thus solutions—are part of a larger system. A system is a group of interrelated entities that receives input which affects it in some way, and produces output to achieve needed purposes. Knowing the interrelationships within and between the elements and dimensions of a system is the value of this principle.

The immediate problem and the broad outlines of its solution are only the tip of the iceberg—what is visible above the surface is often only a small portion of a solution. The hidden part can be devastating. Successful problem solving and problem prevention (good planning) hinge on consideration of all the interrelated elements of the larger system. These can be organized in a systems matrix that clarifies complex relationships.

If the *Titanic* had had radar and sonar, it might have escaped its tragic end. For today's problem solver, the systems matrix is like radar and sonar. It is designed to illuminate the seven-eighths of solution ideas and recommendations that otherwise might be overlooked.

The systems matrix (shown in Figure 7-1) considers eight interrelated elements of a solution (in horizontal rows) in six distinct attributes or dimensions (in vertical columns). Use this systems matrix to define the elements of your solution in each of its six attributes or dimensions. The systems matrix highlights not only the relationships and interdependencies between the various elements of any solution, but also provides the best assurance of including all necessary factors.

A systems matrix organizes a wide variety of details into a usable structure and keeps you aware of the larger context within which you are working. It stimulates you to ask "systems-type" questions as you are developing your solution. Think of it as a "question matrix," as banking management consultant Gail Woodard calls it. Although you never really "fill in" the boxes of the matrix, focusing on each one helps you determine what information you need, regardless of how many other boxes may be affected. In other words, the lines between the elements and dimensions are not *firm* divisions.

Everything is a system.

LIMITED INFORMATION COLLECTION
Become an expert on the solution, not the problem

People often assume a problem can be solved by throwing data and statistics at it. Great quantities of human effort are squandered in learning "everything" about the present systems or problem situation. But information alone is never the substance of thought. If you want to do something with your information other than simply possess it, you must learn to gather it selectively. Avoid analysis-paralysis.

To apply the limited information collection principle, first identify the purposes array, starting with the information you think you need to collect. Awareness of purposes and solutions-after-next will enable you to form the essential base for relevant information gathering or, in many cases, to work on achieving a purpose for which the information needs are much different. Look for the absolute minimum, only the information essential to illuminate the broader dimensions of your problem.

To get beyond the gathering stage, you must hone your information gathering. If you look for all the facts or who to blame for the problem, you will amass a tremendous amount of useless data. *What you look for is what you get.*

Many people assume that measurements are the starting point for solving a problem. Although accurate numbers can be a valuable source of information, too often they relate to a problem you ought not to be working on (the purposes principle), or they are divorced from the context in which they were compiled.

Seizing on raw statistics without sufficient understanding can quickly lead to a struggle to comprehend unneeded data. Such a careful analysis of the statistical context may take more time than the information is worth.

In most problem situations, factual details are of secondary significance; the problem's framework and setting are what govern possible breakthroughs. The limited information required to find a solution stems from questions that arise during probing of the uniqueness, purposes, solution-after-next, and systems principles.

For example, a project in a large insurance company to locate 200 missing claims folders would ordinarily start with the conventional approach of "getting all the facts." Questioning the purpose of such information-collecting led to a purpose hierarchy.

Figure 7-1. Systems Matrix.

	Fundamental basic or physical characteristics: what, how, where, or who	Values goals, motivating beliefs, global de- sires, ethics, morals	Measures performance, objectives	Controls how to evaluate and modify element or system as it operates	Interfaces relation of all dimensions to other systems or elements	Future planned changes and research needs for all dimensions
Purposes mission, aim, need, primary concern, focus						
Inputs people, things, information to start the sequence						
Outputs desired and unde- sired outcomes from the sequence						

Sequence steps for processing inputs, flow, layout, unit operations					
Environment physical and attitudinal setting, organization, etc.					
Human Agents skills, personnel, responsibilities, rewards, etc.*					
Physical Catalysts equipment, facilities, etc.*					
Information Aids books, instructions, etc. *					

*which do not become part of the outputs

The selected purpose at a bigger level was to keep claim folders available. Obviously, the kind of information collected for this purpose is much different than that for locating the missing claims folders. Furthermore, the first purpose is likely to lead to a change which assumes that missing folders are always going to be occurring. The selected purpose is much more likely to produce a system where folders cannot become missing.

Concentrate on information about what *should be,* not details about what is currently wrong. Collect only the data needed now to move ahead. Focus on the solution, not the problem.

PEOPLE DESIGN
Not just involvement, but positive integration

Often raised on a code of "rugged individualism," many Americans seek solutions by force of individual brilliance and willpower.

However, applying that philosophy alone to problem solving will not result in effective solutions because the isolation inherent in the approach leaves out an indispensable resource: other people. The people-design principle is based on the premise that an individual human life means nothing apart from other human beings. The concerns and ideas of others should be treated as the basic fabric of solution finding.

Anyone—not just status players—has the potential to become a valuable contributor to a solution to your problem. The object of this principle is to create an atmosphere that fosters the optimal contribution of each individual.

To do this, you must first throw away all preconceptions about who is qualified to offer what solutions and really listen to what each person has to say. If you do, you'll see the fallacy in the seldom-challenged premise that people don't like change.

People do not resist change *per se.* They resist conventional change. They resist change they don't understand or change that is imposed on them. They resist change that threatens or interferes with their priorities.

People also resist change that involves risks they perceive as greater than the potential benefits. They resist change when Conventional Thinking probes to pinpoint what's wrong and who's to blame, forcing them to protect their status and "turf."

The people-design principle gets people to work on change from the center (themselves) out, rather than just from the outside (others) in. Its uniqueness, purposes, solution-after-next, and systems principles motivate people more than conventional information-overload approaches do. Following this principle can minimize imposed change and turn perceived risk into welcomed opportunity.

For example, having installed a Total Quality Management program, a large engineering and construction company in the United States conducted two-day workshops to train employees in such concepts as the *"Kaizen"* or continuous process improvement philosophy of work-function teams, statistical process control, quality as a strategic weapon, employee involvement, and customer satisfaction. Nevertheless, despite the celebrated success of such teams in Japan, most U.S. teams proved unable to develop effective solutions to the problems they confronted. In fact, using Conventional Thinking, the U.S. teams seldom advanced beyond the stage of problem identification. Calls for participation in our society are overwhelming, but *how* people get involved—with Conventional Thinking or with Full-Spectrum Thinking—will make the difference between ineffective and effective results.

Typically, the teams were stymied by the decision-making paralysis that stems from excessive analysis of problems. However, using the previous principles with the team members, facilitators were able to lead such groups all the way to solution structuring. In some cases, the workshop training groups were even able to devise recommendations successfully implemented by the company.

We all want to be involved in making decisions that influence our lives. We accept and feel good about implementing a solution we help to devise. That's the premise of the people-design principle: Maximize individual participation with the first five principles and secure their commitment to the solution even before it is fully known. This is the means to align people with changes and ensure their effective performance in the new system. It is also an excellent self-development approach.

People designing their own solutions using Full-Spectrum Thinking principles produces commitment.

BETTERMENT TIMELINE
Not just a solution, but continuing change

No action is ultimate. The nature of all systems is dynamic; it is not just a collection of pieces. Solutions should be pictured on a continuum, yielding more and more gratifying rewards as they are continuously fine-tuned. As you implement a design or recommended change, you should also plan to keep changing and improving it. The larger purposes and solutions-after-next prepare you to do this. You should constantly look for and think about breakthroughs.

There is no such thing as a permanent "solution." A better concept is that any good solution carries within it the seeds of its own change. It develops a *positive* disequilibrium for continual change. Treat the solution or change being implemented now as the "current release" or "version 1.0."

"If it isn't broken, don't fix it" is a pseudo-rationale invoked far too often. It gets politicians off the hook. Managers use it to discourage subordinates who propose to change existing systems. Sometimes the expression is used to explain or justify decision-makers' arbitrary priorities; too often the real issue is not priorities, but laziness and smugness.

"Fix it before it breaks" (closely allied to the "do it right the first time" perspective of the quality first movement) is the clarion call of the modern competitive world. The betterment timeline principle epitomizes the "know when to improve it" concept.

Prepare a schedule for change and improvement of a solution as you are implementing it. Identify the elements of the change you are installing that could be changed later to move it toward the present solution-after-next target. Also prepare a schedule for starting all over again to expand purposes and to develop a new solution-after-next target. These two precepts are applicable to all sizes of systems or solutions.

The requirement to set up a timeline and a procedure for bettering the chosen solution after it is implemented is more than simply a scheduled time to consider further changes. In our experience, it also accords with what people involved in the Breakthrough Thinking process become eager to accomplish. Having worked together to bring about change, solve a problem, devise a better system, people look forward to its realization and to additional changes for the better. Setting a timeline creates a positive mind-set about the benefits of change.

If you build a program of continual modification and updating into your solution, you will preserve the solution's vitality and viability. The larger purposes in your hierarchy and the solutions-after-next help you to stimulate interest in continuing change and identify what the next changes should be.

Know when you'll make your next change.

UNDERSTANDING THE PRINCIPLES
Reviewing the following questions will help you think in terms of the assumptions of the new paradigm for creating and restructuring solutions:

Uniqueness: "All problems are not alike."
- Have I approached this problem or opportunity as if it were indeed unique, even if my first impression tells me that it isn't?

- What people, timing, and organizational culture make this situation unique?

- In addressing this problem, have I started with the perceptions of implied and stated assumptions of the person or people who first presented the problem?

You may indeed find later that a previous solution will work in your case. But apply that solution only after you are sure that a new or different one won't work better for the unique situation you confront.

Purposes: "A single or simple purpose rarely exists."

- Have I listed many purposes for working on this problem or opportunity?
- Have I explored the purposes for addressing the problem?
- Have I expanded those purposes?
- Where am I aiming? At what mission? At what larger purposes? What am I trying to accomplish?
- Do I truly know the larger context of purposes?

Ask purpose questions. Assume nothing. You may be missing the real problem altogether. Don't fix what should be eliminated.

Solution-After-Next: "Become a futurist."

- What would be some "fantasy" ideas for achieving the purposes? What "technology fiction" possibilities might lead me to what I could do today?
- Have I generated many alternative solutions-after-next or ideal systems? What regularities can guide the development of the best ideal systems?
- Am I implementing a near-term solution without concern for what might come in the future?
- Am I seeing the right targets toward which our recommendations should lead?
- Have I looked for a second right answer? A third?

A long-term and even "ideal" solution gives direction to your near-term solution. If you look to the future, you will surely meet the present.

Systems: "No problem exists in a vacuum."

- Have we considered our solution as a "system?" (Everything is a system.)
- Have I considered all the dimensions of my problem? Time? Costs? Resources? Controls?
- What are the elements and dimensions of the idea or the proposed solution? Have I used the "Systems Matrix?"

- Have I viewed the solution in the context of the "big picture?"
- Have I considered the "domino effect?" How will my solution affect other functions? Other people—clients, sponsors, target groups? The way we do work?
- Are there related problems that should be addressed at the same time?

The immediate problem and its solution are like the tip of an iceberg—they represent only a small portion of the whole.

Limited Information Collection: "Don't become a problem expert."

- Am I wasting time learning "all there is to know" about the problem?
- What would I do with the information if it were available (what are its purposes)?
- Am I wasting time looking for all the facts or whom to blame?
- Am I gathering only information needed to promote solutions—not bury them?

What you look for is what you get. Information and data are meaningless without ideas and wisdom to shape their collection.

People Design: "Teamwork, individual creativity, change."

- Have I said to myself: "Two thinking heads are better than one"?
- Am I including all the stakeholders or their representatives in defining purposes and generating solution ideas? Communicating to each person in terms of purposes, solutions-after-next, and "systems"?
- Have I given people on the team time to contribute to the change? Do they perceive it as a benefit? What groups or segments need to know the solution? What reward structure would help?

- Am I including a good mix of minds on the team? Experts? Doers? Creative thinkers? Holders of technology information? What is the best way to communicate information? Small groups? Newsletters? Memos? Staff/employee meetings? Video/Audio?
- Who should communicate the recommendation—Team members? Supervisors? Top management?

People with different experiences and abilities need to be a part of the process. Creative thinking, patience, and the principles of Breakthrough Thinking are the key. A solution will work only if people know about, contribute to, and understand it; only if they help in some way to develop it and/or continuously improve it.

Betterment Timeline: "Know when to improve it."

- How and when can we change *this* solution so that it incorporates more of the solution-after-next target?
- Do we have plans to "fix it before it breaks"? Have we prepared a schedule for initiating change and improvement of our solution?
- Does our solution include seeds of its own later change?
- Have we built the needed betterments into the strategic and financial plans?
- When will we try to develop a new solution for a larger purpose?

A breakthrough can occur over a period of time, not just at a given point in time.

A Fusion of West and East: Systems and Mandala

In the 1960s and 1970s, the Japanese were first to realize the benefits of the fusion of Western and Eastern thought that Breakthrough Thinking represents, based on their post-World War II necessity. Today, out of a similar necessity, the West turns toward the East to find the source of its own renaissance. Breakthrough Thinking provides a powerful synthesis of Western and Eastern principles and processes of thought. In the truest sense, it offers the best of the best of both worlds.

In Eastern thought, the concept of holistic understanding is symbolized by the mandala, the sign of wholeness, of self-contained unity, with no beginning and no end. The closest Western equivalent to the mandala is the concept of systems, in which every part of a whole is viewed as interdependent upon all the other parts.

In Eastern thought, the holistic perception of the mandala is achieved by meditation, over a long period of time. If this practice is performed rigorously and with dedication, ultimately you may perceive the mandala in your mind. If you do, you will then see everything, in all of its complex inter-relationships; you will understand all. Understanding the whole, you will also understand all the parts that comprise the whole. Unfortunately, achieving this all-encompassing understanding by means of meditation is difficult, and its success is unpredictable.

Far faster and more certain (if not as spiritually uplifting) is the western equivalent of the mandala concept: the holistic comprehension of systems. From this perspective, which is central to Breakthrough Thinking, everything is considered a system. And every system has a purpose. Moreover, much like those intricate Russian dolls, each of which is hidden inside a slightly larger doll, one system always involves another, which involves another, and so on.

Thus, in order to achieve holistic comprehension of a problem, we need to start by asking about the purposes of finding a solution, then the purpose of the purpose of the purpose of the purpose of the purpose of the purpose. And so forth. Finally, by means of such purpose expansion—much faster than by meditation—you will create a mental hierarchy of purposes to be achieved by the solution. In effect, you will arrive at the mandala. You will comprehend your situation in its entirety. This comprehension is the key to its solution.

In the West, as our research shows, effective people (and effective solution finders) intuitively think this way. Extensive evidence shows that effective people in the West fully understand the uniqueness of each situation, cope well with ambiguity, and focus on the larger purposes served by solving their problems. All of the assumptions of Full-Spectrum Thinking were practiced by the approximately eight percent who are effective people in the West, long before their intuitive solution-finding process was investigated and synthesized. Moreover, extensive research on thinking (Chapter 6) establishes a firm foundation for the fundamentals of the Full-Spectrum Thinking principles and process.

In the East, thanks to Eastern cultural traditions, the principles and process were practiced intuitively, perhaps by a greater percentage of the population. What people in the East lack in this regard is a *structure* to the paradigm that they have long used intuitively. Breakthrough Thinking has gained great acceptance in Japan not because it changes intuitive habits of Eastern thought—it does not—but instead because it provides a codified set of assumptions, and a conscious process by which to understand effective solution finding. It provides a paradigm, a plan to follow.

In the West, those relative few who have used intuitively the new thinking paradigm rally to its principles and process because it provides them with a way of explaining to others their often incomprehensible yet exceptionally effective thinking pattern. Once others understand it, they too can enjoy the benefits of this powerful synthesis of concepts, this fusion of Eastern and Western thought.

NOTES

1. Thomas H. Kuhn, *The Structure of Scientific Revolutions* (Chicago, IL: University of Chicago Press, 1970).

2. Ibid.

3. Ibid.

4. Gerald Nadler, "Design Processes and Their Results," *Design Studies,* Vol. 10, No. 2, (April 1989), pp. 124–127.

Chapter 8

Process of
Reasoning

The seven principles of Breakthrough Thinking provide fundamental assumptions for a new paradigm of thinking. Now we complete the paradigm by showing you how to activate these powerful new assumptions, how to combine them into a strong and flexible approach to solution finding, how to put the new assumptions into practice, how to "pull" people and technology into the most effective *implementable* changes.

Breakthrough Thinking is more than a solution or program. It is a paradigm shift in fundamental thinking that replaces conventional wisdom about planning, designing, improving, and problem-solving, that is, creating and restructuring solutions.

The difficulties each of us—each individual, each group, each organization, each society—has should alert us to question *how* we think about creating and restructuring solutions. The evidence presented in preceding chapters should further arouse your consciousness about the issue.

Decisions Over Time

Both "process" and "reasoning" are time-related. Process is defined in *The American College Dictionary* as "a systematic series of actions directed to some end," "the action of going forward or on." Reasoning is defined as "the act or process of one who reasons (the mental powers . . . to think out a problem)" and "the process of drawing conclusions or inferences from facts or premises."[1]

Like all animals, humans go through life each day making many decisions, large and small. Most animals are programmed to make decisions within a limited range of problem types and solution options. Humans, of course, perceive an immensely varied set of problems and opportunities and have the ability to conceive an almost infinite number of solutions. Consequently, human beings are likely to make more decisions every day than do other animals.

A decision means choosing from among alternatives. The choice leads to action. The overall scheme of making such a decision is to (1) generate alternatives, (2) organize them (for example, by categories, combinations of parts into a distinct whole), and then (3) select your choice. Humans repeat this three-part scheme, some claim, up to 50,000 times each day. To arrive at this number of decisions, you would have to count each word you speak as a point of decision. And it *is*.

In any case, each human being makes many decisions leading to action each day.

Likewise, a project represents a series of many, often minute, decisions made over time. But most critical is what a given decision is intended to accomplish; this is what is meant by the Process of Reasoning.

Making decisions about the steps and sub-steps of the Conventional Thinking reasoning process—what present activity to gather information about, what analysis techniques to use, who is at fault or who should be blamed, what model to use, what existing "solutions" can be copied—is reasoning based on the old paradigm of thinking. Because it does not focus on the intended purpose to be accomplished, the analysis- or rule-based action of Conventional Thinking is a major contributor to the current collapse of solution finding.

The process of reasoning based on the new Full-Spectrum Thinking assumptions detailed in Chapter 7 represents a different set of steps—a series of decisions to be made—to guide each human being, team, group, and organization. The subject of this chapter is the process based on the new principles. It is used to guide all the minute and major decisions made in the new paradigm of thinking.

The Concept of Expantegration

The Breakthrough Thinking process that completes the new paradigm of thinking is primarily based on our concept of "expantegration"—a word we coined to describe the thinking pattern needed for major decisions. As the word implies, you must both expand the options and alternatives regarding the step and integrate them to make the choice for that step.

In terms of the overall concept of the Breakthrough Thinking process, expantegration takes this form: First, you expand the purposes to be achieved for the problem, opportunity, activity, or issue you start with. Ask yourself its purpose, then ask the purpose of that purpose, then its purpose, and so on. Do this until you have gone far beyond any purpose that you are able actually to work on to find a solution. Then (and only then) work backward from this largest purpose to identify that purpose (usually bigger than originally imagined) which will serve to focus you on what you seek to achieve.

Addressing the Future

Because Conventional Thinking depends on finding and analyzing facts that exist in the present and past, it is ineffective for devising solutions that adequately address the future. Since the future does not yet exist, there are no "facts" to be found.

The only way to successfully address the future is to focus on something that *does* exist in the future—solutions—not on the past and present facts of the situation. Specifically, focus on the real *purpose* to be achieved, even the values, goals and objectives that motivate you or your group to *do something*.

For example, one of the 24 nationwide warehouses in a perishable product manufacturing company was experiencing high costs, damaged product, excessive overtime, and late shipments on its outgoing loading dock. Analyzing the current situation—flow diagrams, statistical data on delays, sources of damage, patterns of overtime activities, etc.—led the engineer assigned to the problem to recommend an automated system. It would cost $60,000 and pay for itself in eight months.

The idea seemed so good that it was also recommended for the other 23 loading docks. The vice president who had to approve the total of nearly $1.5 million expenditure asked a staff assistant to review the proposal and recommend whether or not the proposal should be funded. The assistant used Breakthrough Thinking on the project. The proposed expansion started with "to load trucks," and its purpose was to consolidate shipments to dealers, then to transport products to dealers, to deliver products to dealers, to distribute products to dealers, to sell products, to bring products into each home, to have customers use the products, etc.

The Breakthrough Thinking assistant, in conjunction with several supervisors and other staff people, selected "to distribute products to dealers" as the focus or real purpose to accomplish. This led to a solution-after-next target of selling all 24 warehouses! Twenty warehouses were actually sold as the completely new distribution system was installed to stay as close as possible to the target. Finding the solution recommendation took less than two weeks, and achieved far more of the values, goals, and objectives that stimulated the project to start with. So all three types of breakthroughs were achieved—the "ah-ha" change from reengineering the whole distribution system, the much better measurable results than what would have occurred from Conventional Thinking, and the avoidance of using a bad idea (even though the automated system would work, it did not achieve the *real* purpose, found by focusing on and examining the larger purposes of the loading dock).

On the one hand, Conventional Thinking focuses evermore-narrowly inward on ever-smaller parts of a problem and then, from an understanding of a minute part, assumes that answers for each part of a problem can be put together to solve the whole problem. On the other hand, Full-Spectrum Thinking develops outward and follows an ever-expanding hierarchy of purposes to understand first the whole, then, through an understanding of the whole, to comprehend the parts as well. This process often identifies a different "whole" for which the parts are frequently not at all the same as those in the original problem.

Following the principles and process of Breakthrough Thinking—particularly purpose expansion and then integration—greatly diminishes the possibility of finding the "right" solution to the wrong problem.

This "expantegration" should be repeated throughout the entire Breakthrough Thinking process. Doing so expands the number of options to be considered at each step—purpose, measures of purposes accomplishment, ideas for a solution-after-next, major ideal system alternatives, specifications for your solution recommendation, and so on. Repeating expantegration encourages consideration of all the new paradigm principles because many types of breakthroughs can occur in different steps throughout the process.

We propose "expantegration" as the thinking pattern characteristic of Breakthrough Thinking. It is distinct from, but related to certain thinking patterns noted in Chapter 6: for example, divergence and convergence.

In Conventional Thinking, convergent thinking is used to arrive at what is considered the one "right" solution to a problem. Convergence arrives at a general solution, a single, universal truth. This "solution" is a direct result of sub-division and compartmentalization.

Divergent thinking may be thought of as "brainstorming." Applying this pattern of thinking, you can discover many alternative solutions to your problem. However, these solutions will not be arranged in any useful order. All will appear equally possible; thus none will necessarily be more useful than another.

In addition, the end sought by divergent thinking is significantly different in Breakthrough Thinking. Being divergent in your thinking about what the problem or opportunity or issue is (instead of what the purposes are), what the parts of the situation are (instead of what the larger purposes are), the measures of effectiveness of what exists in the situation (instead of measures of the purposes to be accomplished), what ideas would correct or ameliorate the current situation (instead of what the ideal system toward which you move should be), and so on, minimizes the effectiveness of your results.

Expantegration is significantly different from divergence and convergence because the general pattern of reasoning in Full-Spectrum Thinking provides a different set of questions or steps to follow. For example, you expand the scope of your purpose as far as possible in order to arrive at a holistic comprehension of your problem. Then, you integrate the expanded hierarchy of purposes to select a situation-specific, a culturally and environmentally fit purpose.

This focus purpose is the largest possible purpose from the hierarchy that you *should* seek to achieve. It reflects a critical start to Full-Spectrum Creativity and will inevitably address the future as a solution-after-next. Since the focus purpose is smaller than the biggest purpose in the hierarchy, you have a larger context of purposes to guide the development of ideal and innovative solutions-after-next. This assures you that you will not choose a solution that "saws off the limb you are sitting on." At the same time, you will find a solution as far out along the limb of the future as you can safely go. Doing the same thing for each step in the process gives you the broad purview throughout. This is the larger, more inclusive mind-set of Full-Spectrum Creativity that results from following the Breakthrough Thinking pattern of expantegration.

By expanding the options to consider in each step and then integrating them, your thinking will remain oriented in the future, where your solution-after-next will succeed. This allows you not only to "pull" in the technology and other knowledge really needed (as opposed to the conventional "push" of technology into a situation), but also to remain flexible in adopting new technology and knowledge when they become available.

The General Flow of Reasoning

Breakthrough Thinking does more than simply generate "aha!" moments of absolute insight, the usual version of what "creativity" means. These will, of course, sometimes occur. By definition, however, a *process* takes place over time. Stroking a series of well-controlled singles and doubles, an occasional triple, is often more effective than swinging away from the heels, always trying to hit a home run. Similarly, many true breakthroughs are won incrementally by applying the seven principles in concert and by achieving creative results throughout the process of finding solutions.

Because breakthroughs are often gradual, some people grow frustrated by their uncertainty as to which principle to apply when. Given a particular problem or need, they want to know what to do first, what to do second, third, fourth, and so on. But in the Breakthrough Thinking process, all seven principles are used all the time.

In other words, the process that emerges from the new paradigm of thinking is best understood as a *general flow* of reasoning. The stream meanders, sometimes doubling back, then proceeds. It offers pools, eddies, currents, shallows, rapids. You can step into or out of the flowing stream at almost any point you choose along its banks.

Here is a rough topography of that river, landmarks along the general course of its flow, a description of your journey in finding solutions with Full-Spectrum Thinking:

- Identify many purposes for your program, project, problem issue, or opportunity. Go beyond your own situation or organization to the purposes of your customers and their customers. Examine these purposes with the other people involved. Work together to plan the changes, the new system, or the solution you will decide on, as well as the implementation mechanisms for making it happen.

- Open the scope of your investigation to examine ever-larger, more fundamental purposes. Expand your purposes from small scope to large, to create a hierarchy of purposes. Then select the largest achievable purpose(s) and focus your solution-finding efforts on that level. Also select your measures of purpose accomplishment—the criteria that will lead to later acceptance of the recommendation—based on that selected focus level.

- Generate many ideas for solutions-after-next to achieve your focus and larger purpose(s). Think ideal. Keep the options of systems and solutions open for consideration as long as possible.

- Form these options into several major alternative ideas. Assess these alternative solutions. Then choose a long-range, solution-after-next target for the major conditions. "Predicting the future may be impossible, but ignoring it is irresponsible."[2]

- Develop the recommended solution that stays as close as possible to the target while incorporating the minor conditions.

- Using the systems or question matrix in the previous chapter, detail the alternative that best fits the "real world," while coming closest to your target solution-after-next. This is your recommended course of action.

- Design a plan to install and carry out your solution.

- Install the solution, following the installation plan. On the basis of purpose accomplishment and related values, goals, and objectives, measure the results that you achieve.

- Provide for continuing change and improvement in your changes, system, or solution. Schedule a specific time to revise/expand your purpose(s) and solution, to move ever closer toward your solution-after-next target. Use "evolution-ary" tactics to attain the "revolutionary" target solution and to develop (every couple of years) a new revolutionary solution-after-next target to keep advancing evolutionary changes.

This process is used for every desire to create or restructure a solution—setting up a meeting, working on a problem, planning a project, instituting a corporate-wide program, making a telephone call, initiating and designing a team or task force, selecting sponsors for a charitable event, performing each phase in a product's life cycle, training an individual or group, doing strategic planning, prioritizing your activities, handling a professional or personal argument, planning your own or someone else's education. In other words, the process is used for all human purposeful activities and needs.

A clothing stores project was initiated at Canada Post Corporation, the Canadian national postal service, to design administrative systems to support a single clothing store for postal personnel, rather than the three stores that were then in operation. A project team of first-line supervisors from various locations across Canada was established. The project was initiated by a five-day workshop attended by the project team, which utilized the Breakthrough Thinking process.

The output from the workshop included a purpose expansion and purpose hierarchy, the design level (which represented the mission statement for the project), the solution-after-next (which was the vision or target to which the team designed the immediate solution), and an action plan (a betterment timeline) to implement the immediate and system-after-next solutions. The immediate solution consisted of a detailed manual system design to satisfy the needs for a single clothing store. This solution was successfully implemented within three months.

The solution-after-next envisioned Canada Post Corporation providing a national retail organization, such as Sears, Bay, or Eaton, with Canada Post's clothing standards. The appropriate Canada Post employees would then be given credit vouchers to purchase uniforms from the selected firm. This solution eliminated the need for a corporate warehouse and the associated distribution system. Canada Post is now in the process of implementing this long-range solution.

The Breakthrough Thinking process is not algorithmic method. It does not follow a constant pattern of inquiry, a method that is always the same. There is an ebb and flow to the universe and, thus, to all solution finding. In some cases, you or your group may want to start with the step concerning ideal systems, solutions-after-next, detailing a solution idea, or how-we-would-do-it-if-we-started-all-over. But all the principles are involved all of the time in each step.

Regardless of your starting point, our experience shows that the group will usually discover that it lacks a clear view of the purpose that needs to be accomplished, and so it "goes back" to that all-important step: identifying purposes.

For example, a college of engineering had convened a task force to do strategic planning for the next ten years. A Breakthrough Thinking facilitator noted that the task force members wanted to move directly to what the college would be like in ten years time. In other words, most members already had in mind their own ideal system/solution, at least their solution-after-next target.

The Breakthrough Thinking facilitator asked each task-force participant to bring to the next meeting his or her ideas about exactly how the college of engineering should be organized in ten years. All factors were to be considered: administration, curriculum, program, and so on.

As the group discussed these ideas, however, participants began to complain that they did not know the purpose of particular ideas proposed: for example, measuring student effectiveness in terms of grade point averages, as opposed to SAT scores or graduation rate. Or collecting certain information, as opposed to other. Consequently, the members agreed they would do better to examine first the larger purposes of the college of engineering, what they, as representatives of the school, were actually trying to accomplish.

In any situation, the general flow of reasoning based on the new assumptions or principles provides a road map to necessary decisions. This detail of Full-Spectrum Thinking contrasts markedly with Conventional Thinking, which typically provides only overall, inexact admonitions, such as "collect more data."

Instead, depending largely on the type of solution you seek—creating or restructuring a system, operating and supervising an existing system or solution, developing a generalization, learning, or evaluating—you will find yourself adapting the Breakthrough Thinking process in different ways.

In this regard, the seven principles themselves will often guide you. For example, the first principle: "Each and every situation is unique" tells you to treat all the people involved and the problem situation itself from a unique perspective. Don't assume that an imported solution will work in your situation or

that a previously successful technique should be used now simply because "this problem is similar to one where that technique was important."

Above all, determine the purposes of the always-unique
group of people involved. If you are working with a group to
solve a problem and you can't seem to get started, ask group
members what each thinks is the purpose—not of the problem
areas, but of the project itself. For example, the CEO of a
medium large company felt future product development and
corporate growth needed a dedicated strategic planning
process. She had heard about different program models at various conferences and decided she should adopt one for the
company. She called a consultant she knew and asked him to
help her install one of the programs.

The consultant who used Breakthrough Thinking suggested that the immediate need had more to do with designing
the plan to do strategic planning in *that* company rather than
with selecting a particular available program. The top nine executives of the company met with the Breakthrough Thinking
consultant to develop the strategic planning framework for that
specific circumstance. In addition to incorporating ideas from
several available programs as well as new ones the group developed, the strategic planning process now had company executives committed to its success.

THE ITERATIVE NATURE OF THE FLOW
The general flow of reasoning can be thought of as running
through five distinct yet interrelated types of terrain. At any
given moment, the nature of the flow is best understood in relation to the territory through which it is passing. The five
phases explained below are another way to describe the Breakthrough Thinking process.

Yet by following the Breakthrough Thinking flow of reasoning, you will seldom if ever adhere strictly to an explicit formula, a pattern of thinking that is exactly the same in every
problem-solving case. Why? In part, because each problem is
unique. Thus, each solution-finding situation must be addressed
in a slightly but significantly different way.

Moreover, you will find that, as you complete certain steps in the process, you may well return to steps you thought were completed and address them again on the basis of insights discovered during a later step, such as developing ideal alternatives for a solution-after-next. In this way, the process steps are often reiterated, so as to constantly refine the search for the ultimate solution.

A major reason for the iterative nature of the process is that there is really no "correct" or "right" purpose, solution-after-next target, or set of system specifications. The steps point out the directions, and the perceptions and understanding of the people involved determine the appropriateness of each decision needed along the way.

Inherent in the process is continual reassessment of exactly where you are. You know how you arrived at that point and what you have learned along the way. The steps are clear; you'll know what information you need, whether purposes, hierarchy of purposes, measures, or solutions-after-next. Full-Spectrum Thinking provides a detailed process, not just general directions to collect data, subdivide, model, analyze, and so on, as does Conventional Thinking.

The Breakthrough Thinking process may be specified in a lesser or greater number of steps. For example, a core set of three steps might be Purposes-Target solution-Results (PTR). Or it is possible to specify 24 steps, as is done in one reference source on Breakthrough Thinking: *Breakthrough Thinking in Total Quality Management* by Glen D. Hoffherr, John W. Moran, and Gerald Nadler (Prentice Hall, 1994).

The general flow of reasoning is a dialectical process: posing questions based on the new principles and examining alternative answers in preparation for selecting one that leads to the next question, and so on, until you ultimately select and implement a highly effective solution. You will find yourself moving back and forth between various steps in the process, sometimes doubling back, sometimes skipping ahead, but always moving generally forward, following the flow as it passes through different phases, distinct terrain.

The map that Breakthrough Thinking provides in this chapter—a three-step PTR process, five phases, a nine-step general flow of reasoning, up to a detailed 24-step process—covers the same basic thinking process with ever-increasing specificity. For some problems, fields of endeavor, and projects, a broad overview will be sufficient. For others, an awareness of the five phases or the nine steps will be all you need. Sometimes, highly detailed step-by-step guidance is called for. The broad direction supplied by the general flow of reasoning can be guidance enough, and reliance on a specific dictum such as "rule 23 is to be applied after technique such-and-such is utilized" can be completely inappropriate.

As you pursue the Breakthrough Thinking process, remember that interaction with people in the "real world" beyond your problem-solving group or your individual mind-set is essential to effective solution finding. Remember too that playing the "believing game" is especially encouraged in Breakthrough Thinking, not only because it provides an effective mode of interacting with "real-world" groups, but also because it inhibits your impulse to grab immediate answers. The believing game encourages you to seek ways to make a proposed solution work (be an "angel's advocate"), rather than to immediately doubt its potential to solve the problem (be a "devil's advocate").

Because the believing game resists the urge for early closure, it discourages arguments, defensiveness, and possessiveness. At each point along the Breakthrough Thinking flow of reasoning, you will keep your options open for as long as possible.

As the largest underwriter of a large state's worker compensation insurance pool, a major American insurance conglomerate was suffering significant losses. Not only was worker's compensation insurance in one large state unprofitable for the company, but profits on all other products combined could not overcome the losses sustained by the company's share of the state's pool, intended to cover businesses unable to obtain standard market coverage.

Developing a hierarchy of purposes for the problem of absorbing insurance pool losses led the company team to focus on the much larger purpose, "to write all related lines of insurance in the state." After considering many alternatives (different products, different marketing, different training, etc.), the team developed a new system for senior management that enabled diverse profit centers to cross-market effectively for the first time. Team members reasoned that, if single-product customers bought other types of insurance, the broader revenue base would, while absorbing the load imposed by the company's worker compensation obligation, also effect a more favorable product mix for the company.

An additional benefit of the Breakthrough Thinking workshop was that profit-center managers were aligned behind a common purpose (cross-marketing) for the first time. The region's cross-marketing efforts so substantially exceeded the regional vice president's and corporate headquarter's expectations that the cross-marketing scheme was adapted with Breakthrough Thinking to the nationwide property casualty operation, illustrating both the uniqueness and betterment timeline principles of Full-Spectrum Thinking.

A FIVE-PHASE VIEW OF THE PROCESS

Figure 8-1 represents the five-phase version of the general flow of reasoning in the Breakthrough Thinking process. It poses questions and employs devices that cause you to rethink what is to be done. As the flow of reasoning passes through these five phases, it manifests a remarkably high potential for achieving creative solutions.

Even though you will seldom be able to implement your ideal solution, the solution you ultimately choose will be closer to ideal, almost always a better, more inclusive, more future-rooted selection than you could otherwise achieve.

Phase One: Determining the purpose that should be achieved   The intent of Phase One is to ensure that your efforts seek a solution for the "right" purpose of the issue, activity,

Figure 8-1. Breakthrough Thinking Flow of Reasoning: Full-Spectrum Creativity.

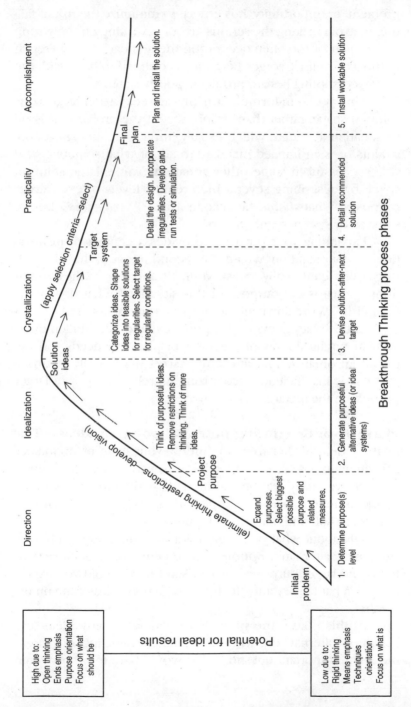

problem, or opportunity. It is crucial to minimize the risk of failure, to avoid making the serious error of working on the wrong one, which far too often occurs "on the first day." As the French Catholic novelist Georges Bernanos is claimed to have said, the worst, corrupting lies are problems poorly stated.

This problem-formulation phase seeks to enlarge your solution space, rather than simply accept the problem or issue or situation as stated, which usually implies technological constraints or is an implied mandate to adopt what someone *said* was successful in some other situation. You enlarge solution space by describing several hierarchical levels of ever larger purposes: What *should* be accomplished? What *should* be the solution or system requirements?

Expanding your purposes provides a context of justification for your solution, which is a second intent of this phase. It forces you continually to ask yourself and others these questions: "What is the purpose of this situation? What does it accomplish?" Write down all the purpose statements.

In this phase, obvious purposes expand into hidden ones. Your hierarchical array of purposes displays the needs and values of an organization, and emphasizes that merely stating a purpose is insufficient. Recognizing its relationship to a larger purpose in the hierarchy is also necessary.

Phase Two: Generating potential solution ideas   This phase should further free you and/or your team of prejudices and limitations and should lead you toward a desired, innovative yet eventually feasible solution. This requires that you develop as many "breakthrough" ideas as possible prior to selecting a solution that you will pursue.

Talk about what you really want to commit to for a future. How many alternative *options* can you envision to achieve your focus and larger purposes? What ideal future would you like to create? What fantasy and "technology fiction" ideas can you develop?

In this phase, the point is to generate many ideas and "phantom alternatives," without detailing, evaluating, or criticizing them. Important questions that would have to be answered if an idea were actually to be used should be noted, but not addressed at this point.

To help you select a target solution, assume "regularities." Regularities represent what *usually* occurs, factors about the selected purpose that are most frequent or important or "constant" through the time horizon being considered.

For example, imagine that you are a manufacturer of men's shirts in Paris in 1919. Despite the existence of thousands of amputee war veterans among your potential clientele, you should nonetheless design your *target* system to make two-armed shirts. Why? Because most of the end-users of your product will still have both arms intact.

By developing a target solution that assumes regularities, you can achieve high levels of innovation and creativity in your systems/solutions. By contrast, it is very difficult to develop creative ideas that will fit all conditions and factors. People too quickly discard ideas that do not "fit" *all* conditions or do not satisfy *all* the factors in a situation. The result is that they focus on the exception rather than the norm, the worst possible situation, as the governing influence in finding a solution.

For example, a university admissions office used Breakthrough Thinking to design an advanced information system for receiving, entering, and processing all the applications it received. In the process of designing the system, the assumption was made that all applications would arrive in the exact format and with complete enclosures as specified in the instructions, *even though this was known not to be entirely true.*

Of course, something still had to be done about the 23 percent of applications that arrived in less-than-complete form. They could not be handled at the beginning of the system designed for regularities. So a second, hand-operated system had to be designed to deal with them. All such applications had to be manually processed and "dummy" forms and information inserted so they could "fit into" the rest of the automated system, the one designed to accommodate 77 percent of the applications received.

The point is that, in designing solutions, you want to stay as close as possible to your ideal solution target. You want to develop ideas and systems for regularity conditions, for the things that occur most frequently, *as if they were the only things that occur.* You want ideas that give you the highest potential for ideal results. Why? Because in Phase Three, you can adjust that regularity solution to accommodate "real world" irregularities. In that way, you can come as close as possible to ideal results. In other words, accommodate your exceptions, but only once you have already developed your rule.

Phase Three: Selecting a feasible ideal solution target
After selecting a target solution for regularity conditions, identify contemplated but presently unfeasible solutions. Use these to stimulate research and development for the period far beyond the time horizon of even your feasible ideal solution target. What can be the *target* vision to achieve our purposes?

Review the ideas you developed in Phase Two to determine which have potential as a major solution and which are components that may fit into several major solutions. Following this review, prepare more detail, give each major idea greater form, so that you can effectively evaluate the likely solutions, while attempting to incorporate needed components. This knowledge allows you to divide your ideas into contemplated and presently feasible systems. The result is that some edge is taken off the "wild" ideal system ideas developed in Phase Two for their potential to achieve high amounts of exceptional results.

Phase Four: Developing a recommended solution   In this phase, develop a workable solution that stays as close as possible to the feasible ideal solution target, yet incorporates components to deal with necessary exceptions or irregularities. The resulting solution tends to preserve the benefits of the feasible ideal solution target developed for regularities, at the same time incorporating close to "optimal" components for accommodating irregularities. Such pluralistic and multi-channeled systems do not attempt to force everyone into a single mode of operation.

Several considerations arise in this phase. One is to determine how the irregularities or infrequent demands can be incorporated without drastically altering the target solution.

A second consideration is how and where the feasible ideal solution target is to be modified to cope with irregularities. An installed solution should come as close as possible to being "all things to all people," as long as irregularities have not modified the core solution-after-next target too significantly. If the loss in utility to your primary purposes is greater than the gain for your secondary purposes, you should not accept the modification.

A third consideration concerns the documentation needed for a solution. In some projects you will need to develop significant detail so that the various parts of your recommended solution can be understood and the workability of the whole can be assured.

A fourth consideration in this phase is to get approval of or agreement to install your recommendation.

Phase Five: Installing today's recommended solution
Nothing in the previous phases guarantees that your solution will work. Experience alone is insufficient to determine a system's adequacy for achieving the desired purpose, reliability of performance, completeness of specification, and effectiveness and stability in the face of real-life input and operating conditions. In this phase, your intent is to intelligently install, adequately measure the performance of, and advisedly plan future changes in your solution. What *course of action* should be followed to install and operate the recommendation? What schedule should be set up for future changes to get closer to the target solution?

Testing those specifications, components, or policies that need to be tested (laboratories, in the field, simulation, etc.) should resolve five questions: (1) Will the forms, equipment, and any other arrangements function as expected? (2) Will irregularities be dealt with reliably and satisfactorily? (3) Will the output or results satisfactorily meet the needs of the customer or user? (4) After training and skill development, can the human elements needed to operate the solution system perform satisfactorily? (5) Will the integrated system do the job as expected under real-life conditions?

Answering all these questions is difficult, but requires your review in this final phase. Fortunately, the Breakthrough Thinking principles and process can be applied to each question. That is, as you address them, you can apply the concept of expantegration again and again.

> *In 1989, Japan experienced a strong construction boom. As a result, many construction companies and design consulting companies urged Showa Ceramic Company, one of the famous wall tile manufacturers of Seto City, to send them samples of tile products. The Showa staff was soon overloaded with urgent requests for sample wall tiles.*
>
> *A meeting was called to use Breakthrough Thinking to solve the problem. They began to expand the purposes of providing sample tiles. They realized that the larger purpose of providing sample tiles was not to send the actual tile, but rather to provide potential customers with tangible awareness of the various reflective properties, shadings, and textures of Showa tiles.*
>
> *After discussing many alternative solutions for this focused larger purpose, they selected the largest feasible target solution, which they called a "stick sample." Their solution revolutionized the conventional concept of tile samples.*
>
> *The "stick sample" increased the productivity of such samples as far as possible toward the ideal solution, namely, samples provided at no time and no cost. The solution reduced the cost of material to almost nothing. Almost no cost or time was spent in handling and packaging. Shipping and transport costs were also greatly reduced, since the new samples sticks are so light and compact that they can easily be sent through the mail.*
>
> *This "stick sample" concept, designed by Showa Ceramic Company on the basis of Breakthrough Thinking, won the Nikkei Advertising Award for 1993.*

Full-Spectrum Creativity

Unusual, innovative, radical "off-the-wall" ideas for solutions are what is expected when creativity is sought in Conventional Thinking. Such ideas are indeed hard to generate when the data about what exists overwhelms us. Full-Spectrum Creativity is representing the future to the present—identifying effective and common purposes, developing "imaginations" of the future for the purposes, incorporating people in a positive way to influence and generate more change, and designing installation plans that assure use of the solution and minimize transition trauma. Simply developing creative idealized solutions (for education, health care, transportation, etc.) is not enough; people must recognize that creativity is needed in all phases of change.

Figure 8-1 helps to reinterpret the conventional notion of creativity. Instead of defining creativity as only the development of significant ideas and changes, the expantegration concept shows how "significant ideas" and solutions are needed and must be developed at all phases of the Breakthrough Thinking process.

The horizontal axis in Figure 8-1 is roughly related to the time spent in solving a problem. However, amounts of time vary greatly for each phase of actual projects.

Our experience shows that approximately 25–35 percent of the time spent in solution finding is spent on the first three of the five phases and 65–75 percent on the last two phases. Detailing and installing your solution are simply more time-consuming.

The curving line interrelates the five phases of solution finding, as each one "flows" purposefully to the next.

The vertical scale reflects the potential for achieving an "ideal" result, for example, a creative solution, great savings, low costs, a high level of commitment by people involved, or outstanding innovation. This scale marks the degree of potential reached toward maximizing the results of your efforts.

In Phase One, determining the real opportunity offered by the situation involves expanding purposes into a hierarchy, exploring purposeful directions, incorporating customer purposes and purposes of the customer's customer, expanding the solution space, and selecting the largest purpose that the project can seek to achieve. Here you want to consciously redefine existing conceptualizations and transcend current formulations of the problem.

This part of the process allows thorough exploration of beliefs, terms of reference, warrants, and charges to assure that work is proceeding satisfactorily. This end is often aided by a group. Starting at this point, questions concerning implementing potential solutions need to be answered.

This first phase immediately pushes the project into a level of high potential for ideal results. It is far more likely than conventional strategies to get consensus among group members on a basic premise through which solutions can be jointly sought. Large and complex systems are dealt with by developing functional components, each of which then requires its own purpose expansion.

Phase Two continues the push toward ideal results by utilizing techniques of individual and group stimulation for what is acknowledged, for the time being, to be a necessary purpose. As many ideal (in terms of values, goals, and objectives), "perfect," or start-all-over-again solutions as possible are now developed to widen choices and to remove thinking restrictions. All ideas should aim toward creating significant difference from current or initially expected levels of performance.

If the differential is negligible, the possibilities for action are remote. An ideal solution is a constant guide for continuing change and improvement. This point of highest potential in Figure 8-1 should be your goal in the remaining three phases.

Phase Three shapes the ideas into possible solutions that you then develop by playing the believing game: How *can* an idea be made operational? In this phase, you select your target solution-after-next—the ideal *feasible* system, for use under regularity conditions. It will be slightly lower in its potential for ideal results, because real conditions will crystallize the parameters of a solution that can actually be implemented. Nonetheless, your ideal target solution represents an excellent blueprint to guide the rest of the project and to stimulate future changes, even after your solution is installed.

In Phase Four, you address the necessary exceptions and irregularities, while seeking to maintain the good qualities of the target solution. After all, why discard an excellent target solution that adequately handles 95 percent of the conditions you face, simply because another 5 percent of the conditions cannot fit into it? By contrast, conventional approaches would have you search for the single arrangement or method that would accommodate both the 95 percent and the 5 percent. Instead, Breakthrough Thinking utilizes three or four integrated arrangements for keeping the recommendations as close as possible to the target for each of the major conditions.

In Phase Five, you maintain high potential for ideal results by keeping in mind your purposes, purpose hierarchy, suggestions for ideal solutions, target solution, and real-life conditions while making essential accommodations—the many, often minor, decisions that are necessary whenever a change is made, a new system installed, or a solution implemented. Especially when working with a group or as part of a larger organization, be sure to keep all interested parties informed as you proceed to develop your solution. Schedule the next changes to achieve more of the target solution and bigger purposes. An organization always thinking about breakthroughs and how to get closer to them is energetic, exciting, and competitive.

From the start of the solution-finding process, continual interchanges between you or your group and members of the "real world" make installation of a new system or implementation of your solution seem natural, rather than a sudden action imposed from the outside. In addition, the information developed through the course of your solution-finding project lends itself to your seeking continuing improvements in and updates of the target solution itself, as well as of the installed solution.

Now, by stark contrast, consider the bottom half of Figure 8-2. Notice how Conventional Thinking influences your flow of reasoning.

Gathering data about the problem and analyzing what exists in the unsatisfactory present and past, determining who is at fault for the current situation, and further probing into the current unsatisfactory system or situation greatly restricts or

Figure 8-2.
Comparison of potential for ideal results between Full-Spectrum Thinking and Conventional Thinking.

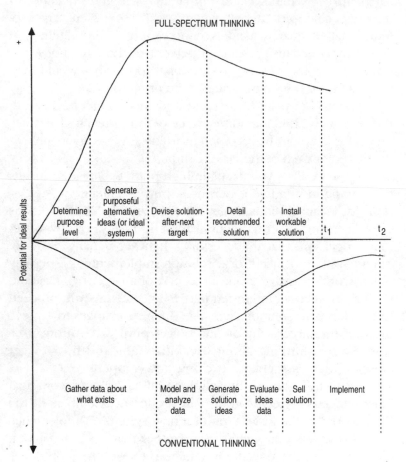

turns negative the potential for ideal results. Worse yet are the many "fad" programs (total quality management, reengineering, management by objectives, cycle-time management, etc.) that "require" you to use a pre-set number of data-gathering and analysis tools right at the beginning of any improvement project. Getting good ideas from the morass of data that paralyzes us is extremely difficult. Even with great effort, escaping this trap is almost impossible. At this point, *any* solution is usually accepted. And that outcome is hardly conducive to innovative solutions. As noted earlier, this probably explains why organizations seek "creativity" in Conventional Thinking efforts.

Remember that no amount of formally recorded data or information about what the existing, unsatisfactory system does or what the current problem situation is will ever equal the knowledge and information base in the minds of the people involved—operators, clients, customers, even prospective users not currently involved. It is *how*—the paradigm of thinking—their knowledge can be effectively utilized. Although many problem-solving strategies indicate that you should be sure that you are working on the right problem, they fail to indicate how collecting a great deal of data will accomplish this essential goal.

By using the knowledge of people involved to develop the purpose hierarchy, generate ideal systems, select target solutions, and so on, Full-Spectrum Thinking allows you to be certain that you are indeed working on the right problem (or purpose) and enhances the solutions implementation. People will accept changes, new systems, and solutions that they help generate. This again demonstrates the inextricable intertwining of the seven principles of Full-Spectrum Thinking into the Breakthrough Thinking process.

Again in Japan, one of the largest computer and communications companies gives top priority to customer satisfaction through relentless efforts to provide better products and services. Using Breakthrough Thinking, the company has engaged in several activities to achieve this purpose: (1) A

"New Champion Product Movement" was established in 1987. Prior to this, product development was the province of professional staff, an isolated group in many ways. Everyone in the company was involved in product development after 1987. Through 1992, an amazing 200,000 new product ideas were submitted by all levels of people in the company. Some successful products from this movement are VoicePoint, TeleMeeting Terminal, and Humming Board.

(2) The year 1990 was designated as the Year of BREAKTHROUGH to enhance the New Champion Product Movement. Breakthrough Thinking was taught to many as advanced creativity to foster sensitivity, customer-oriented creativity, and seeds-oriented creativity (what R&D ought to be performed).

(3) The "Super 21 Movement" started in 1992. The vision of the company was defined first as a purpose or mission (the domain of computer and communications for a holonic—holistic and electronic—society), and then the development of a holonic corporation to achieve that mission with the specific products needed for society. This vision was developed with Breakthrough Thinking at a "Future Conference" in 1990. The company also stated that the entire business is now to be based on "learn from the future" or on a "pull-system" from the future.

Purposes: At the Head of an Expanding Circular Parade

A Breakthrough Thinking effort may begin at any one of several steps. Typically, however, it will begin by questioning the purposes of finding a solution for your situation.

As you expand your understanding of those purposes, you will naturally expand your solution space. For example, what was at first considered a problem of how best to utilize a nursing staff might come to be seen as a problem of how to develop a system of patient care—a larger purpose that *includes* your original conception of the problem. As you expand your purposes, then, you will also expand the values, goals, and objectives by which you will ultimately measure the effectiveness of the solution that you finally select.

For example, if you conceive of your problem as one of nursing staff utilization through Conventional Thinking, you will probably consider that the purpose of your problem-solving effort is to collect data about what the nursing staff now does. In that case, your measures of success would include the amount of data you collect, the completeness of the data, its accuracy, and the extent to which your sample is representative of the entire nursing staff.

However, if you expand the purposes of solving your problem to the bigger level of "develop a system of patient care," your measures of success in accomplishing that larger purpose will also change and expand. In that case, your new measures would probably include the number of patients served per nurse, the indicators of patient satisfaction, improved rates of mortality and morbidity, and cost per patient-day.

By expanding your purposes, you will escape a characteristic trap of Conventional Thinking. You will refuse to lock yourself into less significant measures of improvement in your problem situation. This is essential to finding the most effective possible solution. Why? Because in almost all cases, if you are told to aim for 25 percent improvement, you will achieve no more than that, probably less.

On the other hand, if from the very start of your solution-finding effort, you expand purposes as far as possible, then you are certain to derive a set of success measures far larger and more effective than what you had originally envisioned. If you begin with the inflexible assumption that you want only incremental, not radical change, mere incremental change (or less) is exactly what you'll get. And your "solution" will likely be outdated and prove useless even before it is fully implemented.

In solution finding, as in the rest of life, what we find is what we seek. Conventional Thinking insists that a problem be rigidly classified before a solution can be sought. By contrast, Breakthrough Thinking requires that, rather than limit yourself to a narrow, preexisting definition of the problem, you instead expand as far as possible the purpose you seek to achieve. To paraphrase a Scandinavian proverb: Aim for the stars so that your arrow will be sure to clear the trees.

While the manifestation of current values, goals, and objectives is often your initial impetus to seeking a solution, because your current situation does not conform to your needs, desires, or expectations, effective solution finding requires that you not let existing values, goals, and objectives become the ul- timate measure of your success. Effective solution finding oc- curs at the greatest possible level of expanded purposes. Only on that expanded level is it effectively measured.

Another important reason to focus first on purposes—and their expansion—is that they are an excellent way of identify- ing exactly what type of issue you are confronting. Once you expand as far as possible the purposes of solving your problem, you will clearly see whether your best solution is to be found in terms of creating or restructuring a system or solution, operat- ing and supervising an existing system or solution, developing generalizations, evaluating, or learning.

A third important reason to focus first on purposes is that the level to which you are able to expand your purposes is the one at which you should start to collect information. In fact, it encourages information collection about the bigger purpose levels. These are the levels at which you will find your solution. Thus, at least as regards the solution for your situation, consciously collecting information at lower levels of purpose is a waste of time and energy, not to mention money.

Finally, focusing first on purposes provides powerful moti- vation to exert the effort necessary to find a solution. It shows you early in the process that the results you achieve will be measured in much larger terms than you had anticipated.

As you expand your purposes, you realize that the smaller the purpose you address, the smaller the number of alternative solutions are available. The larger the purpose you envision, the more ideas you will generate for its solution.

A New Paradigm of Thinking Means Results

Both Conventional Thinking and Breakthrough Thinking be- gin with a felt need, an identified dissatisfaction, a desire for something more, something better. Closing the gap between perceived reality and aspiration—closing it on the basis of a consciously chosen solution-finding approach—is a uniquely human goal.

A telling distinction, however, between Conventional Thinking and Full-Spectrum Thinking is that the former is vague about precisely how to follow its steps. It tells you to collect the facts. But exactly which facts? It tells you to analyze the data. But exactly which data? And *how*? Exactly what proposed solution should you model? Exactly which procedures should you represent in your flowchart? In these and other important matters, Conventional Thinking offers little if any specific guidance.

By contrast, Breakthrough Thinking is firmly rooted in purposes. It tells you where and how to begin looking for the information that will help you understand not only your situation, but far more importantly, its best possible solution. Breakthrough Thinking provides a radically different solution-finding culture, a new set of fundamental assumptions, a new process, a new pattern, a new approach—a new paradigm of thinking.

Whenever you try to create a system or artifact, solve problems, make a change, plan, design, improve, or reengineer an existing system or solution, these are the results that you are very likely seeking:

- The most effective solution, system, or recommendation;
- A high likelihood of implementing the solution, system, or recommendation that you select;
- A low cost of resources and time to achieve these results.

In evaluating whether to practice the principles and process of Full-Spectrum Thinking, or whether to continue to rely on Conventional Thinking, simply ask yourself: *How* will I find . . .

THE MOST EFFECTIVE SOLUTIONS/ SYSTEMS/ RECOMMENDATIONS

Does the process (or thinking paradigm) that you now use provide

- Assurance that you are working on the right purpose (problem) at the right time?

- Connection of your purposes to your customers' purposes and your target groups' needs?
- Opportunities for creativity in all phases or steps of the problem-solving project?
- Proven significantly better-than-expected benefits—innovations, new ideas, workable solutions, economic return, quality, customer satisfaction, customer delight?
- Built-in, continual improvement?

A HIGH LIKELIHOOD OF IMPLEMENTING YOUR SOLUTION/SYSTEM/RECOMMENDATION

Does the process (or thinking paradigm) that you now use provide

- Early stakeholders' buy-in, so that implementation starts at the beginning of the problem-solving process and is supported throughout all changes?
- Ways to remove obstacles to simple solutions?
- Identification of all interfaces and consequences of proposed plans?
- Ability to cope with uncertainties, for example, environment, economics, regulations, external forces, etc.—by developing and keeping options available for consideration when needed.

A LOW COST OF RESOURCES AND TIME TAKEN TO ACHIEVE RESULTS

Does the process (or thinking paradigm) that you now use provide

- Clutter-free reasoning?
- Less time required than expected per project?
- Minimal but required information collection, so as to reduce analysis-paralysis?
- Structure for the imaginative mind and freedom for the structured mind?
- Effective, continuing intercommunications among the participants (after completion of the solution-finding project), so as to promote team building, open information exchange, etc.?

We have asked varied audiences and workshop participants these questions. When people answer in relation to the
Conventional Thinking paradigm, their responses are over-
whelmingly "No." When they answer in relation to the new
thinking paradigm—once it has been learned—their responses
are resoundingly "Yes."

In other words, we should change our automatic process
response when starting to find a solution from "Everyone
knows we have to gather facts about what exists, apply analysis
techniques, and pin a label on the problem (it's a personnel or
inventory or communications or accounting problem)" to
"Everyone knows we have to expand purposes to find our
focus and develop solutions-after-next for it."

In addition, the seven principles and the process provide
the foundation for significant individual and organizational
learning. The larger purposes show all larger contexts, solutions-after-next instigate searches for ways to make unusual
ideas workable, the systems matrix identifies what solution
specifications are needed, and so on. Getting everyone involved with the new paradigm of thinking "pulls" all toward
what's coming as the real basis for learning.

Solution finding that effectively accomplishes the results
that people seek to achieve when creating and restructuring
systems is now based on the Breakthrough Thinking concepts.
However, we want to stress once again that we propose this
new paradigm of thinking as an *inclusive,* not an exclusive, alternative. When useful and appropriate, Full-Spectrum Thinking incorporates Conventional Thinking. Chapter 11, the
Multi-Thinker, will expand on this concept.

Chapter 9 will now detail the research of many, including
our own 30 years of investigations, which provide support for
the principles and process of Breakthrough Thinking.

NOTES
1. *The American College Dictionary* (New York: Random House,
   1964).

2. Eberhardt Rechtin, *Systems Architecting: Creating and Building
   Complex Systems* (Englewood Cliffs, NJ: Prentice-Hall, 1991).

Research on Breakthrough Thinking

*T*he philosophy is great. The research is compelling. The principles make sense. The process is stimulating.

But does it work?

Besides our own investigations, evidence derived from the work of many other researchers supports, both directly and indirectly, the validity and value of the principles and process of Breakthrough Thinking. Full-Spectrum Thinking, developed jointly in both East and West, has been shown to produce consistently better results in planning, designing, creating and restructuring systems, and solving problems—in finding solutions—than does Conventional Thinking.

The roots of the formal development of Breakthrough Thinking formulated in this book can be traced back some 45 years. As with many other highly successful achievements, it arose from apparent failure.

A Brief History of Breakthrough Thinking

In 1948, a young industrial engineer, a graduate student working at a food processing plant in the midwestern state of Wisconsin, was assigned his first problem to solve as a professional.

In processing food, the company president explained, a crucial quality aspect is the freshness of the food. The key is to minimize the time between the moment the beans, for example, are picked from the stalk and the time they are canned or blanched before being frozen.

A bottleneck had occurred in the system. The president explained to the eager young engineer that loading dock delays were causing major problems of waste and quality control. "Give me a one-page report on the problem," he instructed. "Tell me what I ought to do."

The young man, steeped in academic techniques and models, had learned well the beauty and utility, indeed the infallibility, of flowcharts and statistical analyses, measurements of work and productivity. Eager to please his first employer, he flawlessly applied all the techniques he had been taught. Proud of his analytical accomplishment, as well as his recommendations, he incorporated all his data and findings in his first professional report, which was ten times longer (and certainly much better) than his boss had expected.

The president called the young man into his office. "Gerry," he said, "know what I think of your report?" With a crisp snap, the president took the young man's ten-page handiwork, tore it in half, and threw it in the wastebasket. Then he asked simply: "If you were in my shoes, how would you solve the problem? That's what I need to know."

At that moment, the seeds of Breakthrough Thinking were sown.

Chastened and puzzled, the young man reduced his report to a single page of recommendations and justification, as ordered. Eventually, his recommendations were adopted, but something far more important had also occurred.

The young man realized that he had done exactly what all his professors had told him to do. He had analyzed the problem exhaustively. He had skillfully applied techniques he had been taught in school. What was wrong?

Over the next several years, he began informally to observe those engineers, managers, and others whom he considered most professionally effective. "What do they do differently from the run-of-the-mill?" he wondered.

At Washington University in St. Louis, Missouri, where he was now a member of an academic faculty, he asked various colleagues—a psychologist, a sociologist, a business professor, an anthropologist—"How do the most effective people you know go about being so effective? How do the best problem-solvers solve problems? How do the best planners and designers go about planning and design?" This small, interdisciplinary group of colleagues, which included such leading scholars as sociologist Alvin Gouldner and anthropologist John Bennett, began interviewing people in their fields whom they considered expert problem solvers.

At that time little if any useful research existed on the topic. What did exist were simply studies of people in the aggregate, general populations of research subjects. In short, the "run-of-the-mill." No one had exclusively studied people recognized as most effective. The question asked was: Did effective people use the same process of reasoning as everybody else? Were they simply smarter, or did they go about their solution finding and implementation differently?

The first research findings were striking. Almost invariably, the effective people noted that, in order to become effective, they first threw out almost everything they had been taught about solving problems. From that point on, they proceeded intuitively.

By compiling and synthesizing common aspects of the shared solution-finding intuitions of their subjects, the investigators were able to identify and synthesize various principles and a solution-finding process that this population of effective problem solvers followed unconsciously.

The initial research results were published by Gerald Nadler: *An Investigation of Design Methodologies,* in the academic journal, *Management Science* in June 1967. From then on, Nadler and his colleagues continued to test their hypotheses with other groups of expert solution finders and to refine the principles and process of what came to be called Breakthrough Thinking.

Although he was still teaching the Conventional Approach to problem solving, Nadler's increasingly firm conviction was that students should be taught what works. In 1959, as the first Lucas Visiting Professor at the University of Birmingham in England, he introduced the concepts of Full-Spectrum Thinking.

These concepts were first published by Nadler in his article "Work Design: A Philosophy for Applying Work Principles," which appeared in the *Journal of Industrial Engineering* (May/June 1959). They were later amplified in his book *Work Design* (Homewood, IL: Richard D. Irwin, 1963).

Soon, Nadler was invited to Tokyo. In 1963, as a visiting professor at Waseda University, Japan's largest private educational institution, he realized that Japanese industialists, executives, and managers had been engaged in activity similar to his own for the previous decade or so. Both he and the Japanese had been striving to understand, improve, and adapt traditional Western ways of thinking.

His host, Japanese professor Ryuichi Yoshiya, tactfully challenged the assumptions in *Work Design*. Yoshiya had been educated in the United States and knew well that Nadler's principles did not represent prevailing thought. After a few weeks of auditing Nadler's course, however, Yoshiya became a devoted champion of *Work Design*.

Vigorously advocating Nadler's new thinking process, Yoshiya personally translated Nadler's book into Japanese and was instrumental in founding the Japan Work Design Society, which studies, practices, and promotes the principles and process of what is called Breakthrough Thinking. To this day, Professor Yoshiya—a ranking expert in Japan and a key consultant to that nation's most successful corporations—regards these ideas as "probably the only appropriate technique for designing large and integrated systems."[1]

Other members of Nadler's first Japanese seminars in 1963 also became staunch advocates of the process then called *Work Design*. Among these were Professor Kozi Morooka of Tokai University; Fujio Umibe, retired president of Toshiba Research Corporation; Professor Teruo Takahashi of Waseda University; and Shigeru Harashina, now president of Systems Giken Company in Tokyo and developer of its Creative Problem Solving Program, based on *Work Design*.

The principles and process of Breakthrough Thinking have since come to play a major role in the development of Japan's most innovative and successful industrial techniques.

Professor Seiji Kurosu of the Systems Science Institute at Waseda University notes in his 1994 article in the Japanese journal *Management Systems,* "Classical Books on Industrial Management: From *Work Design* to *Breakthrough Thinking,*" that "there is still no epoch-making system design method exceeding it."[2]

Yet Nadler had made no conscious effort to incorporate Eastern principles of thought into the developing paradigm of thinking. His quest was simply to identify what exceptionally effective solution finders actually do to solve their problems and exactly how they go about finding their excellent solutions. It came as a surprise, both to Nadler and to his Japanese colleagues, that the principles and process emerging from his research related so well to some characteristic aspects of Eastern thought. For example, Umibe tells the story about an ancient Buddhist priest who went to China to study with a high Chinese priest. The high priest asked him "What is your purpose?" And when he answered, he was asked again and again, "What is the purpose?" Thus, his eyes were opened and he understood what he should do—not just study books and the Buddhist Bibles, but train others. He returned to Japan to start a new school of his own.

While living in Japan Nadler also came to realize how much certain principles he found in his studies mirrored traditional Japanese instincts and patterns of thinking they employ when working on projects. For example, when he visited the offices of IBM Japan to request their technical assistance in performing some statistical computations, he did not receive the immediate, straightforward response he had come to expect from American executives. Instead, he met with a group of four interested persons. Moreover, in an attempt to comprehend completely how they might best meet his needs, all four of the Japanese executives questioned him at length as to the purpose of the computations for which he sought IBM's assistance. Finally, they made no decision on the spot; instead, they told him that they would respond to his request later. They quickly agreed to provide the computer assistance.

Later, as his host, Professor Yoshiya, explained various aspects of the Japanese manner and custom to him, Nadler realized that, in their instinctive response to his request, the IBM Japan executives had manifested at least three of the principles of *Work Design* that he had come to Japan to teach. For example, they invested time up front to find out what it was that Nadler really wanted, what his larger purpose was, what he was trying to accomplish. By contrast, an American executive would simply say: "Tell me what you want and how long it'll take. I'll tell you whether we can do it." The American would consider only activity, not purposes.

In 1966, teaching at the University of Wisconsin, Nadler was pleased to receive into his tutelage a Japanese master's degree candidate who had come to the United States specifically to study with Nadler. Shozo Hibino immediately began to collaborate with Nadler in his research into the principles of thought used intuitively by expert solution finders. These and other advanced findings provided the basis for Nadler's 1981 textbook, *The Planning and Design Approach* (John Wiley & Sons, New York).

After establishing himself in his Japanese academic and consulting career, Hibino returned to Wisconsin in 1979. There, bringing to bear his own extensive knowledge of Eastern philosophies, he again studied and worked with Nadler to develop and refine the principles of Full-Spectrum Thinking.

In 1983, during one of Nadler's frequent trips to Japan to discuss his work with the Japan Work Design Society and many other groups, Nadler and Hibino decided to make their previously academic work available to a wider, indeed global, audience. They coined the phrase "Breakthrough Thinking" to describe Full-Spectrum Thinking for creating and restructuring solutions, problem solving, improving, planning, and design. In 1990, they published the first of their books for a popular audience, *Breakthrough Thinking* (Prima Publishing/St. Martin's Press) now translated into Danish, Korean, and Japanese. (The second edition appeared in 1994.)

As this historical overview demonstrates, intuitive Breakthrough Thinkers have always existed. Yet the principles and process of Full-Spectrum Thinking have been formally established on the basis of research, both empirical and investigative, conducted over some 40 years. The principles and process have also been developed and tested in applications and field research conducted in both Western and Eastern societies, where they have been proven to work with individuals, groups, and large organizations.

The results of those studies and case histories—some of which you may recognize from earlier chapters—comprise direct, scientific support for the principles and process of Breakthrough Thinking. Other case histories and studies conducted in a variety of other fields provide further indirect evidence in support of the new paradigm of thinking. The intuitive Breakthrough Thinkers, approximately 8 percent of people, may say that these concepts are "obvious" and "self-evident." While true for them, our aim is to get each person to change his or her current automatic response when trying to find a solution—"everyone knows you have to start by finding out what's happening now"—to a different automatic response—"everyone knows you have to start by expanding purposes and developing solutions-after-next." The following limited review of direct and indirect support for each principle and the process, in conjunction with the research reported in Chapter 6, should help achieve this aim.

The Uniqueness Principle

DIRECT SUPPORT

Writing in *Management Science,* Ohio State University professor Paul Nutt reported an experimental comparison of the effectiveness of three planning methods; those based on systems (that is, Full-Spectrum Thinking) ideas, those based on behavioral science concepts, and those based on heuristics. Each planning method was applied to develop plans for two distinct problems. The systems method, which produced significantly better quality plans, addressed each problem as unique. Nutt's experiment found that "applying research findings associated with simple problems, like work measurement rate setting, to multidimensional problems, like planning, seems unwise."[3]

Writing in *Archives of Psychiatric Nursing*, Linda K. Tuyn, faculty member of the Decker School of Nursing, State University of New York at Binghamton, describes an approach to psychiatric counseling and therapy that integrates concepts from Martha Rogers' science of unitary human beings with the strategic school of therapy known as brief, solution-oriented therapy. Tuyn notes that, in both Rogerian mental health nursing practice and (in brief) solution-oriented therapy, the principle of uniqueness is center stage.

"The second essential Rogerian concept states that we all have different points of view of reality and we are creating our own realities all the time, an experience Rogers refers to as the relative present (Malinski, 1986). Said another way, each person is a center of consciousness with his or her unique experience of space and time, or, even more simply, 'everyone is an exception' (O'Hanlon, 1990).

"Because of the uniqueness of each person," states Tuyn, "and the fact we are in continuous interaction with our environment, we live in a world of unlimited possibilities. Rogers (1970, 1987) frequently reiterates her long-held view that her ideas are optimistic, but not utopian, which this clinician interprets as meaning there are always possibilities, hope, and options. . . . How we define a problem has everything to do with finding solutions."[4]

In arguing the case for situated cognition, Stanford University psychologist James Greeno (see Chapter 6) proposes three new framing assumptions or premises for research into thinking. Although Greeno's work pertains to how young students learn, his new assumptions, as you will note, are directly applicable to any planning, design, or solution-finding situation.

First, that thinking is situated in physically and socially specific, thus, unique contexts. Consequently, no preexisting assumptions about teaching/learning are acceptable.

Second, that students' personal and social epistemologies differ. Thus, even among siblings, each student brings a unique background to the educational process.

Third, Greeno asserts that—given such differences in learning situations and in personal and social epistemologies—the conceptual competence of each learner will also be unique.[5]

This last point can be seen to be related to Harvard University psychologist Howard Gardner's seven types of intelligence. (See Chapter 6). For example, assuming Gardner's seven types of intelligence, no two individuals are ever likely to have the same amounts and qualities of each type of intelligence. Each individual will bring to any activity a unique intellectual profile, one that is not exactly matched by any other.[6]

Yale University distinguished historian Michael Howard extends the uniqueness concept to understanding the past. He summarizes his study principles in two lessons: "not to generalize from false premises based on inadequate evidence, [and] the past is a foreign country; there is very little we can say about it until we have learned its language and understood its assumptions." Since using this second lesson is an impossible task and has the purpose of simply learning and understanding, the uniqueness of history may delight and inform us; but it presents no guide to action or formula for success.[7]

INDIRECT SUPPORT

Writing in *Academy of Management Review*, University of Southern California researcher S. Mark Young makes a compelling argument for the uniqueness principle, in the context of the misguided, unmodified use by American companies of Japanese manufacturing practices such as *Kaizen,* Total Quality Control, and Just-In-Time (JIT) production. Young states that American firms are rushing to implement Japanese manufacturing practices because these practices have contributed to Japanese preeminence in many areas, including automobiles and consumer electronics. However, the reason that U.S. companies are having problems successfully employing Japanese practices is that they are not being modified to the unique conditions present in each U.S. firm.[8]

For example, the implementation of JIT production techniques may have, in the past, worked miracles in Tokyo; but making half a dozen different delivery runs per day in Los Angeles—where, by law, delivery trucks can only be on city streets during certain non-peak traffic hours—is obviously misguided. Indeed, Tokyo's own monumental traffic jams are today blamed on JIT, which is now being modified to ameliorate the problems it caused.

Also writing in *Academy of Management Review*, University of Colorado at Denver researchers Raymond Zammuto and Edward O'Connor show that different plants operate with different value systems. Thus, one cannot count on an "improvement" in one plant being equally effective or equally accepted in another plant. Each plant has its own value system. Each culture and climate is therefore unique.[9]

Even plants and operational sub-units within the same company need to be viewed as unique. Reporting on a study on the transfer of internally developed technology (software systems) within single organizations, Harvard business researcher Dorothy Leonard-Barton and Purdue University colleague Deepak Sinha show that "effective internal technology transfer depends not only upon the cost, quality, and compatibility of the technology, but also upon two processes of interaction between developers and users. These are user involvement in development and adaptation by the developers and users of both the technical system itself and the workplace."[10]

In the field of economics, that school of thought known as the Austrian School is founded on an application of the uniqueness principle—the disequilibrium of markets. That is, it embraces the uniqueness, rather than the regularity, of markets.

Writing in *Academy of Management Review*, University of Washington professor Robert Jacobson compares the perspective of conventional, industrial organization-based economic strategy with that of the Austrian School:

"Industrial organization-based economic strategy largely ignores, despite their importance, change, uncertainty, and disequilibrium in the business environment. Because these fundamental characteristics are cornerstones of the Austrian School of Economics, this doctrine offers unique strategic perspectives. The Austrian emphasis on 'the market process' and entrepreneurial discovery establishes a framework for both strategy formulation and research."[11]

In other words, things are always more unique than they are similar. Assuming, as it does, the principle of uniqueness, the Austrian School of economic analysis is thus able to cope with ambiguity, soft data, and other factors that bedevil and harrass traditional economic analysis.

Studying the various impacts of corporate cultures upon their participants, Massachusetts Institute of Technology professor Edgar Schein found that different people have different "career anchors" and will eventually gravitate toward their own individual anchor.

"Five anchors were identified as sufficient to unambiguously classify all 44 graduates of the Sloan School 10 to 12 years after their graduation. The anchors are stated in terms of the need/motive which is the ultimate constraint—that which the person is seeking primarily and which he will not give up: (1) Managerial competence; (2) Technical/ functional competence; (3) Creativity; (4) Security/stability; (5) Autonomy.

"The implications of the findings are that one must be cautious in generalizing about the motives and values which underlie careers, determine what anchors are actually operating, and be prepared to vary reward systems and career development systems to permit people with different anchors each to pursue their own career goals."[12]

In other words, people, like their problems, are unique. Part of what makes problems unique are the motives and values of the people involved, the individuality and human differentiation. By contrast, Schein finds that stereotyping—an action fundamentally opposed to the uniqueness principle—is dangerously misleading, an illustration of the indeterminacy of truth.

Says Schein: "I've concluded that every organization has its own particular pattern of assumptions about the world. We would be better served if we tried to represent it accurately instead of looking for a type into which to classify it."[13]

As Breakthrough Thinking puts it: All people are unique. Composed as they are of unique individuals, all groups, organizations, and cultures are unique. Each solution-finding effort is unique. Don't blindly adopt slogans, fads, adages, stereotypes. They deny the uniqueness of individual human beings and solution-finding situations.

The Purposes Principle

DIRECT SUPPORT

As part of a project to improve the performance and management of a 2,500-engineer division of a large aerospace company, our researchers studied the processes used by the effective engineers (identified by peer, subordinate, and superior assessments). The most striking finding was the way they all sought to define the context for each of their assignments. For example, a request from the field test group would want the engineer to calculate the airflow characteristics around a particular wing configuration. The effective engineers would always ask about the purposes being sought by the calculations, what's the larger context of purposes within which the calculated characteristics were to be used. The other engineers would just start their work with the request or problem as stated. Because many small decisions had to be made as the process of, say, calculating the characteristics, was underway, the effective enginers were able to relate their work to the larger purposes of the "customer."

In her doctoral dissertation, industrial engineer M. Güldal Sakman empirically compared three methods of defining problems, that is, of setting up a statement of the problem on which to work. The methods examined were Purpose Expansion, Strategic Assumption Surfacing and Testing, and a modified brainstorming method called Nonstructured, which was the control method for the study.

Sakman studied 72 participants, drawn from the population of professional planners in the Madison and Milwaukee areas in the state of Wisconsin. The methods of problem definition were implemented by randomly formed groups of these participants. She concluded that the Purpose Expansion method of problem definition—a key element of Breakthrough Thinking—proved consistent in its level of effectiveness and produced significantly better problem statements, both for individuals and for organizations.[14]

"Certainly," she writes, "from the responses to the post-test questionnaire, we know that the participants felt that thinking in terms of broader and broader purposes enforces reexamination and redefinition of issues which is so essential for creativity."[15]

"The Purpose Expansion method," explains Sakman, "enforces thinking in terms of a hierarchy of purposes, rather than focusing down on the elements of the problem itself, so that the defined boundary of the problem space is as broad as possible, and so that the defining and solving activities are purposive instead of reactive.

"This 'thinking in broad categories' is reinforced by another aspect of Purpose Expansion: while generating possible purpose statements in order to build the hierarchy, the method encourages the group members to think in terms of verbs instead of nouns. Using verbs which broadly stress functions instead of nouns when naming subjects is a useful aid to thinking in broad categories (Hunt, 1982).

"[The] Purpose Expansion method also acknowledges the plurality of decision making or the political nature of ill-structured problem solving activity. It sets forth a group process, the formation of which is carefully designed, to constructively handle differing views on the situation."[16]

An evaluation of the performance of project teams in 131 hospitals showed a very significant relationship between the establishment of an "overriding theme or set of [superordinate] goals for the project team" and the perceived outcome and team "levels of interaction and cooperation."[17]

INDIRECT SUPPORT

In his book *Discovering,* biochemist and science historian Robert Scott Root-Bernstein wonders why, given the fact that science has flourished since the 1600s, indeed blossomed a millionfold, we are not now witnessing a corresponding million-fold increase in the number of fundamental discoveries about the natural world. Where, he asks rhetorically, are the thousands of Newtons, Darwins, and Einsteins that should now be walking the earth?

Root-Bernstein argues that a plurality of the great inventions and discoveries of the future will take place in "cultures . . . that promote educational and ideological pluralism, intellectual freedom, and idiosyncratic behavior . . ." In our view, these values reflect the larger, expanded purposes of science itself. In other words, following the purposes principle of Breakthrough Thinking, science would now do well to encourage an expansive breadth of intellectual inquiry, rather than the intense and narrow focus that it currently pursues, forcing its students (and too many of its professional practitioners) to march in lockstep through a tedious and deadening succession of prerequisites.[18]

Focusing on and expanding purposes as a means of accurately defining the opportunity, issue, policy, or problem at hand is often instinctively (and wrongly) rejected as a waste of time, at least by those who assume that they already understand what the problem is. However, there is clear evidence that investing a higher percentage of a project's total cost in the initial problem-definition phase ultimately leads to savings in the overall cost.

For example, research by Werner Gruhl at the California Institute of Technology's Jet Propulsion Laboratory indicates that, in projects undertaken by the U.S. National Aeronautical and Space Administration (NASA), when at least 10 percent of the project's total cost was invested early to precisely define project goals and objectives, prior to making budget decisions and external commitments, cost overruns were held to a minimum.

"It is reasonable to hypothesize that the larger the Definition Investment in a new project, within practical limits, the better the plan and estimate," states Gruhl. "The larger the definition resources, the more likely the requirements, scope, design, and complexity will be understood and will provide the necessary foundation for accurate planning and cost/budget estimates that will reflect positively on NASA management ability.

"Findings indicated that inadequate definition prior to NASA budget decisions and external commitments is one of the significant reasons for cost and schedule growth of several NASA projects."[19]

Researchers Allen Bluedorn, Carol Felker Kaufman, and Paul Lane set up measures to provide some indication of organizations' and people's preference for either monochronic or polychronic time.[20] These terms respectively refer to and distinguish between a preference for doing one thing at a time, as opposed to doing two or more things simultaneously. The purposes principle of Breakthrough Thinking is based on a polychronic orientation, in that one must constantly consider not only the task at hand but also the larger purposes of that task.

Experts (in electronics design) illustrate another form of this "keeping your eye on several balls." Engineering design researchers L. J. Ball, J. Evans, and I. Dennis report that experts are likely to follow a top-down, breadth-first pattern of reasoning about the problem. Practitioners follow a depth-first route. The results show that the experts attend to linkages between problems and purposes and their respective solutions, at every level in the hierarchy.[21]

In solution-oriented therapy, explains registered nurse and psychotherapist Denise Webster, assumptions about the "rules" of a given situation are questioned, much as the purposes principle of Breakthrough Thinking requires a constant reconsideration of preexisting problem definitions. Such "reframing" helps strip away nonessential aspects of a problem, says Webster. She explains "reframing" a problem as looking for exceptions to the preexisting definition of the problem.[22]

According to Schein, four primary external issues are faced by every group or organization: consensus on core mission [read "purposes"], primary tasks, manifest functions, and latent functions. Corporate culture, he notes, solves the group's basic problems of survival in and adaptation to the external environment and integration of its internal process to ensure the capacity to continue to survive and adapt.

"Every new group or organization must develop a shared concept of its ultimate survival problem from which is usually derived its most basic sense of core mission, or 'reason to be,'" writes Schein. In other words: What is the purpose of this group coming together in the first place? Behind everything lies the key principle of purpose. "Every organization must define and fulfill its core mission [purpose], or it will not survive."[23]

Investigating some of the factors that differentiate innovative and less innovative companies, industrial engineers Shoukry Saleh and Clement Wang support the need to focus on and agree about the purposes of organized endeavors. They call this creating a "collective orientation."

"Synthesizing and integrating activities within groups, departments, and levels," Saleh and Wang note, "would not be effective without a collective orientation. Such an orientation would provide a sense of community, of purpose, and a feeling of trust, which are important for today's innovative technical organizations."[24]

Writing in the *Journal of Applied Psychology,* University of Arizona management and policy researcher Christina Shalley reports on a study she conducted about the contextual determinants of creative behavior in organizations. She studied environmental factors that might enhance or stifle individual creativity within the organizational context.

Shalley defined creativity as "developing solutions to job-related problems that are judged as novel and appropriate for the situation."[25] She found that the larger the problem is perceived to be, the more creativity and productivity are brought to bear on its solution. Thus, defining a problem in terms of the largest purposes served by its solution will tend to increase both the productivity and creativity of the solution-finding process.

Reinventing Government authors David Osborne and Ted Gaebler likewise show how mission-driven (i.e. purpose-oriented) govermental organizations "are more efficient than rule-driven organizations, . . . more effective (they produce better results), . . . more innovative, . . . more flexible, [and] have higher morale . . ."[26]

As a result of comparing product development at Canon, Inc., and Apple Computer, Inc., Japanese business researcher Ikujiro Nonaka and behavioral scientist Martin Kenney urge that all levels of an organization must have "constant reexamination, reconceptualization, and reorganization [which] entail and require the constant creation of *new meanings*" [emphasis added].[27]

The lack of considering pupeses and the larger context of expanded purposes had led to what economist and former ambassador to India John Kenneth Galbraith calls "the primal role of stupidity in shaping the course of history. . . . Ignorance, stupidity, in great affairs of state is not something that is commonly cited. A certain political and historical correctness requires us to assign some measure of purpose, of rationality, even where, all too obviously, it does not exist!"[28] What an elegant statement of why purposes are needed at the beginning!

Expanding purposes each time a product redesign or system review or policy setting or problem is addressed is a critical concept, one that provides a mechanism that searches for new meaning and increases the levels of positive expectancy for all. Management guru Peter Drucker reiterates this concept in many of his books and articles through his two basic questions: "What is our business?" and "What should our business be?" Looking to larger purposes also builds in a reasonable way to develop "self-fulfilling prophecies."

The Solution-After-Next Principle

DIRECT SUPPORT

The Breakthrough Thinking principle of solution-after-next suggests that, in seeking to achieve focus purpose, you should ask yourself: "What would I do if I could start all over again?" Thus, it directs you to think intuitively, to seek new combinations and relationships, to target—at least initially—the ideal solution for achieving your focus purpose(s).

Kouzes and Posner propose that the essential function of a leader, any leader, is to create a vision. "Every organization, every social movement," they state, "begins with a dream. That dream, that vision, is the force that invents the future."[29] They consider that vision is the word that most aptly describes exactly what it is that effective leaders do. "First of all, [vision] is a 'see' word. It evokes images and pictures. Visual metaphors are very common when we are talking about the long-range plans of an organization. Second, vision suggests a future orientation—a vision is an image of the future. Third, vision connotes a standard of excellence, an ideal. It implies a choice of values. Fourth, it also has the quality of uniqueness. Therefore, we define a vision as *an ideal and unique image of the future*"[30]

Snyder notes that a flexible, multi-dimensional thinker, one who values and actively practices both analytical and intuitive thinking, uses "a mix of modes to both frame problems and solve them. A central finding was the close connection between the use of both modes and the expansion of the network of enterprises. Those with only one mode were found to have more often narrowed their set of concerns and limited their network of enterprises."[31]

Solutions-after-next are not created from thin air. Rather they arise naturally (though not without effort) from a growing awareness of the expanded purposes for finding a solution, as well as from increased awareness of the systematic relationships that affect the solution's success.

Greeno and other proponents of "situated cognition" maintain that creativity occurs naturally when one's situation is restructured. Changes in the environment, they argue, can cause a reorganization of "conceptual structures."

"The assumption of situated cognition says that all of our cognitive activity is connected with situations," Greeno explains. "Creativity, in this view, involves reorganizing the connection the person has with a situation, rather than a reorganization that occurs within the person's mind. The situation with which one's connections are reorganized can be physical, social, or conceptual."[32]

In other words, three thoughts reinforce the Full-Spetrum Thinking principles. First, purpose expansion helps reorganize the connections with a situation. Second, by expanding purposes, creativity in developing solution-after-next or ideal ideas is increased. And third, as the problem-situation changes over time—partly as a result of the successful implementation of a selected solution—the most effective, feasible solution will also change, growing to encompass further possibilities that approach ever closer to your ideal solution.

Referring to the potential impact of visionary leadership on corporate culture, theorists such as Warren Bennis, Charles Kiefer, and Peter Senge have "found that successful leaders in uncertain environments maintained an ongoing vision and commitment that gave an inherent strength to their organizations. . . . Leaders guide the change process by insuring the presence of visioning, experimenting, pattern breaking, and bonding, and by keeping these four elements in balance."[33]

Kouzes and Posner imply the essential relationship between the Breakthrough Thinking principles of expanded purposes and solutions-after-next. Visions, they note, like objects in the distance, get clearer and clearer as we move toward them.[34]

"Ideals reveal our higher-order value preferences. They represent our ultimate economic, technological, political, social, and aesthetic priorities . . . the ones that we seek to attain over the long term. They are statements of the idealized purpose that all our practical actions will enable us to attain."[35]

INDIRECT SUPPORT

As noted by historian of science and biochemist Robert Scott Root-Bernstein, "the period preceding any great breakthrough in science will be characterized by the elaboration of a tremendous diversity of possible solutions."[36]

Such a precedent-shattering, habit-altering mode of thought is also considered essential to success in brief, solution-oriented psychotherapy. As Webster notes, "considerable time is spent helping clients to develop clear descriptions of how they would like things to be [in the future], and how they will know that they are headed in the right direction. Very little time is spent on the past, except to identify resources that may have been forgotten or devalued. The present is explored in the context of noting what small changes are needed to create a more desirable future."[37]

The work of researcher Shalley, noted earlier, points out that awareness of larger purposes and motivation toward objectives recognized as higher and more difficult lead to increases in both the productivity and creativity of solutions devised. Conversely, if you are assigned a task and told you have no goal at all for creativity, that your goal is simply to solve the problem, the results you achieve will not be as good.

Shalley's findings indirectly support both the Purposes and Solution-After-Next principles of Breakthrough Thinking, which together call upon the solution finder to seek the fulfillment of larger purposes and thus achieve wider, more broadly encompassing solutions and better results.[38]

The mathematical and modeling developments in operations research and management science known as "genetic algorithms" and "optimization" emphasize the need to identify and keep viable as long as possible a diverse set of solution ideas—even if you have a "perfect" or optimum solution! The concept is based on the evolutionary process of change. To be effective in the mathematical sense, many alternative solutions are needed to enable one to make an effective choice.

The decision analysis field discusses the concept of "phantom alternatives" as being "unavailable" as solution possibilities because of legal, ethical, environmental, or technological infeasibility factors. Management and decision scientists Peter Farquar and Anthony Pratkanis argue "that phantoms [read: solution-after-next ideas] should be considered explicitly in decision structuring [because] they can provide useful information . . . and help generate new options. . . ."[39]

The Systems Principle

DIRECT SUPPORT

Beyond its support for the efficacy of the uniqueness principle, Nutt's study, "An Experimental Comparison of the Effectiveness of Three Planning Methods," further demonstrates the benefits of a systems approach to problem solving.

"In the systems method," Nutt writes, "objectives [read: purposes] were established in the first phase of the meeting, and used as a basis to structure the development of plans. For example, the intent of the service delivery plan was established before recommendations were developed.

"The results of the experiment indicated that the systems approach produced *better quality* plans, while the behavioral approach produced *more new ideas*. [See People Design Principle, p. 374.] This suggests that involving an organization's clients in planning of services to define their problems provides a rich array of ideas for the planning process, but that systems approaches and experts are needed to formulate these ideas and consolidate them into a viable plan.

"The behavioral approach provided new information and maintained good planner-participant relationships, but produced plans that were judged low in quality by experts, agency decision makers, and agency staff. Thus, distinct planning methods [systems perspectives] were found to produce plans with distinct characteristics."[40]

INDIRECT SUPPORT

The concept of "systems" has been so widely used in the last 50 years that it world appear redundant to provide support for a systems principle. The idea of wholeness and considering all the interrelationships is the key so many researchers, designers, and managers proclaim is necessary regardless of name used—systems analysis, systems approach, systems concept, contingent systems thinking, system design, systems integration, systems modeling, systems planning, systems thinking. The systems principle goes beyond these versions of Conventional Thinking, but acceptance of a systems idea is at least widespread.

Zammuto and O'Connor examined the roles that organization design and culture play in the varying levels of success experienced by organizations that adopt advanced manufacturing technologies (AMTs). They concluded that, in order to increase the chances of implementational success for a particular technology, one needs to understand the organizational, cultural, and structural components of both the technology and its intended environment—the system. Failure to do so will (1) reduce the benefit of the planned change, and (2) compound the difficulties involved with any implementation, since not only a technology but also a new structure and support climate have to be developed.[41]

"Major cultural and structural change efforts are costly and time-consuming," they note, "because of the need to build trust, develop skills, and overcome resistance. If managers . . . want to increase the likelihood of implementation success, they have to cope with the difficulties of both extensive organizational and technological change."[42]

Thus, Zammuto and O'Connor hypothesized that "organizations emphasizing control-oriented values can decrease the likelihood of implementation failure by increasing cultural and structural flexibility prior to technology implementation." That is, the likelihood of success can be increased by evaluating the introduction of any new technique from a systems perspective, prior to its implementation.

Tuyn explains that brief, solution-oriented therapy solves human problems by creative use of a client's strengths and patterns of living. That is, brief therapists use their clients' patterns of living—their systems—as part of the solution to their problems.[43]

"A second principle of brief, solution-oriented therapy," notes Tuyn, "directs us to use a systems perspective in approaching client situations. Especially important are the two systemic axioms that state a change in one part of the system affects the whole system, and small changes tend to lead to other changes. In other words, change within a system has a 'snowball' effect, and knowing this can help us influence change in the desired direction (O'Hanlon & Weiner-Davis, 1989)."[44]

The Limited Information Collection Principle

DIRECT SUPPORT

In their article "Locally Rational Decision Making: The Distracting Effect of Information on Managerial Performance," professors Rashi Glazer, Joel Steckel, and Russell Winer describe a phenomenon in which the mere presence of information may have dysfunctional consequences on managerial performance. This impact occurs even when decision makers process the excessive information *correctly.*

Using the results from an experiment conducted with a strategic market simulation game, the authors found that "the accessibility of information results in a disposition to focus on those components of decision-making most clearly addressed by the information. If these are not the components most closely tied to success, overall performance may in fact suffer. . . . The presence of additional information has a 'seductive' or distracting effect. . . ."[45]

"Furthermore," they note, "we find the rather ironic result that decision makers would be better off in some situations had the information not been available in the first place—i.e., decisions made in the absence of information often result in superior performance than decisions made in the presence of information, even though the information is not in itself processed incorrectly. . . . Teams *without* the additional information generally outperformed those with it. At the same time, decisions made in the presence of the information were on average no worse than decisions made in its absence. This suggests that the poorer performance was less a function of the misuse of the information with respect to specific decisions than of the misdirection of decision makers' attention resulting from the information's accessibility."[46]

"Perhaps the most significant normative implication of the research is an exceedingly simple one: Information should not be used just because it is there! Rather, given what can be predicted about the nature of information-processing biases and the limits on attention, we urge managers to be sure that the information they collect and choose to focus on is related to the correct issues.

"In the final analysis, what is required is better 'quality' information, accompanied by a realization that correct assessment of overall strategic direction (e.g., an understanding of the whole strategic plan) must be made before specific data-gathering consumes valuable resources."[47] In other words, before gathering data, problem solvers should ask these questions: What are the purposes to be achieved, and what solution ideas should guide the information gathering?

In his doctoral dissertation at the University of Wisconsin, Donald Murtha examined three different solution-finding approaches used by environmental designers. The 5-step, 10-step, and 15-step approaches were compared. The 5-step approach was closely related to Conventional Thinking. The 15-step approach resembled Full-Spectrum Thinking.

As Murtha explains, "The 5-Step [process] presented the simplest, most basic approaches . . . The 10-Step [process] was based on a more traditional model of design. . . . The 15-step [process] was developed . . . as a theoretically 'best' design [process], utilizing presumably more systematic concepts. . . ."

Murtha found "an apparent low level of effectiveness for [the 5-step process] . . . demonstrated in part by the additional time required for arriving at a solution, and the apparently random selection and application of information. Overall, the [5-step] subjects did require more time for solution, particularly as compared with the 10-step [process] group. The subjects did demonstrate an apparent uncertainty in beginning problem-solving with a relatively high selection of definition information.

"By contrast, the 15-Step [process] was slightly but consistently more efficient and effective in comparison with the other [processes]. These subjects appeared to establish systematic definitions as indicated by a substantial selection of problem descriptors and a generally high level of definition activity. The subjects did indicate lower levels of information selection in most categories, particularly those less central to problem development. In contrast, the subjects did show high levels of selection and use of conceptual information. The subjects did remain relatively steady on most measures. . . ."[48]

The high levels of effectiveness Murtha found among those subjects using the 15-step approach results in part from its inherent preference for purposes and solutions. This directed but limited information collection, particularly the collection of broadly conceptual, not deeply specific, information, results in large part from initially defining the problem in terms of the largest purposes to be served by its solution.

INDIRECT SUPPORT

The efficacy of brief, solution-oriented therapy as described in Chapter 6 is due in large part to not spending time focusing on the past life of the patient, trying to help the patient comprehend the underlying causes of behavior that results in psychological distress. The central idea is the assumption that the patient currently and consciously holds the key to the solution of his or her problem. So brief therapy focuses on the future, what the patient's life will look like when the problem is solved. Information collection, in other words, is limited to solutions, not problems.

According to Greeno's theory of situated cognition, knowledge is not a self-contained substance, it cannot be separated from context. In other words, data can (even approximately) describe and inform us about only the specific context from which they are drawn.

Data are only a model of reality. They are never the reality itself. By definition, no model can ever be complete and accurate. The only fully accurate model of anything is the object itself. The only complete model of a human being is an actual person.

Even an object as simple as a chair cannot be fully and accurately described in terms of its characteristics of shape, color, size, substance. A particular example of the object called "chair" must and can only speak for itself, as experienced by individual human beings, each filtering that experience through his or her own perspective, personal and social epistemology, not to mention conceptual competence.

Such is the actual complexity of an object as simple as a chair. How much more complex is a system or solution. All the more so, infinitely complex, is an individual human being.

A central tenet of Conventional Thinking is to gather as much data, from as many different sources, as possible. In this way, it is assumed, objectivity will be achieved. And objectivity, it is held, is critical to finding the "correct" solution.

Yet the "objectivity" to which Conventional Thinking aspires is actually a false premise. Objectivity, as such, does not exist. For example, if one person observes and analyzes another, collects endless data about that other person and what he or she is doing, the observer will bring to that study of the observed his or her own premises, prejudices, and assumptions. Since no observer and no method of investigation can ever be ideally objective, the quest for "objectivity" is a fallacious basis for arguing in favor of the collection of as much data as possible.

By involving a variety of individuals, each with his or her own subjective perspective on the situation, guided specifically by the purposes, solutions-after-next, and systems principles and by the process of Breakthrough Thinking—you can identify what information is really needed.

The People-Design Principle

DIRECT SUPPORT

In Nutt's study, "An Experimental Comparison of the Effectiveness of Three Planning Methods" (see "Uniqueness Principle," p. 355 and "Systems Principle," p. 368), what he calls the "behavioral" approach generated more new ideas for problem solution. Why? Because of client involvement in the problem-solving process.

The behavioral approach, which employed client participants along with experts, produced more new information. "Thus, client involvement seemed to be a necessary ingredient when new information was needed in planning efforts."[49]

"Involving an organization's clients in planning of services to define their problems provides a rich array of ideas for the planning process," Nutt concludes.[50] He cautions, however, that for clients to be helpful in the problem-solving process, they must bring to the endeavor appropriate experiences.

"The uncritical use of clients in planning seems universal," he laments. "Clearly, consumer involvement in planning is no panacea. If clients are used, they should be selected carefully to insure they have had experiences which permit them to make contributions. For instance, when planning a new building, users of the current facility may have pertinent comments on its design."[51]

Nutt is not alone in noting that involvement of those with a stake in the outcome of the problem-solving process tends to result in better solutions. That finding has been made so often as by now to appear self-evident.

Moreover, as regards the People Design Principle of Breakthrough Thinking, those involved in the problem-solving process are, by definition, those with a role in the implementation of the chosen solution and so a stake in its outcome. Thus, by definition, they bring "appropriate experiences" to the endeavor. Under such circumstances, our own research indicates that—far from delaying the solution of a problem or increasing the cost of its solution—involving as many such people as possible in the solution-finding process in fact results in spending both less time and less money.

In a 1973 study titled "The Economic Effect of Cost Control Programs in Mid-West Industry," conducted at the University of Wisconsin, researcher O. Friedman found that program costs tend to decrease as participation in the problem-solving effort is widened and coordination of participants' efforts (as opposed to direct leadership by program managers) increases. Friedman concluded that programs that involved people directly affected by the decisions in the decision-making process (purpose-oriented programs) produced better results than conventional programs, in which the decisions were made and imposed by superiors.

Friedman's people-design-related findings showed these benefits: Emphasis on a coordinative role by program management, as opposed to a direct leadership role, tended to produce better economic results; the greater the degree of general management involvement in the program, the better the economic results; and the existence of formal training activities in a program tended to increase the economic results achieved.

Friedman further found that purpose-oriented cost control programs produce better economic results than conventional programs, both in production-centered companies (where production methods, layout, and tooling have the most impact on the firm's effectiveness—its profitability, growth, and development) and in system-centered companies (where engineering and design, as well as interdepartmental relationships, have the main impact on the firm's effectiveness). The average economic results per individual in purpose-oriented programs was greater than the average produced in conventional-approach programs. The role of program management was more frequently coordinative in purpose-oriented than in conventional programs.[52]

Mary Pinto, Jeffrey Pinto, and John Prescott verified the major influence of larger ends on the effectiveness of teams. In addition, the cooperation among team members that resulted from the "overriding theme" [or purposes] produced a significant level of psycho-social outcomes.[53]

INDIRECT SUPPORT

Schein's research concerning the effectiveness of people in groups and their need to feel membership in the group to function effectively within it suggests further evidence in support of the People Design Principle. That is, if you expect the solution you choose to function properly, you must include in its design and selection as many "stakeholders" as possible—those people with direct personal involvement in the successful implementation of the solution.[54]

What criterion for group membership could be more clear and effective than genuine inclusion in the deliberative process of group decision-making? What better way to develop group cohesion and sense of membership than to include all group members in the selection, design, and development of a solution from the very beginning of the solution-finding process, especially when buttressed with the first five principles of Breakthrough Thinking?

Greeno's point concerning the uniqueness of personal and social epistemologies—that is, individual experiential backgrounds leading to individually unique consciousness and knowledge—also supports the People Design Principle. The only way to reach solutions that provide for the breadth of individual experience and make use of the wealth of various perspectives this affords is to involve as many stakeholders as possible in solution finding.

Moreover, those who must "live the solution," whether it be an organizational information system or a land-use plan for a community, must have their "eyes," their "humanity," and their "feel for the real world" incorporated into the solution chosen and implemented. Jargon, high theory, experts, and the successes of others should not be imposed on people.

The celebrated Hawthorne experiments in work productivity—conducted between 1924 and 1932 by Elton Mayo and associates at the Hawthorne Works of Western Electric Company—first demonstrated the significant positive impact of paying attention to people regarding the design of the work they are required to accomplish. Mayo and his colleagues reported that, as working conditions were gradually improved—rest breaks introduced, morning refreshments provided, the variety of electrical relay types the workers were expected to assemble reduced—and the work was thus made easier and faster, productivity improved.

However, even when these experimental improvements were rescinded, productivity *continued* to improve. Mayo concluded that this surprising result occurred simply because the workers had, over the preceding months of the experiment, developed a positive attitude toward their work and a desire to cooperate with the researchers, precisely because the workers had been selected as participants in the experiment. In other words, because they had been acknowledged as human beings, not merely productive units, and had been directly involved in decisions affecting their work.[55]

The negative impact of Conventional Thinking on people's responsiveness to change, notably in the field of organizational dynamics, is illustrated by many authors. For example, even such well-respected experts as Harvard professor Chris Argyris state that fundamental changes in corporate culture may take five years' concentrated effort.[56] By suggesting that the process takes so long a time, Argyris and other consultants on corporate culture seem almost to take pride in the length of time demanded, as if effort expended were necessarily an accurate measure of results obtained.

Similarly, not many years ago, chief executives of American automobile companies insisted that it took five years to develop a new product, from the beginning of the design process until the first such vehicle rolled off the production line. Soon enough, of course, they learned from their Japanese competitors that the five-year timeline was not at all essential.

From our perspective, one of the reasons that organizational changes often does take so long is that most consultants exhaustively study the *existing problem* and its historical roots, not the *needed purpose* and the *future solution.* Given the extensive time involved in the performance of specific data gathering about the past and present, no wonder the desired changes take so long to devise, develop, and implement.

Simply overcoming the natural "defensive routines," as Argyris calls them, routines developed by the people who were studied and/or were involved in the past systems, is almost a guarantee that excessive time will be needed. And even if it appears that acceptance of change has been achieved, lingering residual negativism decreases the likelihood of long-term success of the change.

Moreover, the process-oriented, continuous "double loop" learning that Argyris advocates (as opposed to simply content-oriented "single loop learning) is automatically effected by Full-Spectrum Thinking. The principle of expanded purposes and the solution-after-next principle, in conjunction with the people design principle, are particularly effective in stimulating successful organizational learning.

The Betterment Timeline Principle

DIRECT SUPPORT

Perhaps the most compelling evidence in direct support of the Betterment Timeline Principle is the extraordinary achievement of the Japanese system of industrial production. That performance has been founded upon *Kaizen,* the concept of continual improvement, called "the key to Japan's competitive success."[57]

The Eastern idea of *Kaizen* considers existing systems and solutions from a perspective of gradual, constant, incremental changes that result in undramatic but long-term, long-lasting improvement. From the point of view of *Kaizen,* a quantity of constant, small improvements add up to considerably more than merely the sum of their parts.

Yet Breakthrough Thinking adds a great deal not only to the traditional Western perspective, but also to the Eastern view of *Kaizen.* Its Betterment Timeline Principle provides a model of exactly where the effort toward continual improvement should be heading, a target solution toward which future changes are directed.

Under either the traditional Western system or the Eastern *Kaizen* system, in our experience, when a significant change in systems or operating procedures has recently been made, and yet another change is called for, the worker on the shop floor or behind the word processor is likely to resist the latest change: "What?! Another change? We just changed four months ago!" By contrast, with Breakthrough Thinking, people—actively involved in the solution-finding process from the very beginning—are actually eager to implement constant improvements in the system or solution that they helped design.

For example, we have often enjoyed the experience of returning to a company with which we have recently consulted to find shop floor workers pressing us to find out why a particular improvement or device they helped design as a solution-after-next has not yet been implemented. "What's the hold-up?" they demand. "Tell those guys up at R&D that we're waiting on 'em." That's the sort of eager, continuous improvement that is built into the "schedule the next change" principle of the Betterment Timeline.

INDIRECT SUPPORT

"The central thesis of *The Evolution of Useful Things,* by Duke University professor of engineering Henry Petroski, is that failure, not necessity, is the mother of invention," writes *Los Angeles Times* book reviewer Chris Goodrich. By that, says Goodrich, Petroski means that "somebody, somewhere, has found today's zipper wanting and is already working to improve it or replace it."[58]

Thus, all solutions—even those as elegant, efficient, and effective as the zipper—if they are to remain sufficient to the ever-evolving problem, must be continually reexamined and improved. Just as the zipper itself replaced the hook-and-eye and common button fasteners predominant in earlier years.

Evidence of Petroski's perspective can be found in the increasing prevalence of products designed with future expansion in mind. For example, computer hardware is today designed with excess ports to be applied to future applications; communications standards have been designed with only 19 of a potential 25 leads assigned a current function.

As professional sports have evolved from their origin as high-level athletic contests to high-stakes mass entertainment, continuous change and improvement are also built into the mix. Witness the three-point shot in basketball, the tennis tie-breaker, "sudden death" overtime in football.

As Tuyn points out, brief therapy too focuses on continual change for the better, along a timeline firmly focused on the future. "A third basic principle of the solution-oriented approach directs us to emphasize the future and possibilities for change, instead of exploring the past and details regarding the hypothetical etiology of problems. Said another way, in therapy situations, we do not necessarily need to know the cause to find solutions. . . . All the therapist and client need to know is: 'How will we know when the problem is solved?' "[59]

Similarly, in the field of group management within organizations, Schein calls for "consensus on criteria for measuring results," another form of monitoring for continual change.

"Once the group is performing," Schein insists, "there must be consensus on how to judge its own performance, in order to know what kind of remedial action to take when things do not go as expected. If members of the group hold widely divergent concepts of what to look for and how to evaluate results, they cannot develop coordinated remedial action."[60]

Finally, research into situated cognition by Greeno and others demonstrates that learning—gaining both knowledge and understanding—occurs "over significant periods of time, in ways that involve significant reorganization of conceptual structures.

"Taken together," states Greeno, "these results provide a compelling body of evidence that children should not be considered as mere vessels for receiving knowledge when they learn. Instead, when they arrive at a learning situation, they have rich, albeit largely tacit, structures of conceptual competence."[61]

In other words, human beings (of all ages) do not function as limited receptacles into which to pour a chosen solution. Instead, we have the enviable capacity constantly to elaborate, change, and improve the solution, even as we grow in our knowledge and understanding. Refreshed, sustained, and energized by the solution we have initially chosen, over time, we become ever more able to adapt it to provide us with even more nourishment—a continually evolving and ever better solution.

The Full-Spectrum Thinking Process

DIRECT SUPPORT

Friedman's study of the economic results of cost control programs in American industry (see: People Design Principle, p. 374) also provides impressive direct support for the Full-Spectrum Thinking process. Friedman found that companies using a purpose-oriented approach to improvement had twice the financial benefits per staff person as those using the conventional Approach. That is, companies with, say, $500 million in sales had $5 million in yearly savings when they used Conventional Thinking, but $10 million when they used Full-Spectrum Thinking. From another perspective, the Full-Spectrum Thinking companies could save $5 million with half the number of staff people as the companies using Conventional Thinking.

In his examination of three different processes (See Limited Information Collection Principle, p. 372), Murtha compared 5-step, 10-step, and 15-step approaches used by environmental designers. The 5-step (open-ended) and 10-step (traditional) processes are what we have called Conventional Thinking in this book. The 15-step systematic process is close to the Full-Spectrum Thinking process.

Murtha compares and contrasts the effectiveness of the three processes. "An apparent low level of effectiveness for [the 5-Step process] was demonstrated in part by the additional time required for arriving at a solution, and the apparently random selection and application of information.

"The 10-Step [process] portrayed an apparent uneven performance with an overconcern about details. The data generally indicated low levels of solution quality. . . . [They further] suggest an additional factor of disillusionment or overconfidence. This [process] . . . is apparently workable, but it produces only a moderate level of performance.

"The 15-Step [process] was . . . consistently more efficient and effective in comparison with the other [processes]. The solution ratings were . . . consistently better, particularly on specific criteria such as comprehensiveness and innovativeness, which had been stressed in the problem statements. These results suggest that this is a definitely workable [process] with potential advantages. . . ."[62]

The software design division of a major electronics company, in seeking to achieve a high "process rating" of the Software Engineering Institute, a government sponsored think-tank, compared the Tradition-Based Approach (use past data on time, costs, and resources to estimate what is to be done on a new assignment), the Process Improvement Approach (Conventional Thinking), and Breakthrough Thinking. The results of evaluating the different approaches when used on many projects and of reviewing the concepts involved in each approach, the division concluded that Breakthrough Thinking significantly improved the impact of the three major sources of uncertainty inherent in software projects: pragmatic uncertainty (requirements stated by the client are inadequate), Heisenberg uncertainty (the client will change the requirements during the actual project), and Goedel uncertainty (a fixed and clear set of requirements in the client's mind becomes incomplete or semantically ambiguous when it is described). The division determined that the benefits of Breakthrough Thinking were critical because the managerial and administrative problems of large-scale software development far overshadow the technical challenges.

Direct support for the Breakthrough Thinking process is also provided by the many cases already referred to throughout this book and other books about Full-Spectrum Thinking concepts, especially *Breakthrough Thinking* and *Breakthrough Thinking in Total Quality Management.* Sometimes those illustrations reflect the direct experience of the authors, but mostly that of others trained in Breakthrough Thinking.

All these case histories provide direct support for Full-Spectrum Thinking. Whether they referred to the allocation of hospital capital improvement money, the operation of a loading dock, the utilization of a nursing staff, the development of product samples, the creation of an international voluntary service society, or the organization of an inter-agency task force; whether they occurred in organizations such as an automobile manufacturer, an aerospace firm, an international electronics corporation, a multi-national insurance conglomerate, a national postal service, an urban school district, a county sheriff's department, or a regional mental-health maintenance group; whether they involved the problems of individual human beings, of persons working together in groups, of groups working together in organizations, of racial, religious, and ethnic interests cooperating within communities or nations, or of nations sharing the resources of the planet. Even the first prize winners of a Wisconsin contest for egg and sausage recipes who developed their winning entries with Breakthrough Thinking to those successful in a Japanese Labor Ministry contest for a career development training system.

All of these cases occurred in the field, where Breakthrough Thinkers worked with real people—individuals, groups, and larger task forces—on real issues, opportunities, or problems, in organizations both public and private. In every case, remarkably successful results were achieved. New experiences and cases are reported at an increasing rate and in an expanding array of settings—software engineering, a Swedish crisis information system, a waste-water effluent treatment system, a rocket booster helium supply, and many educational curricula, personal, and community decisions.

Of particular importance is the fact that, in some of these cases, effective solutions had previously been identified yet rejected by the participants in the solution-finding process. Only when Breakthrough Thinking was applied to their dilemma, were participants able to agree—often with astonishing rapidity—on the now obviously effective solution.

Moreover, they were often motivated to immediately implement the Breakthrough Thinking solution. And they proved themselves committed not only to its successful implementation, but also to its continual improvement. Full-Spectrum Thinking resulted not only in startling moments of insight, bolt-of-lightning, "aha!" ideas; not only in much better results, more productive, more cost-effective systems and methods; but, even more importantly, in successful *implementation* of effective solutions.

INDIRECT SUPPORT

"We are caught squarely between two poles," notes organizational researcher Terry Deal, coauthor of *Corporate Cultures.* "What Urie Bronfenbrenner characterizes as 'between a rock and a soft place.' The rock symbolizes an approach to knowledge that involves defining, operationalizing, measuring, testing, and then trying to link culture to outcomes.

"I think that's needed," Deal states, "but we ought to realize that there is another possibility: to name, observe, apprehend, and begin to explore. The 'soft place' is another way of approaching knowledge. It has its own systematic basis, but it's not quite the same as the more rational approach that often governs what researchers do."[63]

We submit that the rock to which Deal and Bronfenbrenner refer may be considered Conventional Thinking. The 'soft place' to which they allude is akin to, at least in tune with, the spirit of Full-Spectrum Thinking.

Management researchers Susanne G. Scott and Reginald A. Bruce investigated the factors which determined individual innovation in the workplace. One factor was "problem-solving style and innovative behavior." They categorized one style as "systematic problem solving (working within established methods or procedures, is likely to generate conventional solutions to problems)" and the other as "intuitive problem-solving (overlapping separate domains of thought simultaneously, a lack of attention to existing rules and disciplinary boundaries, . . . an emphasis on imagery and intuition, [and] likely to generate more problem solutions)." The former style resembles Conventional Thinking, while the latter has many Full-Spectrum Thinking characteristics shown in the next section. Their results showed the systematic problem-solving style had quite a significant negative effect on producing innovative behavior.[64]

In their article "The Management of Innovation: Strategy, Structure, and Organizational Climate," Saleh and Wang propose that innovative companies follow a proactive approach in addressing dynamic and uncertain business environments. Their study focused on the differences in managerial strategy, organizational structure, and organizational climate.

The results showed that innovative companies "use, or have more of the following than the less innovative ones: calculated risk taking; management commitment to entrepreneurial activities and innovation; integration and intermingling of talents in teams and task forces; group and collective orientation; and a reward system that reinforces entrepreneurial behavior."[65]

"An organization that only reacts to its environment," note Saleh and Wang, "[does] not mobilize . . . idea generation and new product development except as a reaction to a crisis or unexpected event. Based on this study, Souder concluded that being reactive is not sufficient to compete successfully in a dynamic world of aggressive innovators.

"This conclusion is supported by Eisenhardt and Bourgeois, who reported that the poor performers of the microcomputer industry were often reactive in their strategic decision processes, 'they reacted to outside events, rather than acting proactively—and they . . . considered few alternatives.' "[66]

Full-Spectrum Thinking, it seems to us, provides precisely the long-term focus and future-oriented, proactive approach to solution-finding that these studies indicate are effective.

Similarly, Full-Spectrum Thinking—particularly the Purposes, Solution-After-Next, and Systems principles—provides a framework for what engineering consultant Robert Glass identifies as the rapid mental modeling and simulation that occur in the course of expert design. (See Chapter 6, p. 232.)

Citing investigations conducted by computer software researchers Bill Curtis and Elliot Soloway, Glass characterizes the solution of problems in design as "a mental process—a very rapid, iterative process—of fast trial and error. The mind forms a solution to the problem, all the while knowing that it will be inadequate, because the mind is not yet able to fully grasp all the facets of the problem.

"The essence of design, then," Glass concludes, "is rapid mental modeling and simulation. A key factor in design is the ability to propose solutions and allow them to fail."[67] And the ideas of genetic models emphasize getting many solution alternatives and keeping them open as long as possible.

Greeno's theory of situated cognition is also evidence of the value and validity of the overall process of Breakthrough Thinking. Particularly in its principles of uniqueness and expanded purposes, Breakthrough Thinking assumes and encourages the specificity of situated cognition, as well as the personal and social epistemologies and conceptual competencies of individuals. The Breakthrough Thinking principles of systems and solutions-after-next place unique individuals and their larger purposes within a context of effective solution finding.

Industry economist and corporate executive Robert Malpas echoes the opinion of many of his colleagues in calling for a radical change of emphasis in the process of obtaining organizational change. He notes that it is necessary to create "technology demand pull from business managers as opposed to push from technologists."[68] The expanded purposes, solutions-after-next, and systems principles of the Breakthrough Thinking process are, of course, organized to do this.

Why Practice Breakthrough Thinking?

As we explained at length in Chapter 8, Breakthrough Thinking means results. The Full-Spectrum Thinking process produces success in achieving the results people seek in solution finding:

- The most effective solution, system, or recommendation.
- A high likelihood of implementing the solution, system, or recommendation that you select.
- A low cost of resources and time spent to achieve your results.

Why is the Full-Spectrum Thinking so successful? Because the seven principles and the process of Breakthrough Thinking pose questions that ensure that you address each situation in the most effective way, thus help close the gap between perceived reality and aspiration. The principles and process provide the paradigm of thinking essential to fulfill the needs of organizations in the future: "Effective managers are change agents, developers, proactive, innovators, team players, boundary-crossers. . . ."[69]

Their choices in decision making are much more likely than those in Conventional Thinking: (1) to incorporate both preferences and consequences of alternatives as well as the "rules" appropriate to the decision maker and the specific situation, (2) to be consistent through each project and from project to project, (3) to involve the key stakeholders or decision makers at the appropriate points in the process to gain commitment to the outcomes whatever they may be, and (4) to reflect the contextual influence of customers and suppliers, the organization itself, key individuals, and community and society.[70]

Breakthrough Thinking is an *inclusive*, not an exclusive, alternative. Whenever useful and appropriate, Breakthrough Thinking incorporates Conventional Thinking. Indeed, the inclusive nature of Full-Spectrum Thinking permits some further definitive comparisons between Conventional Thinking and Breakthrough Thinking for creating and restructuring solutions:

CONVENTIONAL THINKING	BREAKTHROUGH THINKING
Analytical	Expantegration
Why? (Measures)	What purpose?
Focus on past and present problems	Focus on future solutions
Extension of the past	Learn from the future
Doubting game	Believing game
Problem as stated	Right problem
Find "problem area"	Expand solution space
Problem expert —gather data —quality recommendation	Solution expert —information as needed —quality implementation
Knowledge is power	Knowing how to use knowledge is power
Defensive participation	Active participation
Focus on similarities	Focus on uniqueness
Reductionism	Expansion
Zero-sum	Positive-sum
Solve today's problem	Solution-after-next
Hard data only	Soft data as well
Snap-shot	Movie

Some scholars in methodologies claim that the principles and process of Breakthrough Thinking can be "mapped into the classical steps of problem solving." Doing this is possible in theory but defeats the whole purpose of raising the question of the thinking paradigm. The very words used in Conventional Thinking are simply not conducive to the new paradigm. It is inconceivable that people would interpret "gather facts," "find out what's going on now," and "analyze the difficulties" in any way other than their current meanings. It is critical to recognize the need for new words to express the new assumptions and process of the new paradigm of thinking.

Breakthrough Thinking, rooted as it is in purposes, will greatly reduce or eliminate the chance of your falling into one or more of the Eight Basic Errors characteristic of Conventional Thinking in finding solutions:

1. applying *ineffective mental assumptions* to the problem;
2. taking an *ineffective approach* to the problem;
3. involving *ineffective or "standard" people;*
4. trying to solve the *visible or wrong problem;*
5. addressing the problem with *inappropriate timing;*
6. exerting *ineffective control* over the search for a solution;
7. *unfortunately accepting* a predictable or incomplete "solution"; or
8. *inappropriately rejecting* a broader and effective solution

Full-Spectrum Thinking lets you develop the most effective solutions, systems, and recommendations because it provides

- assurance of working on the right issue, need, or problem at the right time;
- expanded solution space;
- links to the purposes of customers and needs of target groups and/or to your own purposes;
- opportunities for creativity in all phases or steps of a project;
- benefits that have proven consistently better than expected— for example, innovation, new ideas, workable solutions, high economic return, quality products and services, customer satisfaction and delight;
- built-in, continual improvement

Full-Spectrum Thinking ensures a high likelihood of successful implementation of your solutions, systems, and recommendations because it provides:

- early buy-in by all stakeholders, so that implementation starts at the beginning of the solution-finding process and is supported throughout all changes;
- ways to remove obstacles to simple solutions;
- identification of all interfaces and consequences of proposed plans;
- ability to cope with uncertainties—for example, environment, economics, regulations, external forces—by developing and keeping options open.

Full-Spectrum Thinking ensures low cost in resources spent and time taken to achieve results because it provides:

- clutter-free reasoning;
- proven less time than expected per project;
- minimal but requisite information collection to reduce "analysis paralysis";
- structure for the imaginative mind and freedom for the structured mind;
- effective, continuing intercommunications among project participants once the solution-finding project is completed— for example, team-building, open information exchange.

Characteristically, when people think about finding solutions, they focus not on the principles and process of their thinking, but rather on the end result. This "solution" is usually imagined in terms of some product or material thing—a computer system, FAX machine, VCR, television, car.

In truth, of course, thinking is invisible, intangible. Thinking is software, not hardware. Yet those invisible, intangible principles and processes of thinking significantly, indeed, decisively impact both the quantity and quality of the visible, tangible ends achieved.

The true measures of quality thinking are invisible. The principles and process of Breakthrough Thinking embody the invisible advantage of Full-Spectrum Creativity, effectively applied to finding solutions. Human beings *do* have a paradigm of thinking when creating and restructuring solutions. It is time to adopt a new paradigm "software."

Quality thinking is Breakthrough Thinking.

NOTES

1. Ryuichi Yoshiya, in correspondence with G. Nadler.

2. Seiji Kurosu, "Classical Books on Industrial Management: From Work Design to Breakthrough Thinking," *Management Systems,* Vol. 3, No. 4 (February 1994) pp. 243–246.

3. Paul C. Nutt, "An Experimental Comparison of the Effectiveness of Three Planning Methods," *Management Science,* Vol. 23, No. 5, (January 1977), p. 511.

4. Linda K. Tuyn, "Solution-Oriented Therapy and Rogerian Nursing Science: An Integrated Approach," *Archives of Psychiatric Nursing,* Vol. VI, No. 2, (April 1992), p. 84.

5. James G. Greeno, "A Perspective on Thinking," *American Psychologist,* (February 1989), pp. 134–141.

6. Howard Gardner, *The Unschooled Mind* (New York: Basic Books, 1991).

7. Michael Howard, *The Lessons of History* (New Haven, CT: Yale University Press, 1991).

8. S. Mark Young, "A Framework for Successful Adoption and Performance of Japanese Manufacturing Practices in the United States," *Academy of Management Review,* Vol. 17, No. 4, (1992), pp. 677–700.

9. Raymond F. Zammuto and Edward J. O'Connor, "Gaining Advanced Manufacturing Technologies' Benefits: The Roles of Organization Design and Culture," *Academy of Management Review,* Vol. 17, No. 4, (1992), pp. 711–712.

10. Dorothy Leonard-Barton and Deepak Sinha, "Developer-User Interaction and User Satisfaction in Internal Technology Transfer," *Academy of Management Journal,* Vol. 36, No. 5, (October 1993), pp. 1125–1139.

11. Robert Jacobson, "The 'Austrian' School of Strategy," *Academy of Management Review,* Vol. 17, No. 4, (1992), p. 785.

12. Edgar H. Schein, "The Stability of Values in the First Ten Years of the Career," a report for the Office of Naval Research, distributed by National Technical Information Service, U.S. Department of Commerce, (September 1975).

13. Edgar H. Schein, "What You Need To Know About Organizational Culture," *Training and Development Journal,* (January 1986), p. 31.

14. M. Güldal Sakman, "An Empirical Study on Three Methods of Problem Definition in Ill-Structured Situations," Ph. D. dissertation, University of Wisconsin, Madison, (1985), p. 137.

15. Ibid.

16. Ibid., pp. 48-49.

17. Mary Pinto, Jeffrey Pinto, and John Prescott, "Antecedents and Consequences of Project Team Cross-Functional Cooperation," *Management Science,* Vol. 39, No. 10, (October 1993), pp. 1281-1296.

18. Robert Scott Root-Bernstein, *Discovering* (Cambridge, MA: Harvard University Press, 1990).

19. Werner Gruhl, "Definition Investment vs. Cost Growth," a report for the National Aeronautics and Space Administration, (March 25, 1985).

20. Allen C. Bluedorn, Carol Felker Kaufman, and Paul M. Lane, "How Many Things Do You Like to Do at Once? An Introduction to Monochronic and Polychronic Time," *Academy of Management Executive,* Vol. 6 No. 4., (1992), p. 17.

21. L. J. Ball, J. Evans, and I. Dennis, "Cognitive Processes in Engineering Design: A Longitudinal Study," *Ergonomics,* in press.

22. Denise C. Webster, "Solution-Focused Approaches in Psychiatric/Mental Health Nursing," *Perspectives in Psychiatric Care,* Vol. 26, No. 4, (1990), pp. 18-19.

23. Edgar H. Schein, "Are You Corporate Cultured?" *Personnel Journal,* (November 1986), pp. 87-88.

24. Shoukry D. Saleh and Clement K. Wang, "The Management of Innovation: Strategy, Structure, and Organizational Climate," *IEEE Transactions On Engineering Management,* Vol. 40, No. 1, (February 1993), p. 18.

25. Christina Shalley, "Effects of Productivity Goals, Creativity Goals, and Personal Discretion on Individual Creativity," *Journal of Applied Psychology,* Vol. 76, No.2, (1991) pp. 179-185.

26. D. Osborne and T. Goebler, *Reinventing Government: How the Entrepreneurial Spirit Is Transforming the Public Sector* (New York: Plume/Penguin Group, 1992).

27. Ikujiro Nonaka and Martin Kenney, "Towards a New Theory of Innovation Management," *Journal of Engineering and Technology Management,* Vol. 8, No. 1, (1991), pp. 67-83.

28. John Kenneth Galbraith, *A Journey Through Economic Time: A Firsthand View* (Boston, MA: Houghton Mifflin, 1994).

29. James M. Kouzes and Barry Z. Posner, *The Leadership Challenge: How to Get Extraordinary Things Done in Organizations* (San Francisco: Jossey-Bass, 1987), p. 9.

30. Ibid., p. 85.

31. Benson R. Snyder, "Literacy and Numeracy: Two Ways of Knowing," *Daedalus: Journal of the American Academy of Arts and Sciences,* (Spring 1990), p. 242.

32. Greeno, "Perspective on Thinking," pp. 138–40.

33. Gloria Barczak, Charles Smith, and David Wilemon, "Managing Large-Scale Organizational Change," *Organizational Dynamics,* Vol. 16, No. 2, (Autumn 1987), p. 23.

34. Kouzes and Posner, *Leadership Challenge,* p. 103.

35. Ibid., p. 90.

36. Root-Bernstein, *Discovering.*

37. Webster, "Solution-Focused Approaches," p. 20.

38. Shalley, "Effects of Productivity Goals."

39. Peter H. Farquar and Anthony R. Pratkanis, "Decision Structuring with Phantom Alternatives," *Management Science,* Vol. 39, No. 10, (October 1993), pp. 1214–1226.

40. Nutt, "Experimental Comparison of Effectiveness of Three Planning Methods," p. 501.

41. Zammuto and O'Connor, "Gaining Advanced Manufacturing Technologies' Benefits," p. 701.

42. Ibid., p. 718.

43. Tuyn, "Solution-Oriented Therapy and Rogerian Nursing Science," p. 83.

44. Ibid., p. 85.

45. Rashi Glazer, Joel Steckel, and Russell Winer, "Locally Rational Decision Making: The Distracting Effect of Information on Managerial Performance," *Management Science,* Vol. 38, No. 2, (February 1992).

46. Ibid., p. 213.

47. Ibid., p. 225.

48. Donald M. Murtha, "A Comparision of Problem-Solving Approaches Used by Environmental Designers," Ph.D. dissertation, University of Wisconsin, (1973), p. 36.

49. Nutt, "Experimental Comparison of Effectiveness of Three Planning Methods," p. 506.

50. Ibid., p. 499.

51. Ibid., p. 510.

52. O. Friedman, "The Economic Effect of Cost Control Programs in Mid-West Industry," Thesis for Master of Science in Industrial Engineering, University of Wisconsin, (1973).

53. Pinto, Pinto, and Prescott, "Antecedents and Consequences."

54. Schein, "Are You Corporate Cultured?", p. 89.

55. William Finlay, "Revelations Reassessed," review of Richard Gillespie, *Manufacturing Knowledge: A History of the Hawthorne Experiments* (New York: Cambridge University Press, 1991), *Science,* Vol. 254, No. 20, (December 1991), pp. 1820–21.

56. Chris Argyris, "Education for Leading-Learning," *Organizational Dynamics,* Vol. 21, No. 3, (Winter 1993), pp. 5–17.

57. Masaaki Imai, *Kaizen: The Key to Japan's Competitive Success* (New York: Random House, 1986).

58. Chris Goodrich, review of Henry Petroski, *The Evolution of Useful Things: How Everyday Artifacts—From Forks and Pins to Paper Clips and Zippers—Came to Be as They Are* (New York: Alfred A. Knopf, 1992) in *Los Angeles Times,* (December 6, 1992).

59. Tuyn, "Solution-Oriented Therapy and Rogerian Nursing Science," p. 85.

60. Schein, "Are You Corporate Cultured?", pp. 86–88.

61. Greeno, "Perspective on Thinking," p. 138.

62. Donald Murtha, "Comparison of Problem-Solving Approaches," pp. 95–97.

63. Terry E. Deal and Allen Kennedy, *Corporate Cultures: The Rites and Rituals of Corporate Life.* (Reading, MA: Addison-Wesley, 1982) excerpted from *Research on Culture* (Washington, DC: ASTD Press, 1986).

64. S. G. Scott and R. A. Bruce, "Determinants of Innovative Behavior: A Path Model of Individual Innovation in the Workplace," *Academy of Management Journal,* Vol. 37, No. 3 (June 1994), pp. 580–607.

65. Saleh and Wang, "The Management of Innovation, p. 14.

66. Ibid., p. 15. [See: W. E. Souder, *Managing New Product Innovations;* (Lexington, MA: Heath; 1987.)]

67. Robert L. Glass, "Software Design: It's All in Your Mind," *Computer World,* Vol. 22, No. 45 (November 7, 1988), p. 107.

68. Robert Malpas, "Technology and Wealth Creation," *The Bridge,* publication of The National Academy of Engineering, (Spring 1994), pp. 9–16.

69. O. Harari and L. Mukai, "A New Decade Demands a New Breed of Managers," *Management Review,* Vol. 79, No. 8, (August 1990), pp. 20–24.

70. James G. March, *A Primer on Decision Making* (New York: The Free Press/Macmillan, 1995).

Part IV

Translating the New Thinking Paradigm into Practice

Chapter 10

Getting Started: Problems, Opportunities, Usual Activities

A new paradigm of thinking—the seven assumptions of Breakthrough Thinking and the solution-finding process to which they lead—is now identified and thoroughly supported. Research, logic, and applications show this paradigm to promote the most effective solutions for most human opportunities and needs. This new mode of thinking is now available to all who choose to learn and practice the following principles and process.

The Uniqueness Principle
Assume initially that your problem or opportunity is different than any other. Don't start by copying preexisting "solutions."

The board of directors of a $2 billion, multi-divisional manufacturing and R&D company, studied four well-promoted models of Total Quality Management programs. It was anxious to get TQM established in the company, but couldn't decide which of the four structures to adopt. The chairman of the board asked a Breakthrough Thinking consultant to help the board pick a model. By asking the board members what purposes they wanted to get accomplished with the TQM *idea*, the consultant found that the board quickly agreed to what the

Breakthrough Thinking consultant already knew—it should not adopt any of the four models, but instead should design its own TQM effort. The board proceeded to do this and found some parts of all four models which could be used, but developed different ideas as well for a much more effective program for its own unique circumstances.

The Purposes Principle
Explore and expand your purposes, to select the largest possible purpose(s) that you ought to achieve. Don't simply fix what shouldn't even exist.

In late 1993, the Knoxville Community Investment Bank sought to develop the bank structure and policies to accommodate a million dollar challenge grant from Green Bay's All-Pro defensive end Reggie White, a former football player at the University of Tennessee, along with nearly $200,000 from the City of Knoxville. The advisory board members were all motivated to achieve the goal of investing in the inner-city and other low-income areas of Knoxville. However, the people involved represented a widely varied, sometimes conflicting set of interests—leaders of the Urban League, advocates for the homeless, commercial bank presidents, educators, clergy, entrepreneurs, and so forth. Indeed, one activist had recently sued another committee member and his entire organization.

Working with a Breakthrough Thinking facilitator, the board identified the following hierarchy of purposes from small to large for their effort: (1) to travel to other cities to see what others are doing, (2) to have a non-intimidating lending location, (3) to provide one-step lending and technical assistance, (4) to provide credit and technical assistance, (5) to develop community-based enterprises, (6) to provide interacting framework for individuals, neighborhoods, and city, (7) to have a framework for meeting the needs of the community, (8) to build an inner-city infrastructure, and (9) to provide "hand-up" and "hand-out" for legal improvement of communities. Beyond purpose level number (4), upon which they chose to focus initially, the larger levels of purpose on which all members agreed provide the context for future individual and group actions.

The Solution-After-Next Principle

Seek many ideal solutions for your selected focus and larger purpose(s). How might you best achieve them if you could start all over again? How might your solution be strengthened the next time (say, three years from now) that you work on creating or restructuring it? Use the future solutions for the needed purposes as your guide to today's actions.

A manufacturer of tools and metal supplies for human joint replacements (hips, knees, etc.) was almost always late in delivering its products and often over cost. After clarifying what purposes had to be accomplished, the consulting team and company personnel developed an ideal "solution-after-next" target system, as if they were designing five years from now. Because some of the essential technology of the ideal system did not yet exist and several parts of the target were too expensive for present budget constraints, the group chose a somewhat less-than-ideal solution to use in the present moment, but a solution that stayed as close as possible to their ideal target. As a result, even their solution for the present virtually eliminated late deliveries and overestimated production capabilities.

The Systems Principle:
Seven-Eighths of Everything Can't Be Seen

Everything is a system. Use a systems framework to identify the elements, dimensions, and interrelationships of your solution. Don't assume the details will work out.

A young accountant, about to graduate from business school, planned her career over the next five years. After developing a purpose hierarchy, selecting her focus purposes, and generating a rough idea of her target solution, she used a systems matrix to detail what she would do. The systems matrix led her to review eight elements—purposes, inputs (information, people), outputs (forms of action), sequence or steps to follow, environment (physical and organizational), human agents (people to help her), physical catalysts, and information aids—defined in six dimensions—fundamental characteristics, values and goals, measures of effectiveness, controls, interfaces, and future. Two-and-a-half-years later, she reports that when she takes a new client, seeks a change in type of assignments, seeks mentoring, and otherwise moves ahead in her career, she is greatly helped by a systems view. She became a senior manager about a year early.

The Limited Information Collection Principle: Don't Become an Expert About the Problem

It is impossible to know everything about the issue, situation, opportunity, or problem. What purposes would any proposed information collection serve? What would you do with all the information if you had it? Seek information about purposes and solutions rather than about who's at fault or what's going on now.

In the late 1950s, after years of exhaustive research, Ford Motor Company introduced its prized "concept car"—the almost-perfect Edsel. Yet a plethora of data had obscured the most pertinent fact. Automotive historians note that the Edsel, one of the most heavily researched cars ever, had only one serious flaw: No one wanted to buy it.

By contrast, when newly appointed Chrysler president Lee Iacocca sought to distinguish his failing company by reintroducing the convertible to U.S. domestic markets, he told his engineers to chop the top off a LeBaron, drive around the streets of Dearborn, and check out the reactions. The positive responses of people who saw the car were sufficient to convince Iacocca to invest in the development of a convertible model. Chrysler's move was immediate, emphatic, and highly successful.

The People-Design Principle

Using the principles above gives everyone with a stake in the outcome the opportunity to contribute to finding the solu-

*tion. People respond positively and enthusiastically and be-
come committed to purposes, solutions-after-next, and a
"whole" system vision. Don't try to overcome resistance to
change; instead, generate interest in achieving results.*

Agricultural specialists in a province of Mexico introduced
a promising new variety of maize that produced two to three
times more grain per acre than the prevalent strains. They persuaded local farmers to plant the new maize, and productivity
increased significantly. By the end of the third year, however,
the farmers had reverted to planting their old seed varieties.
Why? The women who made tortillas from the maize—and
who had not been involved in the first change—didn't like the
new color.

The Betterment Timeline Principle:
Know When to Improve Your Solution
*Install your solution with the seeds of its future change built
in. Use the future orientations of purposes, solutions-after-
next, and systems to stimulate continual improvements in today's solution and even changes in the solution target.*

Nothing is permanent.
Excellent companies become troubled and fail. Sears Roe-
buck had $3.6 billion in annual sales. For a hundred years, the
Sears catalog had been the unquestioned leader in the field, a
beloved and highly successful American institution. It never
changed. It did not even install a toll-free number until one year
before its shocking collapse. In the debacle, 50,000 employees
lost their jobs.
In reality, we should not even use the term "solution." We
should consider it to be the change that we can make right
now, one that includes what the next change should be. The
larger purposes of the community investment bank, the solution-after-next of the manufacturer of joint replacement equipment, and the young accountant's system matrix (especially its
future dimension) provide the advantages for continual improvement sought by this principle.

Such are the seven principles of the new paradigm. The process of solution-finding to which these seven new assumptions lead can be briefly sketched as follows:

Purposes

* Identify many purposes for your program, project, or problem area.
* Expand the scope of your purposes, from smaller purpose to larger, arrange these in a hierarchy, and select the purpose on which you will focus your efforts.

Target

* Develop many options for solutions-after-next (SAN), for the focus and larger purposes.
* Assess these solution-after-next options to select your SAN target.
* Develop recommendations that stay close to your target.

Results

* Detail your recommendations to assure workability.
* Design an installation plan for the recommendations.
* Install your system/solution.
* Set dates for betterment and improvement of the recommended solution, so as to attain your larger purposes and your SAN target.

This new paradigm of thinking (Breakthrough Thinking) is "software for the mind." It leads you to develop a vision of where you need to be and enables you to get there without ponderous data collection. It most effectively creates and restructures solutions. It gives new meaning to the ancient human purposeful activity: to plan, design, reengineer, improve, and solve problems—to create and restructure solutions.

It extends the creativity process to determine the right purposes to be accomplished, generate a large number of imaginative and original options, and develop the systems to implement effective solutions. This Full-Spectrum Creativity provides structure for the imaginative mind and freedom for the structured mind.

It removes obstacles to simple solutions. It forces a fresh look at your options. It requires minimal data collection to reduce "analysis paralysis." It produces answers that provide much greater benefits in terms of quality, economic return, timeliness, and other desirable aspects. In developing these benefits, it requires much less time and cost for projects. It promotes innovative thinking to seek major changes in new personal perspectives, products, systems, and services. It results in systems for the long-term. It causes your recommendations to be actually implemented. It builds natural, long-lasting teams, and personal relationships. By stark contrast, the Conventional Thinking paradigm fails on almost all these counts.

For example, at the close of the twentieth century, writes professor of social sciences and management consultant Peter Drucker, our need is to measure, not count: "Quantification has been the rage in business and economics these past 50 years. Accountants have proliferated as fast as lawyers. Yet we do not have the measurements we need.

"Neither our concepts nor our tools are adequate for the control of operations, or for managerial control. And, so far," says Drucker, "there are neither the concepts nor the tools for business control, [that is] for economic decision-making.

"We need measurements for a company or industry that are akin to the 'leading indicators' and 'lagging indicators' that economists have developed for the economy. A loss of market standing or a failure to innovate do not register in the accountant's figures until the damage has been done."[1]

Full-Spectrum Thinking focuses on the expanded purposes of each human activity, thus leading to the measures indicative of its actual effect. Clearly, counting alone—mere information collection—won't do you any good, not unless you have a clear vision of your purposes, where you want to go and why.

The international financial reporting firm of Dun & Brad-street has noted that "sometimes you have to forget what you know to make a breakthrough." For example, success did not come to Paul MacCready, designer and builder of the first, effective human-powered aircraft "until he approached the problem from a completely different perspective, without mind-numbing preconceptions."[2]

To make similar breakthroughs, you must replace your old Conventional Thinking paradigm with Full-Spectrum Thinking. Like many of our normal paradigms—eating a meal, getting dressed, responding to another in a relationship (whether personal or at work), driving in a car, determining political affiliations—the paradigm of thinking is likely to change in stages. First comes an *Interest* or dissatisfaction or crisis. You manifest this stage by reading this book, for example. Or you are just curious about anyone who says that the paradigm of thinking should be changed or have a general proclivity toward learning and seeking new perspectives in life.

Second is *Understanding*. We hope this book provides this for you in terms of fathoming the assumptions and processes of a new thinking paradigm. Understanding is necessary but not sufficient to actually change your paradigm of thinking.

The third stage is *Belief.* The critical turning point comes when your understanding turns into a solid commitment to try the new paradigm.

Then comes *Use.* Like any paradigm of behavior, using the new paradigm of thinking over and over becomes critical to reinforcing and making it permanent in your actions.

To move to the fifth stage of *Facilitate Others,* more details than this book provides are needed. These are available in a how-to book for the general public, *Breakthrough Thinking: The Seven Principles of Creative Problem Solving,* written by the two of us, and in a book for professional facilitators, *Breakthrough Thinking in Total Quality Management,* written by Glen Hoffherr, Jack Moran, and Gerald Nadler. But using Breakthrough Thinking for your own solution finding can give you a feeling of strength and capability in providing some leadership to others as problems are addressed.

The sixth, seventh and eighth stages, *Teach, Write and Communicate* and *Investigate New Developments,* are those you get to, at least aspire to, but are far beyond what we can cover in this book. At any rate, success at the previous stages leads to recognizing that others will want to learn the ideas. Teaching, preparing materials to communicate the concepts— articles, books, videotapes, computer programs, etc.—and doing research to further the ideas and support the concepts are to be expected in any dynamic concept such as the paradigm of thinking for creating and restructuring solutions, and represent the complete adoption of a paradigm.

What Can I Do?

Once people become aware of the existence of this new paradigm of thinking, once they grasp the fact that a different, exceptionally effective way of thinking does exist, is simply: "Well, all right, great. But how do I actually change my solution-finding behavior, the activities that I do?" To that much of the process, we now offer a beginner's guide.

First of all, consider every question, assignment, problem, request, opportunity, proposed action, idea, issue, need, argument—everything—as the time to use the new paradigm of thinking. Trying to pick an "appropriate" project on which to use Breakthrough Thinking is an indication that you may not fully understand the new assumptions and process. So begin by following the process on your very next decision-making situation—and the very next one, and so on—whether you are on your own or interacting with someone else in the organization, a customer, a supplier, a family member.

Thus, one way to begin is to consider each opportunity or problem challenge you face as unique. Regardless of which type of human purposeful activity it may be, regardless of whatever someone else may call it—research, evaluation, planning, learning, or operation and control—consider your present situation to be without parallel. Do not initially try to fit a previous solution or technique you found successful in the present situation.

Third, you might use the new paradigm to set up a plan of how you will "tackle the situation." Remembering that each such plan is unique, expand your purposes to determine what the project (or other initiating situation) is really supposed to be achieving. This is one of the most beneficial aspects of Full-Spectrum Thinking—making sure that your effort is indeed needed and setting up the implementation perspective right at the beginning. Next, develop several "ideal" planning systems from which you pick a target system. Then stay as close as possible to the target as you proceed.

Surely, you want to pursue and accomplish each human purposeful activity in the most effective way. The drive for achievement is central to human progress. This fact alone may well provide sufficient motivation for a change in your thinking principles and process.

Almost everyone of any age possesses the ability to apply this new and different mode of reasoning. Indeed, the younger the person, the more likely he or she may be to switch to the paradigm of thinking that will most effectively solve the problem at hand.

This reflects both the fact that longstanding habits are harder to break and the fact that youth is naturally open to discovering effective new ways to achieve desired goals. Yet whatever your age or ingrained habits of thinking may be, if you possess the interest and capacity to explore the concepts this book offers, you can no doubt learn and effectively apply the new paradigm of thinking. You have only to choose to do so.

If you make that choice, you will not only more effectively accomplish most of the purposeful activities that you pursue, you will also avoid the common errors of problem solving.

BELIEVE

These specific benefits of the new paradigm of thinking can be yours almost immediately. The only essential ingredient is your willingness to play the "believing game" regarding Full-Spectrum Thinking as you address each decision situation or problem. You know more than you think you do, and now you also know *how* to convert that knowledge to practice.

Of course, it is not easy to "believe" something new. A lifetime of thinking habits are likely to intervene and offer stiff resistance. You have not previously been asked to raise your consciousness in regard to thinking about thinking. Your personal mental computer may well balk at the introduction of this new "software for the mind."

Astonishingly, as Leonard Sayles, senior research scientist at the Center for Creative Leadership, recently reported, "The bad news is that most [American] middle managers have not been trained to take certain initiatives. Management courses ignore managing work systems and coordination and still emphasize clean desks and keeping your eyes upward, on the lookout for cues from the boss. One of America's largest corporations, one that invested heavily in training, recently had to retrain middle managers who had never learned that their jobs included improving systems effectiveness."[3]

Similarly, McGill University professor Henry Mintzberg, in his definitive history of strategic planning, notes ruefully that management's reliance on strategic planning has often narrowed a company's vision with disastrous business consequences. Mintzberg has examined every school of strategic planning and concluded that regardless of the form, shape, or size of the plan, planners have failed to address the strategists' fundamental dilemmas of reconciling concurrent but conflicting needs for change and stability within the organization. For that matter, we might add, within individuals. According to Mintzberg, strategic planning—which too often consists of simply filling out forms designed to indicate strengths and weaknesses, opportunities and threats, as opposed to fundamental purposes and values—can in fact impede commitment, discourage major change, and promote internal politics in organizations.[4]

No wonder, then, as Mintzberg writes, the consequences to business are often disastrous. We directly attribute this self-destructive narrowing of corporate vision to the conventional mode of thinking. Far too many individuals, groups, and organizations, even when they think they're looking toward the future, are in fact firmly shackled to the present and the past. We definitely need to plan, to do strategic planning, to accomplish the human purposeful activity of creating or restructuring solutions. Although Mintzberg correctly shows the failure of current strategic planning, what he really shows is that the process, *how* to go about it, has failed, but not that the *purposes* of strategic planning are not needed. The strategic thinking required is Breakthrough Thinking.

The key to change lies in taking action. Just do it. "Each individual is fundamentally in charge of his or her own life" is the way educator and consultant Stanley Herman states it.[5]

Do it with your very next activity or problem or decision. And the next one. And the next. Effective action comes from taking a stand for the new thinking. The key to learning the new paradigm of thinking is repetition. In all you do, become committed to seeking the three types of breakthroughs—as many "aha!" ideas and recommendations as possible, significantly better quality and quantity of your results, and getting your good ideas *implemented* (or avoiding implementation of a bad idea).

In getting started with Breakthrough Thinking, as with any cerebral activity, it is useful to follow some simple techniques that tend to increase mental acuity. Thus, as noted by psychiatrist Richard Carlton, you are in all cases well advised to take an occasional mental break from rational thinking of either sort, set a time limit for your focused mental activity, protect your sleep, exercise, pay attention to diet, and take vitamins.[6]

Additionally, as educator Susan Newman remarked in a recent seminar, the principles and process of Breakthrough Thinking serve to develop non-threatening questions when dealing with others. Inevitably, Breakthrough Thinking leads you to "play the believing game." A related benefit has been noted by Australian practitioner Jon Elks: "Breakthrough Thinking disturbs a person's comfort zone. But at the same time the *process* of Breakthrough Thinking is a great way to overcome that disturbance." Moreover, Full-Spectrum Thinking leads you away from that excessive comfort in which you avoid the growth and change essential to human survival.

THE SPREAD OF BELIEF

In whatever way the seeds of Breakthrough Thinking are planted, in whatever soil, under whatever conditions, they will adhere and flourish. Usually, a single individual can get the ball rolling. You may be a high school student organizing homework assignments, a coach evaluating the performance of athletes, a retired person finally learning to draw or to speak a foreign language, a corporate CEO determining the five-year direction of a company. Whatever your own situation, you must change your behavior, base your actions on the principles and process of Full-Spectrum Thinking.

For example, a few years ago, we led a strategic planning seminar for the executives of a major international advertising agency. Among the participants was an exceptionally able young executive whose initial skepticism of Full-Spectrum Thinking was apparent, yet whose interest and enthusiasm increased with every hour of our presentation. Evidently, he liked what he heard. More importantly, he began to practice Breakthrough Thinking, not only in his personal life, but at all levels within his organization.

Although we fell out of touch with this particular Breakthrough Thinker for some years, we later learned of his promotion in a most gratifying way. Having ascended to the position of head of international operations, he requested that we present a series of Breakthrough Thinking seminars for all staff of the international office.

In Florida, a university professor, himself convinced of the value of Full-Spectrum Thinking, began a Breakthrough Thinking user's group to focus on planning, improving, and finding solutions in education. Soon the group included a dozen individuals who meet regularly to wrestle with issues such as planning for the implementation of new technologies at all levels of the educational system.

The impact of the new paradigm of thinking can quickly reach beyond the individual. For example, after attending a seminar on Breakthrough Thinking, a middle-school teacher in Connecticut offered the book *Breakthrough Thinking* as one of many possible titles her students might choose for a book report assignment. Two seventh-grade girls read the book, tracked down Nadler, called him on the phone, and asked for further guidance in their own practice of the ideas.

Effects on Decision Making

Anyone, whether child or employee or manager or CEO, will greatly benefit from a clear understanding of the purposes— both immediate and larger—of the activity in which they are engaged. Such an understanding provides an essential framework for all truly effective human endeavors.

One problem in organizations today is that employees are asked, for example, to direct a customer-satisfaction survey . . . and are then simply expected to develop the required questionnaire. Yet when that same well-intentioned (though ill-directed) employee returns with the survey results, his or her superior is likely to reject the work, saying in frustration, *"This* isn't what I wanted."

In most such cases, the only one who knows what the boss actually wants (and what the organization needs) is the boss. Bosses want what they want. So why the confusion? Because only *they* know what their *purposes* actually are. The confusion results directly from the failure to discuss and expand purposes, a central tenet of Full-Spectrum Thinking, with and for the person to whom the assignment is made.

Discussing expanded purposes and agreeing on focus purposes puts human activity, at whatever level, in an essential context of larger purposes. Thus, the many minute decisions we must make in the course of any assigned task—even one apparently directed by computer software—are profoundly guided by the lodestar of agreed larger purposes, the "true north" that provides direction for all effective human activities. Directed by the compass of larger purposes, agreed and understood, we can all contribute effectively to the work of our organizations.

Even something at once as simple and complex as the design of a gear, even a design accomplished with computer-aided engineering software, demands that countless minute decisions be made by the individual using the software. At almost every minute, if you don't understand the context of purposes for the design and existence of the gear you are designing—not only its immediate purposes, but also the larger, ultimate purposes— you are bound to make many of your decisions inappropriately.

On complex projects and systems, when people make decisions, take actions concerning their own assignments within the overall system, and other people working on another aspect of the system make their own decisions, both parties acting from their own, necessarily dissimilar understandings, the outcome is almost certain to be incompatibility between two or more aspects of the system. Typically, the result is known as "satisficing," finding and accepting whatever solution that works, not the solution that is best, from either aspect of the situation. The U.S. Congress (or the Japanese Diet), acting on large and small issues from healthcare system reform to wool and mohair subsidies, provides very good illustrations of satisficing that arise in large part because a context of purposes, solutions-after-next, and systems description is lacking.

Full-Spectrum Thinking rejects satisficing as the guide to finding solutions. No doubt the doubling of factory capacity, which company officers selected to solve their late delivery and high cost problems, *would* be workable—but such satisficing is a poor solution when establishing effective management control systems is the most effective purpose to achieve. No doubt automating a loading dock with many problems *would* work—but such satisficing is a poor solution when selling that warehouse (and 19 others of a company's 24) is a far more effective solution. Satisficing is the opposite of the third type of breakthrough—attaining the implementation of a good idea and/or avoiding the use of a bad idea.

No matter who you are, no matter what your individual or group situation, the key element in getting started is to learn by doing. We urge you to follow the apprenticeship model. Involve yourself in solving not a "canned," pre-existing, case study, but rather a real, tangible problem, one that affects you personally. Not only will you be more motivated to find the most effective possible solution, but as you experience success, you will find yourself increasingly eager to apply Breakthrough Thinking to all aspects of your everyday life. Moreover, you are likely to change the behavior of others, not by a focus on *getting* them to change to the new thinking paradigm, but by conscious illustration of the results you obtain and the new kinds of questions you ask.

Even though the process of group decision making and negotiation are complex, even though they involve multi-player, multi-criteria, ill-structured, evolving, dynamic problems, even in the largest of human organizations, all it takes is one interested person educated in the principles and process of Full-Spectrum Thinking. In accordance with the Breakthrough Thinking principle of uniqueness, however, there is no single, one-size-fits-all way to implement the new thinking paradigm within your organization. Nor is there any way of predicting precisely how and when the new principles and practice will establish themselves. Every organization is unique.

The Impact of You

Only one thing is essential: a single individual who, for whatever reason, whether wisdom or desperation, is *aware of* and *willing* to try a new way. Then, to *act upon* that willingness. You are in charge of your life.

You may try Full-Spectrum Thinking first in your own personal life. And when you take actions based on the new paradigm, you learn how to do it. The more you do it, the more you learn.

Or you may start with a real project in an organization where results must be attained in a specific amount of time. Use the project to get one or more of the types of breakthroughs.

From that point on, there is no single way that Breakthrough Thinking will come to be implemented in an organization. Getting others in an organization "into action" with a new thinking paradigm depends on their readiness for openness and the general organizational culture. Awareness is first achieved somehow, by some single individual. Then others are made aware. (A mid-level manager of a federal department told her team for "reinventing government" about Breakthrough Thinking as they were beginning work on a new design for their department. The operations manager of a very large distribution company read about Breakthrough Thinking and perceived its value to the whole company. He immediately told the director of customer service about its benefits because he knew the director was meeting with worldwide customer service managers to redesign the whole system—and the prospect of using Conventional Thinking frightened him.) The aim is to empower each individual with Full-Spectrum Thinking for his or her use in all solution finding.

For example, the "reinventing government" team agreed that the principles and process of the new thinking paradigm would prove much more effective for their effort. So how did they begin? They applied the concepts of Full-Spectrum Thinking to develop a proposal for using Breakthrough Thinking in the entire effort, a proposal they submitted to the next higher level of authority for approval and funding.

Once a key individual becomes aware of and privately practices Full-Spectrum Thinking, he or she may then send Breakthrough Thinking materials to other executives or managers within the organization. Or they may work with their managers, using Breakthrough Thinking on a particular project. In effect, they may become their own organizational facilitators.

Such managers instinctively recognize that all the many roles they play daily—innovator, broker, producer, director, coordinator, monitor, facilitator, mentor[7]—were, in effect, assigned to them by the "hardware" of an organization. What they urgently need is the "software" that allows them to play those roles effectively—Breakthrough Thinking. Sometimes the chief executive officer is first to become aware of Breakthrough Thinking and is in a position to begin organizational implementation directly by retaining professional Breakthrough Thinking consultants to train key executives and managers. Obviously, the "ball gets rolling" with greater immediate impact when it starts at the top of the mountain.

The top, however, is by no means the only level at which the principles and process of Full-Spectrum Thinking can begin to impact organizational decisions. As recent economic events have demonstrated, "trickle up" often proves more effective than "trickle down."

Even an individual who is isolated and relatively powerless within his or her organization can still positively impact not only his or her individual life, but also the life of the organization, simply by practicing, as much as possible within the parameters of his or her own responsibilities, the principles and process of Full-Spectrum Thinking. The transference of this individual behavior to the actions of others is much more likely when one person—you—actually uses the ideas and is seen as being successful. One man returned to his company after attending a Breakthrough Thinking seminar and used the paradigm on all his assignments. His results were so good after 18 months that the president asked him what he was doing to produce such outstanding solutions. The president then set up workshops for others to learn Breakthrough Thinking.

Even if you find you are unable to convince others in your organization to try the new paradigm of thinking, even if you find yourself doing it alone, you will still perform your organizational function better—to accomplish more and do a better job of it—than you would by following the old thinking paradigm of Conventional Thinking. And thanks to your enhanced individual contribution, your organization (however unconscious it may be) will benefit. Ultimately, then, both you and the benefits of your new way of thinking are likely to be recognized.

As former *New York Times* business writer Isadore Barmash has noted, "Individuals still do count. While it's axiomatic that businesses are not comfortable with geniuses, they clearly recognize individual effort, although sometimes they are slow to show it. But an individual who stands out because of his or her performance, who has the courage to shake things up, to call attention to opportunity, will usually do well.

" 'The purpose of an organization is to enable common men to do uncommon things,' said business guru Peter F. Drucker in his seminal book, *Management.* 'No organization can depend on genius; the supply is always scarce and unreliable. It is the test of an organization to make ordinary human beings perform better than they seem capable of, to bring out whatever strength there is in its members, and to use each man's strength to help all the others perform.' "[8]

Ultimately, organizations are composed of individuals. So as you and other individuals come to value and adopt Full-

Spectrum Thinking as your own new paradigm of thinking, ultimately, the organizational response to any question, assignment, problem, request, opportunity, proposed action, idea, issue, need, argument—in short, to everything—will eventually come to be based on Full-Spectrum Thinking.

At whatever stage of personal development, at whatever level of your organization, the profound change to a new paradigm of thinking begins with a single individual. Why not you?

NOTES

1. Peter F. Drucker, "We Need to Measure, Not Count," *The Wall Street Journal*, (April 13, 1993).

2. Dun & Bradstreet, advertisement in *Fortune*, (April 20, 1992).

3. Leonard R. Sayles, "Middle Managers Can Rescue Business," *New York Times*, (February 14, 1993).

4. Henry Mintzberg, *The Rise and Fall of Strategic Planning* (New York: The Free Press/Macmillan, 1993).

5. Stanley Herman, *A Force of Ones: Reclaiming Individual Power in a TIme of Teams, Work Groups, and Other Crowds*, (San Francisco: Jossey-Bass, 1994).

6. Richard Carlton, M.D., "How To Use Our Minds Much More Effectively," *Bottom Line*, (February 28, 1993).

7. Robert E. Quinn, *PRISM: Personal Reflective Instruments for Successful Management*, (San Francisco: Jossey-Bass, 1992).

8. Isadore Barmash, "Minor vs. Major," *Sky*, (March, 1993).

Chapter 11

The Multi-Thinker

Both basic paradigms of thinking—the analytical Conventional Thinking and the Full-Spectrum Creativity of Breakthrough Thinking—are useful for human advancement and the effective solution of human problems. These complementary approaches are intertwined to varying degrees in addressing each type of problem or opportunity. That is, each helps in different amounts to accomplish the five basic types of human purposeful activity.

The person who seeks to employ and enjoy the full scope, range, and power of his or her mind must learn to use both approaches (and their closely related modifications), each when most appropriate. In short, *you must become a multi-thinker.*

ILLUSTRATIONS OF WHAT
YOU MIGHT FACE

Consider these problems or questions or issues, which are a sample that might concern anyone. How would you approach each of them?

1. You have enrolled your four-year-old child in a highly recommended preschool program. In the last few weeks, however, your child has made two or three slightly disturbing comments about what goes on in the program. Your friends with children in the same program report no similar comments.

419

2. Customer complaints to the company where you work have increased nearly 300 percent in the last few weeks. Although still small per total number of units shipped, the increase could nonetheless tarnish your company's reputation for high quality products.

3. With the revelation that your uncle has contracted colon cancer, you realize that he is the fourth member of a dozen or so close relatives to suffer the disease. This starts you wondering about the relationship between heredity and the occurrence of this affliction.

4. The increasing trade deficit with Japan has caused some members of Congress and several trade organizations to seek the establishment of a U.S. competitiveness policy. Variants of this proposed solution go by other names— technology policy, trade policy, most-favored-nation status, and so on.

5. Your interest in furniture-making as a hobby has led you to produce some quite good yet simple bookshelves, stools, and end tables. To be able to produce more complicated objects—chest of drawers, entertainment center, armoire, dining room table and chairs—you decide to improve your skills.

With all these situations, Conventional Thinking would have you start your search for a solution by gathering data about the existing conditions, applying a "standard" set of techniques, preparing models or abstracting from the data, analyzing the data and models, finding out the causes of the problem and who is to blame, and/or looking for what previous solutions others have already used in apparently similar situations. Doing one or more of these *may* be needed at some step somewhere along the way of the solution-finding process. But this conventional paradigm of thinking is precisely what has led to the solution collapse detailed in the first two parts of this book.

By contrast, Full-Spectrum Thinking is used to *initiate* what the multi-thinker does to address these—and all other— situations. It requires you to check the premises or assumptions of any issue or usual activity. Far too often, we, and our organizations, follow untested premises and assumptions. Full-Spectrum Thinking allows you to determine when Conventional Thinking should be followed.

In illustration #3, for example, you would initially ask the purpose of finding a relationship between colon cancer and heredity . . . and then, the purpose(s) of that purpose. In other words, clarify the hierarchy of purposes for even working on the question or finding a solution. If the focus purpose or purposes selected in the context of the larger hierarchy is to determine a *generalization* about the linkage between heredity and the onset of colon cancer, *then* the Research Approach of Conventional Thinking is likely to predominate in the solution-after-next ideas for achieving the focus purpose(s).

Illustration #5 would be viewed in terms of expanding the purposes for working on the motivation to become an advanced furniture maker. If the selected focus purpose(s) from the hierarchy relate to *learning* new skills, then much of the rest of Full-Spectrum Thinking could be used—purpose hierarchy for the identified new skills, solution-after-next options to obtain the skills (including methods others have found successful), and then the detailing (partially using the Conventional Approach to acquire the identified, needed information) and implementation (the actions you would take).

Similarly, the other illustrations or problems would be initially addressed from the Full-Spectrum Thinking perspective of purpose expansion to determine what purposeful activity is being considered as the way to determine the remaining steps. Illustration #1 might lead to a focus purpose of *evaluation,* which in turn leads to using a combination of Full-Spectrum Thinking and Conventional Thinking (what is the ideal preschool program to serve as a basis for comparison—part of Full-Spectrum Thinking—and then collecting data about the existing program—part of Conventional Thinking—to form the basis for determining differences, both positive and negative, from the ideal).

Expanding the purposes in illustration #2 is likely to lead to the purposeful activity of *operation and supervision,* where finding (within the context of larger purposes) causes and fixing what has gone wrong with an existing good system predominate (Conventional Thinking). Expanding the purposes in illustration #4 is likely to lead to a purposeful activity of *planning and design,* where Full-Spectrum Thinking should be used to create or restructure policies.

The utility of Full-Spectrum Thinking even in the course of scientific inquiry is exemplified by the teaching of Nobel Laureate physicist Richard Feynman. The Cal Tech professor habitually chided graduate students who began working on a scientific problem in the normal way, that is, by following the Research Approach—checking what research had already been done, noting what was already known. That way, Feynman told his students, they almost certainly relinquished the opportunity to discover original truths.[1] The fundamental focus on purposes and expanded purposes lends scope and effectiveness to even the most analytical endeavor.

The most effective thinker—the multi-thinker—integrates both approaches in the solution of most problems. Creating or restructuring solutions (illustration #4, for example) is the purposeful activity most entirely suited to Full-Spectrum Thinking. Similarly, the operation and supervision of an existing system or solution (illustration #2, for example) is generally best accomplished by combining Full-Spectrum Thinking, including the solution-after-next plan of action, ahead of Conventional Thinking.

The evaluation of solutions already in place (illustration #1, for example) partakes of Full-Spectrum Thinking before delving into Conventional Thinking's analytical endeavor. Learning new information and skills (illustration #5, for example) lends itself well to Full-Spectrum Thinking. To succeed in that purposeful activity, you must first identify what you are trying accomplish by the learning (purposes) and where it fits within your framework of understanding (systems).

Recognizing the validity of both approaches, applying each (or both) as indicated by the particular purposeful activity and its larger hierarchy of purposes, few if any solutions to problems lie beyond the scope of human intelligence. Yet however promising its outcome, the process of multi-thinking is not easy, at least not at the beginning. As Thomas J. Watson, founder and long-time chairman of IBM once noted, "All the problems of the world could be settled easily, if men were only willing to think. The trouble is that men often resort to all sorts of devices in order *not* to think. Thinking is such hard work."[2]

During the last 400 years, perhaps the most difficult aspect of thinking, of solution finding, has been the pervasive assumption in the West that any and all problems can best be solved by Conventional Thinking. While this assumption proves increasingly and manifestly false, most people today persist in an approach that is, more often than not, doomed to fail.

That is why, although we absolutely support the usefulness of Conventional Thinking in the finding of generalizations, as well as in certain limited aspects of other human purposeful activities, we find it necessary to proclaim emphatically the far wider applicability of Full-Spectrum Thinking. The future, it seems clear, belongs to the multi-thinker. Yet in order to enjoy that future, we must accept the broader perspectives of Full-Spectrum Thinking, while using Conventional Thinking where needed, just as Newtonian mechanistic views of the world are still useful within the broader and more pervasive Einsteinian nonlinear view.

Intelligence, Information, and Wisdom

Educational psychologist Howard Gardner's theory of multiple types of human intelligence shows how multiple perspectives and thinking paradigms are essential to effective problem solving. Gardner writes: "I have posited that all human beings are capable of at least seven different ways of knowing the world—ways that I have elsewhere labeled the *seven human intelligences.* According to this analysis, we are all able to know the world through language, logical-mathematical analysis, spatial representation, musical thinking, the use of the body to solve problems or to make things, an understanding of other individuals, and an understanding of ourselves. Where individuals differ is in the strength of these intelligences—the so-called *profile of intelligences*—and in the ways in which such intelligences are invoked and combined to carry out different tasks, solve diverse problems, and progress in various domains."

Gardner argues that people learn, represent, and utilize knowledge in many different ways. "To begin with," he notes, "these differences challenge an educational system that assumes that everyone can learn the same materials in the same way and that a uniform, universal measure suffices to test student learning. Indeed, as currently constituted, our educational system is heavily biased toward linguistic modes of instruction and assessment and, to a somewhat lesser degree, toward logical-quantitative modes as well."[3]

As Alan Kantrow of the international consulting firm McKinsey & Company has noted, three basic types of information exist: "know that" (the facts), "know how" (the techniques), and "know why" (purposes). It may be said, then, that knowledge consists of informed understanding in the combination of these three areas, another category.

The further category, of course, is wisdom. And surely part of such wisdom lies in knowing when to apply which paradigm of thinking, knowing how to effectively find solutions— the challenge of our opportunities.

Kantrow believes that the biggest problem of all is the prevailing, pervasive, unvoiced, international assumption that management is basically the same everywhere. That similar "solutions" simply require a tweak here or there to work effectively in any and all situations and settings.[4] Business schools have assumed for nearly 50 years that "a manager is a manager is a manager," regardless of type of organization or in what city or country it is located. These false and increasingly dangerous assumptions are in turn based on the quantifying, compartmentalizing, analytical instincts of Conventional Thinking.

Mismanaging People and Thinking

In fact, the conventional paradigm of thinking can now be seen to have resulted in the mismanagement of the most valuable resource of all: human beings. In his book, *Competitive Advantage Through People: Unleashing the Power of the Work*

Force, Stanford University professor of organizational behavior Jeffrey Pfeffer asserts that all the evidence argues that a knowledgeable and committed work force is essential for firms to remain competitive. Why then do businesses continue to mismanage their most valuable asset?

Pfeffer argues that the answer resides in a complex web of factors, based on perception, history, legislation, and practice that continue to dominate management thought and action. These have led to profound errors that lead to advancing the wrong heroes, the wrong theories, and the wrong language.

"Through much of the past two or three decades, business heroes have been numbers people, rather than people people, and those willing to slash employment levels and take on the work force have received much approbation, even as they were occasionally obtaining less than spectacular results."[5]

For example, during the 1980s, numbers-crunching, bottom-line-focused executives such as airline CEO Frank Lorenzo were lauded by the best of business schools. In fact, however, Lorenzo ran various airlines, Eastern and Texas Air among them, straight into the ground. "He fought unions and his work force with a vigor some describe as ruthless," writes Pfeffer, "and had extracted a fortune of some $40 million, even as the company he controlled was failing."[6] That is certainly the wrong sort of business hero.

With reference to wrong theories, Pfeffer writes: "The view of human behavior promulgated in virtually all economic models of behavior is that workers don't like to work, and without some form of external control or incentive, they will not perform useful labor. Since economic models presume that people don't want to work, and those that employ them want them to, these models highlight the differences in interests between managers and their workers.

"These perspectives on human behavior are realized in numerous policies and practices of the workplace, in which an emphasis on control, discipline, limited individual incentives, and monitoring are evident. These views of human behavior, with their emphasis on optimal incentive contracts, encourage

organizations to seek answers to many, if not most, performance problems by tinkering with the compensation system."[7]

Few companies have as yet taken the fundamentally dis-
tinguishing step of changing the total environment in which
their people work. Such changes, based on the new Full-
Spectrum Thinking paradigm, could quickly draw a profitable
distinction between mere labor (at whatever level of financial
compensation) and the profound, enduring satisfactions of
work.

Of course, both personal experience and observation
will generally indicate that work is essential to human happiness. In fact, people do want to work. But they also want to
exert significant control over their own efforts and to be recognized as important for the work they do. Within agreed production standards, they want to be free to perform their work
as they deem best. Moreover, they want to be part of the design of that work.

"We see things according to how they are described,"
writes Pfeffer. "That is why Disney uses language in its theme
parks that reinforces its employees' understanding that they are
in show business and [purpose-related] terminology that helps
them deliver high quality service. There is no personnel department—employees are hired by 'Central Casting.' People work
'on stage,' and most important, those visiting the park are called
'guests' rather than 'tourists.' "[8]

In this context, Pfeffer suggests, the language of much
economic theory and of traditional management should be
carefully considered. We should ask ourselves: Does this language foster the right feeling? [To which we add, the right purpose.] The right set of expectations? [To which we add, target
solutions.] The right approach to managing the work force? [To
which we add, the right principles and process.]

We contend that the basic dichotomy in these wrong "solutions"—wrong heroes, wrong theories, wrong language—is
that of an essentially negative, constrained, strictly quantifying
scientism as opposed to an essentially positive, expansive, qualitatively focused Full-Spectrum Thinking. We maintain that the
right solutions—the right heroes, right theories, and right lan-

guage, all of which are functions and reflections of effective thinking—become more available and operational by addressing all problems and opportunities with reference to the multi-thinking perspectives of Full-Spectrum Thinking.

To employ the conventional paradigm of thinking is ever to adopt the threadbare, pessimistic role of "devil's advocate." To employ the new paradigm of thinking is to adopt the hopeful, optimistic role of "angel's advocate." Fault-finding and blame-placing play no part in Full-Spectrum Thinking. Why? Because only in a mutually respectful and supportive process of thinking can we arrive at the best possible solution. It is possible to manage yourself (and an organization) to achieve intentional breakthroughs—the "aha!" changes, significantly better quality and quantity of solutions, and installation of good ideas.

However well-intentioned they may be, the many and increasing attempts in organizations, whether for-profit, not-for-profit, or governmental, to tinker with the outmoded rules of the Conventional Thinking paradigm—such "alphabet programs" as TQM (total quality management), CPI (continuous process improvement), TEI (total employee involvement), or BPR (business process reengineering)—defeat themselves. Why? Because any solution—even one which seeks generalizations concerning quantifiable, physical phenomena—will prove less effective, accurate, and successful than if addressed with Full-Spectrum Thinking.

For example, over the last ten years, the emphasis on total quality has led to the development of ISO 9000, a series of international standards for quality assurance management systems. Developed by the Geneva-based International Organizations for Standardization, companies are registered when they pass an audit conducted over time. Such registration is rapidly becoming a condition for competing in the global marketplace.

What is forgotten is that registration in no way means that your organization has good products, low costs, or satisfied and delighted customers. Your organization can comply with *all* the requirements at the 100 percent perfect level and still be ineffective. Why? Because you may succeed in operating a "good" system of quality standards but fail in content of products, services, systems, and purposes.

The new paradigm is a new way of thinking about all "standard" human activities, personal interactions, problems, and opportunities—how to make a telephone call, how to respond to a request for a FAX machine, how to set up and run a meeting, how to build an effective team, how to do performance appraisal of an employee, how to determine if a new product (or acquisition or merger or investment) should be pursued. It lets you see other points of view, be a good and committed follower as well as leader, take the initiative, get the right information for your solution finding, and build good teams and networks.

True creativity in thinking is not to be found in the application of fashionable techniques, adaptations of the existing paradigm, however "liberating" they may initially seem, however cleverly they may be named. True creativity lies in the application of multi-paradigm thinking, in knowing when and how to apply the two basic approaches, how to enter the Age of Multi-Paradigm Thinking Processes.

These processes will tell you when the great number and variety of creativity techniques such as DeBono's "six hats" and "six boots" or the computer program IdeaFisher or Von Oechs' "Whack on the Side of the Head" cards might be useful. With this new thinking, various techniques to stimulate "micro" creativity may or may not be used.

Unbounded Systems Thinking

Others have argued that a new multi-paradigm perspective toward solution finding should be adopted. University of Southern California business policy professor Ian Mitroff and Portland State University systems science professor Harold Linstone argue persuasively for multiple perspectives in decision making.

"The thing that depresses all of us is that we really want to agree. We just can't seem to achieve it. We come from such different educational and professional backgrounds that even when we seem to be using the same words, they mean entirely different things to each of us. The trouble is that we have no choice but to find agreement between us.

"The engineering, marketing, planning, production, and sales teams have to be involved from day one in the design of critical products. We can't afford to have engineering produce designs any longer that customers don't want, and we can't have marketing and sales force through products that are impossible to manufacture economically. We're divided by our differences. Instead of our differences being one of our greatest strengths, they are one of our greatest liabilities. Is there a super model out there somewhere that could integrate our differences into a common framework that we could get behind?"[9]

We suggest that there is a new paradigm (or model) of thinking, new principles, and a new process of thought that can lead to the discovery and development of the common framework so avidly sought. The "unbounded" Full-Spectrum Thinking naturally includes, indeed, relies upon and celebrates, the existence of multiple realities.

Mitroff and Linstone state that "everything interacts with everything." The authors find that, in this way of knowing, "all branches of inquiry depend fundamentally on one another, and that the widest possible array of disciplines, professions, and branches of knowledge—capturing distinctly different paradigms of thought—must be consciously brought to bear on our problems.

"The basis for choosing a particular way of modeling or representing a problem is not governed merely by considerations of conventional logic and rationality. It may also involve considerations of justice and fairness as perceived by various social groups and by considerations of personal ethics or morality as perceived by distinct persons."[10]

Intellectual Wrongheadedness

Similarly, UCLA professor of management and public policy James Q. Wilson argues that we are now paying the price for a century of intellectual wrongheadedness, fundamental errors based largely on exclusive reliance on Conventional Thinking.

In a review of Wilson's book *The Moral Sense,* Alex Raksin notes that "many thinkers such as Hobbes and Freud, who have argued that people's inner drives are selfish and must be sublimated through social institutions, in fact did not distrust human motivations as much as their popularizers have led us to believe. Adam Smith, for example, did indeed argue that we are self-interested. But by this he did not mean that we desire to get ahead at all costs; rather, we desire to be allegiant to the principles that have historically ensured order and prosperity in human society. We yearn not only to be praised, Smith wrote, but to be praiseworthy; not only to be loved, but 'to be lovely.'

"Essentially, [Wilson] argues that the Enlightenment persuaded us to place more faith in the 'objective' viewpoints of science, law and bureaucracy than in our own subjective intuitions, values and moral sentiments. These synthetic ways of seeing and responding to the world left us feeling adrift because they were so callow and undiscerning compared to the naturally occurring moral sense that has historically been our worldly anchor.

"'A good character, however defined, is not life lived according to a rule,' Wilson proposes. 'It is a life lived in a balance . . . that is struck without deliberation or reasoned justifications.' "[11]

Why Single Perspective Thinking Is Limited

Particularly in the United States, the legislative branch of government tends to demand "scientific" evidence on which to base its funding decisions, as if scientifically validated, quantified "truth" lends indisputable moral cover to the public policies they promulgate. These legislators generally ignore the fact that alternative kinds of valuable, accurate evidence exist: cogent and persuasive philosophical argument (does it make sense?), purposes/systems (does it do the job?), intuitive evidence (does it coincide with human experience?), and others. Even without scientific evidence, for example, the interrelationships of elements and dimensions (systems matrix) provides the opportunity to assess future risks and know when they are likely to occur.

Indeed, exclusive reliance on Conventional Thinking leads inevitably to an impasse in the search for certainty. In her book *The History of God,* scholar of comparative religion Karen Armstrong traces the development of a monotheistic concept of divinity in Judaism, Christianity, and Islam. Armstrong studies that development in various contexts—psychological, socioeconomic, philosophical, historical, and anthropological. She finds that the nature of worship has consistently evolved to meet the human needs of the worshippers.

Armstrong's account of radical reformations in each of the three faiths leads her to discuss efforts during the Enlightenment to provide a scientific proof for the existence of God. Of course, as soon as one "scientist" proved the existence of God by means of the skeptical Research Approach, another could use the same scientific skepticism to *dis*prove God's existence.

Armstrong concludes by considering the future of religion in a society where "more and more people have found that it no longer works for them, and when religious ideas cease to be effective, they fade away." She argues that human beings require faith, citing such twentieth-century theologians as Paul Tillich, Karl Barth, and Martin Buber as models of modern piety.[12]

Whether faith in reason, in science, in purposes, in God, in other humans, or in yourself, faith is essential. Unlike most other animals who apparently do what they do unconsciously for the most part, our human burden and blessing of self-consciousness demands that we have faith just to get out of bed in the morning. Thus, the thinking paradigm that human beings require in order to find "working" truth is the positive, optimistic, hopeful, inclusive Full-Spectrum Thinking.

What Multi-Thinking Can Do

The purpose of Full-Spectrum Thinking is to produce the most effective solutions possible for whatever confronts us. It serves as the basis for ethical, moral actions designed to better the human condition.

As such, it reflects the perspective of American philosopher and critic Kenneth Burke, who sought to create a system for analyzing human thought as it manifests itself in expression or communication. Burke held that "man is a symbol-using animal" and that language, the expression and communication of ideas and feelings by means of such symbols, is best understood as the basis for a mode of action.[13] Positive action toward human betterment is the goal of Full-Spectrum Thinking.

The tendency toward the "institutional mentality"—inaction, self-deception, manipulation of others, elitist management styles and attitudes, emphasizing executives' personal interests, and arrogance—that is often characteristic of organizations whose thinking is founded on the command and control style of Conventional Thinking can be observed in the precipitous decline of IBM and in a recent exposé of sinister practices at Procter & Gamble.

In reviewing *Big Blues: The Unmaking of IBM,* a history and analysis of this decline written by Paul Carroll, business reporter Jolie Solomon notes: "Clearly, the market has judged IBM . . . [which] has recently suffered a . . . $75 billion plunge in stock-market value and the loss of about 150,000 jobs. . . . IBM's culture, which once worked so well, failed utterly to adjust to the new realities of fast-moving technology and less loyal customers. The story is something of a Greek tragedy, in that IBM's leaders' passion for their company inspired, but ultimately blinded them. They developed an arrogance that couldn't contemplate change, let alone failure.

"The [IBM] culture was paralyzingly closed and conformist. . . . IBM managers endlessly debated, but did not decide. They were rewarded for presenting ideas, not implementing them. Microsoft wrested dominance of the software industry from IBM by such innovations as cutting the number of characters of computer code to 200 from 33,000; IBM programmers were rated on how much code they wrote, not how fast it ran."[14]

As for Procter & Gamble, writer Alicia Swasy's book *Soap Opera: The Inside Story of Procter & Gamble* reports that P&G practices a ruthless aggression that one former executive terms

"organizational fascism." Swasy details stories of P&G's harass-
ment of environmental activists, its iron grip on employees, and
its arrogant manipulation of competitors, advertising agencies,
and its hometown of Cincinnati. P&G even subpoenaed hundreds of phone records to find out which employees were talking to Swasy. Moreover, she charges that P&G knew how
dangerous its Rely tampon was but resisted acting until women
were sick and dying from toxic-shock syndrome.[15]

Whether missteps or misdeeds, all these past errors could
have been avoided by Full-Spectrum Thinking related to the
corporate cultures and the solution-finding processes of IBM
and Proctor & Gamble and the many other organizations whose
fortunes have declined. Similarly, we can best prepare for success in the future with what is really great internally available
capabilities by turning in the present to the multi-thinking of
Full-Spectrum Thinking.

For example, in his most recent book, *Post-Capitalist Society,* Peter Drucker argues that we are entering a "knowledge"
society, as opposed to one based on capital, land, and labor.
This, he contends, will have a profound effect on how business
is conducted, how and where people work, what role education has to play, and the new kinds of organizations that will be
required to make it all run smoothly.

The essential component in Drucker's knowledge society
is the individual—the actual repository of knowledge and thus
the vessel of the new economic resource—and the individual's
relationship to the highly specialized organizations that will
emerge in the new era. Yet Drucker offers no methodology for
addressing this new state of affairs.[16]

Similarly, other thoughtful experts offer useful and innovative perspectives on what needs to be done in order to reach
effective solutions to problems, yet few if any provide the principles and process to follow. For example, Roger Fisher,
founder of the Harvard Negotiation Project suggests productive
attitudes and useful preparations to make in approaching prin-
cipled negotiations. He proposes that one should "separate the
people from the substantive problem; focus on interests, not
positions; generate a range of options before deciding upon

one; insist on using some legitimate standard of fairness; develop your best alternative to a negotiated agreement; consider what kind of commitment you want; and communicate."[17]

Fine and good advice. But how precisely does one accomplish these laudable and useful goals? What way of thinking is provided for finding a cure for the ills?

With Full-Spectrum Thinking, one accomplishes most if not all of the goals set forth by Fisher. For example, a focus on purposes and their expansion naturally "separates the people from the substantive problem." As has been noted, Breakthrough Thinking works remarkably well even among those who have previously been actively antagonistic toward one another. What are interests if not a range of expanded purposes that automatically take the focus off the individuals involved and place it on solutions. Developing a solution-after-next generates the range of options that Fisher recommends. The principle of people-design ensures that the solution sought will be one that benefits everybody.

All of these worthy goals are naturally accomplished by means of Full-Spectrum Thinking; few if any may be achieved by using Conventional Thinking. Indeed, the conventional paradigm of thinking will actively inhibit your success in solution finding, whether you call the process "negotiation" or use any number of other labels to describe it.

More to the point, we suggest, is the work of those, such as strategy scholar and organizational theorist Daniel R. Gilbert, who look to basic concepts. In his recent book, *The Twilight of Corporate Strategy: A Comparative Ethical Critique,* Gilbert addresses what professor James E. Post correctly describes as

> perhaps *the* fundamental issue in strategic management today: Does the concept of corporate strategy tell us anything about the changing purpose of the modern corporation? Is it even relevant to the dialogue about the kind of institutions our world needs as we move into the 21st century?
>
> These two statements lie at the heart of Gilbert's challenge to strategy researchers: Where are the people, and the humanist values they possess? Why is the richness of human diversity and aspiration so notably missing from

most strategy research today? Why are management scholars in general more infatuated with the abstraction of 'the
organization' than with the uniqueness and specificity of
the humans that are a part of it? . . . [He holds that] the
corporate strategy of [numerically based] models, matri-
ces, and r^2 is hopelessly detached from the quest for
human achievement and fulfillment.

Too often, it seems, scholars miss the point that the
very word 'corporate' means collective, as in the collective
efforts of people to achieve meaningful, shared objectives.
His notion of management responsibility is one of creating
a "conducive context" in which people are central to organizational direction.[18]

Post notes that Gilbert is not alone in wondering about
these issues.

No less an establishment organization than the Alfred P.
Sloan Foundation has launched a research program addressing
"The Changing Purpose of the Modern Corporation." However,
even so timely and essential an inquiry is doomed to relative
failure if it does not at least begin its work with reference to the
thinking assumptions, principles, and process used in planning,
design, and problem-solving—*how* solutions are created,
found, or restructured.

The perspective of the multi-thinker is essential to the effective solution of human problems because—contrary to the
popular opinion that has resulted after 400 years of the conventional paradigm of thinking—the future can never be predicted
with absolute certainty. Not even the rising of the sun tomorrow morning is assured. And since science can never be absolutely certain, the Research Approach ought never to be
considered the only appropriate paradigm of thinking.

Conventional Thinking is insufficient for solution finding in
large measure because it relies upon the division of problems,
tasks, concepts, systems, everything, into ever smaller sub-
divisions of the whole, and their categorizations and measurement *as if they were unrelated entities*. It fails to adequately
address the fact that, in the phrase of Garrett Hardin, emeritus
professor of human ecology at the University of California, Santa

Barbara, "we can never do merely one thing."[19] All things are interrelated. Or as John Muir put it: "When you try to pick out any thing by itself, you find it hitched to everything else in the universe."[20]

In this regard, our continuing failure effectively to solve or even adequately address many of our most fundamental problems has led some, such as Harvard University science professor Edward O. Wilson, to ask the question: "Is humanity suicidal? Is the drive to environmental conquest and self-propagation embedded so deeply in our genes as to be unstoppable?

"This admittedly dour scenario," writes Wilson, "is based on what can be termed the juggernaut theory of human nature, which holds that people are programmed by their genetic heritage to be so selfish that a sense of global responsibility will come too late."

Wilson concludes: "We are smart enough and have time enough to avoid an environmental catastrophe of civilization-threatening dimensions. But the technical problems are sufficiently formidable to require a redirection of much of science and technology, and the ethical issues are so basic as to force a reconsideration of our self-image as a species."[21]

Adoption of Full-Spectrum Thinking for solution finding is essential if Wilson's barely optimistic conclusion is to hold true. Certainly, for centuries, if not millennia to come, most of us are likely to do all we can to protect and enhance ourselves as individuals. But putting our problems into the larger perspective of purposes and expanded purposes helps us overcome our most basic, ultimately suicidal, tendencies toward excessive selfishness, exploitation, fear, and greed.

Indeed, with Full-Spectrum Thinking, we may confidently aspire to the ideal of the Six Nations Iroquois confederacy of Native Americans, whose great law stated: "In every deliberation, we must consider the impact of our decisions on the next seven generations."[22]

In the more immediate, short term as well, multi-thinking is likely to enhance your survival skills. Increasingly, skill-based pay appears to be making its way from blue- to white-collar workers.

According to Professor Edward Lawler of the University of Southern California, "Slowly, but surely, we're becoming a skill-based society where your market value is tied to what you can do and what your skill set is [as opposed to the perceived value of a particular job]. In this new world where skills and knowledge are what really count, it doesn't make sense to treat people as jobholders. It makes sense to treat them as people with specific skills and to pay them for those skills."[23]

In the near future, if not the present, the more skills you have, the more flexible you are, the more you will be paid. With so many different jobs to perform, a person clearly needs to be a multi-thinker.

The real flexibility and strength, of course, is less in knowing how to run a certain machine, than in translating that knowledge into practice. What is it that you need to get accomplished? What are your purposes? How to go about or plan a job and improve it continuously demands Full-Spectrum Thinking.

CHARACTERISTICS OF MULTI-THINKING

To practice Full-Spectrum Thinking is inherently to achieve the highly-prized and highly productive benefits of effective teamwork: shared goals, a common culture, freely shared information, a sense of trust, the ability to resolve conflicts. Indeed, unless one starts *by* dealing with purposes and purposes expansion, then the multi-thinker perspective is not effective. Why? Because however much one wants to achieve effective teamwork, however hard one tries to do so, Conventional Thinking actually inhibits the achievement of these benefits.

By contrast, Texas-based management consultant and corporate creativity expert Ray Slesinski has devised from his own experience a list of ten common traits of creative people (note how almost all of these traits are developed and enhanced by using the principles and process of Full-Spectrum Thinking):

• They come up with many ideas quickly for random requests.
• They are flexible in their thinking styles.
• They tend to be emotional and intuitive.

- They see things differently; that is, they do not automatically accept conventional rules, assumptions, or facts.
- They are motivated more by the nature of the job and its intrinsic satisfaction rather than by such external rewards as money, prestige, or power.
- They push themselves to the limits.
- They gather information and love diverse knowledge and unique experiences.
- They persevere in the light of skepticism and criticism.
- They are not afraid of taking risks or fearful of failure.
- They see themselves as creative, different, playful, and humorous.[24]

Social science researchers Pelton, Sackman, and Boguslaw conclude that, while there may be no hard and fast rules for handling complex, unanalyzable situations (as most, if not all, situations are), executives effective in handling them demonstrate these characteristic habits and abilities (note again how Full-Spectrum Thinking develops and enhances each one):

- Recognize a complex, unanalyzable situation when it emerges.
- Avoid rigid adherence to conventional management "principles" and formulate effective alternatives.
- Develop sensitivity to the differences in the situations confronted by employees.
- Rely on quantitative measures to the degree that they are useful, and abandon them when they are not.
- Develop confidence in using intuition and gut feelings as aids to effective decision making and action.
- Draw productively on experience, but avoid the barriers that experience may present.
- Reconcile the often conflicting demands of organizational goals and their own powerful egos.
- Use available technology as part of the solution to complex, unanalyzable situations, but avoid relying on technology for simple solutions; are not confined by the boundaries imposed by existing technology.

- Change the structure of their organizations when appropriate, such as when experiencing unusual growth or unusual demands on their organizations.
- Master the intricacies of a long-term perspective, including living with contradictions, formulating a relevant time orientation, and achieving an effective balance.
- Develop a useful, coherent image of the future using the planning process.
- Recognize, select, and employ the right people in their operations.
- Use relational management effectively and understand the importance of philosophical compatibility, self-management, teamwork, and critical thought in assembling an effective team.
- Respond to situations with appropriate flexibility, while at the same time know when to remain firm.
- Understand the conditions under which the concept of bottom line is relevant and when it must be modified or abandoned as an impediment to successful operations.
- Draw on the insights and creative management approaches of those who have proven to be effective . . . managers.[25]

Both the traits of creative people and the characteristic habits and abilities of effective executives exhibit the recognition of values, beliefs, and aspirations of the people involved, the uniqueness of each situation. The multi-thinker with Full-Spectrum Thinking knows about and is capable of coping with this reality: There is no such thing as a "value-free" society or situation.

From a parallel perspective, management consultants Coulson and Strickland remind us that problems are best solved when the process is enjoyed. "The more playful people get while problem solving, the more likely they are to come up with good ideas that lead to an implementable solution, one they would have missed if they'd stayed in a serious mode. Creativity flourishes in an environment where there's laughter and a sense of fun."[26] In addition, better solutions are likely to be found under such circumstances because people will define work in terms of its intrinsic worth and enjoyment rather than almost exclusively in terms of economic worth.

Taking pleasure in the process has much in common with the way that professional designers approach the problems they are called upon to solve. Unlike the solution of problems by logical analysis, notes the late University of California, Berkeley, professor Horst Rittel, "the designer's reasoning is much more disorderly . . . not due to intellectual sloppiness, but rather to the nature of design problems. There is no clear separation of the activities of problem definition, synthesis, and evaluation. All of these occur all the time. A design problem keeps changing while it is treated, because the understanding of what ought to be accomplished, and how it might be accomplished is continually shifting. Learning what the problem is *is* the problem."[27]

This is illustrated by the immense number of calls for change in company structure, government, welfare policy, health care, and education, to cite only a few. But is *change* what is wanted? Is change the problem? Full-Spectrum Thinking asks: What is the *purpose* of change? This question requires people to focus on the purposes of getting something accomplished. That is why all of the many seminars, books, lectures, and education on "overcoming resistance to change" are ineffective, if not plain wrong-headed and inappropriate for a multi-thinker. People become committed to accomplishing something that is based on purposes and target solution (the two parts of a vision), not by simply being told they have to change.

For example, a large unit of a Defense Department service was losing many skilled technical people. The commander therefore ordered all divisions and sections to change how people were managed. He sought the worthy goals of a satisfied workforce and improved morale, assuming that achieving these goals would accomplish his objective: to improve the unit's retention of valued personnel. Yet, even though surveys found that "satisfaction" and "morale" did indeed improve after some gimmicks and supervisor/manager techniques were changed, the unit's retention of personnel barely improved at all.

By contrast, Full-Spectrum Thinking would have involved the unit's people in a quest for purposes, solutions-after-next, and systems, so as to develop effective solutions to accomplish their desired results. Then the *measures* of morale, satisfaction, and retention of personnel would have accurately reflected the success—the change—of the system.

You, The Multi-Thinker

Consultant Garfield notes that "the peak performer tolerates confusion and ambiguity up to a point and is willing to let go of a problem now and then, trusting that [in the subconscious mind] creative, productive mental work will take place."[28] Garfield insists that peak performers are able to think in a variety of ways and cultivate their ability to do so.

Business professor Robert Kelley at Carnegie Mellon University and consultant Janet Caplan point out that a "star performer" also is able to see other points of view,[29] a characteristic certain to be enhanced by Full-Spectrum Thinking through its expanding purposes, solution-after-next options, and systems point of view. With Full-Spectrum Thinking, you can significantly improve your own performance and have positive impact on the work of others and of a team. Whenever you interact with others, you deal with the behavior-enhancing and Full-Spectrum Creativity issues raised by the process of Breakthrough Thinking.

For example, a Breakthrough Thinking consultant once asked a sociologist to join a team that was trying to improve the medication administration system in a hospital. The sociologist said, "Sure. I'll survey the attitudes and opinions of the nurses and other professionals before you start. Then after you've made the changes, I'll be able to tell you what went wrong!"

The sociologist's response was instinctively to follow the Research Approach. The consultant did not say that was not the reason a sociologist was desired—to avoid doing something that would go wrong. Instead, the consultant asked, "What's the purpose of finding out what went wrong?" Within ten minutes, the sociologist "saw" the bigger purposes and became an enthusiastic, positive contributor, rather than a negative, data-gathering responder.

For every problem, activity, and solution-finding endeavor, the multi-thinker utilizes many of the heuristics identified by former CEO and current University of Southern California professor Eberhardt Rechtin for systems architecting. Based on his experiences in developing large, complex systems—satellites, rocket launch vehicles, aircraft—Rechtin demonstrates the need to play the role of an architect when working on such extensive projects. In his curriculum for educating people to become systems architects, Rechtin categorizes more than 100 such heuristics or rules-of-thumb.

These heuristics portray the multi-thinker's awareness of the wide range of factors and conditions to be considered. For example:

- If anything can go wrong, it will.
- Relationships among the elements are what give systems their added value.
- The greatest leverage in system architecting is at the interfaces.
- Success is defined by the beholder, not by the architect.
- Organize personnel tasks to minimize the time individuals spend interfacing.
- Be prepared for reality to add a few interfaces of its own.
- Quality cannot be tested in, it has to be built in.[30]

These and many other insights more directly related to systems architecting are remarkably comparable to those of Full-Spectrum Thinking.

In our own experience, by taking the initiative to become a multi-thinker—learning-by-using Full-Spectrum Thinking—you will come to enjoy, indeed relish, your flexible, multi-thinking, "systems architecting," solution-finding efforts. Indeed, you will become much like the master in the art of living described in the Zen Buddhist text: One who "makes little distinction between his work and his play, his labor and his leisure, his mind and his body, his education and his recreation, his love and his religion. He hardly knows which is which. He simply pursues his vision of excellence in whatever he does, leaving others to decide whether he is working or playing. To him, he is always doing both."[31]

It is the grand utility of Full-Spectrum Thinking in all realms of work and play that makes it the paradigm of achieving excellence. You may not become the peak performer, the star performer, the system architect, or the master in the art of living by using the new paradigm of thinking. It does not give you that kind of guarantee. What it does give you is a framework of reasoning, a state of mind, the multi-thinker perspective that serves as the target paradigm of thinking for which you should always strive. Use the assumptions and process of effective people when doing anything—the new paradigm of thinking—rather than the restricting Conventional Thinking. You will find yourself getting significantly better, if not "star" or "peak," results—recommendations, solutions, changes, effective use of time and resources, personal and group interrelationships, and the insights to know that all of them can still be improved. Results that go beyond what was "predicted."

These outcomes cause a deep sense of enjoyment so rewarding people are willing to expend a great deal of energy to achieve it. Remember, you are basically in charge of your own life. As a multi-thinker applying the new paradigm of thinking—the principles and process of Full-Spectrum Thinking— whether in projects or daily tasks, on task forces or strategy issues, you can face the challenges of the future not with resignation or dread, but with joyful expectation.

NOTES

1. James Gleick, *Genius: The Life and Science of Richard Feynman* (New York: Pantheon Books, 1992).

2. Will Rodgers, *Think: A Biography of the Watsons and IBM* (New York: Stein & Day, 1969).

3. Howard Gardner, *The Unschooled Mind* (New York: Basic Books, 1991).

4. Alan Kantrow, Lecture in School of Business Administration, University of Southern California, May 5, 1993.

5. Jeffrey Pfeffer, *Competitive Advantage Through People: Unleashing the Power of the Work Force* (Cambridge, MA: Harvard Business School Press, 1994).

6. Ibid.

7. Ibid.

8. Ibid.

9. Ian I. Mitroff and Harold A. Linstone, *The Unbounded Mind: Breaking the Chains of Traditional Business Thinking* (New York, Oxford University Press, 1993).

10. Ibid.

11. Alex Raksin, review of James Q. Wilson, *The Moral Sense,* in *Los Angeles Times,* (August 2, 1993).

12. Karen Armstrong, *The History of God: The 4,000 Year Quest of Judaism, Christianity and Islam* (New York: Knopf, 1993).

13. Obituary of Kenneth Burke, *New York Times,* (November 21, 1993).

14. Jolie Solomon, review of Paul Carroll, *Big Blues: The Unmaking of IBM* and Alicia Swasy, *Soap Opera: The Inside Story of Procter & Gamble,* in *Newsweek,* (September 27, 1993).

15. Ibid.

16. Peter F. Drucker, *Post-Capitalist Society* (New York: Harper Business, 1993).

17. Roger Fisher, "Advice from the founder of the Harvard Negotiation Project," *Bottom Line Personal,* Vol. 14, No. 18, (September 30, 1993).

18. James E. Post, review of Daniel R. Gilbert, *The Twilight of Corporate Strategy: A Comparative Ethical Critique* (New York: Oxford University Press, 1992), in *Academy of Management Review,* (July 1993), pp. 576–579.

19. Garret Hardin, *Ecology, Economics, and Population Taboos* (New York: Oxford University Press, 1993).

20. Ibid.

21. Edward O. Wilson, "Is Humanity Suicidal," *New York Times Magazine,* (May 30, 1993).

22. The Great Law of the *Hau de no saunee* (Six Nations Iroquois Confederacy), as quoted in Catalog of the Seventh Generation Fund, (1990).

23. Mary Rowland, "It's What You Can Do That Counts," *New York Times,* (June 6, 1993).

24. Ray Slesinski, "10 Traits of Creative People," *Executive Excellence,* (August 10, 1991).

25. W. J. Pelton, S. Sackman, and R. Boguslaw, *Tough Choices: The Decision Styles of America's Top 50 CEOs* (Homewood, IL: Dow-Jones-Irwin, 1990), pp. 148–149.

26. Ted Coulson and Alison Strickland, "Applied Creativity," *Executive Excellence,* (August 8, 1991), p. 9.

27. Horst W. J. Rittel and M. W. Webber, "Dilemmas in a General Theory of Planning," Design Methods Group, *Design Research Society Journal,* Vol. 8, No. 1, (January-March 1974), pp. 31–39.

28. Charles Garfield, *Peak Performers: The New Heroes of American Business* (New York: William Morrow, 1986), p. 156.

29. Robert Kelley and Janet Caplan, "How Bell Labs Create Star Performers," *Harvard Business Review,* Vol. 71, No. 4, (July-August 1993), pp. 128–139.

30. Eberhardt Rechtin, *Systems Architecting: Creating and Building Complex Systems* (Englewood Cliffs, NJ: Prentice-Hall, 1991).

31. Zen Buddhist text, cited by Lester Thurow, *Head To Head* (New York: William Morrow, 1992).

Chapter 12

The Future for Assumptions About Thinking

The past is prologue. We think and act in the present. Our actions prepare the future.

It is *how* we think when we try to create and restructure solutions that opens the window and sheds light on our future.

The Journey Thus Far

Getting you (and everyone) to change your (their) thinking paradigm was our task at the start of this book. We have taken quite an excursion through a lot of territory and are left with reminders of the wonders of our exploration.

Our needs to create and restructure solutions in personal, organizational, national, and societal arenas are not being well satisfied. At whatever level you view the problems, opportunities, policies, issues, difficulties, desires, needs, wants—whatever you call them—almost everyone agrees that we are experiencing a solution collapse in most areas. It's not that we lack solution ideas; a few quite good ones are being promoted by promoters, geniuses, and well-meaning idealists. But the truth is that the vast knowledge base available to us is not being converted to successful solutions.

All of us have mental assumptions about the way most systems or present solutions—organizational structure, education, meal preparation, transportation to work—are supposed to work. So too do we have such mental assumptions or paradigms about how we are to proceed, to think, when seeking to create or restructure one of those solution paradigms.

The link between the relative collapse of solution finding to get results and the current Conventional Thinking paradigm is established through a review of cases and the characteristics of paradigms. The review shows clearly how the anomalies now so prevalent in Conventional Thinking show that a Paradigm Shift in Thinking is needed.

So where did the Conventional Thinking paradigm— gather data, analyze what is happening now, use techniques to model what exists, who is to blame—come from? Thinking paradigms for creating and restructuring solutions can be traced back to the early Greeks, but the rise of science through the philosophies of Descartes and Bacon in the 1600s is the basis of how we now try to find solutions. The methodologies of Descartes and Bacon worked wonderfully for research and science to develop generalizations about the natural world.

But laws and "truths" about physical phenomena are only one kind of result that humans seek. Humans think about other purposes they would like to achieve; four in particular are likewise critical to satisfy human aspirations—operate and supervise existing good systems, evaluate the effectiveness of solutions previously put in place, learn new ideas and knowledge, and, of course, create new and restructure present solutions to satisfy needs and wants. With the different purposes to achieve, the need for different types of thinking is clear.

As you might expect, a great amount of research focuses on finding out what thinking is and how it works. Descartes, as a matter of fact, initially started his philosophical work with an attempt to write "Rules for the Direction of the Mind," which he abandoned after he had 18 rules because it became an impossible task. However, significant findings in the last 30 years show that Conventional Thinking for creating and restructuring solutions needs to and can be superseded by a new thinking paradigm.

Seven principles or mental assumptions as the first part of a new paradigm of thinking are synthesized from the bodies of knowledge in the broad areas of thinking: Uniqueness, expanding purposes, solution-after-next, systems, limited information collection, people design, and betterment timeline. These replace the Conventional Thinking assumptions for creating and restructuring solutions—gathering as much data as possible is necessary, everything can be subdivided into smaller problems, each small problem can be solved, and solving all the small problems will solve the whole problem.

A new flow of reasoning based on the new principles (or the process part of the new thinking paradigm) starts by expanding purposes to find what should be the focus of solution finding, ideal or solution-after-next options to achieve the focus purpose to serve as a guide for the actual recommendation, and a systems framework for specifying the recommendation and building in future changes in what is installed.

Beyond the already reviewed research into paradigms and thinking as the basis for new thinking paradigm assumptions and process, much additional information from investigations, evaluations, and applications is available to show reasons Full-Spectrum Thinking is so valuable.

Because the Conventional Thinking paradigm is so ingrained as an instinct in each of us, some thoughts about how *you* can get started with the new paradigm are offered—use the process on every situation you face or where a decision of any sort is to be made; don't wait to pick a "good" project to try out the new thinking (this means you haven't really understood Full-Spectrum Thinking); ask questions of others based on the process.

At the same time, don't throw away Conventional Thinking. It can be used within Full-Spectrum Thinking when you find your purpose is really to develop a generalization or fix the cause of a deviation in an otherwise good system. Being a multi-thinker is the basic need for each of us, just as it is for the scientists and engineers who have not thrown away the Newtonian model of mechanics just because the Einstein model replaced it in overall utility.

Now, we want to finish our journey by looking at the Full-Spectrum Thinking paradigm in terms of how consciously seeking its improvement is natural both in the scheme of the way

paradigms change and in helping you use Full-Spectrum Thinking more effectively! Full-Spectrum Thinking requires an open
mind, receptiveness to new ideas, tolerance of the unusual, capability of taking advantage of the mysterious moment of inspi-
ration and flash of insight, acceptance of intuition along with a
structure to take advantage of it. In other words, the new "software for the mind" includes the built-in benefit of adapting
from learning about its own use as well as responding to conscious efforts to produce Version 2.0, and 3.0, and 4.0 of the
"software" paradigm.

Problems and Opportunities in the Future

Problems and opportunities will always arise. They will occur
everywhere—in organizations, groups, communities and states,
among peoples and nations, and for all of us as individual human beings. These will be unprecedented challenges, both
problems and opportunities, challenges to our powers of solution finding, of thinking.

What do we face in the future? What will our problems
and opportunities be? No one can say for certain.

In many ways, however, the general outline of our future
problems and opportunities is already discernible. It is the basis
of today's anxieties, uncertainties, and changes: restructured
economies due to new technology and global markets, global
migration patterns from poor countries to rich, concepts of family and community evolving from traditional forms to new, and
foreign policy turmoil resulting from the end of the Cold War.

The list could go on and on, as shown in Chapter 1. Add
to this litany of presently discernible problems and opportunities the future emergence of figurative "earthquakes" such as
the oil embargo of the '70s, the AIDS epidemic of the '80s, and
the rise of ethnic warfare in the '90s. For individual organizations, both for-profit and nonprofit, less-cosmic earthquakes
that radically impact them can occur—a new kind of material, a
completely different type of computer chip, a new global com-
petitor, an exceptional drop (or increase) in interest rates, and

so on. *How* one thinks about such shattering occurrences and the multitude of problems they spawn is critical to success or failure in solution finding.

Prophesied Implications

Many prophets, for the most part self-proclaimed, have proposed "solutions" for these future problems and/or tools with which we might exploit our future opportunities.

Organizations, they tell us, will emphasize increased productivity; will need to design jobs more broadly; will rely more on executives and managers with "people and intuitive skills," as opposed to "number crunchers"; will seek to empower, not command and control, employees on all levels of the organization; will de-emphasize hierarchies and emphasize webs of interrelating responsibility and authority; will increasingly use cross-disciplinary teams to accomplish tasks and achieve goals; will connect strategic thinking with management of operations to emphasize informal learning and personal visions; will demonstrate a true commitment to participation and mutual trust for and among all members of the organization; will coordinate organizational activities through mutually shared values and goals; and will be completely ethical.

American organizations may well strive to foster a modicum of Japan's highly valued social discipline. Japanese organizations may learn to profit from a measure of American individual flexibility and professional mobility.

American organizations will be urged to solve problems of competitiveness, quality, and productivity by changing almost everything—manufacturing systems and strategies, organizational structures, accounting practices, company culture, purposes/services, customer relations, product design, strategic planning, human resource development, marketing, crisis management, and so on. Many of the models urged upon U.S. organizations to guide such changes will be based upon essentially unrelated Japanese or German successes.

Communities and states, it is said, must transform and reinvent their governments based on an "entrepreneurial spirit."

They will newly emphasize issues of "moral infrastructure." Particularly in the U.S., they will focus on values such as lawfulness and honesty, education, thrift, diligence, and strong family bonds. While such basic values are in fact stimulators (not results), motivators to action and measures of success (not actual solutions), these values will, however, very likely lead to simplistic slogan "solutions" such as a policy of "three strikes and you're out" for repeat felons, "taxpayer vouchers" to promote private education at public expense, "zero tolerance" for non-prescription drug use, and "balanced budget" constitutional amendments to force the reduction of public deficits.

Peoples and nations everywhere, so the prophets predict, will continue to emulate the U.S., Japanese, and German economic models, often without questioning the appropriateness or applicability of these models to specific local conditions. Nations created with relation to geography, not common bonds of blood or culture, will be torn between the polarities of violent dissolution, on the one hand, or repressive federation, on the other. The flood of immigration that threatens to inundate many economically developed nations in the northern hemisphere will be stemmed either by increased economic opportunity in southern climes or by new "great walls" and xenophobic laws discriminating against "foreigners." In the future, so they say, regional trading blocs will compete for economic hegemony where political ideologies once did battle. National sovereignty will gradually give way to regional and international political entities, thus forever eliminating the horrors of war.

Some researchers predict that they can so decompose and specialize any sort of business process or other kind of work that, in the future, a "handbook" will enable anyone to compare, analyze, or redesign existing processes or design new ones. They believe that any process is essentially a sequence of events "distributed in time and space" (days, hours, or weeks and internal or external organizational or physical boundaries).

In the future, individual human beings, we are told, will work more in the home and "commute" via the much-vaunted "electronic superhighway." We will come to develop a variety of flexible skills for economic survival, which will prove essential in a working lifetime that will see us change jobs and fields of interest many times. We will foster individual creativity even while learning to work cooperatively in groups. We will come to value the multicultural perspectives of human beings different from ourselves. We will learn to participate effectively in the disparate cultures of other nations. We will value and respect equally both sexes. We will accept the validity of homosexual relationships between consenting adults. We will respect one another's religious beliefs and moral standards. We will foster individual freedoms while protecting the interests of society as a whole. We will do all this in response to the gaping spiritual emptiness perceived particularly by philosophically "communitarian" observers, who find Americans to have become cynical, overworked, and profoundly isolated psychologically and emotionally. Books and journals (*The 1990s Beyond, The Futurist, Technological Forecasting and Social Change*, for example) abound in telling us what is coming.

All these and countless similar prophecies, whether emanating from an informed pundit, visionary soothsayer, well-intentioned crackpot, or self-serving profiteer, are all too readily proposed as *the* "solution" to our future problems, the capital by which we may successfully exploit our future opportunities. Yet few if any of these prophets are able to propose a way for us to get from here to there. All of them violate essential principles of how to create or restructure solutions—uniqueness, expanded purposes, people design, betterment timeline, and even (as in the "prophecy" of the handbook of processes) systems of interrelationships. What their prophecies offer, for good or ill, are simply *solution* paradigms, not the essential new paradigm of *thinking*.

Paradoxically, we argue strongly for the continuous development of such solution paradigms for "the way we ought to do things" or "reinvent government" or the "super-duper widget" or "software that solves all your problems." Just because we point out that none of these answers or solutions or models should be imposed or adopted directly does not imply that people should stop proposing new structures or ideas.

Solution paradigms are necessary prods to stimulate people. Maybe we *should* do something about this problem. Maybe we can include the ideas in one of our alternative solutions-after-next. Maybe we can do research and development on the idea's concept because it might be something we should be doing.

In other words, nothing should be done to quell people's intuitive juices in developing what each may consider a utopia (organization structure, information highway, healthcare system, etc.) or the ideal mousetrap. Each person's "stash of insight" or "light bulb experience" needs to be disseminated so that all of us can benefit.

Nevertheless, in making a change to get "better" results, each of us who listens to, receives information on, hears about, or sees the "save the world" idea must harken to the new paradigm of thinking if positive results are to be obtained. The solution paradigms will not be used if imposed. The new ideas must be learned and made available in our mental (and company and societal) memory banks, in order to be pulled out when the purposes we seek and needs we have so indicate. We know much more than we think we do. The question is "*how* can we convert this knowledge to get results?"

WHAT WILL ACTUALLY OCCUR
In our view, two likely possibilities exist.

The first possible future is that these prophesied "solutions" should and/or will become reality. In that case, the critical question that needs to be answered is this: *How* might human beings best approach the implementation of these solutions and their attendant changes, so as to achieve the most effective solutions or systems, the highest likelihood of putting the chosen solution/system to use, and the most effective use of money, time, and resources available to achieve these results.

The second—and in our view far more likely—possible future is that these prophesied solutions are far from correct or complete, at best misbegotten, and should not or will not become reality. In that case, the main question that needs to be answered is this: *How* might human beings best approach the problems and opportunities that each organization, group, community, state, people, nation, and individual will face, so as to develop the most effective solution or system possible, attain the highest likelihood of getting the chosen solution/system to be actually used, and use most effectively the money, time, and resources available to achieve those beneficial results.

In short, either possible future reality leads inevitably to the essential questions: *How* are we going to approach the opportunity? *How* are human beings going to bridge the gap? *How* are we going to get from here to there? *How* are we going to advance from a perceived need or problem or a recognized opportunity to selecting and successfully implementing the system or solution that will most effectively solve our problem or exploit our opportunity?

In essence, *how* will we think when we seek to create and restructure solutions? Today, our response to these fundamental questions is the new Full-Spectrum Thinking, to foster the creativity essential to an effective and successful human future.

Many self-help suggestions—*I'm OK, You're OK; Time Management; Men Are from Mars, Women Are from Venus; Seven Habits of Highly Effective People; Coping With Difficult People*—are good and useful books to improve behavior and enhance the interpersonal intelligence of individuals. They are certainly better than doing nothing about interrelationships among people and about moving toward some resolution concerning the "how" questions asked above.

The next step up in concepts, however, lies in the paradigm of thinking used to create and restructure solutions. Why? Because even if you successfully practice these self-help nostrums, using Conventional Thinking almost always negates their relationship benefits in terms of the *results* you obtain in achieving changes. Just as Taylor's now outmoded studies of time management at the turn of the century represented an important advance over having no such studies at all, so the practice of these self-help prescriptions is better than doing nothing at all to improve yourself. The time has come, however, for even the best of these inherently limited prescriptions to be superseded by Full-Spectrum Thinking.

Full-Spectrum Creativity

Far too often, creativity is associated simply with the generation of an idea, a technique, a technology—a "solution." What this perspective neglects, to its great disadvantage, is creativity as a *process.*

For example, the creativity essential to assembling a group of people to work together on finding a solution. The creativity essential in face-to-face interactions and group meetings. The creativity essential to the process of identifying what situation you will actually work on to find a solution. The creativity essential to the installation and implementation of the chosen recommendation. And of course, the creativity of generating "aha!" and major (as well as innovative, intermediate) ideas.

In short, true creativity entails far more than merely the generation of ideas, however clever, brilliant, or elegant they may be. Creativity is not limited to "solutions" or products or systems. Truly creative solutions result from selecting the priority problem to work on, the biggest possible purpose to address, with effective and committed people, who apply the broadest set of ideas, use effective purpose-related measures, and devise the complete installation plan.

Creativity is a process, not merely the recognition of a "creative" result. The process of true creativity is defined by Full-Spectrum Thinking.

We contend that the current "thinking environment," defined as it is by exclusive reliance on Conventional Thinking, is altogether incapable of meeting the challenges and opportunities of the future that is already upon us. Exclusive, even primary, reliance on the Conventional Thinking paradigm will certainly condemn us not only to repeat the mistakes of the past but to fail dismally in the future.

None of the prophesied "solutions," however apparently well-reasoned, however clever, however hopeful, will carry the day—at least not until the problems they are supposed to solve are examined in light of Full-Spectrum Thinking. Indeed, these "solutions" may well prove more vexing than the problems they are meant to solve.

For example, consider the much-vaunted "information superhighway." As commentator Robert J. Samuelson has noted, "We are all (it seems) about to be swept into a new world of interactive, multimedia services that will arrive over the superhighway and, somehow, revolutionize our lives. Folks, I'm not holding my breath. The information superhighway may or may not become a truly transforming technology—the likes of the railroad, car or phone. But if it does, the event is many years, and perhaps decades, away.

"What inspires the hoopla is the fascination with the new and the spectacle of massive companies . . . frantically maneuvering, through mergers and joint ventures, to prepare for a future they only dimly perceive. We in the press contribute to the illusion, because our technology writers . . . are wild enthusiasts whose excursions into 'cyberspace' exaggerate its importance.

"What now passes for the information superhighway is a slogan in search of a mission. . . . All new technologies trigger turmoil. True, they foster change. But they also retard it, because they spawn new technical, economic, and legal problems. When these are few, the technology may catch on quickly. In 1945 almost no one had a TV; by 1960 about 86 percent of [U.S.] households did. But typically, the problems are greater, and the spread is slower. This is why new technologies usually make themselves felt only gradually. Alexander Graham Bell invented the telephone in 1876. By 1940 only 40 percent of [U.S.] households had one."[1]

Surely, our ability to cope with the "progress" of new technologies would be greatly enhanced by a thinking paradigm that required us to consider the *uniqueness* of the situation, the *purposes* to be served by the technology, the *solution-after-next* alternatives and then target for the purposes, and the multiple-*systems* perspective of any solution. Full-Spectrum Thinking would diminish the likelihood of new technologies arriving on the scene like squalling infants, demanding of us far more than they can immediately contribute. In Samuelson's assessment of the technology phrase, *information superhighway:* "a slogan in search of a mission." We need to be selective in what technology (and other prophesied nostrums) we adopt, designing it to fit our purposes, needs, and competencies.

Moreover, as machines evolve, they impact the evolution of the human species. As Massachusetts Institute of Technology historian Bruce Mazlish contends, there is compelling evidence that not only the functioning of human societies but our very identities are symbiotically related to the machines that we create yet do not entirely control. Mazlish notes that we can no longer justify the self-flattering notion that we dominate our machines. "Such a need satisfies important psychological and social purposes, yet is a crutch that is best discarded, in order to move closer to reality and away from disabling fantasy."[2]

Indeed, biophysicist Gregory Stock maintains that human beings and machines have by now "co-evolved" into a collective superorganism. While this may not be an entirely attractive prospect, Stock consoles us: "Humankind," he writes, "has before it a long and vital future in a world where the natural environment will be managed, where the nation-state will lose its dominance in world affairs, where technology will penetrate virtually every aspect of human life, where human reproduction will be managed, and where local cultural traditions will merge into a rich global culture."[3]

Maybe. Maybe not. In either case, will what is gained be preferable to what is lost? No one can say.

How is humanity to solve such troubling conundrums? How can we unravel, not hack through, the Gordian knot of our collective futures? For the most part, exclusive practice of Conventional Thinking will not help us resolve these dilemmas.

For example, consider the 1960s, an era perhaps best defined in terms of the state of mind characteristic of its younger generation. It was a decade of disillusionment and consequent search for existential meaning. Its Conventional Thinking led to placing blame, finding faults, and detailing mistakes. Its spirit and values led not only to needed revelation and self-realization, but also to self-indulgence and sometimes self-destruction. In this sense, "The Sixties" can be said to have begun with the assassination of President John F. Kennedy and to have ended with American defeat in the Vietnam War and the resignation of President Richard Nixon.

Among the phrases often heard then and descriptive of that age now was "it seemed like a good idea at the time." In retrospect, of course, some of the "shining paths" taken by youth of that era can now be seen more clearly to have been blind alleys. In fact, the rampant socio-sexual experimentation of the decade has much in common with Conventional Thinking run amuck. If government is to blame, then do away with it. If organized religion has faults, then don't believe in it. If corporations make mistakes, then have no trust in any of them.

While clearly grinding an ideological axe, conservative writer Myron Magnet makes the point that one person's brave and brilliant "solution" is another person's poison. Magnet contends that the American underclass of the 1990s cannot be blamed on the social and economic policies of "benign neglect" popular in the 1980s, not even on the prolonged recession of the early '90s, but rather on the financial, social, and cultural excesses of "The Sixties."[4] As *New York Times* reviewer Sidney Blumenthal puts it, Magnet's thesis is that, 30 years later, America finds itself "strangled by love beads."[5]

Whether or not one agrees with Magnet, the larger question remains: Can all problems be solved, all futures planned, all impacts assessed in advance? The answer: Clearly, no.

However, a change in thinking to Full-Spectrum Thinking seeks to increase significantly the likelihood of doing much better than we have previously done. We ought not make the assumption that we can solve every problem, positively exploit every opportunity. What is important is continually moving toward as much of a change as possible, making major progress, significantly improving our situation.

And we had better improve in a hurry. Much as novelist Charles Dickens viewed the French Revolution, many observers today view the century ahead as "the best of times and the worst of times." At once remarkable and grim.

Some, such as historian John Lukacs, contend that rampant nationalism will give rise to unprecedented barbarity on a planet with too many people increasingly desperate for too few essential resources.[6] Self-described cosmopolitan Michael Ignatieff, journeying to many sites of current ethnic conflicts, is similarly pessimistic: "I cannot help thinking," he writes, "that liberal civilization—the rule of laws, not men, of argument in place of force, of compromise in place of violence—runs deeply against the human grain and is achieved and sustained only by the most unremitting struggle against human nature. The liberal virtues—tolerance, compromise, reason—remain as valuable as ever, but they cannot be preached to those who are mad with fear or mad with vengeance.

"Wherever I went, I found a struggle going on between those who still believe that a nation should be a home to all, and race, color, religion and creed should be no bar to belonging, and those who want their nation to be home only to their own. It's the battle between the civic and the ethnic nation. I know which side I'm on. I also know which side, right now, happens to be winning."[7]

Ignatieff claims these conflicts are driven by what Freud called "the narcissism of minor differences" or the desperate search for identity by essentially similar peoples exaggerating what separates them.

Those more optimistic, such as scholar-scientist C. Owen Paepke, maintain that, while the material advancement of human beings is at an end, the perfection of our species is only beginning.[8] Historian Paul Kennedy concludes that "we face not a 'new world order' but a troubled and fractured planet, whose problems deserve the serious attention of politicians and publics alike."[9]

Whether playing the role of Cassandra or Pollyanna, these prophets all make dutiful attempts to predict the unpredictable. For example, rather obviously, Kennedy stresses three key elements necessary "to prepare global society for the 21st century: the role of education, the place of women, and the need for political leadership."

It seems an innate human tendency to search for "*the* answers," to find *the* pattern that permits "certain" predictions, always to seek (if seldom heed) whomever may have the temerity to forecast our uncertain future. And yet, despite the plethora of "weathermen," all anyone can say for certain is that the winds are blowing harder, in fact, rapidly approaching hurricane force.

Although no certain answers exist, we can do many things to achieve our (expanded) human purposes. Fundamental to affecting the future positively is to change our paradigm of thinking, become multi-thinkers, practice Full-Spectrum Thinking.

The Thinking Paradigm Issue

Our problems will not disappear. We must seek solutions for them. We must exploit our opportunities. Or we will fall farther behind. We must develop new opportunities, not just focus on improving problem situations or transforming existing policies and institutions such as federal defense research laboratories (organizations for which old functions have disappeared), intelligence tests, organizational responsibility assignments, and methods to facilitate children's learning.

We have no time to lose.

We—specific companies, specific countries and states, specific organizations, specifically we as individuals—must take steps to find solutions, to no longer blame others. James Fallows' expert comment on U.S.-Japanese trade relations can be expanded to all sectors of society: "Now, as in the past, economics favors those who are determined to make their own luck."[10] That is, develop their own solutions.

We obviously need to improve the timeliness, creativity, effectiveness, quality, and quantity of our solutions, plans, activities, and systems. And the need for change in our existing systems and solutions leads inevitably to the need for change in our paradigm of thinking.

One way to define excellent thinking is in terms of what it is not. In this light, consider the comments of Meg Greenfield regarding the mid-90s fashionable passion for "rethinking" government in the United States.

"At the simplest level . . . what we solemnly describe as rethinking tends to be little more than personal and institutional damage limitation. At some point in all this frenzy of inquiry and re-examination of first principles, there will presumably have to be some conclusions, and some are already on view. The latter tend to confirm one's suspicions that the 'thinking' part of the rethinking is a bit of a misnomer. People who were really thinking at all simply could not come up with recommendations that read like the opening statement of congressional testimony on behalf of an agency that doesn't want its funds cut. (If you ever faked it on a college essay exam because you hadn't read the book, you will know exactly what this kind of prose presentation sounds like.)

"You can count really only a handful of actual grand 'thinkings' in our post World War II approach to national security and foreign affairs," writes Greenfield. "Our reactions have tended to be less rational than reflexive, less the product of thought than of the stimulus of the moment."[11]

As Greenfield notes, little that should rightly be called thinking at all usually goes into "re-thinking." And that is due in large measure to reliance on Conventional Thinking. If we want actually to "re-think" our policies, institutions, and other fundamental "solutions," we must first re-think our thinking paradigm itself. We must escape from those versions of solution finding characterized by automatic assumptions such as "get more data" or "it's their problem" or "what does the boss want to do?" or "do what the Jones' do" or simply "let a consultant decide."

In discovering (and admitting) that there is no one, single, best answer to every problem and opportunity we confront, we become "affirmative post-modernists," as defined by political theorist Pauline Marie Rosenau. University of Chicago anthropologist Richard A. Shweder explains that Rosenau views affirmative post-modernists as "reacting against modernism, but without the leap into nihilism (the idea of a world without meaning) and without despair. The affirmatives agree with the skeptics that the loose change of daily living does not add up or make consistent sense. They agree that one should not look for life's bottom line, because there is none. They don't try to wrap up the truth in a simple package. However, in contrast to the skeptics, the affirmatives don't play the meaning-of-life game by all-or-nothing rules. The affirmatives honor plurality and multiplicity, delighting in the partial and inconsistent meanings revealed by disparate forms and alternative ways of life."[12]

While it is crucial to stay open in one's thinking, it is equally important to reach workable conclusions. Perfection is desirable as an aim, yet it is not possible to attain. But excellence in developing and implementing changes is. Full-Spectrum Thinking succeeds in both imperatives. As such, it is ideally suited to the "post-modernist" future that we all confront. It is the way to develop the people skills and abilities to put worldwide resources of raw materials, capital, and technology into innovative and competitive, yet learning and evolving, solutions.

The Role of Education in Developing New Paradigms of Thinking

In facing the future, we are severely handicapped by the fact that the Research Approach of Conventional Thinking is taught today at almost all levels of formal education in all but a handful of schools. Even the best schools promote a paradigm of thinking that is clearly outmoded and too often useless in solving most contemporary, not to mention future, problems.

As currently constituted, the educational systems that exist today rely heavily on rote learning—the memorization and regurgitation of "facts," as discovered by Conventional Thinking—rather than developing real solution-finding skills. Generally speaking, this is even more true in England, Germany, and Japan than in the United States. Even with the "Education 2000" goals now legally mandated, U.S. education (hopefully on the path of significant improvement) still faces many problems. Among them, multi-ethnicism, poor-rich differences in financial support, and gender bias.

In the case of the Japanese, despite their reliance on rote learning, a cultural preference for the holistic perspective and the ideographic basis of the Japanese language have proven a strong counterbalance to the impact of the Western-based Conventional Thinking. The result has been to produce students who, while often lacking in individuality and invariably "cut from the same mold" in terms of their formal education, are nonetheless, in their organizational lives, intuitive practitioners of Full-Spectrum Thinking and thus notably creative in their thinking.

Imagine the benefits that would accrue to humanity if, instead of relying exclusively on Conventional Thinking, we formally educated our children that there is more than one way to think, more than one way to find solutions. Experience tells us that children are naturally adept at the multi-thinking perspective of Full-Spectrum Thinking.

An earlier work of Nadler and colleagues, *SPARK: Student Planned Acquisition of Required Knowledge,* clearly demonstrates that elementary and middle school students have no trouble understanding and effectively using Breakthrough Thinking. Indeed, these students grasp it easily, use it well, and thrive with Full-Spectrum Thinking.

Whether education on the principles and process of this new paradigm of thinking takes place formally or as part of an in-house organizational program of job-related education, teaching and learning Full-Spectrum Thinking is well within our personal and public capacities. Education, after all, need not present an either/or proposition, two opposing camps, forever at odds. The multi-thinker perspective of Full-Spectrum Thinking points clearly in this direction.

We must begin to teach the new paradigm of thinking immediately. Since such a realignment of the existing educational system would have the greatest positive impact at the lower grade levels, we must begin with the youngest students. For their part, students are ready, willing, entirely able, and require only our guidance and commitment.

More difficult to change are those more embedded in the ways of Conventional Thinking—those involved in the many in-house, job-related educational programs fostered by various organizations and corporations. Generally, these programs tend to latch onto the latest flavor-of-the-month cureall to make them more competitive, more quality oriented, more just-in-time, more of anything they want to be but don't know how to be. Why do these programs fail? Because they simply reinforce the outmoded Conventional Thinking that quite likely caused the organization to look for "the answer" in the first place.

If the primary role of formal education is, as some see it, to develop the character and moral foundation necessary for both personal success and societal cohesion, Full-Spectrum Thinking again fills the bill. Its widely encompassing, holistic perspective is far more likely to create positive individual and social values than is the exclusive, highly focused pursuit of "fact" that characterizes Conventional Thinking. Full-Spectrum Thinking's principles of uniqueness, purposes and their expansion, people design, and betterment timeline inherently contribute to the development of such virtues as responsibility, self-discipline, compassion, friendship, perseverance, courage, faith, loyalty, honesty, and work.

Not only can education advance Full-Spectrum Thinking, but Full-Spectrum Thinking may be effectively applied to the problem of providing high-quality public education in the United States. According to Gleaves Whitney, an aide to Michigan Governor John Engler, "Once we decide what sort of schools we want and how much it will cost, then we'll figure out how best to pay for it. But we've got to break out of this ossified, ancient way of providing education."[13]

Good idea. But how to do it? One thing is certain: If would-be education reformers continue to apply Conventional Thinking, they will deal with only a few, limited dimensions of a systemic problem. Apparently endless fact-gathering studies of the problem have led to the current impasse. Even the best intentioned efforts have reduced the problem of public education in America to a spurious choice between two conflicting solutions: more "choice" or more money. "Choice is no panacea," writes Klein, "but East Harlem has shown that students can be energized when real choices are offered; more money can also be helpful, but only when spent in a system that works."[14] What better way to devise a system that works than to apply the principles and process of Full-Spectrum Thinking?

Such a project would surely prove more effective than that undertaken by Christopher Whittle, whose late, unlamented Edison Project promised to completely revamp public education in the United States. Whittle recruited Benno Schmidt, then president of Yale University, to join his project. But these self-selected seers disastrously underestimated their ability to raise the $2.5 billion necessary to build or lease the first 100 schools they envisioned. Moreover, they evidently failed to consider the strengths and benefits of the public education system they were determined to supplant, at a handsome personal profit.

According to American Federation of Teachers president Albert Shanker, Whittle was fond of making a certain less-than-enlightening analogy. He "often compared the difference between our current schools and the ones he would invent to the difference between a candle and Thomas Edison's incandescent light. And, as he said, there is no way to make a light bulb out of a candle: 'When Edison invented electric illumination, he didn't tinker with candles to make them burn better. Instead he created something brilliantly new: the light bulb.' "[15]

True enough. And the analogy is compelling, however false. While we wholeheartedly endorse the need to consider fundamental purposes and design systems as if nothing of the sort has previously existed, the case of Christopher Whittle and his astonishingly simplistic metaphor is instructive as a warning against misleading analogies.

Such false analogies violate the principle of uniqueness fundamental to Full-Spectrum Thinking. Effective solution finding and design is never based on analogies, however apt they may seem. Instead, the making of design decisions must be based on purposes and solutions-after-next.

Unfortunately, resorting to this sort of astonishingly false analogy occurs repeatedly among politicians, particularly in Congress, where simplistic "solutions" designed for consumption by particular voters, not nourishment of the general body politic, are in vogue.

Another preexisting, copycat "solution" offered is that proposed by U.S. governors and endorsed and expanded upon by both Presidents Bush and Clinton: national tests and standards for U.S. elementary, middle, and high school students.[16] Growing opposition to these apparently beneficial proposals—even in the face of evidence that national standards and assessments need not strip local school systems of control or introduce other problems stressed by critics—stems from the difference between addressing problems in terms of "what's wrong?" and "*the* answer" (Conventional Thinking) and addressing them in terms of expanding purposes and solutions-after-next (Full-Spectrum Thinking).

Following Full-Spectrum Thinking, purposes, measures of purpose accomplishment, and continual change toward a target solution-after-next inherently respects the uniqueness of individual and local circumstances.

The Role of Full-Spectrum Thinking in Resolving Critical Human Problems

Education is fundamental. Yet far beyond the classroom, we are increasingly confronted by the countless recalcitrant, frightening, and fearfully difficult problems described earlier, apparently resistant to effective solution.

And yet, however "insoluble," these difficulties can be influenced by the way in which one thinks about them, the paradigm of thinking with which they are approached. For example, their evident intractability makes many of them exist in the twilight realm of so-called trade-offs, as if half a loaf was all that any interested party might ever hope to achieve.

Very seldom, if ever, are such situations discussed in terms of the purposes of their solution, not only as regards a specific problem, but also the generic issue. To the contrary, Full-Spectrum Thinking holds out the promise of synergistic solution. As this book makes clear, thinking must always be related to some other activity, some purposes. With Full-Spectrum Thinking, the conflict becomes no longer zero-sum. Instead, one plus one can come to equal three. Or more.

For example, consider trade negotiations between Japan and the United States. Would not the disputing parties be better served by examining the purposes of rice imports and exports, rather than simply insisting on a trade-off between Japan's reluctance to accept imported rice and the U.S. desire to export rice?

Of course, the inevitable confrontation that ensues when such conflicts are addressed solely on the basis of Conventional Thinking is one way to deal with the problem. But what if both parties to the conflict actually considered, for example, the purposes of mohair and wool subsidies in the United States? Or widespread agricultural subsidies in France?

To do so, using Full-Spectrum Thinking, is inevitably to develop a perspective that not only places the purpose of the immediate conflict into a larger context, but also relates that context to still larger purposes and issues. This has proven true not only in the arena of international, national, public, corporate, and organizational concerns, but also in the far more private realm of individual and group psychotherapy. Sufficiently expanded purposes lead inevitably to the discovery of common ground upon which to build mutually satisfactory and effective solutions.

For example, consider an issue that impacts both the most private and most public levels—healthcare reform in the United States. Most of the 1994 suggested reform plans have dealt primarily with costs, allocations, alliances, and insurance. Few have dealt with what health care is supposed to achieve and *how* it is to be delivered.

What if reformers considered the purposes and larger purposes of healthcare delivery? Would they propose the same "solutions"?

To date, healthcare delivery is a system/solution that most people believe must be viewed in the aggregate. Consequently, we have not sufficiently considered what the customer, the individual consumer, really needs. If you were designing a healthcare delivery system for you, as an individual, what purposes would you wish to have accomplished? What would your ideal system be?

Would it be based on access to doctors and nurses in clinics and hospitals? Or might it focus, for example, on the presence of fully-equipped medical vans on constant patrol in every neighborhood? Or would a combination preventive care and medical assistance plan be more effective? Addressed by means of Full-Spectrum Thinking one might envision several different possibilities. But these alternative solutions become obvious only once the issue is addressed from a fundamental premise: What is the *purpose* of healthcare delivery?

On the basis of the answers to the question of what purposes and expanded purposes the healthcare delivery system should achieve, what larger number of alternatives might be developed? Only at that point should cost considerations and payment structure be addressed. Only in that way can the solution ultimately selected reflect a true improvement, an enduring solution-after-next.

Currently, the alternatives we envision are limited.

For example, why is it that we find such a great reluctance to include in a healthcare delivery system certain holistic treatments and other forms of "non-traditional" medical care? The answer can be found in the pervasive influence of the Research Approach and its syndrome of strict "rationality." The "medical metaphor" itself illustrates the difficulties we experience with the healthcare delivery problem: research, analysis, compartmentalization, specialized diagnosis.

Of course, such techniques in themselves are good. Certainly, none of us would want to be attended by a physician who only questioned purposes, to the exclusion of detailed analysis. Yet the fundamental premises of Full-Spectrum Thinking—including appropriately timed and executed application of Conventional Thinking—would allow us to benefit from a variety of alternative healthcare procedures and healing practices.

Now translate this thinking paradigm shift to any other social issue—the homeless, transportation, poverty services, drug traffic, and so on. Let the people in these "categories" take part as "customers" whose purposes must be included in the hierarchy and whose ideas about solutions-after-next need to be considered. "Customer" involvement in shaping the policies and services would not only be likely to yield new and usable solutions but would help the "customer" view the system as relevant and a way out of whatever the morass is.

In order to solve effectively the apparently intractable problems we face, to find new common ground for solutions, the essential point is to accept that we must change not merely our solution paradigm, but first our thinking paradigm itself. We need to change the very process by which we seek solutions.

One arena in which application of Full-Spectrum Thinking would make an immediately tangible positive difference is that of United Nations missions and U.S. foreign policy, particularly the increasingly important role of military peace-keeping missions, such as in Beirut, Somalia, and Bosnia. In the view of Samuel P. Huntington, professor of government and director of the Olin Institute for Strategic Studies at Harvard University, "world politics is entering a new phase in which the fundamental source of conflict will be neither ideological or economic. The great divisions among mankind and the dominating source of conflict will be cultural. The principal conflicts of global politics will occur between nations and groups of different civilizations. The clash of civilizations will dominate global politics."[17]

Noting that only Japan is at once non-Western and modern, Huntington predicts that "the central axis of world politics is likely to be the conflict between 'the West and the rest' and the responses of non-Western civilizations to Western power and values. The most prominent example of anti-Western cooperation is the connection between Confucian and Islamic states that are challenging Western values and power.

"Cultural characteristics and differences," writes Huntington, "are less mutable and hence less easily compromised and resolved than political and economic ones. In the former Soviet Union, Communists can become democrats, the rich can become poor and the poor rich, but Russians cannot become Estonians. A person can be half-French and half-Arab and even a citizen of two countries. It is more difficult to be half Catholic and half Muslim.

"This will require the West to develop a much more profound understanding of the basic religious and philosophical assumptions underlying other civilizations and the ways in which people in those civilizations see their interests. It will require an effort to identify elements of commonality among Western and other civilizations. For the relevant future, there will be no universal civilization but instead a world of different civilizations, each of which will have to learn to co-exist with others."[18]

The Full-Spectrum Thinking focus on people-design and systems—the fact that everything affects everything else—is essential to the solution of problems in such a world, which is to say, the world we already confront. In a world so inextricably interrelated, the conventional paradigm of thinking—based on finding the one "right" answer and the belief that to solve the small problems that supposedly comprise a larger problem is to solve the larger problem itself—is clearly outmoded. In such a world, none of the promises of Conventional Thinking hold true.

Conflict Resolution

Stephen Paskoff, who provides training for companies on workplace legal issues, says: "Programs that focus on [male or female or ethnic] differences can be very divisive. . . . They trivialize the reality that we are complex. The proper way of looking at it is that people manage differently because people are different."[19]

Similarly, the uniqueness principle of Full-Spectrum Thinking maintains that, even if a statistically significant difference were found in the leadership style of men compared to that of women, such a generic difference would nonetheless remain inapplicable with regard to a specific individual. Why? Because an individual man or an individual woman can vary greatly from the supposed norm for his or her gender. Consequently, even studies based on unassailable research methods and that discover statistically significant differences will not avail us in predicting the style of any specific individual from a given category or in developing solutions that ignore the distribution of values from any grouping.

Similarly, because we recognize the need for multi-thinking and the differences between individuals, we do not maintain that everyone *must* learn and apply the principles and process of the Full-Spectrum Thinking. Just as there is not a useful single truth or "solution," neither is there any useful generic "difference" to be drawn between specific individuals.

In our view, if executives and managers used Full-Spectrum Thinking to examine reward systems, incentive plans, and bonus structures in terms of their expanded purposes, they would not make the automatic assumption that reward systems of this sort are necessarily good and useful. With Full-Spectrum Thinking, the probability is much higher that the motivational plan ultimately implemented would actually succeed in increasing productivity, enhancing quality, and so forth. The uniqueness principle will also encourage you to find the mix of incentives and motivators appropriate to the particular circumstances of your own organization. This is the way to set expectations so that they, in effect, can lead to self-fulfilling prophecies. Nadler used this approach when he chaired the executive compensation committee of the board of directors of a $200 million manufacturing company. The plan for executive pay incorporated a wide variety of needed outcomes—long-range plan accomplishments, human resource development, yearly profits, market share, succession planning—which produced a company so successful that it was eagerly merged with another company.

However work performance may be motivated in the future, the nature of work is clearly changing. Moreover, the change is likely to accelerate, not diminish. We are called upon to expand our understanding of the purposes of our work to include the purposes of our "customer."

Now our society is embarking on a new definition of work. Precisely how it will come to be considered remains unclear. Perhaps our future understanding of work will require that it provide the satisfaction of craft, even art. One thing is certain: In order to understand work, we must effectively consider its expanded purposes, with reference to Full-Spectrum Thinking. Why? Because thinking and action, reasoning and purposes are integrated.

And there is no doubt that we must find solutions. Management consultants as diverse as Tom Peters and Peter Drucker have written that the "post-capitalist" future will be startlingly different from the present. Peters notes that "competitive practices required to survive in the '90s—pursuit of "six sigma quality" (99.9997 percent perfect . . .), shrinking innovation and order cycles by orders of magnitude, the use of team-based organizations everywhere and the subcontracting of anything to

anyone from anywhere—are downstream links in a chain of immutable forces sweeping the world's economy."[20] Drucker predicts that "tomorrow's educated person will have to be
prepared for life in a global world. It will be a 'Westernized'
world, but also increasingly a tribalized world."[21]

In such a world, Georgetown University professor of business ethics Thomas Donaldson reminds us, global business
must mind its morals. "So what is the answer?" Donaldson asks.
"Clearly, to steer a middle course between moral relativism and
moral absolutism. But where? Which moral values transcend
national boundaries?" Donaldson continues: "We need rules
that allow us to say to Union Carbide, 'You committed a tragic
mistake in letting safeguards lapse in Bhopal,' while also re-
specting India's culture.

"Many would say the transcendent values are those which
are fundamental to the human condition—freedom, safety, dignity. [Yet] hard thinking is still needed to apply such a standard.
After a company establishes broad moral guidelines, it still must
discover the best tools for making moral choices case by case."[22]
The new thinking paradigm offers the best guide to effective
action.

On a more prosaic level, the Full-Spectrum Thinking emphasis on the development and expansion of purposes and
solutions-after-next provides executives and managers the guidance and justification to take the personal and professional
risks required in finding and implementing effective solutions
and systems. It provides a basis for overcoming and hopefully
avoiding incipient institutional mentality of focusing on personal interests (compensation, management, building, perquisites).
Under the Conventional Thinking paradigm, notes Italian manufacturing manager Mario Levetto, many managers have chosen
to implement the paralyzing theory of PYB management, that
is, "management by protect-your-butt." They do so believing
that "the only way to avoid bad decisions is to avoid all decisions. This is much easier than trying to hide or justify a bad decision." Unfortunately, however useful as a method of personal
career survival, it is also a prescription for failure in meeting the
purposes of the organization.[23] Various observers also contend
that, if the organization is to survive and thrive in a global envi-

ronment, traditional labor/management relations must be "renegotiated," which is to say "re-thought."

The Development of Technology and Its Potential Impact on Paradigms of Thinking

Whether in communications, biochemistry, computer science, neuroscience, or any number of other fields of interest, technology is certain to develop at an accelerating, often astonishing, rate. We can expect such changes to occur with increasing frequency and impact.

The question becomes: How best to cope with this Brave New World?

With the Full-Spectrum Thinking focus on purposes, expansion of purposes, and solutions-after-next, you can see which among alternative technologies are more usefully developed, which yet need to be developed. In other words, you can identify which future technology can most effectively be researched and developed. Full-Spectrum Thinking identifies where to invest your research and development effort most productively.

It allows you to choose more effectively which kind of R&D has the greatest potential to address your chosen purposes. For example, if you can identify the kind of new software package that needs to be developed for your larger purpose, and you learn the impact it will have on your existing system, you can then identify what its impact might be on other systems. Thus, Full-Spectrum Thinking helps to identify and define which technologies to develop and use.

Full-Spectrum Thinking and Technology Transfer

Effective technology and useful knowledge, good systems and solutions, ought to move freely among peoples and nations. There is no reason for Japan or Germany or the U.S. to have effective urban sanitary systems, while Bangladesh may not. Advanced technology must not only be developed, it must be somehow transferred—or adapted—to other countries and cultures, often under different conditions or terrain and climate. Often, the key question becomes, how can an effective and useful technology be installed in a culture unaccustomed to its use?

With Full-Spectrum Thinking, the technology transfer is accomplished in the most effective way. At least, it becomes clear how best to meet the purposes that the technology has been chosen to address. You know what direction to take, what solution to work toward. This avoids the waste occasioned by highly advanced but culturally unsuited technology rusting in Third World urban lots and rural fields.

Typically, the transfer of technology is considered a "push," from the so-called First World to the Third. "We've got the technology. We're going to convince you to use it."

Instead, the more effective perspective would be the "pull" model of Full-Spectrum Thinking. "A need exists. If we can identify the purposes, we can pull in the technology that local people identify as needed." Only in this way do people, both local and foreign, perceive the larger ends to be achieved and thus identify the technologies naturally associated with those larger ends.

When the problem is viewed in light of Full-Spectrum Thinking, "experts" and local people come to see clearly that First World technology may be inappropriate for local circumstances, that the purpose it is designed to serve in Europe or Japan may not be something that needs to be accomplished in Ethiopia.

Future Research on Thinking and Mental Assumptions About Thinking

Is Full-Spectrum Thinking the "final" paradigm of thinking to create or restructure solutions? No.

What will the paradigm that replaces Full-Spectrum Thinking contain? We don't know.

When will it arrive? We don't know.

How will it be found and identified? We don't know.

Who will discover it? We don't know.

Why would we want eventually to change from Full-Spectrum Thinking? Because, then as now, thinking must change. An effective thinking paradigm itself thrives on constant exploration and testing. Even the firmly established assumptions and the paradigm for developing scientific generalizations—the Research Approach—are being questioned and doubted by scientists. "Everything is up for grabs, including the universality of mathematics."[24] Surely, the critical human purposeful activity of creating and restructuring solutions should be continuously questioned.

To maintain exclusive reliance on the absolutism of the current paradigm is, at best, outmoded; at worst, disastrous. The new paradigm of thinking encompasses previously considered either-or assumptions—linear or cyclical, destination- or journey-oriented, maintain equilibrium or create disequilibrium, planned change or evolutionary change. Yet even if one hesitates to embrace fully the radical change in mental assumptions that we propose, it is obvious that considerable room for improvement exists in the current paradigm of thinking.

Not only must Conventional Thinking at last give way to the pressing needs of an uncertain future; Full-Spectrum Thinking must also change and develop to stay abreast of—indeed, ahead of—the changing needs of current and future solution-finding. In particular, Full-Spectrum Thinking will have to develop more insight into how best to identify and select the purposes for solution finders to address. Moreover, we must learn more about how people can best come to recognize and appreciate the full context of their larger purposes. We must adapt to the new kinds of intelligence already identified, the realities of cultural resources and needs, the desires made palpable and available by new technologies, and even the uncertainties of politics.

To that end, we continue to engage in a variety of research efforts. For example, new computer aids for use of Breakthrough Thinking are being investigated. Case studies are being collected in a data base to permit such experiences to be studied for finding other principles or process aids. Based on the systems principle, a detailed framework for evaluating proposed solutions is being developed. It should allow the thinker to recognize aspects such as quality, value, and other interrelated factors in evaluating a chosen solution. Breakthrough Thinking user groups are being set up, even on e-mail, to help people use the ideas.

In this and other ways, Full-Spectrum Thinking is itself open to change and improvement. In no way do we believe it will be *the* final paradigm of thinking. Any such paradigm must welcome and celebrate its own development and change. Pursuing the "truth" of a thinking paradigm for creating and restructuring solutions is better than claiming to possess it.

What impact our own and other research may come to have on the essential, new paradigm of thinking, no one can predict. For the moment, all we know is, if we do not think and work toward it, we may have to endure in the future (though we hope not for another 400 years) needs for solutions of the same severity that we face today, difficulties from which the clear and urgent need for the new Full-Spectrum Thinking paradigm has emerged.

TOMORROW

Our hope in this book is to change your automatic response when you (and your groups) seek solutions. Rather than thinking: "Everybody knows you have to start by finding out what exists, and gathering all the facts," may you think: "Everybody knows you have to start by finding the biggest purpose to achieve and solutions-after-next for accomplishing it."

Replete with problems, splendid with opportunities, the future is already upon us. To master and enjoy that future will demand nothing less than Full-Spectrum Creativity, nothing less than seeking all types of breakthroughs—"ah-ha" or major changes, significantly better results from efforts to create and restructure solutions, and getting good ideas implemented or avoiding bad ideas. Nothing will avail us now, short of Full-Spectrum Thinking.

With it, all things are possible.

NOTES

1. Robert J. Samuelson, "Lost On The Information Superhighway," *Newsweek,* (December 20, 1993).

2. Bruce Mazlish, *The Fourth Discontinuity: The Co-Evolution of Humans and Machines* (New Haven, CT: Yale University Press, 1993).

3. Gregory Stock, *Metaman: The Merging of Humans and Machines Into a Global Superorganism* (New York: Simon & Schuster, 1994).

4. Myron Magnet, *The Dream and the Nightmare: The Sixties' Legacy to the Underclass* (New York: William Morrow, 1993).

5. Sidney Blumenthal, review of Myron Magnet, *The Dream and the Nightmare: The Sixties' Legacy to the Underclass,* in *New York Times Book Review,* (July 25, 1993).

6. John Lukacs, *The End of the Twentieth Century and the End of the Modern Age* (New York: Ticknor & Fields, 1993).

7. Michael Ignatieff, *Blood and Belonging: Journeys Into the New Nationalism* (New York: Farrar, Straus, & Giroux, 1994).

8. C. Owen Paepke, *The Evolution of Progress* (New York: Random House, 1993).

9. Paul Kennedy, *Preparing for the Twenty-first Century* (New York: Random House, 1993).

10. James Fallows, *Looking at the Sun: The Rise of the New East Asian Economic and Political System* (New York: Pantheon, 1994).

11. Meg Greenfield, "Forget About Re-thinking," *Newsweek,* (April 12, 1993).

12. Richard A. Shweder, "Keep Your Mind Open," review of Robert Jay Lifton, *The Protean Self: Human Resilience in an Age of Fragmentation,* in *The New York Times Book Review,* (February 20, 1994).

13. Joe Klein, "Michigan's Tuna Surprise," *Newsweek,* September 6, 1993.

14. Ibid.

15. Albert Shanker, "Where We Stand," advertisement in *The New York Times,* (August 29, 1993).

16. William Celis III, "The Fight Over National Standards," *The New York Times,* (August 1, 1993).

17. Samuel P. Huntington, "The Coming Clash of Civilizations—Or, the West Against the Rest," *The New York Times,* (June 6, 1993).

18. Ibid.

19. Barbara Presley Noble, "The Debate Over *la Difference*," *The New York Times,* (August 15, 1993).

20. Tom Peters, "Prometheus Barely Unbound," *Academy of Management Executive,* Vol.4 No.4, 1990.

21. Peter F. Drucker, *Post-Capitalist Society* (New York: Harper Business/Harper Collins, 1993).

22. Thomas Donaldson, "Global Business Must Mind Its Morals," *The New York Times,* (February 13, 1994).

23. Mario Levetto, "Management By Protect-Your-Butt," *International Management,* (November/December, 1993).

24. George Johnnson, "Cosmic Noise: Scaling Lofty Towers of Belief, Science Checks Its Foundations," *The New York Times,* (July 10, 1994).

Index